Automated
Data Warehouse
Testing

(Beginner's step by step guide)

G. Suden

ISBN-13:   978-1507842010
ISBN-10:   1507842015

Printed by CreateSpace, An Amazon.com Company
Order online at https://www.createspace.com/5297571

Available from Amazon.com, Amazon Europe, other online stores and retail outlets

To my parents, wife and my amazing kids for giving me the support and drive to finish this book. I love you all!

Acknowledgements

The author is grateful to eclipse.org for providing permission to use screen prints in this book. The author is thankful to Lynette Foll for copy editing the manuscript.

Contents

List of Figures

Overview

THIS book aims to assist QA (Quality Assurance) teams in performing data warehouse testing effectively using automation. The complexities and challenges of data warehouse development have evolved over the past few years and testing teams are expected to verify each implementation by running tests multiple times to ensure the system hasn't regressed. Volumes of data are fed into the data warehouse through heterogeneous sources having data quality issues at source. Extract, Transform and Load (ETL) processes have grown too complex. Data warehouse testing is usually associated with a very high cost of quality and any defect slippage has a significant effect on downstream end-user systems. As a result, the ability to perform automated testing becomes extremely useful as it provides testers and the organisation as a whole an added level of confidence.

One good thing about automation is that you can initiate your tests before leaving the office and then, when you get back in the morning, your test results are ready for review!

There are usually millions of records in a data warehouse and it is not possible to check all of this data manually. You may have an automated test that picks up 1000 records from the sales table and verifies the ETL logic while you are getting your tea! Furthermore, this becomes even more powerful when you consider the fact that this test may be picking up a different set of 1000 records each time it is executed, providing additional data coverage on each execution.

"With an automated test in my quiver, I always feel like I have an extra pair of hands."

With each additional automated test you can concentrate on other important tasks while your 'automated buddy' is executing the tests. The help from this 'buddy' becomes even more significant when as a testing team you are given a new build to test at the eleventh hour and in a few hours are asked, "What do you guys think about the new build?" In situations like this, you can feel positive that you have some automated tests that will give you a degree of confidence about the quality of the build.

I have experience working in a Quality Assurance role, on a similar data warehousing project and thought it would help other people like me who perhaps need a helping hand in testing. Automation of data warehouse testing is a powerful, rare and exciting new skill that can benefit any testing team.

This book is aimed at novice to intermediate level testers who want to try their hands at automated testing. It provides a step by step guide that will teach you how to setup an Automation Framework from scratch. As we will see, the framework is quite generic and as such can be applied to most data warehousing projects. This book concentrates on the 'practical side' of automated testing rather than the 'theoretical side'. It includes complete listings of the automated code for the sample data warehouse that we will setup for testing. The code listings explain the logic for the individual tests and generic functions.

As usual, the book is divided into a number of chapters.

- Chapter 1, Getting Started, introduces the data warehouse architecture. It provides a high level explanation of the components of a data warehouse and explains how they fit together. It also summarises the main reasons to automate the testing and provides some golden rules for you to follow when automating tests.

- Chapter 2, Sample Dimensional Data Warehouse, discusses the three models of a system - the business, the logical and the physical model. For automation purposes, we will need an example data warehouse and this chapter sets the scene for this. Throughout this book we will consider one hypothetical system called Order Processing System in its source form (source system) and convert it to a star schema for our dimensional data warehouse (target system). We will then go through an important document called Data Mapping which is a primary input to QA test design, in addition to other documentation available in the project. We will identify the source-to-target mappings required for our sample data warehouse and see how to derive our expected and actual results from this mapping document.

- Chapter 3, Automation Approach, deals with the very important need for a framework which is the driving force behind a successful automation. It looks at the software you will need to set up the Automation Framework and one piece of good news is that all of this is open source and freeware! It also discusses the Automation Framework components. We will write our first automated test in this chapter, and expand on it to add a number of important features to the framework such as logging to a console, files (so that you can refer back when required), sequencing test execution etc.

- Chapter 4, Setting up Sample Data Warehouse, describes how to set up the databases that act as our source systems, staging area and data warehouse. Each database is defined in three stages - creating the database files, defining the schema and finally loading the data.

- Chapter 5, Automating Staging Area, is where the real automation of the data warehouse testing begins, when the data is transferred from the source systems to the staging area and we ensure that the transferred data is correct. Before we finish this chapter we will add a further feature to the Automation Framework i.e. create a test results summary.

- Chapter 6, Automating Dimensional Data Warehouse, deals with automating the testing of the dimension tables and the type of tests that are applicable. We will then automate the fact table in our sample data warehouse and add further important features to the Automation Framework.

- Chapter 7, Automating Other Data Sources, looks at automating the testing of data feeds from commonly used CSV and Excel files. We will cover XLSX and XLS Excel formats.

- Chapter 8, Automated HTML Test Report, describes how to report on the test results. The ability to run a lot of tests is of little benefit if the results of the tests are not easy to understand. We need the framework to automatically generate reports from the tests and present the results in an easy to read format. A report should provide details of where the failures have occurred and what test data was used, including what SQL queries were fired on the source and target systems. This chapter explains how to achieve this and we will generate a formatted HTML report of our testing. The report also generates a test summary for the senior management.

- Chapter 9, Data Profiling, deals with how to automate some of the data quality checking tasks that are very helpful in identifying faults.

Please note that this book aims to teach you how to automate data warehouse testing and provides you with a framework to achieve this. It is not about teaching you "how to design a robust data warehouse" or "how to code effectively in Java". You may find there are better ways to code certain listings shown in the book, so feel free to modify the code and implement this in your framework. In my view, as an experienced automation tester, as long as your code is doing what it is supposed to do and is highlighting bugs or issues in the system you are testing, you are doing a great job. It doesn't need to be a perfectly written piece of code using all the advanced and fancy features of the language. A tester's coding skills do not need to be as comprehensive as a professional programmer to add value. Personally, I don't mind if it takes a few milliseconds, or a few seconds, or for that matter a few minutes to execute an automated test. Once automated, I can add it to my Regression Test Pack and execute it almost without any effort while I'm concentrating on other important tests.

Chapter 1

Getting Started

Getting Started

In this chapter, we will learn about the:

- *Definition of a data warehouse*

- *Components of a data warehouse*

- *Sample data warehouse architecture that we will use for automation purposes*

- *Importance of automated testing*

- *Golden rules to keep in mind while automating data warehouse testing*

So let's get on with it...

A Data Warehouse is a relational database that is designed for query and analysis purposes. It usually contains historical data derived from the transactional data but can also include data from other sources. The primary purpose of a data warehouse is to provide readily accessible information to end-users. It is important to view data warehousing as a process for the delivery of information. The maintenance of a data warehouse is ongoing and iterative in nature. Bill Inmon (recognized by many as the father of the data warehouse) defined a Data Warehouse as:

- Subject Oriented - as it provides information around subjects rather an organisation's ongoing operations e.g. customers, employees, products, sales, revenue etc. for analysis and decision making. The data warehouse provides one-stop shopping and contains information about a variety of subjects.

- Integrated - as it is constructed from heterogeneous sources e.g. relational databases, CSV (Comma Separated Values), Excel files etc. which helps in the effective analysis of the data. Integration of data within a warehouse is achieved by making the data consistent in format, naming and other aspects. For example, the source systems may represent the gender codes by using codes "Male" and "Female", by "M" and "F", or by "1" and "2". The inconsistencies are usually more complex but the data warehouse, on the other hand, stores data in a consistent fashion.

- Time Variant - as it can be used to study trends and changes over a time period. Historical information is of high importance to decision makers.

- Non Volatile - meaning data is non-up-datable. Previous data is not deleted when new data is added. So a data warehouse provides stable information that doesn't change each time an operational process is executed. Information is consistent regardless of when the warehouse is accessed.

We will use the general data warehouse architecture, as shown in Figure 1.1, for the purpose of automated testing. It has a number of areas:

- Source Systems

- Staging Area

- ETL (Extract, Transform and Load)

- Dimensional Data Warehouse

- End User Systems

- Data Marts

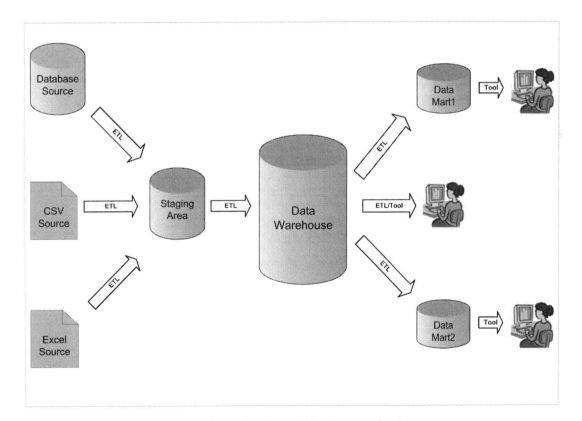

Figure 1.1: Sample Data Warehouse Architecture

1.1   Source Systems

These are the systems that provide the source data for our data warehouse. These systems are all data feeding pipes to the Staging Area. Generally any transformation on the data is performed after the data, in its unchanged form, is taken from the source systems. The data in the source systems can reside in different formats e.g. relational tables, CSV (Comma Separated Values), Excel files etc. In the real world, these source systems may have different naming conventions, measurements, encodings, physical attributes etc. We will consider database tables, CSV and Excel files for automation purposes.

1.2   Staging Area

This is the area where all the data received from the Source Systems is collected. All the required data must be available in the Staging Area before it can be integrated into the warehouse. Ideally the source data remains in its original form in this area but may take a different format in this area based on the design of the data warehouse e.g. source data received in the CSV format is uploaded to a table, or data received in Excel format is loaded into a table.

1.3   ETL (Extract, Transform and Load)

ETL (Extract, Transform and Load) Technology is an important component of the data warehouse architecture. It is used to transfer data from the Source Systems (the operational data) into the data warehouse Staging Area, from the Staging Area into the Data Warehouse and finally from the Data Warehouse into the Data Marts.

1.4   Dimensional Data Warehouse

The purpose of the Data Warehouse in the overall data warehouse architecture is to integrate an organisation's data which usually contains dimension and fact tables. Its structure is optimised for distribution and feeds to one or more data marts or end-users. The data is stored at a granular level of detail e.g. every item that has ever been sold by the organisation is recorded and related to dimensions of interest.

1.5   End User Systems

These are the downstream systems that use data from the warehouse e.g. use a tool to create required reports, data feeds to one or more data marts or the data becomes source to other data warehousing systems.

1.6 Data Mart

This is a subset of the data warehouse that is limited in scope. It is designed to facilitate end-user analysis of the data and is optimised for access. It typically supports a single, analytic application used by a distinct set of users.

1.7 Why Automate?

The need for speed is practically the mantra of the information age. In the real world, automating the data warehouse testing can be very challenging but automating any part of the testing can pay big dividends. Automation usually brings a lot of benefits to the organisation such as:

- Test Efficiency and Accuracy - is usually improved as the comparison of the expected and actual results is performed by computer thereby eliminating human error. Automated tests are fast and, as we will see later, reuse functions & modules within different tests or on different versions of the software.

- Test Coverage - we can achieve better test coverage using automation. As we will see later, we can randomly select records each time we execute a test and thus providing more coverage. Similarly the same tests can be executed when new data arrives.

- Saves Time and Money - automation initially is associated with increased effort but its benefits will pay off in the long run! Regression testing becomes effortless and is highly beneficial for software products with a long maintenance life.

- Tester's Motivation - manual testing can be error-prone and mundane. Automated testing on the other hand is repeatable leaving testers to concentrate on other tasks.

- Reliable - Automated testing is reliable. When a tester writes a test for a defect he or she has found and adds it to the Regression Test Pack, the test just cannot be forgotten. It automatically executes and checks for that peculiar condition where it failed once. A manual tester on the other hand can simply forget to perform this test or may even choose not to perform it due to time pressure or a number of other reasons.

- Quicker Time to Market - In today's competitive environment, time to market is usually the key driver for a number of projects, particularly for revenue generating products. Automation can help reduce time to market by not only shortening the test cycle but helping you meet the deadlines with a reliable product.

1.8 Golden Rules

Here are some golden rules to keep in mind about automation that I have learnt through experience:

1. Start small and simple first. Don't try to automate the complex scenarios first if you are just starting off with automated testing. Take smaller steps before you start walking and finally running.

2. An effective automated test design principle - *always* start the test with a known state.

3. Don't try to automate everything. This simply isn't practical in data warehouse testing, so set realistic expectations.

4. It is typically not a single complex test that uncovers a bug. You may need to perform a combination of simple tests to highlight a bug.

5. Once you are confident of the Automation Framework, test cases with high value and low effort should be automated first.

6. Run your automated tests regularly, if possible with every build. Machines can find flaws.

7. Test your test - make sure you have seen the test case failing at least once - force the failure condition so that you know the required logic works.

8. No matter how much you automate, you still can't replace manual testing or testers. The purpose of automation is not to eliminate testers but to make better use of their time.

9. Ensure that each test has a specific purpose and identifiable results.

10. Log your expected and actual result values for comparison. You never know when you are going to need to look into your test results.

11. All things done well can be done even better. Revising and striving to improve your Automation Framework is a way of improving your skills and driving you on to new heights.

12. Use an Automation Framework that is easy to manage and allows new tests to be added easily.

13. Focus on modularity and re-usability. Build libraries of functions you can reuse in other projects.

14. The *test automation code* has to be used for a long term (just like the *production code*) and hence needs to be easily maintainable. So we need to deploy similar principles and practices in programming the *test automation code* (including coding standards) as we use for the *production code*.

Welcome to the world of automation!

Chapter 2

Sample Dimensional Data Warehouse

Sample Dimensional Data Warehouse

In this chapter, we will learn about:

- *Business, logical and physical models of a system*

- *Source to target data mapping*

- *How data mapping helps us to derive expected and actual results*

So let's get on with it...

BEFORE we can learn to automate the testing of a data warehouse let's first of all understand, at a summary level, how a dimensional data warehouse is implemented. In this book we will setup and automate a sample data warehouse. This sample database is an 'Order Processing System' for a company that sells a broad range of products. To implement our sample data warehouse, we need to understand the following three models of the 'Order Processing System':

- Business Model

- Logical Model

- Physical Model

2.1   Business Model

This is generally a high level Entity Relation Diagram (ERD) of the business. The business model helps us understand what business questions we are trying to answer based on the available information i.e. the attributes and relationship between them. For our Order Processing System (henceforth referred as OPS) we may try answering the following questions:

- Which products were sold?

- Which customers bought products?

- Which employee sold the most products?

- How much discount was applied on sales?

Our Order Processing System is a transactional system where we generally want a very fast response with no redundancy and with the most recent data. Such systems are also called OLTP i.e. On-Line Transaction Processing systems. In contrast, the data warehouse systems that we use to analyse data are called OLAP i.e. On-Line Analytical Processing systems. In order to provide data to these OLAP systems, the operational data required is extracted from the OLTP systems, cleansed and transformed into dimensions and facts. The OLAP data typically has a long time horizon and is non-up-datable.

An OLTP system generally uses a relational data model. It is broken into a number of separate tables to reduce redundancy and eliminate duplicate information. This process is often referred to as 'data normalization'. OLAP on the other hand needs data efficiently organised for end user analysis and will often contain redundancy. This process is generally referred to as 'de-normalization'.

Figure 2.1 shows the ERD of our Order Processing System.

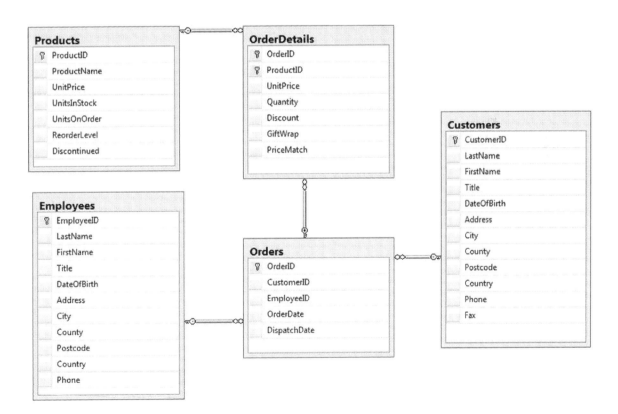

Figure 2.1: Order Processing System ERD

From the diagram we can say that our operational data is divided into four main areas (also sometimes called Subject Areas) – Products, Customers, Employees and Time (order dates etc.) Note that most of the tables feed from the Orders table and this table will be the key in deciding which facts or keys we want to model.

2.2 Logical Model

During Logical Modelling we decompose the data subjects into data entities comprising facts and dimensions. Visualization of the dimensional data model generally happens in the form of a cube of three, four or more dimensions. The slicing and dicing of the cube along its dimensions gives us the desired data. Let's try to visualize the four subject areas we have identified in the business model i.e. Products, Customers, Employees and Time. To make things a bit simpler, let's begin by visualizing the first three subjects i.e. Products, Customers and Employees as shown in Figure 2.2.

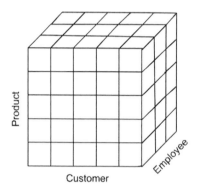

Figure 2.2: Order Processing System - 3 Dimensions

The three dimensional model can be extended to four dimensions by adding the time dimension for the month of year in which a sale was made as shown in Figure 2.3. Imagine there are twelve boxes and each box represents a month from January to December. When the above 3D model is placed in a box say January, the cells within it contain information for January. When the above 3D model is placed in a box say February, the cells within it contain information for February and so on.

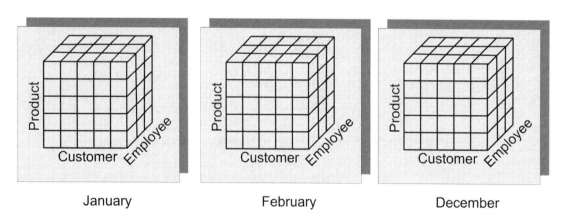

Figure 2.3: Order Processing System - 4 Dimensions

This paradigm can be extended to five or more dimensions.

The data loaded into the warehouse is one of the two types – fact and dimensions. A fact is something that can be measured; they are numeric and generally continuous and are used to calculate some statistic. Dimensions on the other hand are pieces of information that categorize things.

Figure 2.4 shows a possible star-schema model of the Order Processing System based on a central fact table surrounded by a number of dimension tables.

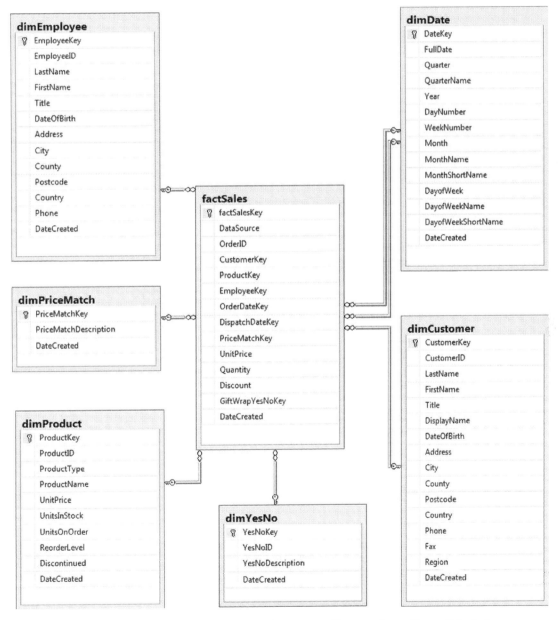

Figure 2.4: Order Processing System - Dimensions Data Model

2.3   Physical Model

Physical Data Model also called schema is the actual model which is created in the database to store data. It includes:

1. Table names

2. All column names of the table along with data type and size

3. Primary and Foreign Keys of a table

4. Indexes and constraints

One of the main goals of physical data warehouse design is good query performance. This goal is usually achieved by facilitating collocated queries and evenly distributing data across all the database partitions.

In the later chapters, we will see how our sample data warehouse is physically implemented.

2.4   Data Mapping

Data Mapping documents how fields in the source (operational) systems are transformed into data warehouse fields. Data Mapping is one of the most important documents you will need as a tester to verify the transformations implemented in the data warehouse. It tells you a number of things like:

- What dimensions and facts are in the data warehouse

- From where each column of the warehouse is being sourced

- What transformation rules are applied to the source data

- Which keys in the dimension and fact are unique

- What default values apply if the source data is not as expected

There is a lot of information in a Data Mapping document. If you don't have this document for the project you are testing, you should definitely ask for one to be created. This mapping document is critical to the successful development and testing of the data warehouse.

For our sample data warehouse, we are working with fictitious data mapping, but in the real world you will see more complex rules than those illustrated here.

The data mapping for our automated testing purposes will contain the following columns:

Dimension or Fact Table name						
Column Name	Source Table	Source Column	Transformation	Unique Key	Unknown Key	Null Value
...	...	...	...	...	...	...
...	...	...	...	...	...	...

Table Header: the name of the dimension or fact table.

Column Name: the name of a column in the dimension or fact table. This is usually taken from the physical implementation of the table schema.

Source Table: the name of the source system table which is feeding into the dimension or fact table.

Source Column: the name of the source table column which is mapped onto the dimension or fact table column. This mapping may be:

- one-to-one (e.g. one source column feeding to one target column) or

- many-to-one (e.g. many source columns feeding to one target column) or

- one-to-many (e.g. one source column feeding to many target columns)

Transformation: this indicates whether or not the source data is transformed in any way before it reaches the target column. Since the data is feeding into the data warehouse from a number of source systems, they may not all have a consistent format e.g. one source system stores Yes/No answers as "Y" and "N" and the another stores it as "Yes" and "No". We may need to transform this diversified data into a single consistent format before it is saved in the data warehouse.

Unique Key: this tells us which columns in the target dimension or fact table contain unique values. It may be a single column or a combination of columns.

Unknown Key: Generally in the dimension table there is an Unknown Key for not known values e.g. our source system column ProductID may have NULL values, so when the fact table is populated all such source keys should be mapped to the Unknown Key.

Null Values: indicates whether the target column can contain null values or not.

Usually there is a lot of additional information in the Data Mapping document and some documents may also list these columns:

Description: a brief description of the column.

Data Type: of the target column.

Primary Key: whether or not the target column is a Primary Key.

Foreign Key: any foreign keys to other tables.

Joins: any links to other tables.

Example: of values in the column.

Let's now see, over the next few pages, what source to target data mapping applies to our sample data warehouse. Note that the mappings are shown for illustration purposes only to demonstrate the different ways a dimension or fact table might get populated and are not necessarily the way it should be populated.

Column Name	Source Table	Source Column	Transformation	Unique Key	Unknown Key	Null Value
EmployeeKey		Generated Key			-1	No
EmployeeID	Employee	EmployeeID		Yes	-1	No
LastName	Employee	LastName			Unknown	No
FirstName	Employee	FirstName			Unknown	No
Title	Employee	Title			Unknown	No
DateOfBirth	Employee	DateOfBirth			Null	Yes
Address	Employee	Address			Unknown	No
City	Employee	City			Unknown	No
County	Employee	County			Unknown	No
Postcode	Employee	Postcode			Unknown	No
Country	Employee	Country			Unknown	No
Phone	Employee	Phone			Unknown	No
DateCreated		getdate()			getdate()	No

dimEmployee

This is the case where the dimension is populated from a source table and there is one-to-one mapping between source to target table and no transformations take place.

dimCustomer

Column Name	Source Table	Source Column	Transformation	Unique	Unknown Key	Null Value
CustomerKey		Generated Key			-1	No
CustomerID	Customer	CustomerID		Yes	-1	No
LastName	Customer	LastName			Unknown	No
FirstName	Customer	FirstName			Unknown	No
Title	Customer	Title			Unknown	No
DisplayName	Customer	LastName, FirstName and Title	Title + ' ' + FirstName + ' ' + LastName		Unknown	No
DateOfBirth	Customer	DateOfBirth			Null	Yes
Address	Customer	Address			Unknown	No
City	Customer	City			Unknown	No
County	Customer	County			Unknown	No
Postcode	Customer	Postcode			Unknown	No
Country	Customer	Country			Unknown	No
Phone	Customer	Phone			Unknown	No
Fax	Customer	Fax			Unknown	No
Region		Postcode	First char of Postcode Between A-G = "North" Between H-N = "South" Between O-R = "East" Between S-Z = "West" otherwise "Unknown"		Unknown	No
DateCreated		getdate()	getdate()			No

Column 'DisplayName' is an example of where many-to-one mapping has been used i.e. many source columns create one target column. Column 'Region' is an example of where the source data is transformed to the target based on the Postcode's value.

Column Name	Source Table	Source Column	dimProduct Transformation	Unique Key	Unknown Key	Null Value
ProductKey		Generated Key			-1	No
ProductID	Products	ProductID		Yes	-1	No
ProductType	Products	ProductID	ProductID ≤ 50 "Domestic" ProductID between 50 and 75 "Commercial" ProductID > 75 "Other" Otherwise "Unknown"		Unknown	No
ProductName	Products	ProductName			Unknown	No
UnitPrice	Products	UnitPrice			-1	No
UnitsInStock	Products	UnitsInStock			-1	No
UnitsOnOrder	Products	UnitsOnOrder			-1	No
ReorderLevel	Products	ReorderLevel			-1	No
Discontinued	Products	Discontinued	Discontinued = 1 then Yes Discontinued = 0 then No Otherwise Unknown		Unknown	No
DateCreated		getdate()			getdate()	No

Column 'ProductType' is another example of where the source data is transformed to the target based on the value of 'ProductID'.

Column Name	Source Table	Source Column	Transformation	Unique Key	Unknown Key	Null Value
DateKey		Generated Key			-1	No
FullDate				Yes	Null	Yes
Quarter					-1	No
QuarterName					Unknown	No
Year					-1	No
DayNumber					-1	No
WeekNumber					-1	No
Month					-1	No
MonthName					Unknown	No
MonthShortName					Unknown	No
DayofWeek					-1	No
DayofWeekName					Unknown	No
DayofWeekShortName					Unknown	No
DateCreated		getdate()			getdate()	No

This is a case where there is no source table but an SQL query is used to populate the dimension. We will learn about this later when we populate this dimension.

dimYesNo

Column Name	Source Table	Source Column	Transformation	Unique Key	Unknown Key	Null Value
YesNoKey		Generated Key			-1	No
YesNoID				Yes	-1	No
YesNoDescription					Unknown	No
DateCreated		getdate()			getdate()	No

This is a case where static text is used to populate the dimension. We will learn about this later when we populate this dimension.

dimPriceMatch

Column Name	Source Table	Source Column	Transformation	Unique Key	Unknown Key	Null Value
PriceMatchKey		Generated Key			-1	No
PriceMatchDescription	OrderDetails	PriceMatch	Distinct PriceMatch values from OrderDetails	Yes	Unknown	No No
DateCreated		getdate()			getdate()	No

This is a case where distinct values of a field in the source table are used to populate the dimension. We will learn about this later when we populate this dimension.

Column Name	Source Table	Source Column	Transformation	Unique Key	Unknown Key	Null Value
factSalesKey		Generated Key				No
DataSource			Generated based on data source	Yes		No
OrderID	Orders	OrderID		Yes		No
CustomerKey	Orders	CustomerID	dimCustomer	Yes		No
ProductKey	OrderDetails	ProductID	dimProduct			No
EmployeeKey	Orders	EmployeeID	dimEmployee			No
OrderDateKey	Orders	OrderDate	dimDate			No
DispatchDateKey	Orders	DispatchDate	dimDate			No
PriceMatchKey	OrderDetails	PriceMatch	dimPriceMatch			No
UnitPrice	OrderDetails	UnitPrice				No
Quantity	OrderDetails	Quantity				No
Discount	OrderDetails	Discount				No
GiftWrapYesNoKey	OrderDetails	GiftWrap	dimYesNo			No
DateCreated		getdate()				No

factSales

The fact table has various keys pointing to the dimension tables. Note that there is no 'Unknown Key' in the fact table.

Chapter 2

2.5   Expected Vs. Actual

Ok, let's explore a little bit about how we are going to know what is the expected result and the actual result of our tests so that we can compare both the values and decide whether the result is a pass or fail. Let us take the example of Products table which feeds to dimProduct in the data warehouse via data mapping as shown in Figure 2.5.

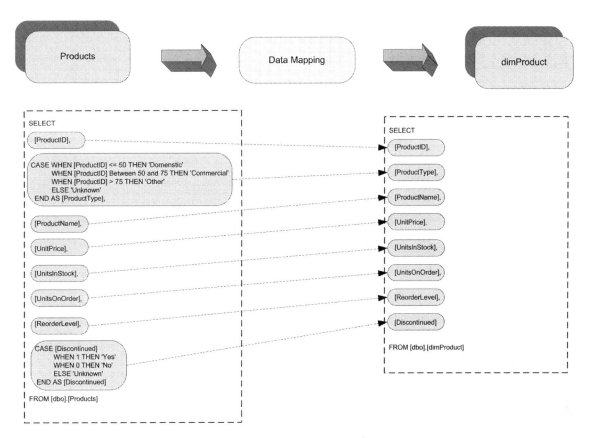

Figure 2.5: Expected vs. Actual

Based on the Data Mapping of table 'dimProduct', let's look at the 'ProductType' column. The following case statement executed on the source table 'Products' provides us with the *Expected Result*.

```
CASE WHEN [ProductID] <= 50 THEN 'Domestic'
   WHEN [ProductID] Between 50 and 75 THEN 'Commercial'
   WHEN [ProductID] > 75 THEN 'Other'
   ELSE 'Unknown'
END AS [ProductType]
```

Column 'ProductType' in the target table 'dimProduct' provides the *Actual Result*.

Now if our *Expected Result* from the source table 'Products' matches the *Actual Result* from target table 'dimProduct' it means 'ProductType' has been successfully loaded in the data warehouse. In other words, when we apply data mapping transformation(s) on the source table column we get the *Expected Result*. The value in the target dimension or fact table is our *Actual Result*. When these two values match we get a Test Step Pass result otherwise it is a Test Step Fail result. As mentioned earlier, the source-to-target mapping could be one-to-one, one-to-many or many-to-one. As a tester you need to understand how each column of the data warehouse dimension or fact table is sourced, so that you can verify its population.

Chapter 3

Automation Approach

Automation Approach

In this chapter, we will learn:

- *Which software we need to automate data warehouse testing*

- *About the Automation Framework that we are going to develop*

- *How to write our first automated test*

- *About adding some important features to our Automation Framework*

So let's get on with it...

WHAT is an Automation Framework? An Automation Framework is an application that allows you to write tests without worrying about the constraints of the underlying test tools. As in Software Development Life Cycle (SDLC) to develop software applications, framework design plays a vital role in building the test approach for automation. The need for a well-defined and designed test framework is especially important in automated testing.

A well designed automation framework makes test automation more efficient, reduces test automation effort, lowers the cost of maintenance and provides a higher Return On Investment (ROI). It is very important to have a framework that enhances efficiency in the development of automated test scripts through modular, reusable and maintainable code. The framework should ensure a uniformity of design across multiple test scripts. Adding more features to the framework should not disturb the existing tests.

Effective test reporting is another important feature and enhances the value of framework. The framework should support the production of both summary, high level views of all the tests executed as well as detailed reports providing a step by step view of various steps in the test.

Similarly log generation is another important part of the test execution. The framework should provide the means to create debug logs which can help find a problem quickly. Execution reports and logs are important for any automation execution and should be stored for future reference.

First of all let's start identify the environment and software we will need to automate the testing.

3.1   Automation Environment and Software

I work on a Windows 7 workstation with the following software on it:

1. Microsoft® SQL Server® 2012 Express – for data warehouse databases.
   `http://www.microsoft.com/en-gb/download/details.aspx?id=29062`

2. Java™ Platform, Standard Edition Development Kit (JDK™) - jdk 1.7 (jdk-7u40-windows-x64.exe)
   `http://www.oracle.com/technetwork/java/javase/downloads/java-archive-downloads-javase7-521261.html#jdk-7u40-oth-JPR`

   Note: If you don't want to use HTML Reporting then you may want to install Java Standard Edition Runtime Environment 1.7 only.

3. Eclipse – an Integrated Development Environment which we will use to write our JUnit tests. The version on my workstation is Eclipse Standard/SDK Version: Kepler Service Release 2.
   `http://sourceforge.net/projects/eclipse.mirror/files/Eclipse%204.3.2/`

   Extract to 'C:\Program Files' or any other location you prefer.

   Make a desktop shortcut of 'eclipse.exe' for quick access. Just right click on 'eclipse.exe' and select Send to ⇒ Desktop (create shortcut)

4. Apache Log4j - a logging library for Java.
   `http://logging.apache.org/log4j/2.x/download.html`

   Extract to 'C:\log4j'

5. Microsoft JDBC Drivers for SQL Server (sqljdbc_4.0.2206.100_enu.exe) - for database connectivity.
   `http://www.microsoft.com/en-us/download/details.aspx?id=11774`

   Extract to 'C:\sqljdbc_4.0'

6. Apache Poi - Java library for Excel operations.
   `http://poi.apache.org/download.html#POI-3.10.1`

   Extract to 'C:\poi-3.10.1'

7. 7-Zip - an open source utility for creating archives.
   `http://www.7-zip.org/download.html`

   Install to 'C:\Program Files\7-Zip'

You will need the corresponding software on your workstation, according to the operating system you are using.

3.2   Automation Framework

We will develop our Automation Framework as we move through this book. Figure 3.1 shows the Automation Framework in its simplest form. We will add more components to this as we progress through its development.

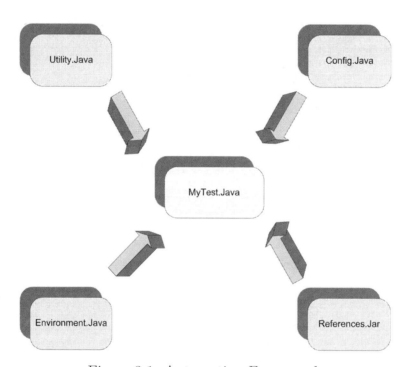

Figure 3.1: Automation Framework

Let me start by explaining the framework components.

3.2.1   Configuration File

The Configuration File is used to store a number of configuration parameters for your framework that are used throughout your testing. Some examples of these parameters are:

```
public static final int STEP_PASS = 0;
public static final int STEP_FAIL = 1;
```

3.2.2 Utility File

The Utility File holds any general purpose functions that are to be used throughout your testing. An example of such a function is:

```
public static void ReportExpectedVsActual(String exp, String act)
```

This function accepts two arguments, the expected outcome and the actual outcome, and reports the result. If the expected and actual outcomes are the same it will pass the step, otherwise it will fail it. The next section provides more information on this.

3.2.3 Environment File

The Environment File contains a number of environment parameters e.g. the names and user ids of the databases you need to connect to during testing, the location of the test files to be loaded into the system etc. An example of such a parameter is:

```
public static final String DB_SOURCE = "<DB Connection details>";
```

3.2.4 Reference Files

The Automation Framework uses a number of reference files and libraries. You will learn how to attach these to the framework in later sections of the book. .

3.2.5 MyTest File

This is the actual JUnit Java File that contains one or more tests. Figure 3.2 shows the structure of an automated test file. As you can see, each test script has a number of important parts:

- Before Test Script Setup - this is the code that is executed **once** before **any** of the test methods are executed e.g. setting up our test result summary file.

- Before Test Setup - this is the code that is executed before **each test** is executed e.g. to reset selected parameters before each test starts.

- Each test will have its own logic to verify. For each test step, once we have derived the expected and actual results, we will make a call to a generic function 'ReportExpectedVsActual' to report the outcome of the test step.

- Report Overall Test result will report the final result of the current test. If any test step has failed, the overall result of that test will be Fail.

- After Test Script Steps - these steps will be executed at the end of all the tests e.g. to close the results file.

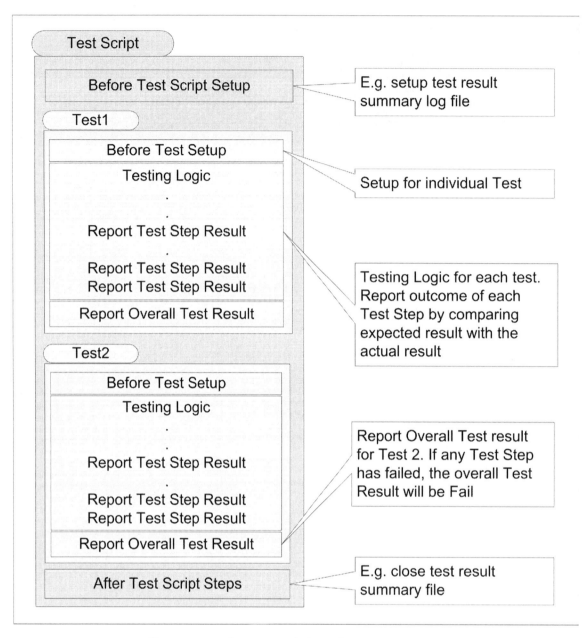

Figure 3.2: Automated Test Script Structure

The above structure will be followed for writing all the tests which gives us a consistent approach. Don't worry, if you don't understand the flow at this stage. Just keep the script structure in mind for the time being. Things will become more apparent when we start writing our first test in the next section!

At this stage, the book assumes that you have successfully downloaded and installed the required software as stated in the beginning of this chapter.

3.3   Your First Automated Test

Let's get on with writing your first automated test, using the following steps.

Step 1: Launch Eclipse from its installed location or from the desktop shortcut you created. You may be asked to choose a workspace folder as shown in Figure 3.3. A workspace is a directory on your hard drive in which Eclipse stores the projects that you define. Simply -

- Click the 'Browse...' button

- Select the C: drive

- Click the 'Make New Folder' button

- Type the folder name as Workspace

- Click the OK button

- Tick the 'Use this as the default and do not ask again' check box

- Click the OK button

You may want to set up the folder on a different drive with a different name. This book uses 'C:\Workspace' as the default workspace location.

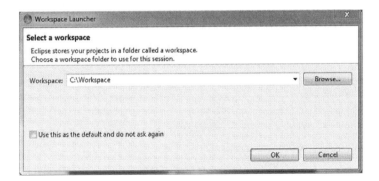

Figure 3.3: Workspace Location

Step 2: Create a new project.

- Go to File ⇒ New ⇒ Project...

- Select 'Java Project' as shown in Figure 3.4

- Click the Next button

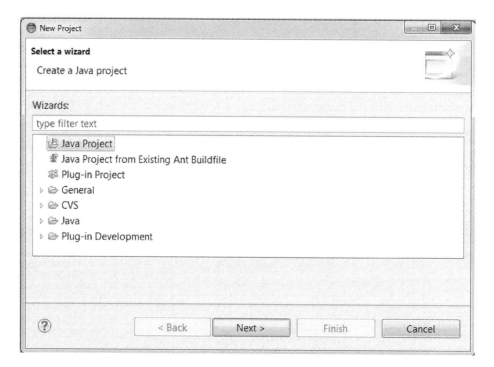

Figure 3.4: Select Java Project

- Type AutoDW in the 'Project Name' edit box as shown in Figure 3.5 and leave everything else as default.

- Click the Finish button.

Figure 3.5: Project AutoDW

Step 3: Now let's setup the Configuration file.

- In the 'Package Explorer' on the left hand side, right click on the folder name 'src' and select New ⇒ Class

- Type autoDW in the 'Package' edit box as shown in Figure 3.6. Packages can be thought of as Java's equivalent of namespaces in other languages like C# and C++. Putting classes in a particular package ensures that there won't be a name conflict between your class and another.

- Type Config in the 'Name' edit box

- Click the Finish button

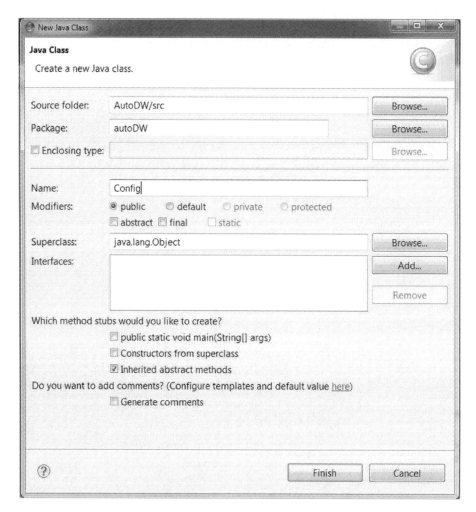

Figure 3.6: Add Config Class

Step 4: Add Listing 8.1 code to the Config.java file.

Listing 3.1: Code for Config.java

```
1  package autoDW;
2
3  public class Config {
4      public static String TestResult;
5      public static final String PASS = "PASS";
6      public static final String FAIL = "FAIL";
7  }
```

Let me explain the code:

Line 4: Configuration variable 'TestResult' will store the overall test result of a test.

Line 5 and 6: Define the PASS and FAIL configuration variables used throughout the framework.

Step 5: Setup Test Script file.

- In the 'Package Explorer', right click on the folder name 'src' and select New ⇒ Other...

- Select Java ⇒ 'JUnit Test Case' as shown in Figure 3.7

- Click the Next button

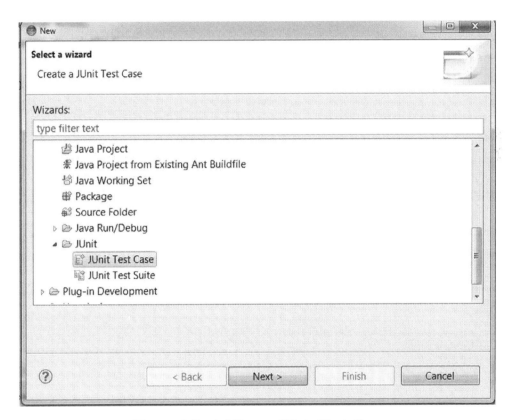

Figure 3.7: Adding a JUnit Test Case

- Type myTest in the 'Name' edit box as shown in Figure 3.8

- Click the Finish button

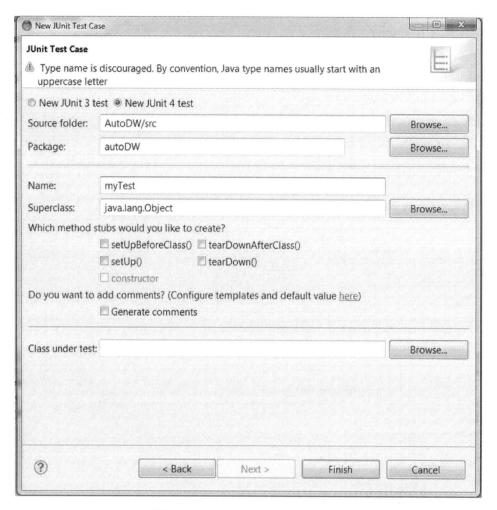

Figure 3.8: Adding myTest

You may be asked to add the JUnit 4 library to the build path, as shown in Figure 3.9. If so, select 'Add JUnit 4 library to the build path' option and press the OK button.

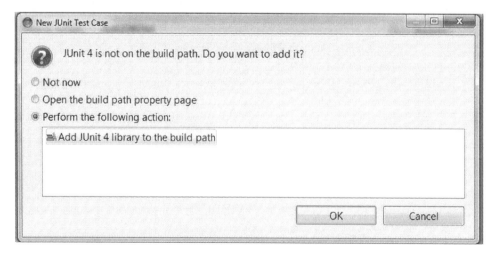

Figure 3.9: Add JUnit 4 library to the Build Path

Step 6: Setup Utility file.

- In the 'Package Explorer', right click on the folder name 'src' and select New ⇒ Class

- Type Utility in the 'Name' edit box as shown in Figure 3.10

- Click the Finish button

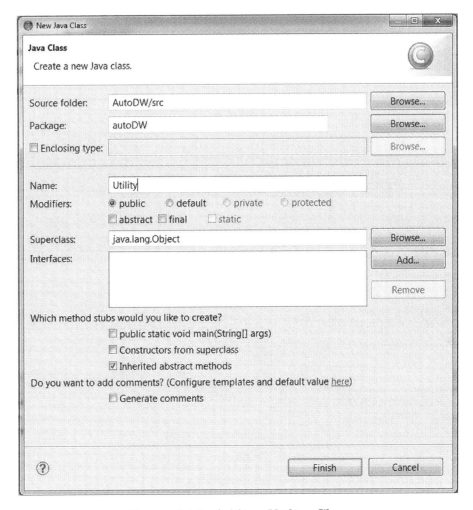

Figure 3.10: Adding Utility Class

Step 7: Let's now define two general purpose functions in our Utility file as follows:

ReportExpectedVsActual - Reports the outcome of expected and actual result comparison for a Test Step		
Input Parameters	*strExpected*	Expected Result passed as a String
	strActual	Actual Result passed as a String
Return Value	*void*	Returns nothing.

ReportResult - Reports the final result (Pass or Fail) of a Test.		
Input Parameters	*none*	No parameter
Return Value	*void*	Returns nothing.

Add Listing 3.2 code to the Utility.java file.

Listing 3.2: Code for Utility.java

```
1  package autoDW;
2
3  import static org.junit.Assert.*;
4
5  public class Utility
6  {
7     public static void ReportExpectedVsActual(String ←
          ↪ strExpected, String strActual)
8     {
9        strExpected = strExpected.trim();
10       strActual = strActual.trim();
11
12       if (strExpected.equals(strActual))
13       {
14          System.out.println("[Expected:] " + strExpected ←
              ↪ + "    [Actual:] " + strActual + "    [Step ←
              ↪ Passed]");
15       }
16       else
17       {
18          System.out.println("[Expected:] " + strExpected ←
              ↪ + "    [Actual:] " + strActual + "    [Step ←
              ↪ FAILED]");
19          Config.TestResult = Config.FAIL;
20       }
21    }
22
23    public static void ReportResult()
24    {
25       System.out.println("Reporting result.... ");
26
27       if (Config.TestResult.equals(Config.FAIL))
28       {
29          System.out.println("Test Failed.... Check error ←
              ↪ log.");
```

```
30                assertFalse(true);
31            }
32        else
33        {
34                System.out.println("Test Passed.");
35                assertTrue(true);
36        }
37    }
38 }
```

Line 3: Import statement to support the required functionality.

Line 9 and 10: Remove any leading or trailing spaces from the parameters.

Line 12: If Expected value equals Actual value, report Pass.

Line 16: If Expected value isn't equal to Actual value, report Fail.

Line 19: Set the overall test result to Fail.

Line 23: Function to be called at the end of each test to report overall result.

Line 25: It is always good to log some useful messages to help in debugging while going through the logs.

Line 27: If any step has failed, report Failure.

Line 32: Otherwise Report Pass.

Step 8: In the 'Package Explorer', double click on the myTest.java file and add Listing 3.3 code to it.

Listing 3.3: Code for myTest.java

```
1  package autoDW;
2
3  import org.junit.Before;
4  import org.junit.Test;
5
6  public class myTest
7  {
8      @Before
9      public void setUp() throws Exception
10     {
11         Config.TestResult = Config.PASS;
12     }
13
14     @Test
15     public void testOne()
16     {
17         Utility.ReportExpectedVsActual("1", "1");
18         Utility.ReportResult();
```

```
19      }
20  }
```

Line 8: @Before annotation indicates that the attached method will be run before any test in the class.

Line 11: Note that we declared the configuration variable 'TestResult' in the Config.Java class. Before each test is run we must reset its value to 'Pass' so that it doesn't report failures from the previous tests.

Line 14: @Test annotation identifies a method as a test method.

Line 17: This test simply calls our generic function 'ReportExpectedVsActual' with two identical values the result of which should be a Pass.

Line 18: 'ReportResult' will report the final result of the test execution which in this case is Pass. We will call this generic function at the end of each test.

☞ Sometimes when you are entering code in the Editor, you may need to include some additional import statements. When you hover over the failing code you will see a little popup window as shown in Figure 3.11 that states *'AfterClass cannot be resolved to a type'*. Click on the *Import 'AfterClass' (org.junit)* link and it should automatically add the required import statement to the code.

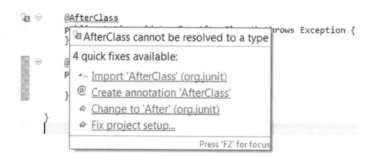

Figure 3.11: Resolving Import Issues

Step 9: By now you have successfully written your first automated test in its simplest form! So let's run it.

- In the 'Package Explorer', right click on the testOne and select Run As ⇒ JUnit Test

- From the top menu select Window ⇒ Show View ⇒ Console.

You will see a Console window as shown in Figure 3.12. The Console indicates that the expected value was '1', the actual value was also '1' and the test step passed. Thus the overall result was Pass.

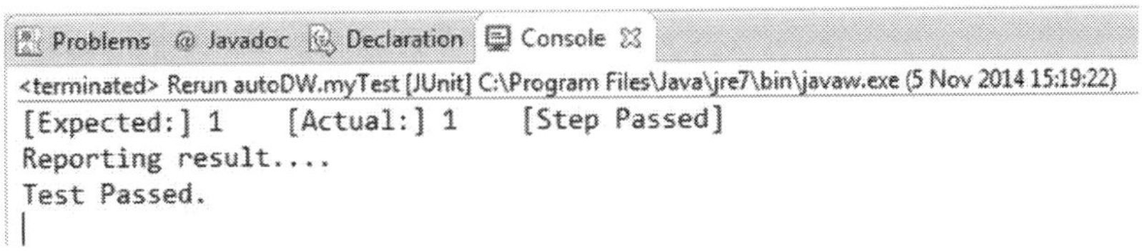

Figure 3.12: Console Output - testOne

Now let's add another test to our test file. Go back to myTest.java and add a new test 'testTwo' as shown in Listing 3.4.

Listing 3.4: Code for myTest.java

```
1  package autoDW;
2
3  import org.junit.Before;
4  import org.junit.Test;
5
6  public class myTest {
7      @Before
8      public void setUp() throws Exception {
9          Config.TestResult = Config.PASS;
10     }
11
12     @Test
13     public void testOne() {
14
15         Utility.ReportExpectedVsActual("1", "1");
16         Utility.ReportResult();
17     }
18
19     @Test
20     public void testTwo() {
21
22         Utility.ReportExpectedVsActual("1", "2");
23         Utility.ReportResult();
24     }
25 }
```

Line 19: Note the @Test annotation before this new test.
Line 22: Let's compare '1' with '2' this time the result of which should be Fail.

Now let's run the testTwo as we did previously i.e.

- In the 'Package Explorer', right click on the testTwo and select Run As ⇒ JUnit Test

- From the top menu select Window ⇒ Show View ⇒ Console.

You will see a console window as shown in Figure 3.13.

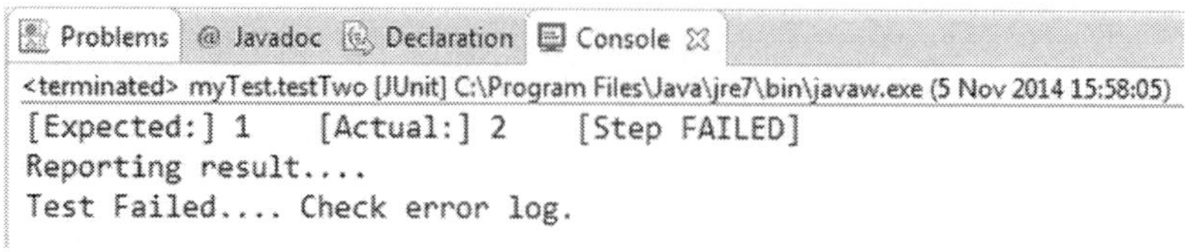

```
Problems   @ Javadoc   Declaration   Console ⊠
<terminated> myTest.testTwo [JUnit] C:\Program Files\Java\jre7\bin\javaw.exe (5 Nov 2014 15:58:05)
[Expected:] 1    [Actual:] 2     [Step FAILED]
Reporting result....
Test Failed.... Check error log.
```

Figure 3.13: Console Output - testTwo

The console indicates that the expected value was '1' but the actual value was '2' and the test step failed. The overall test result was Fail. We will learn about error logging in the next section.

Now let's add another test 'testThree' to our myTest.java file.

Listing 3.5: Code for myTest.java

```
1  package autoDW;
2
3  import org.junit.Before;
4  import org.junit.Test;
5
6  public class myTest
7  {
8      @Before
9      public void setUp() throws Exception
10     {
11         Config.TestResult = Config.PASS;
12     }
13
14     @Test
15     public void testOne()
16     {
17
18         Utility.ReportExpectedVsActual("1", "1");
19         Utility.ReportResult();
20     }
21
22     @Test
23     public void testTwo()
24     {
```

```
25
26          Utility.ReportExpectedVsActual("1", "2");
27          Utility.ReportResult();
28      }
29
30      @Test
31      public void testThree()
32      {
33
34          Utility.ReportExpectedVsActual("4", "4");
35          Utility.ReportExpectedVsActual("4", "5");
36          Utility.ReportExpectedVsActual("5", "5");
37          Utility.ReportResult();
38      }
39  }
```

Line 34: Comparing '4' with '4' so the test step should Pass.
Line 35: Comparing '4' with '5' so the test step should Fail.
Line 36: Comparing '5' with '5' so the test step should Pass.
Line 37: Overall test result should Fail because one of the test steps has failed.

Finally let's run the test as we did previously i.e.

- In the 'Package Explorer', right click on testThree and select Run As ⇒ JUnit Test

- From the top menu select Window ⇒ Show View ⇒ Console.

You will see a Console window as shown in 3.14:

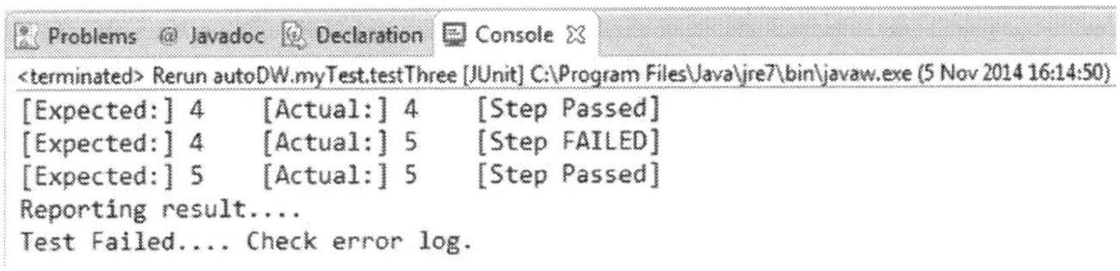

Figure 3.14: Console Output - testThree

As you can see two test steps have passed and one has failed. The overall test result is Fail.

3.4   Logging Information

So as you saw in the previous section, we developed a simple Automation Framework and it works! Log generation is an important part of the test execution. It is very important to generate debug information at various points in a test. This information can help you identify problem areas quickly and also reduce the bug fixing time for developers.

In the previous example, the framework used the 'System.out' function for logging information. However, we need our framework to provide a robust logging mechanism so that we can log different types of message e.g..

- Info i.e. informational messages

- Error i.e. error messages

- Debug i.e. debug messages

Logging different types of message provides better control over the flow of the test script. We will use Apache Log4j as the mechanism for logging different types of message as it is very easy to use. So let's see how to extend the Automation Framework to include logging.

First of all let's add the required reference libraries.

- Right click on the 'src' folder select Build Path ⇒ Configure Build Path

- Go to Libraries and click on 'Add External JARs'

- Select 'log4j-api-2.1.jar' and 'log4j-core-2.1.jar' as shown in the Figure 3.15. The files should be in folder 'C:\log4j\apache-log4j-2.1-bin'. Remember, we extracted the files in 'C:\log4j'.

- Press Open and then press the OK button.

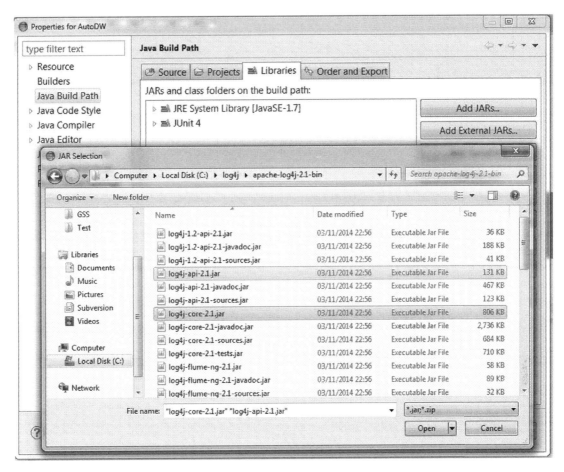

Figure 3.15: Adding Log4j Libraries

3.4.1 Logging to Console via Logger

In the first instance, let's log our messages to the Console Output window. Open the Utility.java file and make the changes shown in Listing 3.6.

Listing 3.6: Code for Utility.java

```
1  package autoDW;
2
3  import static org.junit.Assert.*;
4  import org.apache.logging.log4j.LogManager;
5  import org.apache.logging.log4j.Logger;
6
7  public class Utility {
8
9      public static Logger log = ↵
          ↪ LogManager.getLogger("MyLogger");
10
```

```
11    public static void ReportExpectedVsActual(String ↵
          ↪ strExpected, String strActual)
12    {
13        strExpected = strExpected.trim();
14        strActual = strActual.trim();
15
16        if (strExpected.equals(strActual))
17        {
18            log.info("[Expected:] " + strExpected + "        ↵
                  ↪ [Actual:] " + strActual + "     [Step ↵
                  ↪ Passed]");
19        }
20        else
21        {
22            log.error("[Expected:] " + strExpected + "        ↵
                  ↪ [Actual:] " + strActual + "     [Step ↵
                  ↪ FAILED]");
23            Config.TestResult = Config.FAIL;
24        }
25    }
26
27    public static void ReportResult()
28    {
29        log.info("Reporting result.... ");
30
31        if (Config.TestResult.equals(Config.FAIL))
32        {
33            log.error("Test Failed.... Check error log.");
34            assertFalse(true);
35        }
36        else
37        {
38            log.info("Test Passed.");
39            assertTrue(true);
40        }
41    }
42 }
```

Line 4 and 5: Additional imports required to support the logging mechanism.

Line 9: Logger declaration which is used throughout the Automation Framework.

Line 18, 29 and 38: Change the 'System.out.println' calls to the new logger function 'log.info' to display informational messages.

Line 22 and 33: Change the 'System.out.println' calls to the new logger function 'log.error' to display error messages.

We now need to create a configuration file for the logger. Open the Notepad (or any text editor of your choice) and create a 'log4j2.xml' file in folder 'C:\Workspace\AutoDW\src' as shown in the Listing 3.7.

Listing 3.7: Code for log4j2.xml

```
1  <?xml version="1.0" encoding="UTF-8"?>
2  <Configuration status="WARN">
3    <Appenders>
4     <Console name="Console" target="SYSTEM_OUT">
5        <PatternLayout pattern="%d{HH:mm:ss.SSS} [%t] ←
             ↪ %-5level %logger{36} - %msg%n"/>
6     </Console>
7    </Appenders>
8    <Loggers>
9     <Root level="trace">
10       <AppenderRef ref="Console"/>
11    </Root>
12   </Loggers>
13 </Configuration>
```

The 'log4j2.xml' file has three main components:

- **Appender** - is responsible for publishing the logging information to the preferred destination. We define the appender first with a name which in our case is 'Console'. This is the name used to refer to the appender in the rest of the configuration file. The target method is used to choose which console stream to print messages to, which in our case is 'SYSTEM_OUT'.

- **Layout** - is responsible for formatting the logging information in the preferred style. The format of the result depends on the conversion pattern. For example, in our case we use [%t] which outputs the name of the thread that generated the logging event.

- **Logger** - is responsible for capturing the logging information to the desired appender. We have a 'root' logger that is configured to level 'trace'. The appender 'console' is attached to it. Since all loggers inherit from 'root', all trace or higher messages from all loggers will be printed to the 'Console' appender.

Once you have created the file, within Eclipse IDE, right click AutoDW in the 'Package Explorer' and select Refresh. You should now see the 'log4j2.xml' file in the 'Package Explorer'.

Now let's run the test as we did previously i.e.

- In the 'Package Explorer', right click on the testOne and select Run As ⇒ JUnit Test

- From the top menu select Window ⇒ Show View ⇒ Console.

You will see a Console Output window as shown in Figure 3.16. The Console window now shows a timestamp for each test step. The test steps that were logged as 'log.info' are displayed as INFO along with the name of the logger 'MyLogger'.

```
Problems   @ Javadoc   Declaration   Console ⌗
<terminated> myTest.testOne [JUnit] C:\Program Files\Java\jre7\bin\javaw.exe (7 Nov 2014 19:12:20)
19:12:21.916 [main] INFO  MyLogger - [Expected:] 1     [Actual:] 1     [Step Passed]
19:12:21.916 [main] INFO  MyLogger - Reporting result....
19:12:21.916 [main] INFO  MyLogger - Test Passed.
```

Figure 3.16: Logger Console Output - testOne

Let's execute the testThree that includes a failure step. You will see a console output as shown in Figure 3.17. The test steps that were logged as 'log.error' are displayed as ERROR. The Console window now displays ERROR for an error and INFO for an informational message so we have a better control on the logging mechanism.

```
Problems   @ Javadoc   Declaration   Console ⌗
<terminated> myTest.testThree [JUnit] C:\Program Files\Java\jre7\bin\javaw.exe (7 Nov 2014 19:30:03)
19:30:04.361 [main] INFO  MyLogger - [Expected:] 4     [Actual:] 4     [Step Passed]
19:30:04.361 [main] ERROR MyLogger - [Expected:] 4     [Actual:] 5     [Step FAILED]
19:30:04.361 [main] INFO  MyLogger - [Expected:] 5     [Actual:] 5     [Step Passed]
19:30:04.361 [main] INFO  MyLogger - Reporting result....
19:30:04.361 [main] ERROR MyLogger - Test Failed.... Check error log.
```

Figure 3.17: Logger Console Output - testThree

3.4.2   Logging to a File

So far we have extended the Automation Framework to use our own logger to log additional information in the Console window. However, it lacks one important feature which is the ability to save the test results to an output file (because the console is refreshed as soon as you run the next test and all of the information is lost).

We need all the test results to be saved automatically so that we can refer to them at a later stage for investigation purposes. Also, they are your proof that the test has been executed and can be used as evidence or for audit purposes. I personally log a lot of information for each test execution as it often proves very handy when you need to refer back to logs at a later stage. So, how do we extend our Automation Framework to automatically save logs at the end of the test execution?

Here is how to save the console information in a log file. Modify 'log4j2.xml' created previously, as shown in Listing 3.8.

```
1  <?xml version="1.0" encoding="UTF-8"?>
2  <Configuration status="WARN">
3     <Appenders>
4        <Console name="Console" target="SYSTEM_OUT">
5           <PatternLayout pattern="%d{HH:mm:ss.SSS} [%t] ↵
                ↪ %-5level %logger{36} - %msg%n"/>
6        </Console>
7        <File name="MyFile" fileName="temp/DetailLog.csv" ↵
                ↪ append="false">
8           <PatternLayout pattern="%d{HH:mm:ss.SSS} [%t], ↵
                ↪ %-5level, %logger{36} - %msg%n"/>
9        </File>
10    </Appenders>
11    <Loggers>
12       <Root level="trace">
13          <AppenderRef ref="Console"/>
14          <AppenderRef ref="MyFile"/>
15       </Root>
16    </Loggers>
17  </Configuration>
```

Let's see what changes have been made to the file log4j2.xml.

We have defined a new 'Appender' called 'MyFile' that writes to a file 'DetailLog.csv' in the 'temp' folder. We have set the append mode to false so that the file will be cleared before new records are written to it. We are using the same layout pattern as the console.

Under 'Loggers' we have attached 'MyFile' appender to the 'root'. Since all the loggers inherit from 'root', all trace or higher messages from our logger will be logged to the file.

Refresh the workspace – right click AutoDW in the 'Package Explorer' and then select Refresh.

Now let's run the test as we did previously i.e.

- In the 'Package Explorer', right click on the testOne and select Run As ⇒ JUnit Test

- From the top menu select Window ⇒ Show View ⇒ Console.

- Go to folder 'C:\Workspace\AutoDW\temp'. You will see a 'DetailLog.csv' file as shown in Figure 3.18.

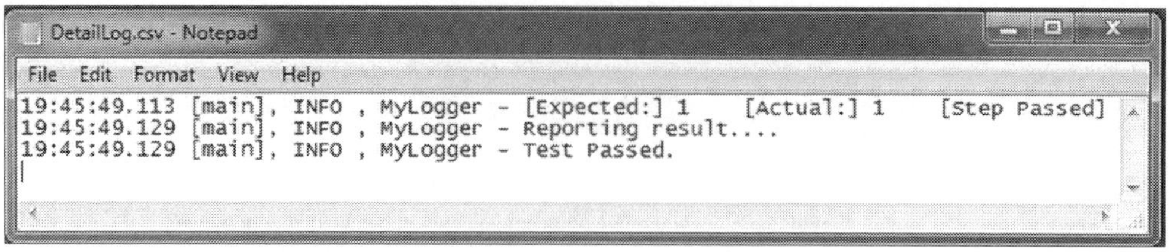

Figure 3.18: Log File - DetailLog.csv

Now all the runtime console information is also available in the 'DetailLog.csv'. However we still have the problem of this log file being overwritten every time we run the test. We need to save a copy this file after each run, as follows.

First of all, add some new declarations to the Config.java file as shown in Listing 3.9.

Listing 3.9: Config.java - specify locations

```
1  public static final String WORKSPACE_LOCATION = ↵
       ↪ "C:/Workspace/AutoDW";
2  public static final String LOG_FILE_LOCATION = ↵
       ↪ "C:/AutoLogs";
```

Line 1: Specify the location of our workspace folder.
Line 2: Specify the log file storage location. I have used "C:\AutoLogs" but you may want to save log files in a different location.

Now we define two new generic functions in the Utility.java file as follows:

CreateFolder - Creates a folder on the specified path, if it doesn't exist		
Input Parameters	*folderName*	Name of the folder to be created
Return Value	*void*	Returns nothing.

SaveLog - Saves a log file by the name specified in the parameter		
Input Parameters	*fileName*	File name to be used for the saved log file
Return Value	*void*	Returns nothing.

Listing 3.10: Utility.java - Saving logs

```
1  import java.io.File;
```

```
2  import java.nio.file.Files;
3  import java.sql.Timestamp;
4
5  public static void CreateFolder(String folderName)
6  {
7      File theDir = new File(folderName);
8
9      if (!theDir.exists())
10     {
11         Utility.log.info("Creating directory: " + folderName);
12         boolean result = theDir.mkdir();
13
14         if(!result)
15             ReportExpectedVsActual("Create Folder", ↵
                    ↪ "Couldnot Create Folder");
16     }
17 }
18
19 public static void SaveLog(String fileName) throws Exception
20 {
21     java.util.Date date= new java.util.Date();
22     String dt = new Timestamp(date.getTime()).toString();
23     dt = dt.replace(":", "_");
24     dt = dt.replace(".", "_");
25     dt = dt.replace("-", "_");
26
27     Utility.log.info("Result File: " + fileName + "_" + dt ↵
           ↪ + ".csv");
28
29     File oldfile = new File(Config.WORKSPACE_LOCATION + ↵
           ↪ "/temp/DetailLog.csv");
30
31     String outDir = Config.LOG_FILE_LOCATION;
32     CreateFolder(outDir);
33
34     File newfile = new File(outDir + "/" + fileName + ↵
           ↪ "_Detail_" + dt + ".csv");
35
36     Files.copy(oldfile.toPath(), newfile.toPath());
37 }
```

Lines 1 - 3: Imports needed to support the new functionality.

Line 9: Create the folder if it doesn't exist.

Line 14: Report an error if the folder cannot be created.

Line 22: Get the system date and timestamp.

Line 23 - 25: Remove any unnecessary characters.

Line 32: Call the 'CreateFolder' function to create the log folder, if it doesn't exist.

Line 34: Setup the detail log file including the date and timestamp in the name.

Line 36: Copy the log file from the temporary location to the log file location.

Let's make some further modifications to myTest.java as shown in Listing 3.11.

Listing 3.11: myTest.java - Saving logs

```
1  package autoDW;
2
3  import org.junit.AfterClass;
4  import org.junit.Before;
5  import org.junit.Test;
6
7  public class myTest {
8      @Before
9      public void setUp() throws Exception {
10         Config.TestResult = Config.PASS;
11     }
12
13     @AfterClass
14     public static void tearDownAfterClass() throws ←
         ↪ Exception {
15         Utility.SaveLog("MyTest");
16     }
17
18     @Test
19     public void testOne() {
20
21         Utility.ReportExpectedVsActual("1", "1");
22         Utility.ReportResult();
23     }
24
25     @Test
26     public void testTwo() {
27
28         Utility.ReportExpectedVsActual("1", "2");
29         Utility.ReportResult();
30     }
31
32     @Test
33     public void testThree() {
34
```

```
35          Utility.ReportExpectedVsActual("4", "4");
36          Utility.ReportExpectedVsActual("4", "5");
37          Utility.ReportExpectedVsActual("5", "5");
38          Utility.ReportResult();
39      }
40 }
```

Line 3: Additional import required to support functionality.

Line 13: @AfterClass annotation indicates that this method is to be executed once, after all the other tests have finished i.e. we want to save the log file once all of the tests are complete.

Line 15: The parameter in 'SaveLog' function identifies the file name to be used for the saved log file. Later on in this book we will see how to derive the log file name automatically from the class name, but for now we are passing a hardcoded value i.e. 'myTest'.

Re-execute testOne. This time a copy of the CSV log file will be saved in the logs folder (configured in the Config.java file) with a date timestamp as shown in Figure 3.19. The Console window also displays the name of file created.

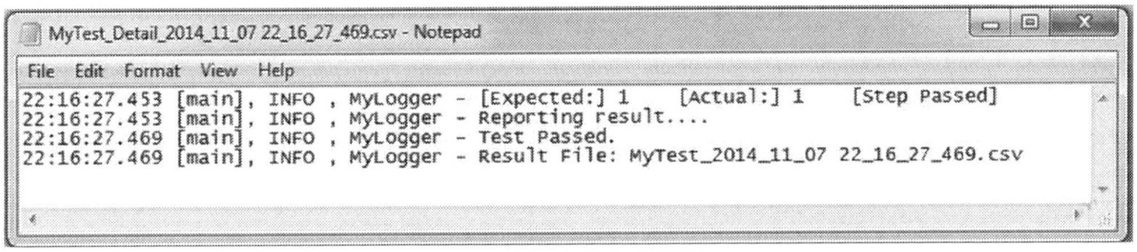

Figure 3.19: CSV Log File in Log Folder

Now in the 'Package Explorer' right click on the myTest.java and select Run As ⇒ JUnit Test. All three tests in myTest.java will be executed and the Console will display information on all three tests. A copy of the detailed log in CSV format is also saved in the logs folder with a date and timestamp as shown in Figure 3.20.

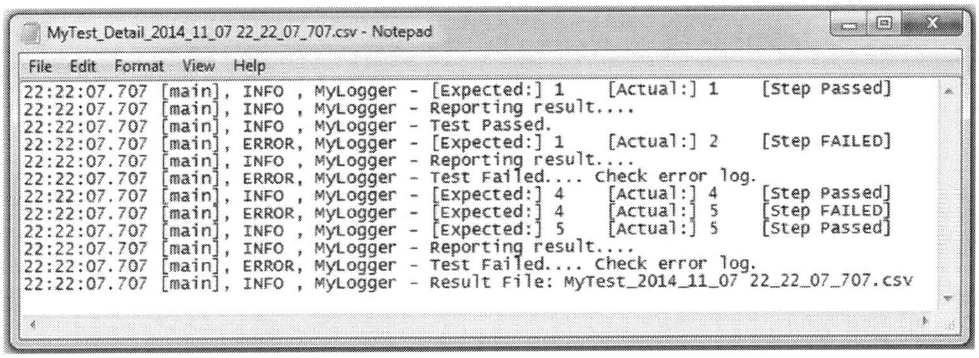

Figure 3.20: CSV Log File in Log Folder - All Tests Executed

3.4.3 Logging Test Name

Let's smarten up the log file a little. What we want is for each test to announce that it has started so that the log is more readable (particular useful when we go through a large test result file). Open the myTest.java file and make the changes shown in Listing 3.12.

Listing 3.12: myTest.java - Announcing test starts

```
1  package autoDW;
2
3  import org.junit.AfterClass;
4  import org.junit.Before;
5  import org.junit.Rule;
6  import org.junit.Test;
7  import org.junit.rules.TestName;
8
9  public class myTest
10 {
11     @Rule public TestName name = new TestName();
12
13     @Before
14     public void setUp() throws Exception
15     {
16         Config.TestResult = Config.PASS;
17     }
18
19     @AfterClass
20     public static void tearDownAfterClass() throws Exception
21     {
22         Utility.SaveLog("MyTest");
23     }
24
25     @Test
26     public void testOne()
27     {
28         Utility.log.info("***********   Starting Test: " + ↵
                ↪ name.getMethodName());
29
30         Utility.ReportExpectedVsActual("1", "1");
31         Utility.ReportResult();
32     }
33
34     @Test
```

```
35    public void testTwo()
36    {
37        Utility.log.info("***********    Starting Test: " + ↵
          ↪ name.getMethodName());
38
39        Utility.ReportExpectedVsActual("1", "2");
40        Utility.ReportResult();
41    }
42
43    @Test
44    public void testThree()
45    {
46        Utility.log.info("***********    Starting Test: " + ↵
          ↪ name.getMethodName());
47
48        Utility.ReportExpectedVsActual("4", "4");
49        Utility.ReportExpectedVsActual("4", "5");
50        Utility.ReportExpectedVsActual("5", "5");
51        Utility.ReportResult();
52    }
53 }
```

Line 5 and 7: Additional imports required to support the functionality.

Line 11: @Rule annotation lets you create objects that can be used and configured in your test methods. We have created an object to hold the test name.

Line 28, 37 and 46: Add code to the beginning of each test to announce its start.

Now when you execute the tests, each test displays its name which is very useful when you are going through a large test result file. Figure 3.21 shows the outcome of the Console window with the above changes.

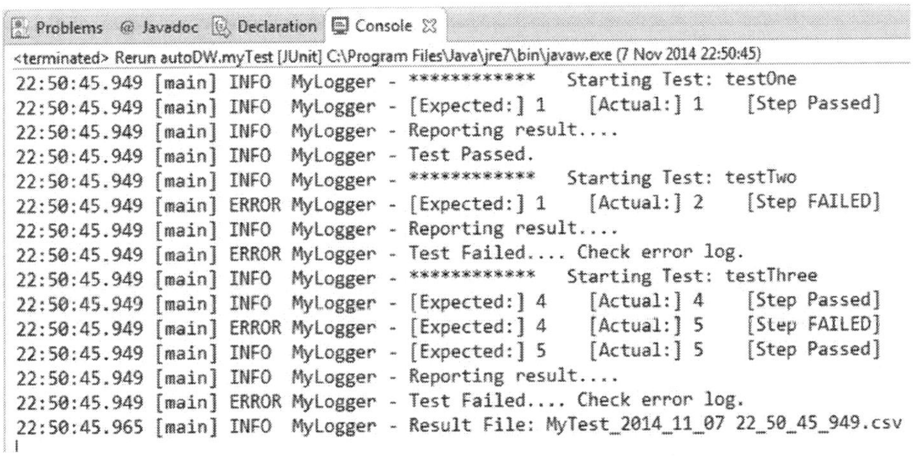

Figure 3.21: Console Output With Test Names

3.4.4 Sequencing Test Execution

One important technique I use is to control the sequence in which the tests are executed, rather than run them in the order in which they are defined in the test file. To achieve this, I assign each test a sequential name e.g. _010_checkCounts, _020_checkChecksums, _030_checkDetails etc. so that they can be executed in the ascending order of their name, regardless of how they appear or are defined in the test file.

Let's assume you want to execute tests in the following sequence - testTwo, testOne and then finally testThree. Let's rename our tests in myTests.java as _010_testTwo, _020_testOne and _030_testThree. If you execute all the tests the test execution sequence still remains as _020_testOne, _010_testTwo and _030_testThree as shown in Figure 3.22.

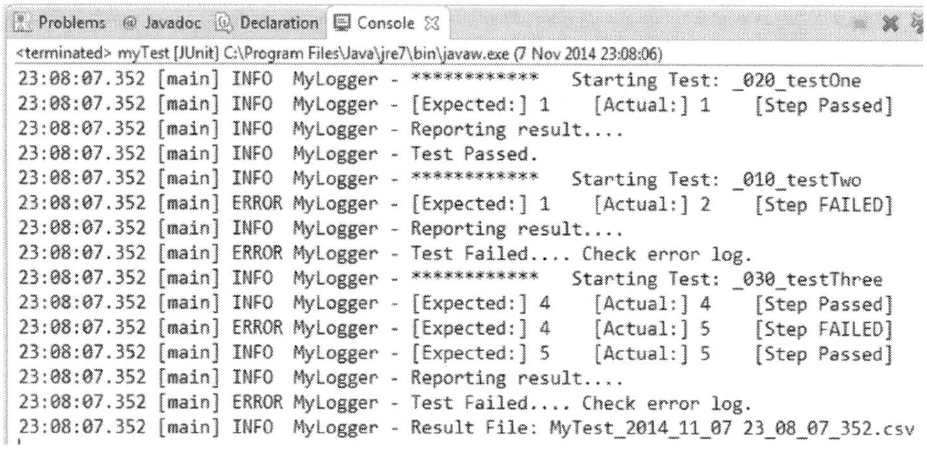

Figure 3.22: Console Output Incorrect Execution Sequence

In order to execute tests in the sequence we want, we need to make some modifications to the myTest.java file as shown in Listing 3.13.

Listing 3.13: myTest.java - Sequence test execution

```
1  package autoDW;
2
3  import org.junit.AfterClass;
4  import org.junit.Before;
5  import org.junit.Rule;
6  import org.junit.Test;
7  import org.junit.rules.TestName;
8  import org.junit.FixMethodOrder;
9  import org.junit.runners.MethodSorters;
10
11 @FixMethodOrder(MethodSorters.NAME_ASCENDING)
12 public class myTest {
```

```
13      @Rule public TestName name = new TestName();
14
15      @Before
16      public void setUp() throws Exception {
17          Config.TestResult = Config.PASS;
18      }
19
20      @AfterClass
21      public static void tearDownAfterClass() throws ↵
            ↪ Exception {
22          Utility.SaveLog("MyTest");
23      }
24
25      @Test
26      public void _020_testOne() {
27          Utility.log.info("***********   Starting Test: " + ↵
                ↪ name.getMethodName());
28
29          Utility.ReportExpectedVsActual("1", "1");
30          Utility.ReportResult();
31      }
32
33      @Test
34      public void _010_testTwo() {
35          Utility.log.info("***********   Starting Test: " + ↵
                ↪ name.getMethodName());
36
37          Utility.ReportExpectedVsActual("1", "2");
38          Utility.ReportResult();
39      }
40
41      @Test
42      public void _030_testThree() {
43          Utility.log.info("***********   Starting Test: " + ↵
                ↪ name.getMethodName());
44
45          Utility.ReportExpectedVsActual("4", "4");
46          Utility.ReportExpectedVsActual("4", "5");
47          Utility.ReportExpectedVsActual("5", "5");
48          Utility.ReportResult();
49      }
50 }
```

Line 8 and 9: Additional imports required to support the functionality.

Line 11: @FixMethodOrder - annotation to define that the test methods are sorted by method name, in lexicographic order.

So now when you execute all the tests, they will be executed in the required sequence i.e. _010_testTwo, _020_testOne and finally _030_testThree as shown in Figure 3.23.

```
 Problems  @ Javadoc  Declaration  Console 
<terminated> myTest [JUnit] C:\Program Files\Java\jre7\bin\javaw.exe (7 Nov 2014 23:20:48)
23:20:49.076 [main] INFO  MyLogger - ************  Starting Test: _010_testTwo
23:20:49.076 [main] ERROR MyLogger - [Expected:] 1    [Actual:] 2    [Step FAILED]
23:20:49.076 [main] INFO  MyLogger - Reporting result....
23:20:49.076 [main] ERROR MyLogger - Test Failed.... Check error log.
23:20:49.091 [main] INFO  MyLogger - ************  Starting Test: _020_testOne
23:20:49.091 [main] INFO  MyLogger - [Expected:] 1    [Actual:] 1    [Step Passed]
23:20:49.091 [main] INFO  MyLogger - Reporting result....
23:20:49.091 [main] INFO  MyLogger - Test Passed.
23:20:49.091 [main] INFO  MyLogger - ************  Starting Test: _030_testThree
23:20:49.091 [main] INFO  MyLogger - [Expected:] 4    [Actual:] 4    [Step Passed]
23:20:49.091 [main] ERROR MyLogger - [Expected:] 4    [Actual:] 5    [Step FAILED]
23:20:49.091 [main] INFO  MyLogger - [Expected:] 5    [Actual:] 5    [Step Passed]
23:20:49.091 [main] INFO  MyLogger - Reporting result....
23:20:49.091 [main] ERROR MyLogger - Test Failed.... Check error log.
23:20:49.091 [main] INFO  MyLogger - Result File: MyTest_2014_11_07 23_20_49_091.csv
```

Figure 3.23: Console Output Correct Execution Sequence

3.4.5   Overall Test Execution Status

Imagine a scenario where you have 100 java test files and they are all executed in one test cycle. There will be 100 test result files created in the log folder. If you need to look at the log files a few days later, you will find 100 test log files and in order to know which tests passed or failed, you will need to open up all of these log files to check the outcome. What would be ideal is if each log file stated, as part of its name, whether the overall test result was Pass or Fail. So let's see how we can achieve this.

First of all add a new declaration to the Config.java file as shown in Listing 3.14.

Listing 3.14: Config.java - Define overall test execution status

```
1  public static String OverAllTestResult = Config.PASS;
```

Line 1: Variable to hold overall test execution status - initially set to Pass.

Now we update two existing functions in the Utility.java file as shown in Listing 3.15.

Listing 3.15: Utility.java - Incorporate overall test execution status

```
1  public static void ReportExpectedVsActual(String ↵
       ↪ strExpected, String strActual)
2  {
3      strExpected = strExpected.trim();
```

```
4      strActual = strActual.trim();
5
6      if (strExpected.equals(strActual))
7      {
8         log.info("[Expected:] " + strExpected + "        ↵
          ↪ [Actual:] " + strActual + "        [Step ↵
          ↪ Passed]");
9      }
10     else
11     {
12        log.error("[Expected:] " + strExpected + "        ↵
          ↪ [Actual:] " + strActual + "        [Step ↵
          ↪ FAILED]");
13        Config.TestResult = Config.FAIL;
14        Config.OverAllTestResult = Config.FAIL;
15     }
16 }
17
18 public static void SaveLog(String fileName) throws Exception
19 {
20     java.util.Date date= new java.util.Date();
21     String dt =  new Timestamp(date.getTime()).toString();
22     dt = dt.replace(":", "_");
23     dt = dt.replace(".", "_");
24     dt = dt.replace("-", "_");
25
26     Utility.log.info("Result File: " + fileName + "_(" + ↵
          ↪ Config.OverAllTestResult + ")_" + dt + ".csv");
27
28     File oldfile = new File(Config.WORKSPACE_LOCATION + ↵
          ↪ "/temp/DetailLog.csv");
29
30     String outDir = Config.LOG_FILE_LOCATION;
31     CreateFolder(outDir);
32
33     File newfile = new File(outDir + "/" + fileName + ↵
          ↪ "_Detail_(" + Config.OverAllTestResult + ")_" + ↵
          ↪ dt + ".csv");
34
35     Files.copy(oldfile.toPath(), newfile.toPath());
36 }
```

Line 14: Set the overall test execution status to Fail if any test step fails.
Line 26 and 33: Incorporate the overall test status in the log file name.

Now whenever you execute tests, the overall result status is appended to the file name e.g. MyTest_Detail_(FAIL)_2014_11_08 00_02_55_21.csv so by looking at the log file name you can tell whether the overall test status was Pass or Fail.

Chapter 4

Setting up Sample Data Warehouse

Setting up Sample Data Warehouse

In this chapter, we shall:

- *Create a source system database and its schema and load test data into it*

- *Create a staging system database and its schema and load test data into it*

- *Create a data warehouse database and its schema and load test data into it*

So let's get on with it...

BEFORE we can automate data warehouse testing, we need some databases - source systems, staging area and the data warehouse itself. So let's set these databases up.

 You can download a copy of the SQL Scripts and Test Data files used in this chapter from http://www.arkenstone-ltd.com/. Navigate to the *Downloads* link and follow the on-screen instructions.

Each database is set up in three stages - creating the database, defining the schema and finally loading test data into the database.

You can use 'SQL Server Management Studio', as I have done, to execute the SQL scripts provided in this chapter. I have used the 'sa' login to execute the scripts but you can use any login that has database create/update permission. The scripts create all of the required databases in the 'C:\AutoDB' folder. However, you can change the destination folder in the scripts to your preferred location. Make sure the folder 'C:\AutoDB' exists before you execute the first SQL script.

4.1   Source System Database

This is our Source Database which provides data to the Staging Area as per Figure 1.1.

 As a tester in a real environment, you probably wouldn't need to create this database as it should already exist but here we need to create this database as we need something to automate our tests against. If you don't understand any of the code here, don't worry. You are not a database administrator! Just execute these SQL scripts to create the environment you need to be able to start writing your automated tests.

4.1.1 Creating Source System Database

Listing 4.1 will create the Source System Database (OPS) files in 'C:\AutoDB' folder.

Listing 4.1: Creating Source System Database

```
1  USE [master]
2  GO
3
4  CREATE DATABASE [OPS] ON  PRIMARY
5     ( NAME = N'OPS', FILENAME = N'C:\AutoDB\OPS.mdf' , ↵
          ↪ SIZE = 5504KB , MAXSIZE = UNLIMITED, FILEGROWTH = ↵
          ↪ 10%)
6     LOG ON
7     ( NAME = N'OPS_log', FILENAME = N'C:\AutoDB\OPS.ldf' , ↵
          ↪ SIZE = 3456KB , MAXSIZE = UNLIMITED, FILEGROWTH = ↵
          ↪ 10%)
8  GO
9
10 ALTER DATABASE [OPS] SET COMPATIBILITY_LEVEL = 90
11
12 IF (1 = FULLTEXTSERVICEPROPERTY('IsFullTextInstalled'))
13 begin
14    EXEC [OPS].[dbo].[sp_fulltext_database] @action = ↵
          ↪ 'disable'
15 end
16
17 ALTER DATABASE [OPS] SET ANSI_NULL_DEFAULT OFF
18 ALTER DATABASE [OPS] SET ANSI_NULLS OFF
19 ALTER DATABASE [OPS] SET ANSI_PADDING OFF
20 ALTER DATABASE [OPS] SET ANSI_WARNINGS OFF
21 ALTER DATABASE [OPS] SET ARITHABORT OFF
22 ALTER DATABASE [OPS] SET AUTO_CLOSE ON
23 ALTER DATABASE [OPS] SET AUTO_CREATE_STATISTICS ON
24 ALTER DATABASE [OPS] SET AUTO_SHRINK OFF
25 ALTER DATABASE [OPS] SET AUTO_UPDATE_STATISTICS ON
26 ALTER DATABASE [OPS] SET CURSOR_CLOSE_ON_COMMIT OFF
27 ALTER DATABASE [OPS] SET CURSOR_DEFAULT  GLOBAL
28 ALTER DATABASE [OPS] SET CONCAT_NULL_YIELDS_NULL OFF
```

```
29  ALTER DATABASE [OPS] SET NUMERIC_ROUNDABORT OFF
30  ALTER DATABASE [OPS] SET QUOTED_IDENTIFIER OFF
31  ALTER DATABASE [OPS] SET RECURSIVE_TRIGGERS OFF
32  ALTER DATABASE [OPS] SET ENABLE_BROKER
33  ALTER DATABASE [OPS] SET AUTO_UPDATE_STATISTICS_ASYNC OFF
34  ALTER DATABASE [OPS] SET DATE_CORRELATION_OPTIMIZATION OFF
35  ALTER DATABASE [OPS] SET TRUSTWORTHY OFF
36  ALTER DATABASE [OPS] SET ALLOW_SNAPSHOT_ISOLATION OFF
37  ALTER DATABASE [OPS] SET PARAMETERIZATION SIMPLE
38  ALTER DATABASE [OPS] SET READ_COMMITTED_SNAPSHOT OFF
39  ALTER DATABASE [OPS] SET HONOR_BROKER_PRIORITY OFF
40  ALTER DATABASE [OPS] SET READ_WRITE
41  ALTER DATABASE [OPS] SET RECOVERY SIMPLE
42  ALTER DATABASE [OPS] SET MULTI_USER
43  ALTER DATABASE [OPS] SET PAGE_VERIFY TORN_PAGE_DETECTION
44  ALTER DATABASE [OPS] SET DB_CHAINING OFF
45  GO
```

4.1.2 Creating Source System Schema

Listing 4.2 will create the Source System Schema tables and foreign keys.

Listing 4.2: Creating Source System Schema

```
1   USE [OPS]
2   GO
3
4   SET ANSI_NULLS ON
5   SET QUOTED_IDENTIFIER ON
6   CREATE TABLE [dbo].[Employees](
7       [EmployeeID] [int] IDENTITY(1,1) NOT NULL,
8       [LastName] [nvarchar](20) NOT NULL,
9       [FirstName] [nvarchar](15) NOT NULL,
10      [Title] [nvarchar](30) NULL,
11      [DateOfBirth] [datetime] NULL,
12      [Address] [nvarchar](50) NULL,
13      [City] [nvarchar](15) NULL,
14      [County] [nvarchar](25) NULL,
15      [Postcode] [nvarchar](10) NULL,
16      [Country] [nvarchar](15) NULL,
17      [Phone] [nvarchar](24) NULL,
18    CONSTRAINT [PK_Employees] PRIMARY KEY CLUSTERED
19  (
```

```
20      [EmployeeID] ASC
21 )WITH (PAD_INDEX  = OFF, STATISTICS_NORECOMPUTE  = OFF, ←
       ↪ IGNORE_DUP_KEY = OFF, ALLOW_ROW_LOCKS   = ON, ←
       ↪ ALLOW_PAGE_LOCKS  = ON) ON [PRIMARY]
22 ) ON [PRIMARY]
23 GO
24
25 SET ANSI_NULLS ON
26 SET QUOTED_IDENTIFIER ON
27 CREATE TABLE [dbo].[Customers](
28      [CustomerID] [nchar](5) NOT NULL,
29      [LastName] [nvarchar](20) NOT NULL,
30      [FirstName] [nvarchar](15) NOT NULL,
31      [Title] [nvarchar](30) NULL,
32      [DateOfBirth] [datetime] NULL,
33      [Address] [nvarchar](50) NULL,
34      [City] [nvarchar](15) NULL,
35      [County] [nvarchar](25) NULL,
36      [Postcode] [nvarchar](10) NULL,
37      [Country] [nvarchar](15) NULL,
38      [Phone] [nvarchar](24) NULL,
39      [Fax] [nvarchar](24) NULL,
40   CONSTRAINT [PK_Customers] PRIMARY KEY CLUSTERED
41 (
42      [CustomerID] ASC
43 )WITH (PAD_INDEX  = OFF, STATISTICS_NORECOMPUTE  = OFF, ←
       ↪ IGNORE_DUP_KEY = OFF, ALLOW_ROW_LOCKS   = ON, ←
       ↪ ALLOW_PAGE_LOCKS  = ON) ON [PRIMARY]
44 ) ON [PRIMARY]
45 GO
46
47 SET ANSI_NULLS ON
48 SET QUOTED_IDENTIFIER ON
49 CREATE TABLE [dbo].[Products](
50      [ProductID] [int] IDENTITY(1,1) NOT NULL,
51      [ProductName] [nvarchar](40) NOT NULL,
52      [UnitPrice] [money] NULL,
53      [UnitsInStock] [smallint] NULL,
54      [UnitsOnOrder] [smallint] NULL,
55      [ReorderLevel] [smallint] NULL,
56      [Discontinued] [bit] NOT NULL,
57   CONSTRAINT [PK_Products] PRIMARY KEY CLUSTERED
58 (
59      [ProductID] ASC
60 )WITH (PAD_INDEX   = OFF, STATISTICS_NORECOMPUTE  = OFF, ←
```

```
          ↪ IGNORE_DUP_KEY = OFF, ALLOW_ROW_LOCKS   = ON, ↩
          ↪ ALLOW_PAGE_LOCKS  = ON) ON [PRIMARY]
61  ) ON [PRIMARY]
62  GO
63
64  SET ANSI_NULLS ON
65  SET QUOTED_IDENTIFIER ON
66  CREATE TABLE [dbo].[Orders](
67      [OrderID] [int] IDENTITY(1,1) NOT NULL,
68      [CustomerID] [nchar](5) NULL,
69      [EmployeeID] [int] NULL,
70      [OrderDate] [datetime] NULL,
71      [DispatchDate] [datetime] NULL,
72   CONSTRAINT [PK_Orders] PRIMARY KEY CLUSTERED
73  (
74      [OrderID] ASC
75  )WITH (PAD_INDEX  = OFF, STATISTICS_NORECOMPUTE  = OFF, ↩
          ↪ IGNORE_DUP_KEY = OFF, ALLOW_ROW_LOCKS   = ON, ↩
          ↪ ALLOW_PAGE_LOCKS  = ON) ON [PRIMARY]
76  ) ON [PRIMARY]
77  GO
78
79  SET ANSI_NULLS ON
80  SET QUOTED_IDENTIFIER ON
81  CREATE TABLE [dbo].[OrderDetails](
82      [OrderID] [int] NOT NULL,
83      [ProductID] [int] NOT NULL,
84      [UnitPrice] [money] NOT NULL,
85      [Quantity] [smallint] NOT NULL,
86      [Discount] [real] NOT NULL,
87      [GiftWrap] [nchar](5) NULL,
88      [PriceMatch] [nvarchar](50) NULL,
89   CONSTRAINT [PK_Order_Details] PRIMARY KEY CLUSTERED
90  (
91      [OrderID] ASC,
92      [ProductID] ASC
93  )WITH (PAD_INDEX  = OFF, STATISTICS_NORECOMPUTE  = OFF, ↩
          ↪ IGNORE_DUP_KEY = OFF, ALLOW_ROW_LOCKS   = ON, ↩
          ↪ ALLOW_PAGE_LOCKS  = ON) ON [PRIMARY]
94  ) ON [PRIMARY]
95  GO
96
97  ALTER TABLE [dbo].[OrderDetails] ADD  CONSTRAINT ↩
          ↪ [CT_OrderDetails_UnitPrice]  DEFAULT (0) FOR ↩
          ↪ [UnitPrice]
```

```
 98 ALTER TABLE [dbo].[OrderDetails] ADD  CONSTRAINT ↵
    ↪ [CT_OrderDetails_Quantity]  DEFAULT (1) FOR [Quantity]
 99 ALTER TABLE [dbo].[OrderDetails] ADD  CONSTRAINT ↵
    ↪ [CT_OrderDetails_Discount]  DEFAULT (0) FOR [Discount]
100 ALTER TABLE [dbo].[Products] ADD  CONSTRAINT ↵
    ↪ [CT_Products_UnitPrice]  DEFAULT (0) FOR [UnitPrice]
101 ALTER TABLE [dbo].[Products] ADD  CONSTRAINT ↵
    ↪ [CT_Products_UnitsInStock]  DEFAULT (0) FOR ↵
    ↪ [UnitsInStock]
102 ALTER TABLE [dbo].[Products] ADD  CONSTRAINT ↵
    ↪ [CT_Products_UnitsOnOrder]  DEFAULT (0) FOR ↵
    ↪ [UnitsOnOrder]
103 ALTER TABLE [dbo].[Products] ADD  CONSTRAINT ↵
    ↪ [CT_Products_ReorderLevel]  DEFAULT (0) FOR ↵
    ↪ [ReorderLevel]
104 ALTER TABLE [dbo].[Products] ADD  CONSTRAINT ↵
    ↪ [CT_Products_Discontinued]  DEFAULT (0) FOR ↵
    ↪ [Discontinued]
105 ALTER TABLE [dbo].[Employees]  WITH NOCHECK ADD  ↵
    ↪ CONSTRAINT [CC_Birthdate] CHECK  (([DateOfBirth] < ↵
    ↪ getdate()))
106 ALTER TABLE [dbo].[Employees] CHECK CONSTRAINT ↵
    ↪ [CC_Birthdate]
107 ALTER TABLE [dbo].[OrderDetails]  WITH NOCHECK ADD  ↵
    ↪ CONSTRAINT [CC_Discount] CHECK  (([Discount] >= 0 ↵
    ↪ and [Discount] <= 1))
108 ALTER TABLE [dbo].[OrderDetails] CHECK CONSTRAINT ↵
    ↪ [CC_Discount]
109 ALTER TABLE [dbo].[OrderDetails]  WITH NOCHECK ADD  ↵
    ↪ CONSTRAINT [CC_Quantity] CHECK  (([Quantity] > 0))
110 ALTER TABLE [dbo].[OrderDetails] CHECK CONSTRAINT ↵
    ↪ [CC_Quantity]
111 ALTER TABLE [dbo].[OrderDetails]  WITH NOCHECK ADD  ↵
    ↪ CONSTRAINT [CC_UnitPrice] CHECK  (([UnitPrice] >= 0))
112 ALTER TABLE [dbo].[OrderDetails] CHECK CONSTRAINT ↵
    ↪ [CC_UnitPrice]
113 ALTER TABLE [dbo].[Products]  WITH NOCHECK ADD  ↵
    ↪ CONSTRAINT [CC_Products_UnitPrice] CHECK  ↵
    ↪ (([UnitPrice] >= 0))
114 ALTER TABLE [dbo].[Products] CHECK CONSTRAINT ↵
    ↪ [CC_Products_UnitPrice]
115 ALTER TABLE [dbo].[Products]  WITH NOCHECK ADD  ↵
    ↪ CONSTRAINT [CC_ReorderLevel] CHECK  (([ReorderLevel] ↵
    ↪ >= 0))
116 ALTER TABLE [dbo].[Products] CHECK CONSTRAINT ↵
```

```
              ↪ [CC_ReorderLevel]
117  ALTER TABLE [dbo].[Products]  WITH NOCHECK ADD  ←
              ↪ CONSTRAINT [CC_UnitsInStock] CHECK  (([UnitsInStock] ←
              ↪ >= 0))
118  ALTER TABLE [dbo].[Products] CHECK CONSTRAINT ←
              ↪ [CC_UnitsInStock]
119  ALTER TABLE [dbo].[Products]  WITH NOCHECK ADD  ←
              ↪ CONSTRAINT [CC_UnitsOnOrder] CHECK  (([UnitsOnOrder] ←
              ↪ >= 0))
120  ALTER TABLE [dbo].[Products] CHECK CONSTRAINT ←
              ↪ [CC_UnitsOnOrder]
121  ALTER TABLE [dbo].[OrderDetails]  WITH NOCHECK ADD  ←
              ↪ CONSTRAINT [FK_OrderDetails_Orders] FOREIGN ←
              ↪ KEY([OrderID])
122  REFERENCES [dbo].[Orders] ([OrderID])
123  ALTER TABLE [dbo].[OrderDetails] CHECK CONSTRAINT ←
              ↪ [FK_OrderDetails_Orders]
124  ALTER TABLE [dbo].[OrderDetails]  WITH NOCHECK ADD  ←
              ↪ CONSTRAINT [FK_OrderDetails_Products] FOREIGN ←
              ↪ KEY([ProductID])
125  REFERENCES [dbo].[Products] ([ProductID])
126  ALTER TABLE [dbo].[OrderDetails] CHECK CONSTRAINT ←
              ↪ [FK_OrderDetails_Products]
127  ALTER TABLE [dbo].[Orders]  WITH NOCHECK ADD  CONSTRAINT ←
              ↪ [FK_Orders_Customers] FOREIGN KEY([CustomerID])
128  REFERENCES [dbo].[Customers] ([CustomerID])
129  ALTER TABLE [dbo].[Orders] CHECK CONSTRAINT ←
              ↪ [FK_Orders_Customers]
130  ALTER TABLE [dbo].[Orders]  WITH NOCHECK ADD  CONSTRAINT ←
              ↪ [FK_Orders_Employees] FOREIGN KEY([EmployeeID])
131  REFERENCES [dbo].[Employees] ([EmployeeID])
132  ALTER TABLE [dbo].[Orders] CHECK CONSTRAINT ←
              ↪ [FK_Orders_Employees]
133  GO
```

4.1.3   Loading Source System Data

In the real world, loading the source database is performed by a frontend application – desktop, website or some other means. A number of validation checks are usually performed on the data before it is finally stored in the database. Some applications apply these validation checks at the client side, others may apply them at the server side (also called the business layer), or at the database level in the form of triggers, stored procedures, constraints etc. Some applications may use a combination of all of these methods.

To make things simpler for our sample database, we will directly insert some test data into our source system OPS (Order Processing System) using the BULK INSERT statement. Sample test data for each table in the OPS is provided in the Appendix.

Listing 4.3 loads the sample test data in the OPS database. The script assumes that the test data (in CSV format) is in 'C:\Workspace\TestData' folder.

Listing 4.3: Loading Source System Data

```
1  USE [OPS]
2  GO
3
4  ALTER TABLE [dbo].[OrderDetails] DROP CONSTRAINT ↵
       ↪ [FK_OrderDetails_Orders]
5  ALTER TABLE [dbo].[OrderDetails] DROP CONSTRAINT ↵
       ↪ [FK_OrderDetails_Products]
6  ALTER TABLE [dbo].[Orders] DROP CONSTRAINT ↵
       ↪ [FK_Orders_Customers]
7  ALTER TABLE [dbo].[Orders] DROP CONSTRAINT ↵
       ↪ [FK_Orders_Employees]
8  GO
9
10 SET DATEFORMAT dmy;
11 GO
12
13 truncate table dbo.[Products]
14 BULK INSERT dbo.[Products] FROM ↵
       ↪ 'C:\Workspace\TestData\Products.csv' WITH (FIRSTROW ↵
       ↪ = 2, FIELDTERMINATOR = ',', ROWTERMINATOR = '\n')
15 GO
16
17 truncate table dbo.[Employees]
18 BULK INSERT dbo.[Employees] FROM ↵
       ↪ 'C:\Workspace\TestData\Employees.csv' WITH ↵
       ↪ (FIRSTROW = 2, FIELDTERMINATOR = ',', ROWTERMINATOR ↵
       ↪ = '\n')
19 GO
20
21 truncate table dbo.[Customers]
22 BULK INSERT dbo.[Customers] FROM ↵
       ↪ 'C:\Workspace\TestData\Customers.csv' WITH ↵
       ↪ (FIRSTROW = 2, FIELDTERMINATOR = ',', ROWTERMINATOR ↵
       ↪ = '\n')
23 GO
24 truncate table dbo.[Orders]
```

```
25  BULK INSERT dbo.[Orders] FROM ↵
      ↪ 'C:\Workspace\TestData\Orders.csv'  WITH (FIRSTROW = ↵
      ↪ 2, FIELDTERMINATOR = ',', ROWTERMINATOR = '\n')
26  GO
27
28  truncate table dbo.[OrderDetails]
29  BULK INSERT dbo.[OrderDetails] FROM ↵
      ↪ 'C:\Workspace\TestData\OrderDetails.csv'  WITH ↵
      ↪ (FIRSTROW = 2, FIELDTERMINATOR = ',', ROWTERMINATOR ↵
      ↪ = '\n')
30  GO
31
32  ALTER TABLE [dbo].[OrderDetails]  WITH NOCHECK ADD  ↵
      ↪ CONSTRAINT [FK_OrderDetails_Orders] FOREIGN ↵
      ↪ KEY([OrderID])
33  REFERENCES [dbo].[Orders] ([OrderID])
34  ALTER TABLE [dbo].[OrderDetails] CHECK CONSTRAINT ↵
      ↪ [FK_OrderDetails_Orders]
35  ALTER TABLE [dbo].[OrderDetails]  WITH NOCHECK ADD  ↵
      ↪ CONSTRAINT [FK_OrderDetails_Products] FOREIGN ↵
      ↪ KEY([ProductID])
36  REFERENCES [dbo].[Products] ([ProductID])
37  ALTER TABLE [dbo].[OrderDetails] CHECK CONSTRAINT ↵
      ↪ [FK_OrderDetails_Products]
38  ALTER TABLE [dbo].[Orders]  WITH NOCHECK ADD  CONSTRAINT ↵
      ↪ [FK_Orders_Customers] FOREIGN KEY([CustomerID])
39  REFERENCES [dbo].[Customers] ([CustomerID])
40  ALTER TABLE [dbo].[Orders] CHECK CONSTRAINT ↵
      ↪ [FK_Orders_Customers]
41  ALTER TABLE [dbo].[Orders]  WITH NOCHECK ADD  CONSTRAINT ↵
      ↪ [FK_Orders_Employees] FOREIGN KEY([EmployeeID])
42  REFERENCES [dbo].[Employees] ([EmployeeID])
43  ALTER TABLE [dbo].[Orders] CHECK CONSTRAINT ↵
      ↪ [FK_Orders_Employees]
44  GO
```

4.2   Staging Database

This is our Staging Area which gets data from the Source Systems as per Figure 1.1.

4.2.1   Creating Staging Database

Listing 4.4 will create the Staging Database (OPS_STG) files in 'C:\AutoDB' folder.

Listing 4.4: Creating Staging Database

```
 1  USE [master]
 2  GO
 3
 4  CREATE DATABASE [OPS_STG] ON  PRIMARY
 5     ( NAME = N'OPS_STG', FILENAME = ↵
          ↪ N'C:\AutoDB\OPS_STG.mdf' , SIZE = 5504KB , ↵
          ↪ MAXSIZE = UNLIMITED, FILEGROWTH = 10%)
 6     LOG ON
 7     ( NAME = N'OPS_STG_log', FILENAME = ↵
          ↪ N'C:\AutoDB\OPS_STG.ldf' , SIZE = 3456KB , ↵
          ↪ MAXSIZE = UNLIMITED, FILEGROWTH = 10%)
 8  GO
 9
10  ALTER DATABASE [OPS_STG] SET COMPATIBILITY_LEVEL = 90
11
12  IF (1 = FULLTEXTSERVICEPROPERTY('IsFullTextInstalled'))
13  begin
14  EXEC [OPS_STG].[dbo].[sp_fulltext_database] @action = ↵
       ↪ 'disable'
15  end
16
17  ALTER DATABASE [OPS_STG] SET ANSI_NULL_DEFAULT OFF
18  ALTER DATABASE [OPS_STG] SET ANSI_NULLS OFF
19  ALTER DATABASE [OPS_STG] SET ANSI_PADDING OFF
20  ALTER DATABASE [OPS_STG] SET ANSI_WARNINGS OFF
21  ALTER DATABASE [OPS_STG] SET ARITHABORT OFF
22  ALTER DATABASE [OPS_STG] SET AUTO_CLOSE ON
23  ALTER DATABASE [OPS_STG] SET AUTO_CREATE_STATISTICS ON
24  ALTER DATABASE [OPS_STG] SET AUTO_SHRINK OFF
25  ALTER DATABASE [OPS_STG] SET AUTO_UPDATE_STATISTICS ON
26  ALTER DATABASE [OPS_STG] SET CURSOR_CLOSE_ON_COMMIT OFF
27  ALTER DATABASE [OPS_STG] SET CURSOR_DEFAULT  GLOBAL
28  ALTER DATABASE [OPS_STG] SET CONCAT_NULL_YIELDS_NULL OFF
29  ALTER DATABASE [OPS_STG] SET NUMERIC_ROUNDABORT OFF
30  ALTER DATABASE [OPS_STG] SET QUOTED_IDENTIFIER OFF
31  ALTER DATABASE [OPS_STG] SET RECURSIVE_TRIGGERS OFF
32  ALTER DATABASE [OPS_STG] SET ENABLE_BROKER
33  ALTER DATABASE [OPS_STG] SET AUTO_UPDATE_STATISTICS_ASYNC ↵
       ↪ OFF
34  ALTER DATABASE [OPS_STG] SET ↵
       ↪ DATE_CORRELATION_OPTIMIZATION OFF
35  ALTER DATABASE [OPS_STG] SET TRUSTWORTHY OFF
```

```
36  ALTER DATABASE [OPS_STG] SET ALLOW_SNAPSHOT_ISOLATION OFF
37  ALTER DATABASE [OPS_STG] SET PARAMETERIZATION SIMPLE
38  ALTER DATABASE [OPS_STG] SET READ_COMMITTED_SNAPSHOT OFF
39  ALTER DATABASE [OPS_STG] SET HONOR_BROKER_PRIORITY OFF
40  ALTER DATABASE [OPS_STG] SET READ_WRITE
41  ALTER DATABASE [OPS_STG] SET RECOVERY SIMPLE
42  ALTER DATABASE [OPS_STG] SET MULTI_USER
43  ALTER DATABASE [OPS_STG] SET PAGE_VERIFY TORN_PAGE_DETECTION
44  ALTER DATABASE [OPS_STG] SET DB_CHAINING OFF
45  GO
```

4.2.2 Creating Staging Schema

Listing 4.5 will create the Staging Schema tables.

Listing 4.5: Creating Staging Schema

```
1   USE [OPS_STG]
2   GO
3
4   SET ANSI_NULLS ON
5   SET QUOTED_IDENTIFIER ON
6   CREATE TABLE [dbo].[Employees](
7      [EmployeeID] [int] IDENTITY(1,1) NOT NULL,
8      [LastName] [nvarchar](20) NOT NULL,
9      [FirstName] [nvarchar](15) NOT NULL,
10     [Title] [nvarchar](30) NULL,
11     [DateOfBirth] [datetime] NULL,
12     [Address] [nvarchar](50) NULL,
13     [City] [nvarchar](15) NULL,
14     [County] [nvarchar](25) NULL,
15     [Postcode] [nvarchar](10) NULL,
16     [Country] [nvarchar](15) NULL,
17     [Phone] [nvarchar](24) NULL,
18    CONSTRAINT [PK_Employees] PRIMARY KEY CLUSTERED
19   (
20     [EmployeeID] ASC
21   )WITH (PAD_INDEX  = OFF, STATISTICS_NORECOMPUTE  = OFF, ↵
        ↪ IGNORE_DUP_KEY = OFF, ALLOW_ROW_LOCKS  = ON, ↵
        ↪ ALLOW_PAGE_LOCKS  = ON) ON [PRIMARY]
22   ) ON [PRIMARY]
23   GO
24
```

```
25  SET ANSI_NULLS ON
26  SET QUOTED_IDENTIFIER ON
27  CREATE TABLE [dbo].[Customers](
28     [CustomerID] [nchar](5) NOT NULL,
29     [LastName] [nvarchar](20) NOT NULL,
30     [FirstName] [nvarchar](15) NOT NULL,
31     [Title] [nvarchar](30) NULL,
32     [DateOfBirth] [datetime] NULL,
33     [Address] [nvarchar](50) NULL,
34     [City] [nvarchar](15) NULL,
35     [County] [nvarchar](25) NULL,
36     [Postcode] [nvarchar](10) NULL,
37     [Country] [nvarchar](15) NULL,
38     [Phone] [nvarchar](24) NULL,
39     [Fax] [nvarchar](24) NULL,
40   CONSTRAINT [PK_Customers] PRIMARY KEY CLUSTERED
41  (
42     [CustomerID] ASC
43  )WITH (PAD_INDEX  = OFF, STATISTICS_NORECOMPUTE  = OFF, ↵
          ↪ IGNORE_DUP_KEY = OFF, ALLOW_ROW_LOCKS  = ON, ↵
          ↪ ALLOW_PAGE_LOCKS  = ON) ON [PRIMARY]
44  ) ON [PRIMARY]
45  GO
46
47
48  SET ANSI_NULLS ON
49  SET QUOTED_IDENTIFIER ON
50  CREATE TABLE [dbo].[Products](
51     [ProductID] [int] IDENTITY(1,1) NOT NULL,
52     [ProductName] [nvarchar](40) NOT NULL,
53     [UnitPrice] [money] NULL,
54     [UnitsInStock] [smallint] NULL,
55     [UnitsOnOrder] [smallint] NULL,
56     [ReorderLevel] [smallint] NULL,
57     [Discontinued] [bit] NOT NULL,
58   CONSTRAINT [PK_Products] PRIMARY KEY CLUSTERED
59  (
60     [ProductID] ASC
61  )WITH (PAD_INDEX  = OFF, STATISTICS_NORECOMPUTE  = OFF, ↵
          ↪ IGNORE_DUP_KEY = OFF, ALLOW_ROW_LOCKS  = ON, ↵
          ↪ ALLOW_PAGE_LOCKS  = ON) ON [PRIMARY]
62  ) ON [PRIMARY]
63  GO
64
65  SET ANSI_NULLS ON
```

```
66  SET QUOTED_IDENTIFIER ON
67  CREATE TABLE [dbo].[Orders](
68     [OrderID] [int] IDENTITY(1,1) NOT NULL,
69     [CustomerID] [nchar](5) NULL,
70     [EmployeeID] [int] NULL,
71     [OrderDate] [datetime] NULL,
72     [DispatchDate] [datetime] NULL,
73   CONSTRAINT [PK_Orders] PRIMARY KEY CLUSTERED
74  (
75     [OrderID] ASC
76  )WITH (PAD_INDEX  = OFF, STATISTICS_NORECOMPUTE  = OFF, ↵
        ↪ IGNORE_DUP_KEY = OFF, ALLOW_ROW_LOCKS  = ON, ↵
        ↪ ALLOW_PAGE_LOCKS  = ON) ON [PRIMARY]
77  ) ON [PRIMARY]
78  GO
79
80  SET ANSI_NULLS ON
81  SET QUOTED_IDENTIFIER ON
82  CREATE TABLE [dbo].[OrderDetails](
83     [OrderID] [int] NOT NULL,
84     [ProductID] [int] NOT NULL,
85     [UnitPrice] [money] NOT NULL,
86     [Quantity] [smallint] NOT NULL,
87     [Discount] [real] NOT NULL,
88     [GiftWrap] [nchar](5) NULL,
89     [PriceMatch] [nvarchar](50) NULL,
90   CONSTRAINT [PK_Order_Details] PRIMARY KEY CLUSTERED
91  (
92     [OrderID] ASC,
93     [ProductID] ASC
94  )WITH (PAD_INDEX  = OFF, STATISTICS_NORECOMPUTE  = OFF, ↵
        ↪ IGNORE_DUP_KEY = OFF, ALLOW_ROW_LOCKS  = ON, ↵
        ↪ ALLOW_PAGE_LOCKS  = ON) ON [PRIMARY]
95  ) ON [PRIMARY]
96  GO
97
98  SET ANSI_NULLS ON
99  SET QUOTED_IDENTIFIER ON
100 CREATE TABLE [dbo].[VersionInfo](
101    [ReleaseVersion] [nvarchar](20) NOT NULL,
102    [DateCreated] [datetime] NOT NULL DEFAULT getdate()
103 ) ON [PRIMARY]
104 GO
105
106 INSERT INTO [dbo].[VersionInfo] ([ReleaseVersion])
```

```
107     VALUES ('1.0.0.0')
108 GO
```

4.2.3 Loading Staging Data

In the real world, loading data into the Staging Area is performed via an ETL tool but to make things easier for our sample data warehouse we will just use the BULK INSERT statement.

Listing 4.6 loads the sample test data in the OPS_STG database. We will use the same data we loaded into the source system OPS. As before, the script assumes that the test data (in CSV format) is in 'C:\Workspace\TestData' folder.

Listing 4.6: Loading Staging Data

```
1  USE [OPS_STG]
2  GO
3
4  SET DATEFORMAT dmy;
5  GO
6
7  Truncate Table dbo.[Products]
8  BULK INSERT dbo.[Products] FROM ↵
       ↪ 'C:\Workspace\TestData\Products.csv'  WITH (FIRSTROW ↵
       ↪ = 2, FIELDTERMINATOR = ',', ROWTERMINATOR = '\n')
9  GO
10
11 Truncate Table dbo.[Employees]
12 BULK INSERT dbo.[Employees] FROM ↵
       ↪ 'C:\Workspace\TestData\Employees.csv'  WITH ↵
       ↪ (FIRSTROW = 2, FIELDTERMINATOR = ',', ROWTERMINATOR ↵
       ↪ = '\n')
13 GO
14
15 Truncate Table dbo.[Customers]
16 BULK INSERT dbo.[Customers] FROM ↵
       ↪ 'C:\Workspace\TestData\Customers.csv'  WITH ↵
       ↪ (FIRSTROW = 2, FIELDTERMINATOR = ',', ROWTERMINATOR ↵
       ↪ = '\n')
17 GO
18
19 Truncate Table dbo.[Orders]
```

```
20 BULK INSERT dbo.[Orders] FROM ↵
      ↳ 'C:\Workspace\TestData\Orders.csv'  WITH (FIRSTROW = ↵
      ↳ 2, FIELDTERMINATOR = ',', ROWTERMINATOR = '\n')
21 GO
22
23 Truncate Table dbo.[OrderDetails]
24 BULK INSERT dbo.[OrderDetails] FROM ↵
      ↳ 'C:\Workspace\TestData\OrderDetails.csv'  WITH ↵
      ↳ (FIRSTROW = 2, FIELDTERMINATOR = ',', ROWTERMINATOR ↵
      ↳ = '\n')
25 GO
```

4.3   Data Warehouse Database

This is our actual Data Warehouse which gets data from the Staging Area as per Figure 1.1.

4.3.1   Creating Data Warehouse Database

Listing 4.7 will create the Data Warehouse Database (OPS_DWS) files in 'C:\AutoDB' folder.

Listing 4.7: Creating Data Warehouse Database

```
1 USE [master]
2 GO
3
4 CREATE DATABASE [OPS_DWS] ON  PRIMARY
5    ( NAME = N'OPS_DWS', FILENAME = ↵
        ↳ N'C:\AutoDB\OPS_DWS.mdf' , SIZE = 5504KB , ↵
        ↳ MAXSIZE = UNLIMITED, FILEGROWTH = 10%)
6    LOG ON
7    ( NAME = N'OPS_DWS_log', FILENAME = ↵
        ↳ N'C:\AutoDB\OPS_DWS.ldf' , SIZE = 3456KB , ↵
        ↳ MAXSIZE = UNLIMITED, FILEGROWTH = 10%)
8 GO
9
10 ALTER DATABASE [OPS_DWS] SET COMPATIBILITY_LEVEL = 90
11
12 IF (1 = FULLTEXTSERVICEPROPERTY('IsFullTextInstalled'))
13 begin
14    EXEC [OPS_DWS].[dbo].[sp_fulltext_database] @action = ↵
        ↳ 'disable'
```

```
15  end
16
17  ALTER DATABASE [OPS_DWS] SET ANSI_NULL_DEFAULT OFF
18  ALTER DATABASE [OPS_DWS] SET ANSI_NULLS OFF
19  ALTER DATABASE [OPS_DWS] SET ANSI_PADDING OFF
20  ALTER DATABASE [OPS_DWS] SET ANSI_WARNINGS OFF
21  ALTER DATABASE [OPS_DWS] SET ARITHABORT OFF
22  ALTER DATABASE [OPS_DWS] SET AUTO_CLOSE ON
23  ALTER DATABASE [OPS_DWS] SET AUTO_CREATE_STATISTICS ON
24  ALTER DATABASE [OPS_DWS] SET AUTO_SHRINK OFF
25  ALTER DATABASE [OPS_DWS] SET AUTO_UPDATE_STATISTICS ON
26  ALTER DATABASE [OPS_DWS] SET CURSOR_CLOSE_ON_COMMIT OFF
27  ALTER DATABASE [OPS_DWS] SET CURSOR_DEFAULT  GLOBAL
28  ALTER DATABASE [OPS_DWS] SET CONCAT_NULL_YIELDS_NULL OFF
29  ALTER DATABASE [OPS_DWS] SET NUMERIC_ROUNDABORT OFF
30  ALTER DATABASE [OPS_DWS] SET QUOTED_IDENTIFIER OFF
31  ALTER DATABASE [OPS_DWS] SET RECURSIVE_TRIGGERS OFF
32  ALTER DATABASE [OPS_DWS] SET ENABLE_BROKER
33  ALTER DATABASE [OPS_DWS] SET AUTO_UPDATE_STATISTICS_ASYNC ↵
      ↪ OFF
34  ALTER DATABASE [OPS_DWS] SET ↵
      ↪ DATE_CORRELATION_OPTIMIZATION OFF
35  ALTER DATABASE [OPS_DWS] SET TRUSTWORTHY OFF
36  ALTER DATABASE [OPS_DWS] SET ALLOW_SNAPSHOT_ISOLATION OFF
37  ALTER DATABASE [OPS_DWS] SET PARAMETERIZATION SIMPLE
38  ALTER DATABASE [OPS_DWS] SET READ_COMMITTED_SNAPSHOT OFF
39  ALTER DATABASE [OPS_DWS] SET HONOR_BROKER_PRIORITY OFF
40  ALTER DATABASE [OPS_DWS] SET READ_WRITE
41  ALTER DATABASE [OPS_DWS] SET RECOVERY SIMPLE
42  ALTER DATABASE [OPS_DWS] SET MULTI_USER
43  ALTER DATABASE [OPS_DWS] SET PAGE_VERIFY TORN_PAGE_DETECTION
44  ALTER DATABASE [OPS_DWS] SET DB_CHAINING OFF
45  GO
```

4.3.2 Creating Data Warehouse Schema

Listing 4.8 will create the Data Warehouse Schema tables and foreign keys.

Listing 4.8: Creating Data Warehouse Schema

```
1  USE [OPS_DWS]
2  GO
3
```

```
4  SET ANSI_NULLS ON
5  SET QUOTED_IDENTIFIER ON
6  CREATE TABLE [dbo].[dimEmployee](
7    [EmployeeKey] [int] IDENTITY(1,1) NOT NULL,
8    [EmployeeID] [int] NOT NULL,
9    [LastName] [nvarchar](20) NOT NULL,
10   [FirstName] [nvarchar](15) NOT NULL,
11   [Title] [nvarchar](30) NULL,
12   [DateOfBirth] [datetime] NULL,
13   [Address] [nvarchar](50) NULL,
14   [City] [nvarchar](15) NULL,
15   [County] [nvarchar](25) NULL,
16   [Postcode] [nvarchar](10) NULL,
17   [Country] [nvarchar](15) NULL,
18   [Phone] [nvarchar](24) NULL,
19   [DateCreated] [datetime] NOT NULL DEFAULT getdate(),
20  CONSTRAINT [PK_Employees] PRIMARY KEY CLUSTERED
21 (
22   [EmployeeKey] ASC
23 )WITH (PAD_INDEX  = OFF, STATISTICS_NORECOMPUTE  = OFF, ↵
      ↪ IGNORE_DUP_KEY = OFF, ALLOW_ROW_LOCKS  = ON, ↵
      ↪ ALLOW_PAGE_LOCKS  = ON) ON [PRIMARY]
24 ) ON [PRIMARY]
25 GO
26
27 SET ANSI_NULLS ON
28 SET QUOTED_IDENTIFIER ON
29 CREATE TABLE [dbo].[dimCustomer](
30   [CustomerKey] [int] IDENTITY(1,1) NOT NULL,
31   [CustomerID] [nchar](5) NOT NULL,
32   [LastName] [nvarchar](20) NOT NULL,
33   [FirstName] [nvarchar](15) NOT NULL,
34   [Title] [nvarchar](30) NULL,
35   [DisplayName] [nvarchar](65) NULL,
36   [DateOfBirth] [datetime] NULL,
37   [Address] [nvarchar](50) NULL,
38   [City] [nvarchar](15) NULL,
39   [County] [nvarchar](25) NULL,
40   [Postcode] [nvarchar](10) NULL,
41   [Country] [nvarchar](15) NULL,
42   [Phone] [nvarchar](24) NULL,
43   [Fax] [nvarchar](24) NULL,
44   [Region] [nvarchar](20) NULL,
45   [DateCreated] [datetime] NOT NULL DEFAULT getdate(),
46  CONSTRAINT [PK_Customers] PRIMARY KEY CLUSTERED
```

```
47 (
48     [CustomerKey] ASC
49 )WITH (PAD_INDEX  = OFF, STATISTICS_NORECOMPUTE  = OFF, ↵
       ↪ IGNORE_DUP_KEY = OFF, ALLOW_ROW_LOCKS  = ON, ↵
       ↪ ALLOW_PAGE_LOCKS  = ON) ON [PRIMARY]
50 ) ON [PRIMARY]
51 GO
52
53 SET ANSI_NULLS ON
54 SET QUOTED_IDENTIFIER ON
55 CREATE TABLE [dbo].[dimProduct](
56     [ProductKey] [int] IDENTITY(1,1) NOT NULL,
57     [ProductID] [int] NOT NULL,
58     [ProductType] [nvarchar](25) NOT NULL,
59     [ProductName] [nvarchar](40) NOT NULL,
60     [UnitPrice] [money] NULL,
61     [UnitsInStock] [smallint] NULL,
62     [UnitsOnOrder] [smallint] NULL,
63     [ReorderLevel] [smallint] NULL,
64     [Discontinued] [nvarchar](10) NOT NULL,
65     [DateCreated] [datetime] NOT NULL DEFAULT getdate(),
66   CONSTRAINT [PK_Products] PRIMARY KEY CLUSTERED
67 (
68     [ProductKey] ASC
69 )WITH (PAD_INDEX  = OFF, STATISTICS_NORECOMPUTE  = OFF, ↵
       ↪ IGNORE_DUP_KEY = OFF, ALLOW_ROW_LOCKS  = ON, ↵
       ↪ ALLOW_PAGE_LOCKS  = ON) ON [PRIMARY]
70 ) ON [PRIMARY]
71 GO
72
73 SET ANSI_NULLS ON
74 SET QUOTED_IDENTIFIER ON
75 CREATE TABLE [dbo].[dimDate](
76     [DateKey] [int] NOT NULL,
77     [FullDate] [date] NULL,
78     [Quarter] [int] NULL,
79     [QuarterName] [varchar](50) NULL,
80     [Year] [int] NULL,
81     [DayNumber] [int] NULL,
82     [WeekNumber] [int] NULL,
83     [Month] [int] NULL,
84     [MonthName] [varchar](50) NULL,
85     [MonthShortName] [varchar](50) NULL,
86     [DayofWeek] [int] NULL,
87     [DayofWeekName] [varchar](50) NULL,
```

```
88      [DayofWeekShortName] [varchar](50) NULL,
89      [DateCreated] [datetime] NOT NULL DEFAULT getdate(),
90   CONSTRAINT [PK_dimDate] PRIMARY KEY CLUSTERED
91   (
92      [DateKey] ASC
93   )WITH (PAD_INDEX = OFF, STATISTICS_NORECOMPUTE = OFF, ↵
        ↪ IGNORE_DUP_KEY = OFF, ALLOW_ROW_LOCKS = ON, ↵
        ↪ ALLOW_PAGE_LOCKS = ON) ON [PRIMARY]
94   ) ON [PRIMARY]
95   GO
96
97   SET ANSI_NULLS ON
98   SET QUOTED_IDENTIFIER ON
99   CREATE TABLE [dbo].[dimYesNo](
100     [YesNoKey] [int] IDENTITY(1,1) NOT NULL,
101     [YesNoID] [int] NOT NULL,
102     [YesNoDescription] [varchar](50) NOT NULL,
103     [DateCreated] [datetime] NOT NULL DEFAULT getdate(),
104  CONSTRAINT [PK_dimYesNo] PRIMARY KEY CLUSTERED
105  (
106     [YesNoKey] ASC
107  )WITH (PAD_INDEX = OFF, STATISTICS_NORECOMPUTE = OFF, ↵
        ↪ IGNORE_DUP_KEY = OFF, ALLOW_ROW_LOCKS = ON, ↵
        ↪ ALLOW_PAGE_LOCKS = ON) ON [PRIMARY]
108  ) ON [PRIMARY]
109
110  GO
111
112  SET ANSI_NULLS ON
113  SET QUOTED_IDENTIFIER ON
114  CREATE TABLE [dbo].[dimPriceMatch](
115     [PriceMatchKey] [int] IDENTITY(1,1) NOT NULL,
116     [PriceMatchDescription] [varchar](50) NOT NULL,
117     [DateCreated] [datetime] NOT NULL DEFAULT getdate(),
118  CONSTRAINT [PK_PriceMatch] PRIMARY KEY CLUSTERED
119  (
120     [PriceMatchKey] ASC
121  )WITH (PAD_INDEX = OFF, STATISTICS_NORECOMPUTE = OFF, ↵
        ↪ IGNORE_DUP_KEY = OFF, ALLOW_ROW_LOCKS = ON, ↵
        ↪ ALLOW_PAGE_LOCKS = ON) ON [PRIMARY]
122  ) ON [PRIMARY]
123
124  GO
125
126  SET ANSI_NULLS ON
```

```
127  SET QUOTED_IDENTIFIER ON
128  CREATE TABLE [dbo].[factSales](
129     [factSalesKey] [int] IDENTITY(1,1) NOT NULL,
130     [DataSource] [nvarchar](40) NOT NULL,
131     [OrderID] [int] NOT NULL,
132     [CustomerKey] [int] NOT NULL,
133     [ProductKey] [int] NOT NULL,
134     [EmployeeKey] [int] NOT NULL,
135     [OrderDateKey] [int] NOT NULL,
136     [DispatchDateKey] [int] NOT NULL,
137     [PriceMatchKey] [int] NOT NULL,
138     [UnitPrice] [money] NOT NULL,
139     [Quantity] [smallint] NOT NULL,
140     [Discount] [real] NOT NULL,
141     [GiftWrapYesNoKey] [int] NOT NULL,
142     [DateCreated] [datetime] NOT NULL DEFAULT getdate(),
143   CONSTRAINT [PK_Orders] PRIMARY KEY CLUSTERED
144  (
145     [factSalesKey] ASC
146  )WITH (PAD_INDEX  = OFF, STATISTICS_NORECOMPUTE  = OFF, ↵
        ↪ IGNORE_DUP_KEY = OFF, ALLOW_ROW_LOCKS  = ON, ↵
        ↪ ALLOW_PAGE_LOCKS  = ON) ON [PRIMARY]
147  ) ON [PRIMARY]
148  GO
149
150  ALTER TABLE [dbo].[factSales]  WITH NOCHECK ADD  ↵
        ↪ CONSTRAINT [FK_factSales_Customer] FOREIGN ↵
        ↪ KEY([CustomerKey])
151  REFERENCES [dbo].[dimCustomer] ([CustomerKey])
152  ALTER TABLE [dbo].[factSales] CHECK CONSTRAINT ↵
        ↪ [FK_factSales_Customer]
153  ALTER TABLE [dbo].[factSales]  WITH NOCHECK ADD  ↵
        ↪ CONSTRAINT [FK_factSales_Product] FOREIGN ↵
        ↪ KEY([ProductKey])
154  REFERENCES [dbo].[dimProduct] ([ProductKey])
155  ALTER TABLE [dbo].[factSales] CHECK CONSTRAINT ↵
        ↪ [FK_factSales_Product]
156  ALTER TABLE [dbo].[factSales]  WITH NOCHECK ADD  ↵
        ↪ CONSTRAINT [FK_factSales_Employee] FOREIGN ↵
        ↪ KEY([EmployeeKey])
157  REFERENCES [dbo].[dimEmployee] ([EmployeeKey])
158  ALTER TABLE [dbo].[factSales] CHECK CONSTRAINT ↵
        ↪ [FK_factSales_Employee]
159  ALTER TABLE [dbo].[factSales]  WITH NOCHECK ADD  ↵
        ↪ CONSTRAINT [FK_factSales_OrderDate] FOREIGN ↵
```

```
        ↪ KEY([OrderDateKey])
160 REFERENCES [dbo].[dimDate] ([DateKey])
161 ALTER TABLE [dbo].[factSales] CHECK CONSTRAINT ↵
        ↪ [FK_factSales_OrderDate]
162 ALTER TABLE [dbo].[factSales]  WITH NOCHECK ADD  ↵
        ↪ CONSTRAINT [FK_factSales_DispatchDate] FOREIGN ↵
        ↪ KEY([DispatchDateKey])
163 REFERENCES [dbo].[dimDate] ([DateKey])
164 ALTER TABLE [dbo].[factSales] CHECK CONSTRAINT ↵
        ↪ [FK_factSales_DispatchDate]
165 ALTER TABLE [dbo].[factSales]  WITH NOCHECK ADD  ↵
        ↪ CONSTRAINT [FK_factSales_GiftWrapYesNoKey] FOREIGN ↵
        ↪ KEY([GiftWrapYesNoKey])
166 REFERENCES [dbo].[dimYesNo] ([YesNoKey])
167 ALTER TABLE [dbo].[factSales] CHECK CONSTRAINT ↵
        ↪ [FK_factSales_GiftWrapYesNoKey]
168 ALTER TABLE [dbo].[factSales]  WITH NOCHECK ADD  ↵
        ↪ CONSTRAINT [FK_factSales_PriceMatch] FOREIGN ↵
        ↪ KEY([PriceMatchKey])
169 REFERENCES [dbo].[dimPriceMatch] ([PriceMatchKey])
170 ALTER TABLE [dbo].[factSales] CHECK CONSTRAINT ↵
        ↪ [FK_factSales_PriceMatch]
171 GO
172
173 SET ANSI_NULLS ON
174 SET QUOTED_IDENTIFIER ON
175 CREATE TABLE [dbo].[VersionInfo](
176    [ReleaseVersion] [nvarchar](20) NOT NULL,
177    [DateCreated] [datetime] NOT NULL DEFAULT getdate()
178 ) ON [PRIMARY]
179 GO
180
181 INSERT INTO [dbo].[VersionInfo]  ([ReleaseVersion])
182     VALUES ('1.0.0.0')
183 GO
```

4.3.3   Loading Data Warehouse Data

In the real world, loading data into the data warehouse is performed via an ETL tool but to make things easier for our sample data warehouse we will use insert statements to load data from the staging area (OPS_STG) into the data warehouse (OPS_DWS).

Listing 4.9: Loading dimProduct

```
1  ALTER TABLE [OPS_DWS].[dbo].[factSales] DROP CONSTRAINT ↵
       ↪ [FK_factSales_Product]
2  GO
3
4  Truncate Table [OPS_DWS].[dbo].[dimProduct]
5  GO
6
7  SET IDENTITY_INSERT [OPS_DWS].[dbo].[dimProduct] ON
8
9  INSERT INTO [OPS_DWS].[dbo].[dimProduct]
10            (ProductKey
11            ,[ProductID]
12            ,[ProductType]
13            ,[ProductName]
14            ,[UnitPrice]
15            ,[UnitsInStock]
16            ,[UnitsOnOrder]
17            ,[ReorderLevel]
18            ,[Discontinued])
19       VALUES
20            (-1
21            ,-1
22            ,'Unknown'
23            ,'Unknown'
24            ,-1
25            ,-1
26            ,-1
27            ,-1
28            ,'Unknown')
29
30  SET IDENTITY_INSERT [OPS_DWS].[dbo].[dimProduct] OFF
31  GO
32
33  INSERT INTO [OPS_DWS].[dbo].[dimProduct]
34  SELECT [ProductID],
35       CASE WHEN [ProductID] <= 50 THEN 'Domenstic'
36            WHEN [ProductID] Between 50 and 75 THEN ↵
                 ↪ 'Commercial'
37            WHEN [ProductID] > 75 THEN 'Other'
38            ELSE 'Unknown'
39       END AS [ProductType],
40       [ProductName],[UnitPrice],[UnitsInStock],
41       [UnitsOnOrder],[ReorderLevel],
42       CASE [Discontinued]
```

```
43          WHEN 1 THEN 'Yes'
44          WHEN 0 THEN 'No'
45          ELSE 'Unknown'
46       END AS [Discontinued],
47       GETDATE()
48  FROM [OPS_STG].[dbo].[Products]
49  GO
50
51  ALTER TABLE [OPS_DWS].[dbo].[factSales]  WITH NOCHECK ADD ←
        ↪  CONSTRAINT [FK_factSales_Product] FOREIGN ←
        ↪ KEY([ProductKey])
52  REFERENCES [OPS_DWS].[dbo].[dimProduct] ([ProductKey])
53  ALTER TABLE [OPS_DWS].[dbo].[factSales] CHECK CONSTRAINT ←
        ↪ [FK_factSales_Product]
54  GO
```

Listing 4.10: Loading dimEmployee

```
1  ALTER TABLE [OPS_DWS].[dbo].[factSales] DROP CONSTRAINT ←
       ↪ [FK_factSales_Employee]
2  Truncate Table [OPS_DWS].[dbo].[dimEmployee]
3  GO
4
5  SET IDENTITY_INSERT [OPS_DWS].[dbo].[dimEmployee] ON
6
7  INSERT INTO [OPS_DWS].[dbo].[dimEmployee]
8           ([EmployeeKey]
9           ,[EmployeeID]
10          ,[LastName]
11          ,[FirstName]
12          ,[Title]
13          ,[DateOfBirth]
14          ,[Address]
15          ,[City]
16          ,[County]
17          ,[Postcode]
18          ,[Country]
19          ,[Phone])
20     VALUES
21          (-1
22          ,-1
23          ,'Unknown'
24          ,'Unknown'
```

```
25              ,'Unknown'
26              ,NULL
27              ,'Unknown'
28              ,'Unknown'
29              ,'Unknown'
30              ,'Unknown'
31              ,'Unknown'
32              ,'Unknown')
33
34  SET IDENTITY_INSERT [OPS_DWS].[dbo].[dimEmployee] OFF
35  GO
36
37  INSERT INTO [OPS_DWS].[dbo].[dimEmployee]
38  SELECT [EmployeeID], [LastName], [FirstName], [Title], ↵
        ↪ [DateOfBirth], [Address], [City], [County], ↵
        ↪ [Postcode], [Country], [Phone], GETDATE()
39  FROM [OPS_STG].[dbo].[Employees]
40  GO
41
42  ALTER TABLE [OPS_DWS].[dbo].[factSales]  WITH NOCHECK ADD ↵
        ↪  CONSTRAINT [FK_factSales_Employee] FOREIGN ↵
        ↪ KEY([EmployeeKey])
43  REFERENCES [OPS_DWS].[dbo].[dimEmployee] ([EmployeeKey])
44  ALTER TABLE [OPS_DWS].[dbo].[factSales] CHECK CONSTRAINT ↵
        ↪ [FK_factSales_Employee]
45  GO
```

Listing 4.11: Loading dimCustomere

```
1  ALTER TABLE [OPS_DWS].[dbo].[factSales] DROP CONSTRAINT ↵
       ↪ [FK_factSales_Customer]
2  Truncate table [OPS_DWS].[dbo].[dimCustomer]
3  GO
4
5  SET IDENTITY_INSERT [OPS_DWS].[dbo].[dimCustomer] ON
6
7  INSERT INTO [OPS_DWS].[dbo].[dimCustomer]
8            ([CustomerKey]
9            ,[CustomerID]
10           ,[LastName]
11           ,[FirstName]
12           ,[Title]
13           ,[DisplayName]
```

```
14              ,[DateOfBirth]
15              ,[Address]
16              ,[City]
17              ,[County]
18              ,[Postcode]
19              ,[Country]
20              ,[Phone]
21              ,[Fax]
22              ,[Region])
23      VALUES
24              (-1
25              ,-1
26              ,'Unknown'
27              ,'Unknown'
28              ,'Unknown'
29              ,'Unknown'
30              ,NULL
31              ,'Unknown'
32              ,'Unknown'
33              ,'Unknown'
34              ,'Unknown'
35              ,'Unknown'
36              ,'Unknown'
37              ,'Unknown'
38              ,'Unknown')
39
40 SET IDENTITY_INSERT [OPS_DWS].[dbo].[dimCustomer] OFF
41 GO
42
43 INSERT INTO [OPS_DWS].[dbo].[dimCustomer]
44 SELECT [CustomerID],[LastName],[FirstName],[Title]
45        , Rtrim(Ltrim([Title] + ' ' + [FirstName] + ' ' + ↵
             ↪ [LastName])) AS [DisplayName]
46        ,[DateOfBirth],[Address]
47        ,[City],[County],[Postcode],[Country],[Phone],[Fax],
48        CASE WHEN UPPER(LEFT([Postcode],2)) Between 'A' and ↵
             ↪ 'G' THEN 'North'
49            WHEN UPPER(LEFT([Postcode],2)) Between 'H' and ↵
                 ↪ 'N' THEN 'South'
50            WHEN UPPER(LEFT([Postcode],2)) Between 'O' and ↵
                 ↪ 'R' THEN 'East'
51            WHEN UPPER(LEFT([Postcode],2)) Between 'S' and ↵
                 ↪ 'Z' THEN 'West'
52            ELSE 'Unknown'
53        END AS [Region],
```

```
54          GETDATE()
55 FROM [OPS_STG].[dbo].[Customers]
56 GO
57
58 ALTER TABLE [OPS_DWS].[dbo].[factSales]  WITH NOCHECK ADD ↵
   ↳  CONSTRAINT [FK_factSales_Customer] FOREIGN ↵
   ↳ KEY([CustomerKey])
59 REFERENCES [OPS_DWS].[dbo].[dimCustomer] ([CustomerKey])
60 ALTER TABLE [OPS_DWS].[dbo].[factSales] CHECK CONSTRAINT ↵
   ↳ [FK_factSales_Customer]
```

Listing 4.12: Loading dimYesNo

```
1 ALTER TABLE [OPS_DWS].[dbo].[factSales] DROP CONSTRAINT ↵
   ↳ [FK_factSales_GiftWrapYesNoKey]
2 Truncate Table [OPS_DWS].[dbo].[dimYesNo]
3 GO
4
5 SET IDENTITY_INSERT [OPS_DWS].[dbo].[dimYesNo] ON
6
7 INSERT INTO [OPS_DWS].[dbo].[dimYesNo]
8          (YesNoKey,[YesNoID],[YesNoDescription])
9     VALUES
10          (-1, -1, 'Unknown')
11
12 SET IDENTITY_INSERT [OPS_DWS].[dbo].[dimYesNo]  OFF
13 GO
14
15 INSERT INTO [OPS_DWS].[dbo].[dimYesNo]
16    ([YesNoID], [YesNoDescription], [DateCreated])
17 VALUES
18    (1, 'Yes', GETDATE()),
19    (2, 'No', GETDATE())
20 GO
21
22 ALTER TABLE [OPS_DWS].[dbo].[factSales]  WITH NOCHECK ADD ↵
   ↳  CONSTRAINT [FK_factSales_GiftWrapYesNoKey] FOREIGN ↵
   ↳ KEY([GiftWrapYesNoKey])
23 REFERENCES [OPS_DWS].[dbo].[dimYesNo] ([YesNoKey])
24 ALTER TABLE [OPS_DWS].[dbo].[factSales] CHECK CONSTRAINT ↵
   ↳ [FK_factSales_GiftWrapYesNoKey]
25 GO
```

Listing 4.13: Loading dimDate

```
1  ALTER TABLE [OPS_DWS].[dbo].[factSales] DROP CONSTRAINT ↵
       ↪ [FK_factSales_OrderDate]
2  ALTER TABLE [OPS_DWS].[dbo].[factSales] DROP CONSTRAINT ↵
       ↪ [FK_factSales_DispatchDate]
3  Truncate Table [OPS_DWS].[dbo].[dimDate]
4  GO
5
6  INSERT INTO [OPS_DWS].[dbo].[dimDate]
7              ([DateKey]
8              ,[FullDate]
9              ,[Quarter]
10             ,[QuarterName]
11             ,[Year]
12             ,[DayNumber]
13             ,[WeekNumber]
14             ,[Month]
15             ,[MonthName]
16             ,[MonthShortName]
17             ,[DayofWeek]
18             ,[DayofWeekName]
19             ,[DayofWeekShortName])
20      VALUES
21             (-1
22             ,NULL
23             ,-1
24             ,'Unknown'
25             ,-1
26             ,-1
27             ,-1
28             ,-1
29             ,'Unknown'
30             ,'Unknown'
31             ,-1
32             ,'Unknown'
33             ,'Unknown')
34 GO
35
36 DECLARE @StartDate DATE = '1985-01-01'
37 DECLARE  @EndDate DATE = '2014-08-31'
38 ;
39
40 WITH Stage AS
```

```
41  (
42  SELECT CAST(@StartDate AS DATETIME) MyDate
43  UNION ALL
44  SELECT MyDate + 1
45  FROM Stage
46  WHERE MyDate + 1 <= @EndDate
47  )
48  INSERT INTO [OPS_DWS].[dbo].[dimDate]
49  SELECT CAST(CONVERT(CHAR(8),CAST(MyDate AS DATETIME),112) ↵
    ↪ AS INT) AS DateKey
50  ,MyDate
51  ,Case
52      When MONTH(MyDate) Between 1 and 3 Then 1
53      When MONTH(MyDate) Between 4 and 6 Then 2
54      When MONTH(MyDate) Between 7 and 9 Then 3
55      When MONTH(MyDate) Between 10 and 12 Then 4
56  End As [Quarter]
57  ,Case
58      When MONTH(MyDate) Between 1 and 3 Then 'Quarter 1'
59      When MONTH(MyDate) Between 4 and 6 Then 'Quarter 2'
60      When MONTH(MyDate) Between 7 and 9 Then 'Quarter 3'
61      When MONTH(MyDate) Between 10 and 12 Then 'Quarter 4'
62  End As QuarterName
63  , YEAR(MyDate) AS [Year]
64  , DATEPART(dy, MyDate) AS DayNumber
65  , DATEPART(wk, MyDate) AS WeekNumber
66  , MONTH(MyDate) AS [Month]
67  , DATENAME(mm, MyDate) AS [MonthName]
68  , CONVERT(VARCHAR(3), DATENAME(MONTH, MyDate), 100) AS ↵
    ↪ MonthShortName
69  , DAY(MyDate) AS DayOfWeek
70  , DATENAME(dw, MyDate) AS DayOfWeekName
71  , CONVERT(VARCHAR(3), DATENAME(dw, MyDate)) AS ↵
    ↪ DayOfWeekShortName
72  , GETDATE()
73  FROM Stage
74  OPTION (MAXRECURSION 0)
75  GO
76
77  ALTER TABLE [OPS_DWS].[dbo].[factSales]  WITH NOCHECK ADD ↵
    ↪  CONSTRAINT [FK_factSales_OrderDate] FOREIGN ↵
    ↪ KEY([OrderDateKey])
78  REFERENCES [OPS_DWS].[dbo].[dimDate] ([DateKey])
79  ALTER TABLE [OPS_DWS].[dbo].[factSales] CHECK CONSTRAINT ↵
    ↪ [FK_factSales_OrderDate]
```

```
80  ALTER TABLE [OPS_DWS].[dbo].[factSales]  WITH NOCHECK ADD ↵
    ↪  CONSTRAINT [FK_factSales_DispatchDate] FOREIGN ↵
    ↪ KEY([DispatchDateKey])
81  REFERENCES [OPS_DWS].[dbo].[dimDate] ([DateKey])
82  ALTER TABLE [OPS_DWS].[dbo].[factSales] CHECK CONSTRAINT ↵
    ↪ [FK_factSales_DispatchDate]
83  GO
```

Line 36 and 37: You may want to specify dates as per your test data range.

Listing 4.14: Loading dimPriceMatch

```
1   ALTER TABLE [OPS_DWS].[dbo].[factSales] DROP CONSTRAINT ↵
    ↪ [FK_factSales_PriceMatch]
2   Truncate Table [OPS_DWS].[dbo].[dimPriceMatch]
3   GO
4
5   SET IDENTITY_INSERT [OPS_DWS].[dbo].[dimPriceMatch] ON
6
7   INSERT INTO [OPS_DWS].[dbo].[dimPriceMatch]
8           (PriceMatchKey,[PriceMatchDescription])
9       VALUES
10           (-1, 'Unknown')
11
12  SET IDENTITY_INSERT [OPS_DWS].[dbo].[dimPriceMatch]  OFF
13  GO
14
15  INSERT INTO [OPS_DWS].[dbo].[dimPriceMatch]
16  SELECT Distinct PriceMatch,GETDATE()
17  FROM [OPS_STG].[dbo].[OrderDetails]
18  Where PriceMatch is not Null
19  GO
20
21  ALTER TABLE [OPS_DWS].[dbo].[factSales]  WITH NOCHECK ADD ↵
    ↪  CONSTRAINT [FK_factSales_PriceMatch] FOREIGN ↵
    ↪ KEY([PriceMatchKey])
22  REFERENCES [OPS_DWS].[dbo].[dimPriceMatch] ([PriceMatchKey])
23  ALTER TABLE [OPS_DWS].[dbo].[factSales] CHECK CONSTRAINT ↵
    ↪ [FK_factSales_PriceMatch]
24  GO
```

Listing 4.15: Loading factSales

```
 1  ALTER TABLE [OPS_DWS].[dbo].[factSales] DROP CONSTRAINT ↵
        ↪ [FK_factSales_Customer]
 2  ALTER TABLE [OPS_DWS].[dbo].[factSales] DROP CONSTRAINT ↵
        ↪ [FK_factSales_Product]
 3  ALTER TABLE [OPS_DWS].[dbo].[factSales] DROP CONSTRAINT ↵
        ↪ [FK_factSales_Employee]
 4  ALTER TABLE [OPS_DWS].[dbo].[factSales] DROP CONSTRAINT ↵
        ↪ [FK_factSales_OrderDate]
 5  ALTER TABLE [OPS_DWS].[dbo].[factSales] DROP CONSTRAINT ↵
        ↪ [FK_factSales_DispatchDate]
 6  ALTER TABLE [OPS_DWS].[dbo].[factSales] DROP CONSTRAINT ↵
        ↪ [FK_factSales_GiftWrapYesNoKey]
 7  ALTER TABLE [OPS_DWS].[dbo].[factSales] DROP CONSTRAINT ↵
        ↪ [FK_factSales_PriceMatch]
 8  Truncate Table [OPS_DWS].[dbo].[factSales]
 9  GO
10
11  INSERT INTO [OPS_DWS].[dbo].[factSales]
12  SELECT 'Table Order'
13         ,o.[OrderID]
14         ,ISNULL(c.CustomerKey, -1) CustomerKey
15         ,ISNULL(p.ProductKey, -1)  ProductKey
16         ,ISNULL(e.EmployeeKey, -1) EmployeeKey
17         ,ISNULL(dtOrd.DateKey, -1) OrderDateKey
18         ,ISNULL(dtShp.DateKey, -1) DispatchDateKey
19         ,ISNULL(pm.PriceMatchKey, -1) PriceMatchKey
20         ,od.UnitPrice
21         ,od.Quantity
22         ,od.Discount
23         ,ISNULL(yn.YesNoKey, -1) GiftWrapYesNoKey
24         ,GETDATE()
25  FROM [OPS_STG].[dbo].[Orders] o
26  INNER JOIN [OPS_STG].[dbo].[OrderDetails] od on ↵
        ↪ od.[OrderID] = o.[OrderID]
27  LEFT JOIN [OPS_DWS].[dbo].[dimCustomer] c on c.CustomerID ↵
        ↪ = o.CustomerID
28  LEFT JOIN [OPS_DWS].[dbo].[dimProduct] p on p.ProductID = ↵
        ↪ od.ProductID
29  LEFT JOIN [OPS_DWS].[dbo].[dimEmployee] e on e.EmployeeID ↵
        ↪ = o.EmployeeID
30  LEFT JOIN [OPS_DWS].[dbo].[dimDate] dtOrd on ↵
        ↪ dtOrd.FullDate = o.OrderDate
```

```
31  LEFT JOIN [OPS_DWS].[dbo].[dimDate] dtShp on ←
        ↪ dtShp.FullDate = o.DispatchDate
32  LEFT JOIN [OPS_DWS].[dbo].[dimYesNo] yn on ←
        ↪ yn.YesNoDescription = od.GiftWrap
33  LEFT JOIN [OPS_DWS].[dbo].[dimPriceMatch] pm on ←
        ↪ pm.[PriceMatchDescription] = od.PriceMatch
34  GO
35
36  ALTER TABLE [OPS_DWS].[dbo].[factSales]  WITH NOCHECK ADD ←
        ↪  CONSTRAINT [FK_factSales_Customer] FOREIGN ←
        ↪ KEY([CustomerKey])
37  REFERENCES [OPS_DWS].[dbo].[dimCustomer] ([CustomerKey])
38  ALTER TABLE [OPS_DWS].[dbo].[factSales] CHECK CONSTRAINT ←
        ↪ [FK_factSales_Customer]
39  ALTER TABLE [OPS_DWS].[dbo].[factSales]  WITH NOCHECK ADD ←
        ↪  CONSTRAINT [FK_factSales_Product] FOREIGN ←
        ↪ KEY([ProductKey])
40  REFERENCES [OPS_DWS].[dbo].[dimProduct] ([ProductKey])
41  ALTER TABLE [OPS_DWS].[dbo].[factSales] CHECK CONSTRAINT ←
        ↪ [FK_factSales_Product]
42  ALTER TABLE [OPS_DWS].[dbo].[factSales]  WITH NOCHECK ADD ←
        ↪  CONSTRAINT [FK_factSales_Employee] FOREIGN ←
        ↪ KEY([EmployeeKey])
43  REFERENCES [OPS_DWS].[dbo].[dimEmployee] ([EmployeeKey])
44  ALTER TABLE [OPS_DWS].[dbo].[factSales] CHECK CONSTRAINT ←
        ↪ [FK_factSales_Employee]
45  ALTER TABLE [OPS_DWS].[dbo].[factSales]  WITH NOCHECK ADD ←
        ↪  CONSTRAINT [FK_factSales_OrderDate] FOREIGN ←
        ↪ KEY([OrderDateKey])
46  REFERENCES [OPS_DWS].[dbo].[dimDate] ([DateKey])
47  ALTER TABLE [OPS_DWS].[dbo].[factSales] CHECK CONSTRAINT ←
        ↪ [FK_factSales_OrderDate]
48  ALTER TABLE [OPS_DWS].[dbo].[factSales]  WITH NOCHECK ADD ←
        ↪  CONSTRAINT [FK_factSales_DispatchDate] FOREIGN ←
        ↪ KEY([DispatchDateKey])
49  REFERENCES [OPS_DWS].[dbo].[dimDate] ([DateKey])
50  ALTER TABLE [OPS_DWS].[dbo].[factSales] CHECK CONSTRAINT ←
        ↪ [FK_factSales_DispatchDate]
51  ALTER TABLE [OPS_DWS].[dbo].[factSales]  WITH NOCHECK ADD ←
        ↪  CONSTRAINT [FK_factSales_GiftWrapYesNoKey] FOREIGN ←
        ↪ KEY([GiftWrapYesNoKey])
52  REFERENCES [OPS_DWS].[dbo].[dimYesNo] ([YesNoKey])
53  ALTER TABLE [OPS_DWS].[dbo].[factSales] CHECK CONSTRAINT ←
        ↪ [FK_factSales_GiftWrapYesNoKey]
```

```
54  ALTER TABLE [OPS_DWS].[dbo].[factSales]  WITH NOCHECK ADD ↩
      ↪  CONSTRAINT [FK_factSales_PriceMatch] FOREIGN ↩
      ↪ KEY([PriceMatchKey])
55  REFERENCES [OPS_DWS].[dbo].[dimPriceMatch] ([PriceMatchKey])
56  ALTER TABLE [OPS_DWS].[dbo].[factSales] CHECK CONSTRAINT ↩
      ↪ [FK_factSales_PriceMatch]
57  GO
```

By now you should have the three databases fully populated with test data and we are ready for automation!

Chapter 5

Automating Staging Area

Automating Staging Area

In this chapter, we will learn how to:

- *Connect to a database*

- *Automate data transfer test scenarios from the source database to the staging area*

- *Enhance the Automation Framework to produce a Test Results Summary Report*

So let's get on with it. . .

W$_{\text{HEN}}$ data is transferred from the source database to the staging area, we need to ensure that the correct data is received i.e. nothing has been lost or corrupted during the transfer. Using our sample architecture defined in the Figure 1.1 we need to automate the following data sources:

1. Database tables from the source system are received in the staging area.

2. CSV files from the source systems are received in the staging area.

3. Excel files from the source systems are received in the staging area.

In this chapter we will concentrate on the first type of data transfer only i.e. database tables. The other two types are covered in later chapters. So let's see what individual tests can be performed when tables are transferred from the source systems to the staging area. There are often many different tests you will need to perform, based on the model of the system you are testing but here are some tests you should certainly perform. Note that you may want to deploy some or all of these tests, or add additional tests, depending on what you need to verify.

We created all of the required databases in the previous chapter. So let's now enhance the Automation Framework to connect to the databases we created.

5.1 Connecting to a Database

First we need to add the necessary libraries to support the SQL database connection.

- Right click on the 'src' folder and select Build Path ⇒ Configure Build Path.

- Go to Libraries and click on 'Add External JARs'.

- Select 'sqljdbc4.jar'. Remember we extracted the files in 'C:\sqljdbc_4.0'. The files should be in the folder 'C:\sqljdbc_4.0\enu'.

- Click Open and then click OK.

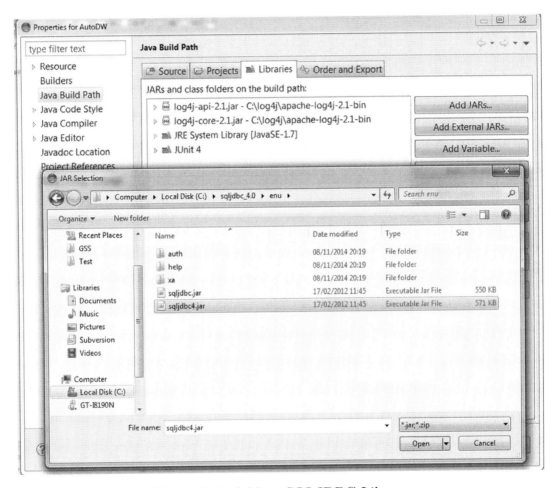

Figure 5.1: Adding SQLJDBC Library

Let's now add a new class to our Automation Framework called Environment.java.

- Within 'Package Explorer', right click on the folder name 'src' and select New ⇒ Class.

- Type Environment in the 'Name' edit box as shown in Figure 5.2

- Click on the Finish button.

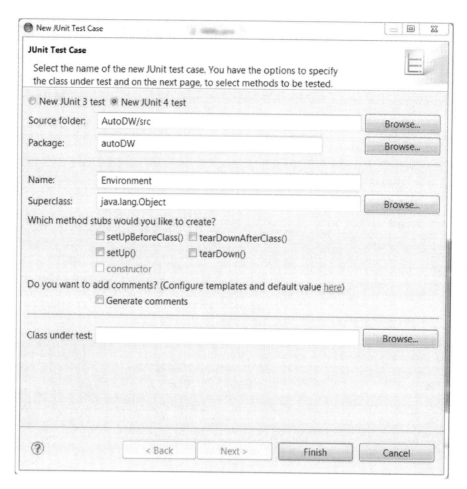

Figure 5.2: Adding Environment Class

Add the code shown in Listing 5.1 to the Environment.java file.

Listing 5.1: Code for Environment.java

```
1  package autoDW;
2
3  public class Environment {
4
5      public static final String DB_OPS_SOURCE = ↵
            ↪ "jdbc:sqlserver://localhost; databaseName=OPS";
6      public static final String DB_OPS_STAGING = ↵
            ↪ "jdbc:sqlserver://localhost; ↵
            ↪ databaseName=OPS_STG";
7      public static final String DB_OPS_DWS = ↵
            ↪ "jdbc:sqlserver://localhost; ↵
            ↪ databaseName=OPS_DWS";
```

```
 8
 9      public static final String DB_USERID = "sa";
10      public static final String DB_PWD = "sa";
11  }
```

Line 5: Connection string for the source database (OPS).
Line 6: Connection string for the staging database (OPS_STG).
Line 7: Connection string for the data warehouse (OPS_DWS).
Line 9: Database userid. Change its value to the credentials you are using.
Line 10: Database password. Change its value to the credentials you are using.

Now let's add a new generic function to the Utility.java as shown in Listing 5.2.

GetDBName - Gets the database name		
Input Parameters	*none*	No parameters
Return Value	*dbName*	Returns the database name it is connected to

Listing 5.2: Utility.java - Code for GetDBName

```
 1  import java.sql.Connection;
 2  import java.sql.DriverManager;
 3  import java.sql.ResultSet;
 4  import java.sql.Statement;
 5
 6  public static String GetDBName()
 7  {
 8  String dbName = "";
 9
10  try
11  {
12      Class.forName("com.microsoft.sqlserver.jdbc. ↵
            ↪ SQLServerDriver");
13      Connection conn = DriverManager.getConnection( ↵
            ↪ Environment.DB_OPS_SOURCE, Environment.DB_USERID, ↵
            ↪ Environment.DB_PWD);
14      Utility.log.info("DB connected..." + ↵
            ↪ Environment.DB_OPS_SOURCE);
15      Statement statement = conn.createStatement();
16      String queryString = "SELECT db_name()";
17      Utility.log.info("SQL is: " + queryString);
18      ResultSet rs = statement.executeQuery(queryString);
19
```

```
20      while (rs.next())
21      {
22          dbName= rs.getString(1);
23      }
24
25  }
26  catch (Exception e)
27  {
28      e.printStackTrace();
29      Utility.ReportExpectedVsActual("Exception occurred" + ↵
            ↪ e.getMessage(), "Failing test");
30  }
31
32  return dbName;
33  }
```

Line 12: Register JDBC driver with the DriverManager.
Line 13: Insert the name, user id and password of the database you want to connect.
Line 14: It is always good practice to log the database name it is connecting to.
Line 16: Construct the SQL Query to be executed on the database.
Line 17: It is also always good practice to log the SQL Query you are executing.
Line 22: Retrieve the query result - i.e. the first value in string format.
Line 26: Exception handling. Fail the test if anything goes wrong. Note the call to function 'ReportExpectedVsActual' which will always fail in this instance!
Line 32: Return the database name.

Now add a new test to the myTest.java file as shown in Listing 5.3.

Listing 5.3: myTest.java - Code for testDBConnection

```
1  @Test
2  public void testDBConnection() {
3      Utility.log.info("***********  Starting Test: " + ↵
            ↪ name.getMethodName());
4
5      Utility.log.info("Database Name is: " + ↵
            ↪ Utility.GetDBName());
6      Utility.ReportResult();
7  }
```

Line 5: Call the 'GetDBName' function.

Finally execute the newly created test testDBConnection. You will see a Console output window as shown in Figure 5.3.

```
Problems  @ Javadoc  Declaration  Console ⋈
<terminated> Rerun autoDW.myTest.testDBConnection [JUnit] C:\Program Files\Java\jre7\bin\javaw.exe (8 Nov 2014 21:31:02)
21:31:02.726 [main] INFO  MyLogger - ************   Starting Test: testDBConnection
21:31:03.104 [main] INFO  MyLogger - DB connected...jdbc:sqlserver://localhost;databaseName=OPS
21:31:03.119 [main] INFO  MyLogger - SQL is: SELECT db_name()
21:31:03.150 [main] INFO  MyLogger - Database Name is: OPS
21:31:03.150 [main] INFO  MyLogger - Reporting result....
21:31:03.150 [main] INFO  MyLogger - Test Passed.
21:31:03.150 [main] INFO  MyLogger - Result File: MyTest_(PASS)_2014_11_08 21_31_03_15.csv
```

Figure 5.3: Console Output - Database Connection

Hurray! We have successfully connected to our database and the test displays its name.

5.2   Automating Table Load Scenario

As a tester in a real environment, before running these tests you would first have executed an ETL job that transfers data from the source database to the staging area. In Figure 1.1 of our sample data warehouse, the data in the OPS database tables would have been transferred to OPS_STG database tables. However, for the purposes of this book, you don't need to execute any ETL job as we already have populated our databases in Section 4.1.3 and 4.2.3.

Let's now see what tests we can apply to verify this transfer.

5.2.1   Test 1 - Compare Record Counts

This test verifies that the record count of a table in the source database is the same as in the staging area. So how do we do it?

We will add a new function GetCountOfRecords to the Utility.java file.

GetCountOfRecords - Gets count of records in a table		
Input Parameters	*dbName*	Name of the database
	dbSchema	Name of the schema
	tblName	Name of the table
Return Value	*count*	Count of records in the table

Listing 5.4: Utility.java - Code for GetCountOfRecords

```
1 public static int GetCountOfRecords(String dbName, String ↵
    ↪ dbSchema, String tblName)
2 {
3    int count = -99;
4
```

```
5    try
6    {
7        Connection conn;
8        Class.forName("com.microsoft.sqlserver. ↵
            ↪ jdbc.SQLServerDriver");
9        conn = DriverManager.getConnection(dbName, ↵
            ↪ Environment.DB_USERID, Environment.DB_PWD);
10       Utility.log.info("DB connected: " + dbName);
11       Statement statement = conn.createStatement();
12       String queryString = "SELECT COUNT(*) from "    + ↵
            ↪ dbSchema + "." + tblName ;
13       Utility.log.info("SQL is: " + queryString);
14       ResultSet rs = statement.executeQuery(queryString);
15       while (rs.next())
16       {
17           count= rs.getInt(1);
18       }
19   }
20   catch (Exception e)
21   {
22       e.printStackTrace();
23       Utility.ReportExpectedVsActual("Exception occurred" ↵
            ↪ + e.getMessage(), "Failing test");
24   }
25
26   return count;
27 }
```

Line 3: Default value to return.
Line 12: Construct SQL Query to get count of records.
Line 17: Get the result as an integer.
Line 26: Return count of records.

Let's add another function CompareCountOfRecords to the Utility.java file.

CompareCountOfRecords - Compares count of records in two tables and reports the outcome		
Input Parameters	sourcDBName	Name of the source database
	sourceSchemaName	Name of the source schema
	sourceTblName	Name of the source table
	targetDBName	Name of the target database
	targetSchemaName	Name of the target schema
	targetTblName	Name of the target table
Return Value	void	Returns nothing.

Listing 5.5: Utility.java - Code for CompareCountOfRecords

```
1  public static void CompareCountOfRecords(String ←
       ↪ sourcDBName, String sourceSchemaName, String ←
       ↪ sourceTblName, String targetDBName, String ←
       ↪ targetSchemaName, String targetTblName)
2  {
3      Utility.log.info("targetTblName: " + targetTblName);
4      int exp, act;
5
6      exp = Utility.GetCountOfRecords(sourcDBName, ←
          ↪ sourceSchemaName, sourceTblName);
7      act = Utility.GetCountOfRecords(targetDBName, ←
          ↪ targetSchemaName, targetTblName);
8
9      Utility.ReportExpectedVsActual(String.valueOf(exp), ←
          ↪ String.valueOf(act));
10 }
```

Line 6: Get the number of records in the source table.

Line 7: Get the number of records in the target table.

Line 9: Report the comparison outcome. Note the use of String.valueOf() function which converts an integer to a string, as our 'ReportExpectedVsActual' function accepts only string values.

Now let's add a new test.

- Within 'Package Explorer', right click on the folder name 'src' and select New ⇒ Other...

- Select JUnit Test Case and click Next.

- Type the 'Name' as sourceDataLoad and click Finish.

Add Listing 5.6 code to the sourceDataLoad.java file.

Listing 5.6: sourceDataLoad.java - Code for record counts

```
1  package autoDW;
2
3  import org.junit.AfterClass;
4  import org.junit.Before;
5  import org.junit.FixMethodOrder;
6  import org.junit.runners.MethodSorters;
7  import org.junit.Rule;
```

```
8   import org.junit.Test;
9   import org.junit.rules.TestName;
10
11  @FixMethodOrder(MethodSorters.NAME_ASCENDING)
12
13  public class sourceDataLoad
14  {
15      @Rule public TestName name = new TestName();
16
17      @Before
18      public void setUp() throws Exception
19      {
20          Config.TestResult = Config.PASS;
21      }
22
23      @AfterClass
24      public static void tearDownAfterClass() throws Exception
25      {
26          Utility.SaveLog("sourceDataLoad");
27      }
28
29      @Test
30      public void _10_test_TableRecorddCounts()
31      {
32          Utility.log.info("************   Starting Test: " + ↵
              ↪ name.getMethodName());
33
34          Utility.CompareCountOfRecords( ↵
              ↪ Environment.DB_OPS_SOURCE,"dbo","Customers", ↵
              ↪ Environment.DB_OPS_STAGING,"dbo","Customers");
35          Utility.ReportResult();
36      }
37  }
```

Line 34: Call the generic function to compare source (DB_OPS_SOURCE) and target (DB_OPS_STAGING) record counts for table "Customers".

Now execute the test _10_test_TableRecordCounts. You will see a Console output as shown in Figure 5.4.

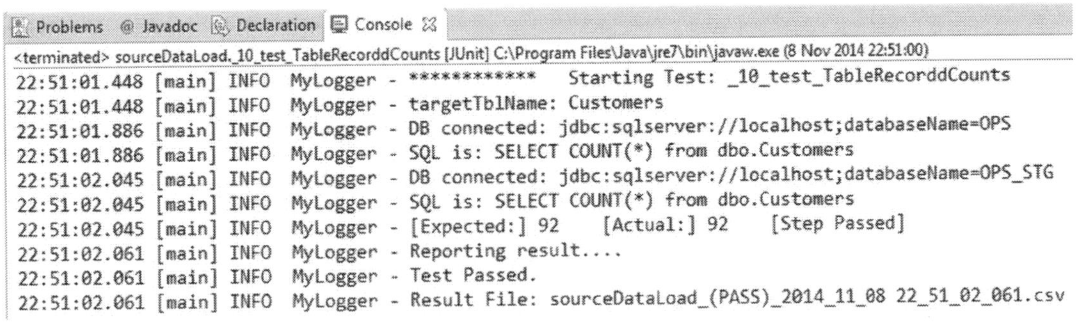

Figure 5.4: Console Output - Count of Records

We have just successfully executed our first automated data warehouse test.

Now let's modify our test _10_test_TableRecordCounts to include the rest of the tables in the source database that are transferred to the staging area.

☞ This introduces the modularity and re-usability aspect of our Automation Framework because, not only within this test but in all our other tests, we will reuse the general purpose functions - CompareCountOfRecords and GetCountOfRecords. In fact, all the functions defined in the Utility file fall into this category.

Listing 5.7: sourceDataLoad.java: _10_test_TableRecorddCounts

```
@Test
public void _10_test_TableRecorddCounts() {
    Utility.log.info("************   Starting Test: " + ↵
        name.getMethodName());

    Utility.CompareCountOfRecords( ↵
        Environment.DB_OPS_SOURCE,"dbo","Customers", ↵
        Environment.DB_OPS_STAGING,"dbo","Customers");
    Utility.CompareCountOfRecords( ↵
        Environment.DB_OPS_SOURCE,"dbo","Employees", ↵
        Environment.DB_OPS_STAGING,"dbo","Employees");
    Utility.CompareCountOfRecords( ↵
        Environment.DB_OPS_SOURCE,"dbo","Products", ↵
        Environment.DB_OPS_STAGING,"dbo","Products");
    Utility.CompareCountOfRecords( ↵
        Environment.DB_OPS_SOURCE,"dbo","Orders", ↵
        Environment.DB_OPS_STAGING,"dbo","Orders");
    Utility.CompareCountOfRecords( ↵
        Environment.DB_OPS_SOURCE,"dbo","OrderDetails", ↵
        Environment.DB_OPS_STAGING,"dbo","OrderDetails");
```

```
11      Utility.ReportResult();
12  }
```

Now re-execute the test and you will see a Console output as shown in Figure 5.5.

```
Problems  @ Javadoc  Declaration  Console ✕
<terminated> Rerun autoDW.sourceDataLoad._10_test_TableRecorddCounts [JUnit] C:\Program Files\Java\jre7\bin\javaw.exe (8 Nov 2014 22:56:51)
22:56:52.164 [main] INFO  MyLogger - ***********    Starting Test: _10_test_TableRecorddCounts
22:56:52.164 [main] INFO  MyLogger - targetTblName: Customers
22:56:52.739 [main] INFO  MyLogger - DB connected: jdbc:sqlserver://localhost;databaseName=OPS
22:56:52.757 [main] INFO  MyLogger - SQL is: SELECT COUNT(*) from dbo.Customers
22:56:52.945 [main] INFO  MyLogger - DB connected: jdbc:sqlserver://localhost;databaseName=OPS_STG
22:56:52.945 [main] INFO  MyLogger - SQL is: SELECT COUNT(*) from dbo.Customers
22:56:52.945 [main] INFO  MyLogger - [Expected:] 92    [Actual:] 92    [Step Passed]
22:56:52.945 [main] INFO  MyLogger - targetTblName: Employees
22:56:52.961 [main] INFO  MyLogger - DB connected: jdbc:sqlserver://localhost;databaseName=OPS
22:56:52.961 [main] INFO  MyLogger - SQL is: SELECT COUNT(*) from dbo.Employees
22:56:52.993 [main] INFO  MyLogger - DB connected: jdbc:sqlserver://localhost;databaseName=OPS_STG
22:56:52.993 [main] INFO  MyLogger - SQL is: SELECT COUNT(*) from dbo.Employees
22:56:53.009 [main] INFO  MyLogger - [Expected:] 9    [Actual:] 9    [Step Passed]
22:56:53.009 [main] INFO  MyLogger - targetTblName: Products
22:56:53.024 [main] INFO  MyLogger - DB connected: jdbc:sqlserver://localhost;databaseName=OPS
22:56:53.024 [main] INFO  MyLogger - SQL is: SELECT COUNT(*) from dbo.Products
22:56:53.024 [main] INFO  MyLogger - DB connected: jdbc:sqlserver://localhost;databaseName=OPS_STG
22:56:53.024 [main] INFO  MyLogger - SQL is: SELECT COUNT(*) from dbo.Products
22:56:53.024 [main] INFO  MyLogger - [Expected:] 77    [Actual:] 77    [Step Passed]
22:56:53.024 [main] INFO  MyLogger - targetTblName: Orders
22:56:53.040 [main] INFO  MyLogger - DB connected: jdbc:sqlserver://localhost;databaseName=OPS
22:56:53.040 [main] INFO  MyLogger - SQL is: SELECT COUNT(*) from dbo.Orders
22:56:53.055 [main] INFO  MyLogger - DB connected: jdbc:sqlserver://localhost;databaseName=OPS_STG
22:56:53.055 [main] INFO  MyLogger - SQL is: SELECT COUNT(*) from dbo.Orders
22:56:53.055 [main] INFO  MyLogger - [Expected:] 100    [Actual:] 100    [Step Passed]
22:56:53.055 [main] INFO  MyLogger - targetTblName: [OrderDetails]
22:56:53.055 [main] INFO  MyLogger - DB connected: jdbc:sqlserver://localhost;databaseName=OPS
22:56:53.055 [main] INFO  MyLogger - SQL is: SELECT COUNT(*) from dbo.OrderDetails
22:56:53.071 [main] INFO  MyLogger - DB connected: jdbc:sqlserver://localhost;databaseName=OPS_STG
22:56:53.071 [main] INFO  MyLogger - SQL is: SELECT COUNT(*) from dbo.[OrderDetails]
22:56:53.071 [main] INFO  MyLogger - [Expected:] 453    [Actual:] 453    [Step Passed]
22:56:53.071 [main] INFO  MyLogger - Reporting result....
22:56:53.071 [main] INFO  MyLogger - Test Passed.
22:56:53.071 [main] INFO  MyLogger - Result File: sourceDataLoad_(PASS)_2014_11_08 22_56_53_071.csv
```

Figure 5.5: Console Output - Count of Records All Tables

This completes our first test which compares the record counts of all the tables in the source database with the staging area.

5.2.2   Test 2 - Compare Column Checksums

This second test verifies that the SUM of SQL CHECKSUM of each individual column in the source database table is the same as in the staging area table. Although the CHECKSUM can potentially produce duplicate results with different data, in my experience this test has been very useful in highlighting issues so I always apply this test. Here is how we do it.

First of all, we need to add a new configuration parameter in our Config.java file which will be used throughout the framework.

Listing 5.8: Code for Config.java

```
1  public static final String MY_NULL = "9";
```

Sometime NULL values are included in the data and we need to replace these so that we can carry out certain operations on the data. I've used a value of "9" but you may want to use some other value.

We will now add a new function GetTableChecksum to the Utility.java file.

GetTableChecksum - Gets Sum of Checksum of columns in a table		
Input Parameters	dbName	Name of the database
	dbSchema	Name of the schema
	tblName	Name of the table
	ignoreColumns	Columns to be ignored for Checksum
	targetClause	Where clause to be applied to the table
Return Value	Checksum	Returns a list of Sum of Checksum of columns in the table

Listing 5.9: Utility.java - Code for GetTableChecksum

```
1  import java.util.ArrayList;
2  import java.util.Arrays;
3  import java.util.List;
4
5  public static List<String> GetTableChecksum(String ↵
       ↪ dbName, String dbSchema, String tblName, String ↵
       ↪ ignoreColumns, String targetClause)
6  {
7      Utility.log.info("GetTableChecksum... " + tblName);
8
9      List<String> resultColumns = new ArrayList<String>();
10     List<String> myChksum = new ArrayList<String>();
11     List<String> ignoreColmList = ↵
          ↪ Arrays.asList(ignoreColumns.split(","));
12
13     try
14     {
```

```
15      Connection conn;
16      Class.forName("com.microsoft.sqlserver.jdbc. ↵
            ↪ SQLServerDriver");
17      conn = DriverManager.getConnection(dbName, ↵
            ↪ Environment.DB_USERID, Environment.DB_PWD);
18      Utility.log.info("DB connected: " + dbName);
19      Statement statement = conn.createStatement();
20
21      String queryString = "select COLUMN_NAME from ↵
            ↪ information_schema.columns where table_name = ↵
            ↪ '" + tblName + "'";
22
23      //Utility.log.info("SQL is: " + queryString);
24      ResultSet rs = statement.executeQuery(queryString);
25
26      while (rs.next())
27      {
28          if (ignoreColmList.contains ↵
                ↪ (rs.getString("COLUMN_NAME")))
29              Utility.log.info("**** Ignoring column **** : ↵
                    ↪ " + rs.getString("COLUMN_NAME"));
30          else
31              resultColumns.add( ↵
                    ↪ rs.getString("COLUMN_NAME"));
32      }
33
34      for(int j=0; j<resultColumns.size();j++)
35      {
36          Connection conn1;
37          Class.forName("com.microsoft.sqlserver.jdbc. ↵
                ↪ SQLServerDriver");
38          conn1 = DriverManager.getConnection(dbName, ↵
                ↪ Environment.DB_USERID, Environment.DB_PWD);
39          Utility.log.info("Going for column...."+ ↵
                ↪ resultColumns.get(j));
40          Statement statement1 = conn1.createStatement();
41
42          String queryString1 = "select ↵
                ↪ Sum(Cast(CHECKSUM(CAST(ISNULL(" + ↵
                ↪ resultColumns.get(j) + "," + Config.MY_NULL ↵
                ↪ + ") as varchar(max))) as Decimal(32,0))) ↵
                ↪ as MySum from "  + dbSchema + "." + ↵
                ↪ tblName;
43
44          if (!targetClause.equals(""))
```

```
45          queryString1 += " Where " + targetClause;
46
47      Utility.log.info("SQL is: " + queryString1);
48      ResultSet rs1 = ↵
            ↪ statement1.executeQuery(queryString1);
49
50      while (rs1.next()) {
51          myChksum.add(resultColumns.get(j) + ": " + ↵
                ↪ rs1.getString("MySum"));
52      }
53      }
54  }
55  catch (Exception e)
56  {
57  e.printStackTrace();
58  Utility.ReportExpectedVsActual("Exception occurred" + ↵
        ↪ e.getMessage(), "Failing test");
59  }
60
61  return myChksum;
62 }
```

Line 11: Columns to be ignored are passed as a comma separated 'String' so convert it to a 'List'.

Line 21: Construct a SQL Query to retrieve a list of the columns in the table from the information_schema.

Line 23: Uncomment this statement if you want to log the query.

Line 28: If the column name is in the ignore list, don't add it to the Checksum list.

Line 29: Log some details to identify the columns that are being ignored.

Line 31: Make a list of the columns for which we are calculating the Checksum.

Line 34: Loop through the list.

Line 42: Construct a SQL Query to determine the sum of the Checksum. Note the use of Config.MY_NULL in case the returned value is NULL.

Line 44: If a 'where' clause is supplied; append it to the SQL Query.

Line 51: Add the result to the Checksum list. Note how we have explicitly specified the column name instead of the column number in 'rs1.getString("MySum")'

Line 61: Return the sum of Checksum values as a List.

Let's add another function CompareChecksums to the Utility.java file.

CompareChecksums - Compares Sum of Checksum of columns of two tables and reports the outcome		
Input Parameters	*sourcDBName*	Name of the source database
	sourceSchemaName	Name of the source schema
	sourceTblName	Name of the source table
	targetDBName	Name of the target database
	targetSchemaName	Name of the target schema
	targetTblName	Name of the target table
	ignoreTargetCols	Columns to be ignored in the target table
	targetClause	Where clause to be applied to the target table
Return Value	*void*	Returns nothing.

Listing 5.10: Utility.java - Code for CompareChecksums

```
1  public static void CompareChecksums(String sourceDBName, ↵
       ↪ String sourceSchemaName, String sourceTblName, ↵
       ↪ String targetDBName, String targetSchemaName, String ↵
       ↪ targetTblName, String ignoreTargetCols, String ↵
       ↪ targetClause)
2  {
3      Utility.log.info("targetTblName: " + targetTblName);
4
5      List<String> expChksum = new ArrayList<String>();
6      List<String> actChksum = new ArrayList<String>();
7
8      expChksum = Utility.GetTableChecksum(sourceDBName, ↵
           ↪ sourceSchemaName, sourceTblName, "", "");
9      actChksum = Utility.GetTableChecksum(targetDBName, ↵
           ↪ targetSchemaName, targetTblName, ↵
           ↪ ignoreTargetCols, targetClause);
10
11     Utility.ReportExpectedVsActual("Column Count: " + ↵
           ↪ String.valueOf(expChksum.size()), "Column Count: ↵
           ↪ " + String.valueOf(actChksum.size()));
12
13     for(int g=0; g<expChksum.size();g++)
14     {
15         Utility.ReportExpectedVsActual(expChksum.get(g), ↵
               ↪ actChksum.get(g));
16     }
17 }
```

Line 8: Get the Sum of Checksum of the source table. Note that no value has been specified for parameters 'ignoreTargetCols' and 'targetClause'.

Line 9: Get the Sum of Checksum of the target table.

Line 11: Report a failure if the column count doesn't match.

Line 15: Report the comparison outcome.

Add Listing 5.11 code to the sourceDataLoad.java file.

Listing 5.11: sourceDataLoad.java - Code for compare Checksums

```
1  @Test
2  public void _20_test_TableChecksums () {
3      Utility.log.info("************  Starting Test: " + ↵
          ↪ name.getMethodName());
4
5      Utility.CompareChecksums(Environment.DB_OPS_SOURCE , ↵
          ↪ "dbo", "Customers", Environment.DB_OPS_STAGING , ↵
          ↪ "dbo", "Customers", "", "");
6
7      Utility.ReportResult();
8  }
```

Line 6: Call to 'CompareChecksums' function. Note that no value has been specified for ignoreTargetCols and targetClause. We will use these parameters in later chapters.

Now execute the test _20_test_TableChecksums. You will see a Console output as shown in Figure 5.6.

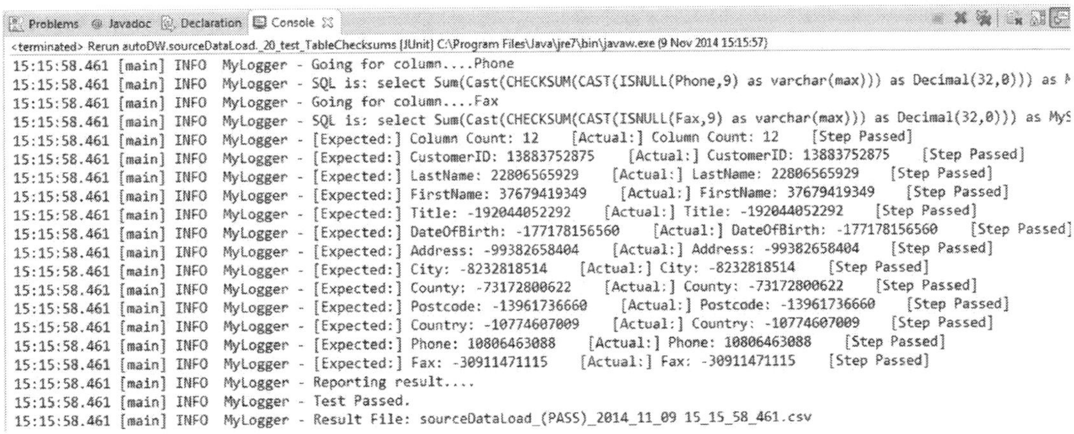

Figure 5.6: Console Output - Checksums

Now let's modify our test _20_test_TableChecksums to include the rest of the tables.

Listing 5.12: sourceDataLoad.java - _20_test_TableChecksums

```
1  @Test
2  public void _20_test_TableChecksums() {
3      Utility.log.info("***********   Starting Test: " + ←
       ↪ name.getMethodName());
4
5      Utility.CompareChecksums(Environment.DB_OPS_SOURCE, ←
       ↪ "dbo", "Customers", Environment.DB_OPS_STAGING, ←
       ↪ "dbo", "Customers", "", "");
6      Utility.CompareChecksums(Environment.DB_OPS_SOURCE, ←
       ↪ "dbo", "Employees", Environment.DB_OPS_STAGING, ←
       ↪ "dbo", "Employees", "", "");
7      Utility.CompareChecksums(Environment.DB_OPS_SOURCE, ←
       ↪ "dbo", "Products", Environment.DB_OPS_STAGING, ←
       ↪ "dbo", "Products", "", "");
8      Utility.CompareChecksums(Environment.DB_OPS_SOURCE, ←
       ↪ "dbo", "Orders", Environment.DB_OPS_STAGING, ←
       ↪ "dbo", "Orders", "", "");
9      Utility.CompareChecksums(Environment.DB_OPS_SOURCE, ←
       ↪ "dbo", "OrderDetails", ←
       ↪ Environment.DB_OPS_STAGING, "dbo", ←
       ↪ "OrderDetails", "", "");
10
11     Utility.ReportResult();
12 }
```

Finally let's execute the test _20_test_TableChecksums and check the log.

5.2.3 Test 3 - Check For Empty Source Tables

This test may sound very unnecessary but at times, it helps a lot. How? Consider the scenario where the source table has no rows due to some issues. The dimension table that is populated from this source table may become empty too (depending on how the developer has coded it). When you run all the previous tests they should all pass but you know there is something wrong and your automated testing should have told you so. In this situation this test comes in handy. So how do we do it?

Add a new function CheckForEmptyTable to the Utility.java file.

CheckForEmptyTable - Checks if the table is empty and reports the outcome		
Input Parameters	*dbName*	Name of the database
	dbSchema	Name of the schema
	tblName	Name of the table
Return Value	*void*	Returns nothing.

Listing 5.13: Utility.java - Code for CheckForEmptyTable

```
1  public static void CheckForEmptyTable(String dbName,
       String dbSchema, String tblName)
2  {
3      String exp = "No Data";
4
5      try
6      {
7          Connection conn;
8          Class.forName("com.microsoft.sqlserver.jdbc
              .SQLServerDriver");
9
10         conn = DriverManager.getConnection(dbName,
              Environment.DB_USERID, Environment.DB_PWD);
11
12         Utility.log.info("DB connected: " + dbName);
13         Statement statement = conn.createStatement();
14         String queryString = "SELECT COUNT(*) from "  +
              dbSchema + "." + tblName;
15         Utility.log.info("SQL is: " + queryString);
16         ResultSet rs = statement.executeQuery(queryString);
17
18         while (rs.next())
19         {
20             Utility.log.info("Rows in table: " + rs.getInt(1));
21             if (rs.getInt(1)>0)
22                 exp = "Data Present";
23         }
24     }
25     catch (Exception e)
26     {
27         e.printStackTrace();
28         Utility.ReportExpectedVsActual("Exception occurred"
              + e.getMessage(), "Failing test");
29     }
```

```
30
31     Utility.log.info("Checking for Empty Table....." + ↵
       ↪ tblName);
32     Utility.ReportExpectedVsActual(exp, "Data Present");
33 }
```

Line 3: Set the initial value to "No Data".
Line 14: Construct the SQL Query to get a count of the records in the table.
Line 21: Check if data is present in the table.
Line 32: Report the outcome.

Add Listing 5.14 to the sourceDataLoad.java file.

Listing 5.14: Code for _05_test_CheckForEmptySourceTables

```
1 @Test
2 public void _05_test_CheckForEmptySourceTables() {
3     Utility.log.info("***********    Starting Test: " + ↵
      ↪ name.getMethodName());
4
5     Utility.CheckForEmptyTable(Environment.DB_OPS_SOURCE, ↵
      ↪ "dbo", "Customers");
6
7     Utility.ReportResult();
8 }
```

Now execute test _05_test_CheckForEmptySourceTables. You will see a Console output as shown in Figure 5.7.

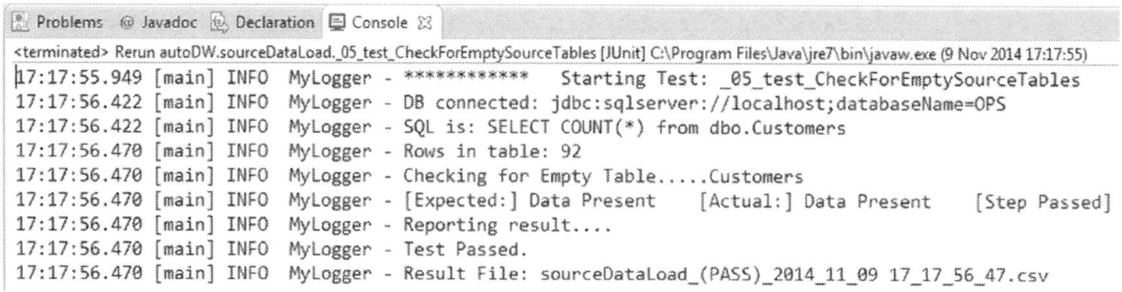

Figure 5.7: Console Output - Checksums

Let's modify our test _05_test_CheckForEmptySourceTables to include the rest of the tables.

Listing 5.15: Code for _05_test_CheckForEmptySourceTables

```
1  @Test
2  public void _05_test_CheckForEmptySourceTables() {
3      Utility.log.info("************   Starting Test: " + ↵
           ↪ name.getMethodName());
4
5      Utility.CheckForEmptyTable(Environment.DB_OPS_SOURCE, ↵
           ↪ "dbo", "Customers");
6      Utility.CheckForEmptyTable(Environment.DB_OPS_SOURCE, ↵
           ↪ "dbo", "Employees");
7      Utility.CheckForEmptyTable(Environment.DB_OPS_SOURCE, ↵
           ↪ "dbo", "Products");
8      Utility.CheckForEmptyTable(Environment.DB_OPS_SOURCE, ↵
           ↪ "dbo", "Orders");
9      Utility.CheckForEmptyTable(Environment.DB_OPS_SOURCE, ↵
           ↪ "dbo", "OrderDetails");
10
11     Utility.ReportResult();
12 }
```

Now let's execute test _05_test_CheckForEmptySourceTables and check the log.

5.2.4   Test 4 - Check For Empty Target Tables

As with the source tables, it is a good practice to check that the target tables are not empty too, as follows.

Listing 5.16: Code for _08_test_CheckForEmptyTargetTables

```
1  @Test
2  public void _08_test_CheckForEmptyTargetTables() {
3      Utility.log.info("************   Starting Test: " + ↵
           ↪ name.getMethodName());
4
5      Utility.CheckForEmptyTable(Environment.DB_OPS_STAGING, ↵
           ↪ "dbo", "Customers");
6      Utility.CheckForEmptyTable(Environment.DB_OPS_STAGING, ↵
           ↪ "dbo", "Employees");
7      Utility.CheckForEmptyTable(Environment.DB_OPS_STAGING, ↵
           ↪ "dbo", "Products");
8      Utility.CheckForEmptyTable(Environment.DB_OPS_STAGING, ↵
           ↪ "dbo", "Orders");
```

```
9      Utility.CheckForEmptyTable(Environment.DB_OPS_STAGING, ↵
       ↪ "dbo", "OrderDetails");
10       Utility.ReportResult();
11   }
```

Execute test _08_test_CheckForEmptyTargetTables and you will see a Console output as shown in Figure 5.8.

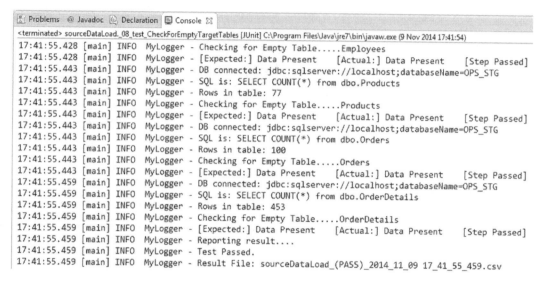

Figure 5.8: Console Output - Check for empty target tables

Note that I deliberately added the two tests - _05_test_CheckForEmptySourceTables and _08_test_CheckForEmptyTargetTables later to illustrate how to order the tests when running them all together. If you now run all of the tests in 'sourceDataLoad' (make sure to right click on the 'sourceDataLoad' rather than an individual test), you will see that the tests are executed in the following order, rather than the order they are defined in the file:

- _05_test_CheckForEmptySourceTables

- _08_test_CheckForEmptyTargetTables

- _10_test_TableRecorddCounts

- _20_test_TableChecksums

There are more test scenarios we can add but we will cover them in later chapters. For now, it is time to add some more features to our Automation Framework.

5.3   Creating Test Result Summary

Previously we added a feature that included the overall test result outcome in the test result file name. This told us whether the final result was a Pass or Fail. If the overall result was a Fail and we look at the result file at some later stage, we will need to go through the entire file to identify the test(s) that failed. This may be quite a cumbersome task if there are a lot of tests to scroll through. It would be really helpful if the test execution provided a summary of the outcome for each test i.e. whether it passed or failed. So, let's enhance our Automation Framework to generate a test result summary file.

In order to do so, we need to declare two more configuration variables in the Config.java file as shown in Listing 5.17.

Listing 5.17: Code for Config.java

```
1  public static String SummaryFile;
2  public static final String newLine = ↵
       ↪ System.getProperty("line.separator");
```

Line 1: Global parameter to hold the test result summary filename.
Line 2: New line character to display long strings e.g. display long SQL Queries on multiple lines.

Now define two more generic functions in the Utility.java file - CreateSummaryFileEntry and SetupSummaryFile.

CreateSummaryFileEntry - Creates an entry into the Test Result Summary File		
Input Parameters	*strData*	Data to be logged into the summary file
Return Value	*void*	Returns nothing

SetupSummaryFile - Sets up a Test Result Summary File		
Input Parameters	*fileName*	Name of the summary file
Return Value	*void*	Returns nothing

Listing 5.18: Code for CreateSummaryFileEntry and SetupSummaryFile

```
1  import java.io.BufferedWriter;
2  import java.io.FileWriter;
3
```

```
4  public static void CreateSummaryFileEntry(String strData) ↵
   ↪ throws Exception
5  {
6      File file = new File(Config.LOG_FILE_LOCATION + "/" + ↵
       ↪ Config.SummaryFile);
7
8      if(!file.exists()){
9          file.createNewFile();
10     }
11
12     FileWriter fileWritter = new ↵
       ↪ FileWriter(file.getPath(),true);
13     BufferedWriter bufferWritter = new ↵
       ↪ BufferedWriter(fileWritter);
14     bufferWritter.write(strData + Config.newLine);
15     bufferWritter.close();
16 }
17
18 public static void SetupSummaryFile(String fileName) ↵
   ↪ throws Exception
19 {
20     java.util.Date date= new java.util.Date();
21     String dt =  new Timestamp(date.getTime()).toString();
22     dt = dt.replace(":", "_");
23     dt = dt.replace(".", "_");
24     dt = dt.replace("-", "_");
25
26     Config.SummaryFile = fileName + "_Summary_()_" + dt + ↵
       ↪ ".csv";
27     CreateSummaryFileEntry("Date Time, Test Name, Test ↵
       ↪ Result");
28 }
```

Line 6: Setup the test result summary file in the LOG_FILE_LOCATION.
Line 8: Create the file if it doesn't exist.
Line 14: Write data to the file.
Line 15: Close the file.
Line 26: Create file name with date timestamp.
Line 27: Create the header entry.

As you know, we already have a general purpose function called 'ReportResult' that instructs the Automation Framework to report the final test result. Let's add another generic function 'ReportResultWithSummary' that will also log each test's result in the result summary file. We could have modified the existing 'ReportResult' function to include the additional logic, but we will just create another function so that it doesn't break our existing tests and we will use this new function as and when required.

ReportResultWithSummary - Reports the test result outcome with an entry into the Test Result Summary File.		
Input Parameters	*testName*	Name of the test to report result about
Return Value	*void*	Returns nothing.

Listing 5.19: Utility.java - Code for ReportResultWithSummary

```java
1  public static void ReportResultWithSummary(String testName)
2  {
3     try {
4        log.info("Reporting result.... ");
5        java.util.Date date= new java.util.Date();
6          String dt =  new ↵
                ↪ Timestamp(date.getTime()).toString();
7
8        if (Config.TestResult.equals(Config.FAIL))
9        {
10          log.error("Test Failed.... Check Error(s) in the ↵
                ↪ log.");
11          CreateSummaryFileEntry(dt + "," + testName + ↵
                ↪ ",FAIL");
12          assertFalse(true);
13       }
14       else
15       {
16          log.info("Test Passed.");
17          CreateSummaryFileEntry(dt + "," + testName + ↵
                ↪ ",PASS");
18          assertTrue(true);
19       }
20    } catch (Exception e) {
21      e.printStackTrace();
22      Utility.ReportExpectedVsActual("Exception occurred" + ↵
            ↪ e.getMessage(), "Failing test");
23    }
24 }
```

Line 11: Create a summary file entry for the failed test.
Line 17: Create a summary file entry for the passed test.

We will include the Pass/Fail status of the overall test execution in the summary file name too, as we did earlier. So let's add a new function to Utility.java as shown in Listing 5.20.

SaveLogWithSummary - Saves the log file with summary		
Input Parameters	*fileName*	File name to be used for the saved log file
Return Value	*void*	Returns nothing.

Listing 5.20: Utility.java - Code for SaveLogWithSummary

```java
1  public static void SaveLogWithSummary(String fileName) ↵
     ↪ throws Exception
2  {
3      java.util.Date date= new java.util.Date();
4      String dt =  new ↵
          ↪ Timestamp(date.getTime()).toString();
5      dt = dt.replace(":", "_");
6      dt = dt.replace(".", "_");
7      dt = dt.replace("-", "_");
8
9      Utility.log.info("Result File: " + fileName + "_(" + ↵
          ↪ Config.OverAllTestResult + ")_" + dt + ".csv");
10
11     File oldfile = new File(Config.WORKSPACE_LOCATION + ↵
          ↪ "/temp/DetailLog.csv");
12
13     String outDir = Config.LOG_FILE_LOCATION;
14     CreateFolder(outDir);
15
16     File newfile = new File(outDir + "/" + fileName + ↵
          ↪ "_Detail_(" + Config.OverAllTestResult + ")_" + ↵
          ↪ dt + ".csv");
17
18     Files.copy(oldfile.toPath(), newfile.toPath());
19
20     //Insert overall result in the summary filename
21     String tmp = Config.SummaryFile;
22     tmp = tmp.replace("()", "(" + Config.OverAllTestResult ↵
          ↪ + ")");
23
24     File oldsummfile =new File(Config.LOG_FILE_LOCATION + ↵
          ↪ "/" + Config.SummaryFile);
25     File newsummfile =new File(Config.LOG_FILE_LOCATION + ↵
          ↪ "/"  + tmp);
```

```
26
27    if(!oldsummfile.renameTo(newsummfile)){
28        Utility.log.info("oldsummfile: " + ↵
            ↪ oldsummfile.getAbsolutePath());
29        Utility.log.info("newsummfile: " + ↵
            ↪ newsummfile.getAbsolutePath() );
30        Utility.ReportExpectedVsActual("Summary file rename ↵
            ↪ failed" , "Failing test");
31    }
32 }
```

Line 22: Insert the overall test result status in the summary filename.
Line 27: Rename the summary file and report an error if the rename fails.

Ok, there is now one more general function to be added to the Utility.java file.

GetName - Returns short name of the class from the full name		
Input Parameters	*strFullName*	Full name of the class e.g. autoDW.dimYesNo
Return Value	*shortName*	Returns short name of the class e.g. dimYesNo

Listing 5.21: Utility.java - Code for GetName

```
1 public static String GetName(String strFullName) throws ↵
     ↪ Exception
2 {
3    int i = strFullName.lastIndexOf('.');
4    return strFullName.substring(i+1);
5 }
```

Line 3: Get the last position of dot.
Line 4: Return substring from the last position of dot plus one.

Now update the sourceDataLoad.java file as shown in Listing 5.22.

Listing 5.22: Modifications to sourceDataLoad.java

```
1 import org.junit.BeforeClass;
2
3 public class sourceDataLoad {
4    @Rule public TestName name = new TestName();
```

```
 5
 6      @Before
 7      public void setUp() throws Exception {
 8          Config.TestResult = Config.PASS;
 9      }
10
11       @BeforeClass
12       public static void setUpBeforeClass() throws ↵
              ↳ Exception {
13         Utility.SetupSummaryFile(Utility.GetName( ↵
              ↳ Thread.currentThread().getStackTrace()[1]. ↵
              ↳ getClassName()));
14       }
15
16       @AfterClass
17       public static void tearDownAfterClass() throws ↵
              ↳ Exception {
18         Utility.SaveLogWithSummary(Utility.GetName( ↵
              ↳ Thread.currentThread().getStackTrace()[1]. ↵
              ↳ getClassName()));
19       }
20  }
```

Line 1: Additional import required to support the functionality.

Line 11: @BeforeClass annotation indicates that this method is executed only once, before the start of all tests.

Line 13: Setup the summary file. Note the parameter passed to the GetName function.

Line 18: Saving the log file with a summary along with the overall test result outcome in the summary file name.

In the 'sourceDataLoad.java' file, replace all occurrences of

```
Utility.ReportResult();
```

With the new function call as

```
Utility.ReportResultWithSummary(name.getMethodName());
```

Now right click on sourceDataLoad and select Run as ⇒ JUnit Test.

You will see this time that a new summary file has been created in 'C:\AutoLogs' folder with the status of each test - as either Pass or Fail. As shown in Figure 5.9, the summary file also records the overall test result status in the name.

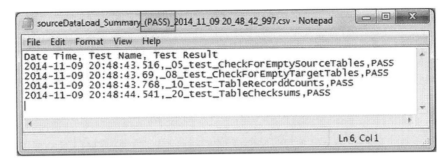

Figure 5.9: Test Results Summary File

In the next chapter, we will see how we can reuse some of the existing functions to write new tests when we automate the testing of dimension and fact tables.

Chapter 6

Automating Dimensional Data Warehouse

Automating Dimensional Data Warehouse

In this chapter, we will learn how to:

- *Automate the testing of dimension and fact tables*

- *Create a Test Runner to run a test suite*

- *Add more features to our Automation Framework*

So let's get on with it...

L ET'S see how we can automate the testing of dimension and fact tables. As a tester in real environment, you would have executed an ETL job which transfers data from the staging database to the warehouse database before running these tests. In Figure 1.1 of our sample data warehouse, the data in the OPS_STG database tables would have been populated to the OPS_DWS database tables. However, for the purposes of this book, you don't need to execute any ETL job as we already have populated our database in Section 4.3.3.

6.1   Automating Dimension Tables

We'll start by automating 'dimEmployee' and see what tests apply.

6.1.1   Test 1 - Check For Empty Staging Source Table

In the previous chapter, we wrote a general purpose function to verify whether or not a table is empty. We don't need to do much here apart from calling that generic function with the name of the staging table that feeds our dimension Employee. First of all, let's add a new test.

- Within 'Package Explorer', right click on the folder name 'src' and select New ⇒ Other...

- Select Java ⇒ JUnit Test Case as shown in Figure 6.1.

- Click the Next button.

- Type dimEmployee in the 'Name' edit box and click Finish.

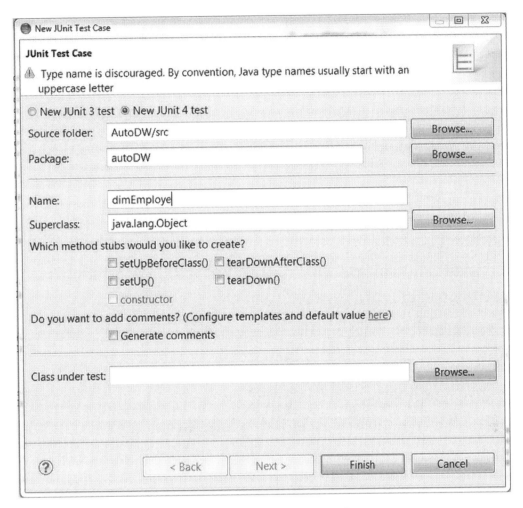

Figure 6.1: Adding dimEmployee

Add Listing 6.1 code to the dimEmploye.java file.

Listing 6.1: dimEmployee - Code for _05_test_CheckForEmptySourceTables

```
1 package autoDW;
2
3 import org.junit.AfterClass;
4 import org.junit.Before;
5 import org.junit.BeforeClass;
6 import org.junit.FixMethodOrder;
7 import org.junit.runners.MethodSorters;
8 import org.junit.Rule;
```

```
 9  import org.junit.Test;
10  import org.junit.rules.TestName;
11
12  @FixMethodOrder(MethodSorters.NAME_ASCENDING)
13
14  public class dimEmploye
15  {
16
17      @Rule public TestName name = new TestName();
18
19      @Before
20      public void setUp() throws Exception
21      {
22          Config.TestResult = Config.PASS;
23      }
24
25      @BeforeClass
26      public static void setUpBeforeClass() throws Exception
27      {
28          Utility.SetupSummaryFile(Utility.GetName ↵
                ↪ (Thread.currentThread().getStackTrace()[1]. ↵
                ↪ getClassName()));
29      }
30
31      @AfterClass
32      public static void tearDownAfterClass() throws Exception
33      {
34          Utility.SaveLogWithSummary(Utility.GetName ↵
                ↪ (Thread.currentThread().getStackTrace()[1]. ↵
                ↪ getClassName()));
35      }
36
37      @Test
38      public void _05_test_CheckForEmptySourceTables()
39      {
40          Utility.log.info("***********   Starting Test: " + ↵
                ↪ name.getMethodName());
41
42          Utility.CheckForEmptyTable(Environment.DB_OPS_STAGING, ↵
                ↪ "dbo", "Employees");
43          Utility.ReportResultWithSummary(name.getMethodName());
44      }
45
46  }
```

Line 42: Note the database name the test is connecting to i.e. Environment.DB_OPS_-STAGING.

Now execute the test _05_test_CheckForEmptySourceTables and you will see a Console output as shown in Figure 6.2.

```
🔲 Problems  @ Javadoc  🔍 Declaration  🖳 Console ☒
<terminated> Rerun autoDW.dimEmploye._05_test_CheckForEmptySourceTables [JUnit] C:\Program Files\Java\jre7\bin\javaw.exe (9 Nov 2014 22:13:52)
22:13:53.316 [main] INFO  MyLogger - ***********   Starting Test: _05_test_CheckForEmptySourceTables
22:13:53.744 [main] INFO  MyLogger - DB connected: jdbc:sqlserver://localhost;databaseName=OPS_STG
22:13:53.759 [main] INFO  MyLogger - SQL is: SELECT COUNT(*) from dbo.Employees
22:13:53.807 [main] INFO  MyLogger - Rows in table: 9
22:13:53.807 [main] INFO  MyLogger - Checking for Empty Table.....Employees
22:13:53.807 [main] INFO  MyLogger - [Expected:] Data Present    [Actual:] Data Present    [Step Passed]
22:13:53.807 [main] INFO  MyLogger - Reporting result....
22:13:53.807 [main] INFO  MyLogger - Test Passed.
22:13:53.807 [main] INFO  MyLogger - Result File: dimEmploye_(PASS)_2014_11_09_22_13_53_807.csv
```

Figure 6.2: Console Output - dimEmployee - Empty Source Table

6.1.2   Test 2 - Check For Empty Target Dimension Table

It is good practice to check that the target dimension table is also not empty, as follows.

Listing 6.2: dimEmployee - Code for _10_test_CheckForEmptyTargetTables

```
1  @Test
2  public void _10_test_CheckForEmptyTargetTables()
3  {
4      Utility.log.info("***********   Starting Test: " + ←
           ↪ name.getMethodName());
5
6      Utility.CheckForEmptyTable(Environment.DB_OPS_DWS, ←
           ↪ "dbo", "dimEmployee");
7      Utility.ReportResultWithSummary(name.getMethodName());
8  }
```

Now execute the test _10_test_CheckForEmptyTargetTables and you will see a Console output as shown in Figure 6.3.

```
Problems  @ Javadoc  Declaration  Console ⬚
<terminated> Rerun autoDW.dimEmploye_10_test_CheckForEmptyTargetTables [JUnit] C:\Program Files\Java\jre7\bin\javaw.exe (9 Nov 2014 22:24:34)
22:24:34.781 [main] INFO   MyLogger - ************   Starting Test: _10_test_CheckForEmptyTargetTables
22:24:35.189 [main] INFO   MyLogger - DB connected: jdbc:sqlserver://localhost;databaseName=OPS_DWS
22:24:35.206 [main] INFO   MyLogger - SQL is: SELECT COUNT(*) from dbo.dimEmployee
22:24:35.252 [main] INFO   MyLogger - Rows in table: 10
22:24:35.252 [main] INFO   MyLogger - Checking for Empty Table.....dimEmployee
22:24:35.252 [main] INFO   MyLogger - [Expected:] Data Present    [Actual:] Data Present    [Step Passed]
22:24:35.252 [main] INFO   MyLogger - Reporting result....
22:24:35.252 [main] INFO   MyLogger - Test Passed.
22:24:35.252 [main] INFO   MyLogger - Result File: dimEmploye_(PASS)_2014_11_09 22_24_35_252.csv
```

Figure 6.3: Console Output - dimEmployee - Empty Target Dimension Table

6.1.3 Test 3 - Check For Unique Key In Dimension Table

This test verifies that the dimension table has unique values for the column specified in the Data Mapping document. First of all, we need to create another generic function in the Utility.java file.

GetCountOfDistinctRecordsSourceSQL - Gets a count of distinct records in a table via SQL Query		
Input Parameters	*dbName*	Name of the database
	queryString	SQL Query to get a count of distinct records
Return Value	*count*	Count of distinct records

Listing 6.3: Utility.java - GetCountOfDistinctRecordsSourceSQL

```java
1  public static int GetCountOfDistinctRecordsSourceSQL( ↵
        ↪ String dbName, String queryString)
2  {
3     int count = -99;
4
5     try
6     {
7        Connection conn;
8        Class.forName("com.microsoft.sqlserver.jdbc. ↵
            ↪ SQLServerDriver");
9
10       conn = DriverManager.getConnection(dbName, ↵
            ↪ Environment.DB_USERID, Environment.DB_PWD);
11
12       Utility.log.info("DB connected: " + dbName);
13       Statement statement = conn.createStatement();
14
15       Utility.log.info("SQL is: " + queryString);
16
```

```
17        ResultSet rs = statement.executeQuery(queryString);
18
19        while (rs.next())
20        {
21            count= rs.getInt(1);
22        }
23      }
24    catch (Exception e)
25    {
26        e.printStackTrace();
27        Utility.ReportExpectedVsActual("Exception occurred" ↵
             ↪ + e.getMessage(), "Failing test");
28    }
29
30    return count;
31 }
```

Line 17: Execute the SQL Query passed as a parameter.

Now let's create another generic function which uses the above function.

CheckForUniqueKey - Checks for the Unique key in a table and reports the outcome		
Input Parameters	dbName	Name of the database
	schemaName	Name of the schema
	tblName	Name of the table
	uniqueKeyName	Unique key to be checked
Return Value	void	Returns nothing

Listing 6.4: Utility.java - CheckForUniqueKey

```
1 public static void CheckForUniqueKey(String dbName, ↵
     ↪ String schemaName, String tblName, String ↵
     ↪ uniqueKeyName)
2 {
3    Utility.log.info("CheckForUniqueKey - tblName: " + ↵
       ↪ tblName);
4
5    int exp, act;
6
7    String sql = "select count(distinct " + uniqueKeyName ↵
       ↪ + ") from " + schemaName + "." + tblName;
8
```

```
9     exp = ↵
          ↳ Utility.GetCountOfDistinctRecordsSourceSQL(dbName, ↵
          ↳ sql);
10    act = Utility.GetCountOfRecords(dbName, schemaName, ↵
          ↳ tblName);
11
12    Utility.ReportExpectedVsActual(String.valueOf(exp), ↵
          ↳ String.valueOf(act));
13 }
```

Line 7: Construct the unique key query.

Line 9: Get a count of distinct records.

Line 10: Get a count of all records.

Line 12: Compare both the values and make sure they match. Note the use of String.valueOf() to convert an integer value to a string.

Now add a new test to the dimEmployee.java file as shown in Listing 6.5.

Listing 6.5: dimEmployee.java - Code for _15_test_CheckForUniqueKey

```
1 @Test
2 public void _15_test_CheckForUniqueKey()
3 {
4     Utility.log.info("***********   Starting Test: " + ↵
          ↳ name.getMethodName());
5
6     Utility.CheckForUniqueKey(Environment.DB_OPS_DWS, ↵
          ↳ "dbo", "dimEmployee", "EmployeeID");
7
8     Utility.ReportResultWithSummary(name.getMethodName());
9 }
```

Line 6: Note the parameter value "EmployeeID" for Unique Key check as per the Data Mapping document.

Execute the test _15_test_CheckForUniqueKey and you will see a Console output as shown in Figure 6.4.

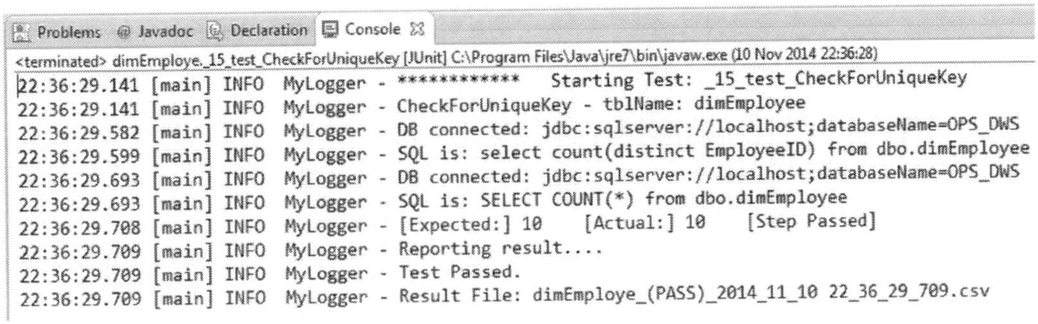

Figure 6.4: Console Output - dimEmployee - Check For Unique Key

6.1.4 Test 4 - Check For NULL Values In Dimension Table

This test checks that the column doesn't contain Null values as per the Data Mapping document. First of all let's create another generic function in the Utilty.java file which will be used throughout our Automation Framework.

CheckForNullValues - Checks for Null values in a table and reports the outcome		
Input Parameters	*dbName*	Name of the database
	dbSchema	Name of the schema
	tblName	Name of the table
	ignoreColumn	Ignore specified columns for checking
	targetClause	Condition to be added
Return Value	*void*	Returns nothing

Listing 6.6: Utility.java - Code for CheckForNullValues

```
1  public static void CheckForNullValues(String dbName, ↵
       ↪ String dbSchema, String tblName, String ↵
       ↪ ignoreColumn, String targetClause)
2  {
3      Utility.log.info("CheckForNullValues... ");
4
5      List<String> resultColumns = new ArrayList<String>();
6      List<String> ignoreColmList = ↵
           ↪ Arrays.asList(ignoreColumn.split(","));
7
8      try {
9          Connection conn;
10         Class.forName("com.microsoft.sqlserver.jdbc. ↵
               ↪ SQLServerDriver");
11
```

```
12      conn = DriverManager.getConnection(dbName, ←
           ↪ Environment.DB_USERID, Environment.DB_PWD);
13
14      Utility.log.info("DB connected: " + dbName);
15      Statement statement = conn.createStatement();
16      String queryString = "select COLUMN_NAME from ←
           ↪ information_schema.columns where table_name = ←
           ↪ '" + tblName + "'";
17
18      Utility.log.info("SQL is: " + queryString);
19      ResultSet rs = statement.executeQuery(queryString);
20
21      while (rs.next())
22      {
23          if (ignoreColmList.contains( ←
               ↪ rs.getString("COLUMN_NAME")))
24              Utility.log.info("**** Ignoring column **** : ←
                   ↪ " + rs.getString ("COLUMN_NAME"));
25          else
26              resultColumns.add(rs.getString("COLUMN_NAME")); ←
                   ↪
27      }
28
29      if (resultColumns.size()== 0)
30      {
31          Utility.ReportExpectedVsActual("Something wrong ←
               ↪ as no data found", "Failing test");
32      }
33
34      for(int j=0; j<resultColumns.size();j++)
35      {
36          Connection conn1;
37          Class.forName("com.microsoft.sqlserver. ←
               ↪ jdbc.SQLServerDriver");
38
39          conn1 = DriverManager.getConnection(dbName, ←
               ↪ Environment.DB_USERID, Environment.DB_PWD);
40
41          Utility.log.info("Going for column...."+ ←
               ↪ resultColumns.get(j));
42          Statement statement1 = conn1.createStatement();
43          String queryString1 = "select Count(*) as ←
               ↪ MyCheck from " + dbSchema + "." + tblName ;
44          queryString1 += " Where " + resultColumns.get(j) ←
               ↪ + " Is NULL";
```

```
45
46          if (!targetClause.equals(""))
47              queryString1 += " And " + targetClause;
48
49          Utility.log.info("SQL is: " + queryString1);
50          ResultSet rs1 = ↵
               ↪ statement1.executeQuery(queryString1);
51
52          int cnt = -9;
53
54          while (rs1.next())
55          {
56              cnt = rs1.getInt("MyCheck");
57          }
58
59          Utility.ReportExpectedVsActual("Nulls for Column ↵
               ↪ " + resultColumns.get(j) + " = 0", "Nulls ↵
               ↪ for Column " + resultColumns.get(j) + " = " ↵
               ↪ + cnt);
60      }
61  }
62  catch (Exception e)
63  {
64      e.printStackTrace();
65      Utility.ReportExpectedVsActual("Exception occurred" ↵
           ↪ + e.getMessage(), "Failing test");
66  }
67 }
```

Line 6: Convert comma separated string of 'columns to be ignored' into a List.

Line 16: Get the table column names from the information_schema.

Line 23: If a column is in the 'ignore list' skip it and log a message.

Line 26: Otherwise, add it to the list of columns to be checked for Nulls.

Line 29: If no columns are to be checked then report an error.

Line 44: Construct SQL Query to check count of Null values.

Line 46: Add the condition if specified.

Line 59: Check that the Null count is zero.

Now add a new test to dimEmployee.java class as shown in Listing 6.7.

Listing 6.7: dimEmployee.java - Code for _20_test_CheckForNullValues

```
1 @Test
2 public void _20_test_CheckForNullValues()
```

```
3  {
4      Utility.log.info("***********   Starting Test: " + ↵
          ↪ name.getMethodName());
5
6      Utility.CheckForNullValues(Environment.DB_OPS_DWS, ↵
          ↪ "dbo", "dimEmployee", "", "EmployeeKey <> -1");
7
8      Utility.ReportResultWithSummary(name.getMethodName());
9  }
```

Line 6: Note the inclusion of target clause "EmployeeKey <> -1". We will exclude this record because the 'DateOfBirth' column can have a Null value as per the Data Mapping document.

Execute the test _20_test_CheckForNullValues and you will see a Console output as shown in Figure 6.5.

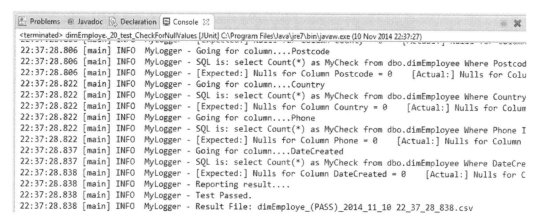

Figure 6.5: Console Output - dimEmployee - Check For NULL Values

6.1.5   Test 5 - Compare Record Counts With Dimension Table

Let's now compare the count of records between the staging and the dimension table. First of all we must create another generic function GetCountOfRecordsWithCondition as follows:

GetCountOfRecordsWithCondition - Gets a count of records in a table with a specified condition		
Input Parameters	dbName	Name of the database
	dbSchema	Name of the schema
	tblName	Name of the table
	condition	Where clause condition to be included
Return Value	count	Returns a count of records

```
1  public static int GetCountOfRecordsWithCondition(String ↵
       ↪ dbName, String dbSchema, String tblName, String ↵
       ↪ condition)
2  {
3      int count = -99;
4
5      try
6      {
7          Connection conn;
8          Class.forName("com.microsoft.sqlserver.jdbc. ↵
               ↪ SQLServerDriver");
9          conn = DriverManager.getConnection(dbName, ↵
               ↪ Environment.DB_USERID, Environment.DB_PWD);
10         Utility.log.info("DB connected: " + dbName);
11         Statement statement = conn.createStatement();
12         String queryString = "SELECT COUNT(*) from "    + ↵
               ↪ dbSchema + "." + tblName ;
13         if (!condition.equals(""))
14             queryString += " Where " + condition;
15         Utility.log.info("SQL is: " + queryString);
16         ResultSet rs = statement.executeQuery(queryString);
17         while (rs.next())
18         {
19             count= rs.getInt(1);
20         }
21     } catch (Exception e)
22     {
23         e.printStackTrace();
24         Utility.ReportExpectedVsActual("Exception occurred" ↵
               ↪ + e.getMessage(), "Failing test");
25     }
26     return count;
27  }
```

Line 14: Add the condition to the where clause.

Now let's define another general purpose function to compare the count of records in two tables and use the above function.

CompareCountOfRecordsWIthCondition - Compares count of records in two tables with a condition and reports the outcome		
Input Parameters	*sourcDBName*	Name of the source database
	sourceSchemaName	Name of the source schema
	sourceTblName	Name of the source table
	targetDBName	Name of the target database
	targetSchemaName	Name of the target schema
	targetTblName	Name of the target table
	targetCondition	Condition to be included for the target table.
Return Value	*void*	Returns nothing

Listing 6.9: Code for CompareCountOfRecordsWIthCondition

```
 1  public static void CompareCountOfRecordsWIthCondition( ←
        ↪ String sourcDBName , String sourceSchemaName , String ←
        ↪ sourceTblName , String targetDBName , String ←
        ↪ targetSchemaName , String targetTblName , String ←
        ↪ targetcondition )
 2  {
 3      Utility.log.info("targetTblName: " + targetTblName);
 4      int exp, act;
 5
 6      exp = Utility.GetCountOfRecords(sourcDBName , ←
            ↪ sourceSchemaName , sourceTblName );
 7      act = ←
            ↪ Utility.GetCountOfRecordsWithCondition(targetDBName , ←
            ↪ targetSchemaName , targetTblName , ←
            ↪ targetcondition );
 8
 9      Utility.ReportExpectedVsActual(String.valueOf(exp), ←
            ↪ String.valueOf(act));
10  }
```

Line 7: Note the inclusion of the condition for the target i.e. dimension table.

Now add a new test to dimEmployee.java as shown in Listing 6.10.

Listing 6.10: dimEmployee - Code for _25_test_CheckTableRecoundCounts

```
1  @Test
2  public void _25_test_CheckTableRecoundCounts()
```

```
3  {
4      Utility.log.info("***********    Starting Test: " + ↵
           ↪ name.getMethodName());
5
6      Utility.CompareCountOfRecordsWIthCondition( ↵
           ↪ Environment.DB_OPS_STAGING, "dbo", "Employees", ↵
           ↪ Environment.DB_OPS_DWS, "dbo", "dimEmployee", ↵
           ↪ "EmployeeKey <> -1");
7      Utility.ReportResultWithSummary(name.getMethodName());
8  }
```

Line 6: Note the inclusion of condition "EmployeeKey <> -1" for dimension table as this record doesn't exist in the source table.

Execute the test _25_test_CheckTableRecoundCounts and you will see a Console output as shown in Figure 6.6.

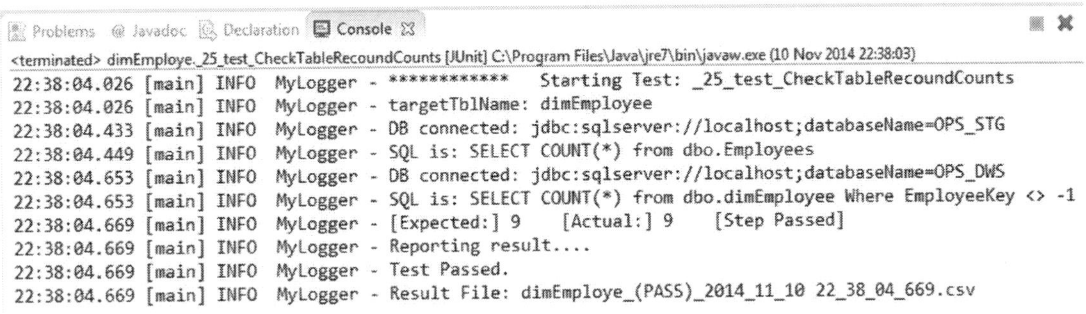

Figure 6.6: Console Output - dimEmployee - Compare Table Record Counts

6.1.6   Test 6 - Compare Checksums

As we did earlier, let's compare the Sum of CHECKSUM of columns in the staging and dimension tables.

Add a new test to the dimEmployee.java as shown in Listing 6.11.

Listing 6.11: dimEmployee - Code for _25_test_CheckTableRecoundCounts

```
1  @Test
2  public void _30_test_CheckTableChecksums()
3  {
4      Utility.log.info("***********    Starting Test: " + ↵
           ↪ name.getMethodName());
```

```
5
6      Utility.CompareChecksums( Environment.DB_OPS_STAGING, ↵
          ↪ "dbo", "Employees", Environment.DB_OPS_DWS, ↵
          ↪ "dbo", "dimEmployee", "EmployeeKey,DateCreated", ↵
          ↪ "EmployeeKey <> -1");
7
8      Utility.ReportResultWithSummary(name.getMethodName());
9  }
```

Line 6: Note the ignore columns parameter. We will ignore columns EmployeeKey and DateCreated because they don't exist in the source table.

Execute the test _25_test_CheckTableRecoundCounts and you will see the following output in the Console window:

```
 Problems  @ Javadoc  Declaration  Console ⅏                                          ⬛ ✖ ⅏
<terminated> dimEmploye._30_test_CheckTableChecksums [JUnit] C:\Program Files\Java\jre7\bin\javaw.exe (10 Nov 2014 22:38:29)
22:38:30.732 [main] INFO  MyLogger - [Expected:] Column Count: 11    [Actual:] Column Count: 11    [Step Pa:
22:38:30.732 [main] INFO  MyLogger - [Expected:] EmployeeID: 927      [Actual:] EmployeeID: 927    [Step Passe
22:38:30.732 [main] INFO  MyLogger - [Expected:] LastName: 205118431    [Actual:] LastName: 205118431    [St
22:38:30.732 [main] INFO  MyLogger - [Expected:] FirstName: -7518172567     [Actual:] FirstName: -7518172567
22:38:30.732 [main] INFO  MyLogger - [Expected:] Title: -11349175580      [Actual:] Title: -11349175580    [St
22:38:30.732 [main] INFO  MyLogger - [Expected:] DateOfBirth: -19220779050     [Actual:] DateOfBirth: -19220;
22:38:30.732 [main] INFO  MyLogger - [Expected:] Address: -9722216583    [Actual:] Address: -9722216583    [
22:38:30.732 [main] INFO  MyLogger - [Expected:] City: -6782424802      [Actual:] City: -6782424802    [Step F
22:38:30.732 [main] INFO  MyLogger - [Expected:] County: -16310019870      [Actual:] County: -16310019870    [
22:38:30.732 [main] INFO  MyLogger - [Expected:] Postcode: -10105068767     [Actual:] Postcode: -10105068767
22:38:30.732 [main] INFO  MyLogger - [Expected:] Country: 9303052134      [Actual:] Country: 9303052134    [St
22:38:30.732 [main] INFO  MyLogger - [Expected:] Phone: 11942035200     [Actual:] Phone: 11942035200    [Step
22:38:30.732 [main] INFO  MyLogger - Reporting result....
22:38:30.732 [main] INFO  MyLogger - Test Passed.
22:38:30.747 [main] INFO  MyLogger - Result File: dimEmploye_(PASS)_2014_11_10 22_38_30_747.csv
```

Figure 6.7: Console Output - dimEmployee - Compare Checksums

6.1.7   Test 7 - Check For Unknown Record

Remember the Data Mapping document had a column for 'Unknown Key'? This test verifies that the dimension table contains that 'Unknown Key' record.

Add a new test to dimEmployee.java as shown in Listing 6.12.

Listing 6.12: dimEmployee.java - Code for _35_test_CheckForUnknownRecord

```
1  import java.util.ArrayList;
2  import java.util.List;
3  import java.sql.Connection;
4  import java.sql.DriverManager;
5  import java.sql.ResultSet;
6  import java.sql.Statement;
```

```
7
8  @Test
9  public void _35_test_CheckForUnknownRecord() {
10     Utility.log.info("***********   Starting Test: " + ↵
           ↪ name.getMethodName());
11     List<String> resultExpEmployeeID = new ↵
           ↪ ArrayList<String>();
12     List<String> resultActEmployeeID = new ↵
           ↪ ArrayList<String>();
13     List<String> resultExpLastName = new ArrayList<String>();
14     List<String> resultActLastName = new ArrayList<String>();
15     List<String> resultExpFirstName = new ↵
           ↪ ArrayList<String>();
16     List<String> resultActFirstName = new ↵
           ↪ ArrayList<String>();
17     List<String> resultExpTitle = new ArrayList<String>();
18     List<String> resultActTitle = new ArrayList<String>();
19     List<String> resultExpDateOfBirth = new ↵
           ↪ ArrayList<String>();
20     List<String> resultActDateOfBirth = new ↵
           ↪ ArrayList<String>();
21     List<String> resultExpAddress = new ArrayList<String>();
22     List<String> resultActAddress = new ArrayList<String>();
23     List<String> resultExpCity = new ArrayList<String>();
24     List<String> resultActCity = new ArrayList<String>();
25     List<String> resultExpCounty = new ArrayList<String>();
26     List<String> resultActCounty = new ArrayList<String>();
27     List<String> resultExpPostcode = new ArrayList<String>();
28     List<String> resultActPostcode = new ArrayList<String>();
29     List<String> resultExpCountry = new ArrayList<String>();
30     List<String> resultActCountry = new ArrayList<String>();
31     List<String> resultExpPhone = new ArrayList<String>();
32     List<String> resultActPhone = new ArrayList<String>();
33
34     //Expected Result from Data Mapping document
35     resultExpEmployeeID.add("EmployeeID ==> -1");
36     resultExpLastName.add("LastName ==> Unknown");
37     resultExpFirstName.add("FirstName ==> Unknown");
38     resultExpTitle.add("Title ==> Unknown");
39     resultExpDateOfBirth.add("DateOfBirth ==> null");
40     resultExpAddress.add("Address ==> Unknown");
41     resultExpCity.add("City ==> Unknown");
42     resultExpCounty.add("County ==> Unknown");
43     resultExpPostcode.add("Postcode ==> Unknown");
44     resultExpCountry.add("Country ==> Unknown");
```

```
45     resultExpPhone.add("Phone ==> Unknown");
46
47     //Find Actual Result
48     try
49     {
50         Class.forName("com.microsoft.sqlserver.jdbc. ↵
               ↪ SQLServerDriver");
51         Connection conn = ↵
               ↪ DriverManager.getConnection(Environment. ↵
               ↪ DB_OPS_DWS, Environment.DB_USERID, ↵
               ↪ Environment.DB_PWD);
52         Utility.log.info("DB connected..." + ↵
               ↪ Environment.DB_OPS_DWS);
53         Statement statement = conn.createStatement();
54         String queryString = "Select EmployeeID, LastName, ↵
               ↪ FirstName, Title, DateOfBirth," + Config.newLine;
55         queryString += "Address, City, County, Postcode, ↵
               ↪ Country, Phone" + Config.newLine;
56         queryString += "From dbo.dimEmployee" + ↵
               ↪ Config.newLine;
57         queryString += "Where EmployeeKey = -1";
58
59         Utility.log.info("SQL is: " + queryString);
60         ResultSet rs = statement.executeQuery(queryString);
61         while (rs.next())
62         {
63             resultActEmployeeID.add("EmployeeID ==> " + ↵
                   ↪ rs.getString("EmployeeID"));
64             resultActLastName.add("LastName ==> " + ↵
                   ↪ rs.getString("LastName"));
65             resultActFirstName.add("FirstName ==> " + ↵
                   ↪ rs.getString("FirstName"));
66             resultActTitle.add("Title ==> " + ↵
                   ↪ rs.getString("Title"));
67             resultActDateOfBirth.add("DateOfBirth ==> " + ↵
                   ↪ rs.getString("DateOfBirth"));
68             resultActAddress.add("Address ==> " + ↵
                   ↪ rs.getString("Address"));
69             resultActCity.add("City ==> " + ↵
                   ↪ rs.getString("City"));
70             resultActCounty.add("County ==> " + ↵
                   ↪ rs.getString("County"));
71             resultActPostcode.add("Postcode ==> " + ↵
                   ↪ rs.getString("Postcode"));
72             resultActCountry.add("Country ==> " + ↵
```

```
                         ↪ rs.getString("Country"));
73            resultActPhone.add("Phone ==> " + ↩
                         ↪ rs.getString("Phone"));
74        }
75
76    }
77    catch (Exception e)
78    {
79        e.printStackTrace();
80        Utility.ReportExpectedVsActual("Exception occurred. ↩
              ↪ " + e.getMessage(), "Failing test");
81    }
82
83    Utility.log.info("Verifying EmployeeID.....");
84    if (resultExpEmployeeID.size() != ↩
          ↪ resultActEmployeeID.size())
85    {
86            Utility.log.error("Size mismatch EmployeeID....");
87            Utility.ReportExpectedVsActual( ↩
                  ↪ String.valueOf(resultExpEmployeeID.size()), ↩
                  ↪ String.valueOf(resultActEmployeeID.size()));
88    }
89
90    for(int j=0; j<resultExpEmployeeID.size();j++)
91    {
92        Utility.ReportExpectedVsActual( ↩
              ↪ resultExpEmployeeID.get(j), ↩
              ↪ resultActEmployeeID.get(j));
93    }
94
95    Utility.log.info("Verifying LastName.....");
96    if (resultExpLastName.size() != resultActLastName.size())
97    {
98        Utility.log.error("Size mismatch LastName....");
99        Utility.ReportExpectedVsActual( ↩
              ↪ String.valueOf(resultExpLastName.size()), ↩
              ↪ String.valueOf(resultActLastName.size()));
100   }
101
102   for(int j=0; j<resultExpLastName.size();j++)
103   {
104       Utility.ReportExpectedVsActual( ↩
              ↪ resultExpLastName.get(j), ↩
              ↪ resultActLastName.get(j));
105   }
```

```
106
107    Utility.log.info("Verifying FirstName.....");
108    if (resultExpFirstName.size() != ↵
           ↪ resultActFirstName.size())
109    {
110        Utility.log.error("Size mismatch FirstName....");
111        Utility.ReportExpectedVsActual( ↵
               ↪ String.valueOf(resultExpFirstName.size()), ↵
               ↪ String.valueOf(resultActFirstName.size()));
112    }
113
114    for(int j=0; j<resultExpFirstName.size();j++)
115    {
116        Utility.ReportExpectedVsActual( ↵
               ↪ resultExpFirstName.get(j), ↵
               ↪ resultActFirstName.get(j));
117    }
118
119    Utility.log.info("Verifying Title.....");
120    if (resultExpTitle.size() != resultActTitle.size())
121    {
122        Utility.log.error("Size mismatch Title....");
123        Utility.ReportExpectedVsActual( ↵
               ↪ String.valueOf(resultExpTitle.size()), ↵
               ↪ String.valueOf(resultActTitle.size()));
124    }
125
126    for(int j=0; j<resultExpTitle.size();j++)
127    {
128        Utility.ReportExpectedVsActual( ↵
               ↪ resultExpTitle.get(j), resultActTitle.get(j));
129    }
130
131    Utility.log.info("Verifying DateOfBirth.....");
132    if (resultExpDateOfBirth.size() != ↵
           ↪ resultActDateOfBirth.size())
133    {
134        Utility.log.error("Size mismatch DateOfBirth....");
135        Utility.ReportExpectedVsActual( ↵
               ↪ String.valueOf(resultExpDateOfBirth.size()), ↵
               ↪ String.valueOf(resultActDateOfBirth.size()));
136    }
137
138    for(int j=0; j<resultExpDateOfBirth.size();j++)
139    {
```

```
140         Utility.ReportExpectedVsActual( ←
               ↪ resultExpDateOfBirth.get(j), ←
               ↪ resultActDateOfBirth.get(j));
141     }
142
143     Utility.log.info("Verifying Address.....");
144     if (resultExpAddress.size() != resultActAddress.size())
145     {
146         Utility.log.error("Size mismatch Address....");
147         Utility.ReportExpectedVsActual( ←
               ↪ String.valueOf(resultExpAddress.size()), ←
               ↪ String.valueOf(resultActAddress.size()));
148     }
149
150     for(int j=0; j<resultExpAddress.size();j++)
151     {
152         Utility.ReportExpectedVsActual( ←
               ↪ resultExpAddress.get(j), ←
               ↪ resultActAddress.get(j));
153     }
154
155     Utility.log.info("Verifying City.....");
156     if (resultExpCity.size() != resultActCity.size())
157     {
158         Utility.log.error("Size mismatch City....");
159         Utility.ReportExpectedVsActual( ←
               ↪ String.valueOf(resultExpCity.size()), ←
               ↪ String.valueOf(resultActCity.size()));
160     }
161
162     for(int j=0; j<resultExpCity.size();j++)
163     {
164         Utility.ReportExpectedVsActual( ←
               ↪ resultExpCity.get(j), resultActCity.get(j));
165     }
166
167     Utility.log.info("Verifying County.....");
168     if (resultExpCounty.size() != resultActCounty.size())
169     {
170         Utility.log.error("Size mismatch County....");
171         Utility.ReportExpectedVsActual( ←
               ↪ String.valueOf(resultExpCounty.size()), ←
               ↪ String.valueOf(resultActCounty.size()));
172     }
173
```

```
174    for(int j=0; j<resultExpCounty.size();j++)
175    {
176        Utility.ReportExpectedVsActual( ←
              ↪ resultExpCounty.get(j), resultActCounty.get(j));
177    }
178
179    Utility.log.info("Verifying Postcode.....");
180    if (resultExpPostcode.size() != resultActPostcode.size())
181    {
182        Utility.log.error("Size mismatch Postcode....");
183        Utility.ReportExpectedVsActual( ←
              ↪ String.valueOf(resultExpPostcode.size()), ←
              ↪ String.valueOf(resultActPostcode.size()));
184    }
185
186    for(int j=0; j<resultExpPostcode.size();j++)
187    {
188        Utility.ReportExpectedVsActual( ←
              ↪ resultExpPostcode.get(j), ←
              ↪ resultActPostcode.get(j));
189    }
190
191    Utility.log.info("Verifying Country.....");
192    if (resultExpCountry.size() != resultActCountry.size())
193    {
194        Utility.log.error("Size mismatch Country....");
195        Utility.ReportExpectedVsActual( ←
              ↪ String.valueOf(resultExpCountry.size()), ←
              ↪ String.valueOf(resultActCountry.size()));
196    }
197
198    for(int j=0; j<resultExpCountry.size();j++)
199    {
200        Utility.ReportExpectedVsActual( ←
              ↪ resultExpCountry.get(j), ←
              ↪ resultActCountry.get(j));
201    }
202
203    Utility.log.info("Verifying Phone.....");
204    if (resultExpPhone.size() != resultActPhone.size())
205    {
206        Utility.log.error("Size mismatch Phone....");
207        Utility.ReportExpectedVsActual( ←
              ↪ String.valueOf(resultExpPhone.size()), ←
              ↪ String.valueOf(resultActPhone.size()));
```

```
208    }
209
210    for(int j=0; j<resultExpPhone.size();j++)
211    {
212        Utility.ReportExpectedVsActual( ↵
            ↪ resultExpPhone.get(j), resultActPhone.get(j));
213    }
214
215    Utility.ReportResultWithSummary(name.getMethodName());
216 }
```

Line 11 - 32: Define Expected and Actual Lists for the columns we want to compare. These are typically columns in your dimension or fact table.

Line 35 - 45: Build Lists of Expected Results from the Data Mapping document. Here we have used Lists (instead of String) as in some cases you may have more than one record that falls into the Unknown category e.g. the dimension has two keys -1 and -2 to differentiate two types of unknown.

Line 54 - 57: Construct the SQL Query to fetch data from the dimension table. Note the where clause - it fetches 'Unknown' record only.

Line 63 - 73: Build Lists of Actual Results fetched from the dimension table.

Line 84: First of all compare the size of both the Expected and Actual Result List. If they are not the same there is something wrong and the step has failed.

Line 90: Go through the entire list and compare the expected and actual values. Report any failures.

Line 95: Similarly go through all the other columns.

Execute the test _35_test_CheckForUnknownRecord and you will see a Console output as shown in Figure 6.8.

Figure 6.8: Console Output - dimEmployee - Check For Unknown Record

6.1.8   Test 8 - Check For Dimension Details

This test verifies that the field level details of all the records (other than 'Unknown') in the dimension table are as per the Data Mapping document once transferred from the staging area to the dimensional table. This verification should also include any ETL transformations applied to the data.

Add a new test to the dimEmployee.java class shown in Listing 6.13.

Listing 6.13: dimEmployee.java - Code for _40_test_CheckEmployeeDetails

```
1  @Test
2  public void _40_test_CheckEmployeeDetails() {
3     Utility.log.info("***********   Starting Test: " + ↵
          ↪ name.getMethodName());
4
5     List<String> resultExpEmployeeID = new ↵
          ↪ ArrayList<String>();
6     List<String> resultActEmployeeID = new ↵
          ↪ ArrayList<String>();
7     List<String> resultExpLastName = new ArrayList<String>();
8     List<String> resultActLastName = new ArrayList<String>();
9     List<String> resultExpFirstName = new ↵
          ↪ ArrayList<String>();
10    List<String> resultActFirstName = new ↵
          ↪ ArrayList<String>();
11    List<String> resultExpTitle = new ArrayList<String>();
12    List<String> resultActTitle = new ArrayList<String>();
13    List<String> resultExpDateOfBirth = new ↵
          ↪ ArrayList<String>();
14    List<String> resultActDateOfBirth = new ↵
          ↪ ArrayList<String>();
15    List<String> resultExpAddress = new ArrayList<String>();
16    List<String> resultActAddress = new ArrayList<String>();
17    List<String> resultExpCity = new ArrayList<String>();
18    List<String> resultActCity = new ArrayList<String>();
19    List<String> resultExpCounty = new ArrayList<String>();
20    List<String> resultActCounty = new ArrayList<String>();
21    List<String> resultExpPostcode = new ArrayList<String>();
22    List<String> resultActPostcode = new ArrayList<String>();
23    List<String> resultExpCountry = new ArrayList<String>();
24    List<String> resultActCountry = new ArrayList<String>();
25    List<String> resultExpPhone = new ArrayList<String>();
26    List<String> resultActPhone = new ArrayList<String>();
```

```
27
28      //Find Expected Result
29       try {
30           Class.forName("com.microsoft.sqlserver.jdbc. ↵
                  ↪ SQLServerDriver");
31           Connection conn = DriverManager.getConnection( ↵
                  ↪ Environment.DB_OPS_STAGING, ↵
                  ↪ Environment.DB_USERID, Environment.DB_PWD);
32           Utility.log.info("DB connected..." + ↵
                  ↪ Environment.DB_OPS_STAGING);
33           Statement statement = conn.createStatement();
34
35           String queryString = "Select EmployeeID, ↵
                  ↪ LastName, FirstName, Title, DateOfBirth," + ↵
                  ↪ Config.newLine;
36           queryString += "Address, City, County, Postcode, ↵
                  ↪ Country, Phone" + Config.newLine;
37           queryString += "From dbo.Employees" + ↵
                  ↪ Config.newLine;
38           queryString += "Order by EmployeeID";
39
40           Utility.log.info("SQL is: " + queryString);
41
42           ResultSet rs = statement.executeQuery(queryString);
43
44           while (rs.next()) {
45             resultExpEmployeeID.add("EmployeeID ==> " + ↵
                    ↪ rs.getString("EmployeeID"));
46             resultExpLastName.add("LastName ==> " + ↵
                    ↪ rs.getString("LastName"));
47             resultExpFirstName.add("FirstName ==> " + ↵
                    ↪ rs.getString("FirstName"));
48             resultExpTitle.add("Title ==> " + ↵
                    ↪ rs.getString("Title"));
49             resultExpDateOfBirth.add("DateOfBirth ==> " + ↵
                    ↪ rs.getString("DateOfBirth"));
50             resultExpAddress.add("Address ==> " + ↵
                    ↪ rs.getString("Address"));
51             resultExpCity.add("City ==> " + ↵
                    ↪ rs.getString("City"));
52             resultExpCounty.add("County ==> " + ↵
                    ↪ rs.getString("County"));
53             resultExpPostcode.add("Postcode ==> " + ↵
                    ↪ rs.getString("Postcode"));
54             resultExpCountry.add("Country ==> " + ↵
```

```
                        ↳ rs.getString("Country"));
55              resultExpPhone.add("Phone ==> " + ↵
                        ↳ rs.getString("Phone"));
56          }
57
58      } catch (Exception e) {
59          e.printStackTrace();
60          Utility.ReportExpectedVsActual("Exception ↵
                ↳ occurred. " + e.getMessage(), "Failing test");
61      }
62
63  //Find Actual Result
64    try {
65          Class.forName("com.microsoft.sqlserver.jdbc. ↵
                ↳ SQLServerDriver");
66          Connection conn = DriverManager.getConnection( ↵
                ↳ Environment.DB_OPS_DWS, ↵
                ↳ Environment.DB_USERID, Environment.DB_PWD);
67          Utility.log.info("DB connected..." + ↵
                ↳ Environment.DB_OPS_DWS);
68          Statement statement = conn.createStatement();
69          String queryString = "Select EmployeeID, ↵
                ↳ LastName, FirstName, Title, DateOfBirth," + ↵
                ↳ Config.newLine;
70          queryString += "Address, City, County, Postcode, ↵
                ↳ Country, Phone" + Config.newLine;
71          queryString += "From dbo.dimEmployee" + ↵
                ↳ Config.newLine;
72          queryString += "Where EmployeeKey <> -1" + ↵
                ↳ Config.newLine;
73          queryString += "Order by EmployeeID";
74
75          Utility.log.info("SQL is: " + queryString);
76          ResultSet rs = statement.executeQuery(queryString);
77          while (rs.next()) {
78           resultActEmployeeID.add("EmployeeID ==> " + ↵
                ↳ rs.getString("EmployeeID"));
79           resultActLastName.add("LastName ==> " + ↵
                ↳ rs.getString("LastName"));
80           resultActFirstName.add("FirstName ==> " + ↵
                ↳ rs.getString("FirstName"));
81           resultActTitle.add("Title ==> " + ↵
                ↳ rs.getString("Title"));
82           resultActDateOfBirth.add("DateOfBirth ==> " + ↵
                ↳ rs.getString("DateOfBirth"));
```

```
83          resultActAddress.add("Address ==> " + ↩
                ↪ rs.getString("Address"));
84          resultActCity.add("City ==> " + ↩
                ↪ rs.getString("City"));
85          resultActCounty.add("County ==> " + ↩
                ↪ rs.getString("County"));
86          resultActPostcode.add("Postcode ==> " + ↩
                ↪ rs.getString("Postcode"));
87          resultActCountry.add("Country ==> " + ↩
                ↪ rs.getString("Country"));
88          resultActPhone.add("Phone ==> " + ↩
                ↪ rs.getString("Phone"));
89          }
90
91      } catch (Exception e) {
92          e.printStackTrace();
93          Utility.ReportExpectedVsActual("Exception ↩
                ↪ occurred. " + e.getMessage(), "Failing test");
94      }
95
96      Utility.log.info("Verifying EmployeeID.....");
97      if (resultExpEmployeeID.size() != ↩
            ↪ resultActEmployeeID.size())
98      {
99          Utility.log.error("Size mismatch EmployeeID....");
100         Utility.ReportExpectedVsActual( ↩
                ↪ String.valueOf(resultExpEmployeeID.size()), ↩
                ↪ String.valueOf(resultActEmployeeID.size()));
101     }
102
103     for(int j=0; j<resultExpEmployeeID.size();j++){
104         Utility.ReportExpectedVsActual( ↩
                ↪ resultExpEmployeeID.get(j), ↩
                ↪ resultActEmployeeID.get(j));
105     }
106
107     Utility.log.info("Verifying LastName.....");
108     if (resultExpLastName.size() != ↩
            ↪ resultActLastName.size())
109     {
110         Utility.log.error("Size mismatch LastName....");
111         Utility.ReportExpectedVsActual( ↩
                ↪ String.valueOf(resultExpLastName.size()), ↩
                ↪ String.valueOf(resultActLastName.size()));
112     }
```

```
113
114     for(int j=0; j<resultExpLastName.size();j++){
115        Utility.ReportExpectedVsActual( ↵
              ↪ resultExpLastName.get(j), ↵
              ↪ resultActLastName.get(j));
116        }
117
118     Utility.log.info("Verifying FirstName.....");
119     if (resultExpFirstName.size() != ↵
           ↪ resultActFirstName.size())
120     {
121        Utility.log.error("Size mismatch FirstName....");
122        Utility.ReportExpectedVsActual( ↵
              ↪ String.valueOf(resultExpFirstName.size()), ↵
              ↪ String.valueOf(resultActFirstName.size()));
123        }
124
125     for(int j=0; j<resultExpFirstName.size();j++){
126        Utility.ReportExpectedVsActual( ↵
              ↪ resultExpFirstName.get(j), ↵
              ↪ resultActFirstName.get(j));
127        }
128
129     Utility.log.info("Verifying Title.....");
130     if (resultExpTitle.size() != resultActTitle.size())
131     {
132        Utility.log.error("Size mismatch Title....");
133        Utility.ReportExpectedVsActual( ↵
              ↪ String.valueOf(resultExpTitle.size()), ↵
              ↪ String.valueOf(resultActTitle.size()));
134        }
135
136     for(int j=0; j<resultExpTitle.size();j++){
137        Utility.ReportExpectedVsActual( ↵
              ↪ resultExpTitle.get(j), resultActTitle.get(j));
138        }
139
140     Utility.log.info("Verifying DateOfBirth.....");
141     if (resultExpDateOfBirth.size() != ↵
           ↪ resultActDateOfBirth.size())
142     {
143        Utility.log.error("Size mismatch DateOfBirth....");
144        Utility.ReportExpectedVsActual( ↵
              ↪ String.valueOf(resultExpDateOfBirth.size()), ↵
              ↪ String.valueOf(resultActDateOfBirth.size()));
```

```
145        }
146
147        for(int j=0; j<resultExpDateOfBirth.size();j++){
148          Utility.ReportExpectedVsActual( ↵
                 ↪ resultExpDateOfBirth.get(j), ↵
                 ↪ resultActDateOfBirth.get(j));
149        }
150
151        Utility.log.info("Verifying Address.....");
152        if (resultExpAddress.size() != resultActAddress.size())
153        {
154          Utility.log.error("Size mismatch Address....");
155          Utility.ReportExpectedVsActual( ↵
                 ↪ String.valueOf(resultExpAddress.size()), ↵
                 ↪ String.valueOf(resultActAddress.size()));
156        }
157
158        for(int j=0; j<resultExpAddress.size();j++){
159          Utility.ReportExpectedVsActual( ↵
                 ↪ resultExpAddress.get(j), ↵
                 ↪ resultActAddress.get(j));
160        }
161
162        Utility.log.info("Verifying City.....");
163        if (resultExpCity.size() != resultActCity.size())
164        {
165          Utility.log.error("Size mismatch City....");
166          Utility.ReportExpectedVsActual( ↵
                 ↪ String.valueOf(resultExpCity.size()), ↵
                 ↪ String.valueOf(resultActCity.size()));
167        }
168
169        for(int j=0; j<resultExpCity.size();j++){
170          Utility.ReportExpectedVsActual( ↵
                 ↪ resultExpCity.get(j), resultActCity.get(j));
171        }
172
173        Utility.log.info("Verifying County.....");
174        if (resultExpCounty.size() != resultActCounty.size())
175        {
176          Utility.log.error("Size mismatch County....");
177          Utility.ReportExpectedVsActual( ↵
                 ↪ String.valueOf(resultExpCounty.size()), ↵
                 ↪ String.valueOf(resultActCounty.size()));
178        }
```

```
179
180    for(int j=0;  j<resultExpCounty.size();j++){
181      Utility.ReportExpectedVsActual( ↵
              ↪ resultExpCounty.get(j), resultActCounty.get(j));
182      }
183
184    Utility.log.info("Verifying Postcode.....");
185    if (resultExpPostcode.size() != ↵
          ↪ resultActPostcode.size())
186    {
187      Utility.log.error("Size mismatch Postcode....");
188      Utility.ReportExpectedVsActual( ↵
              ↪ String.valueOf(resultExpPostcode.size()), ↵
              ↪ String.valueOf(resultActPostcode.size()));
189    }
190
191    for(int j=0;  j<resultExpPostcode.size();j++){
192      Utility.ReportExpectedVsActual( ↵
              ↪ resultExpPostcode.get(j), ↵
              ↪ resultActPostcode.get(j));
193      }
194
195    Utility.log.info("Verifying Country.....");
196    if (resultExpCountry.size() != resultActCountry.size())
197    {
198      Utility.log.error("Size mismatch Country....");
199      Utility.ReportExpectedVsActual( ↵
              ↪ String.valueOf(resultExpCountry.size()), ↵
              ↪ String.valueOf(resultActCountry.size()));
200    }
201
202    for(int j=0;  j<resultExpCountry.size();j++){
203      Utility.ReportExpectedVsActual( ↵
              ↪ resultExpCountry.get(j), ↵
              ↪ resultActCountry.get(j));
204      }
205
206    Utility.log.info("Verifying Phone.....");
207    if (resultExpPhone.size() != resultActPhone.size())
208    {
209      Utility.log.error("Size mismatch Phone....");
210      Utility.ReportExpectedVsActual( ↵
              ↪ String.valueOf(resultExpPhone.size()), ↵
              ↪ String.valueOf(resultActPhone.size()));
211    }
```

```
212
213      for(int j=0; j<resultExpPhone.size();j++){
214        Utility.ReportExpectedVsActual( ←
               ↪ resultExpPhone.get(j), resultActPhone.get(j));
215        }
216
217      Utility.ReportResultWithSummary(name.getMethodName());
218 }
```

Line 35 - 38: Construct the Expected Result SQL Query to fetch data from the source table. Note the order by clause.

Line 45 - 55: Build the Lists of Expected Results from the source table.

Line 69 - 73: Construct the Actual Result Query to fetch data from the dimension table. Note the order by clause which is the same as for the Expected Result Query.

Execute the test _40_test_CheckEmployeeDetails and you will see a Console output as shown in Figure 6.9.

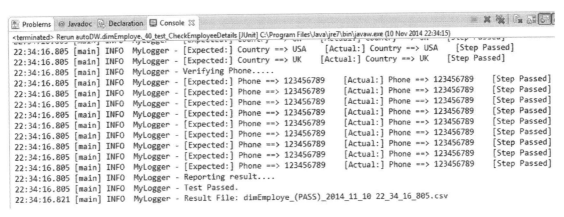

Figure 6.9: Console Output - dimEmployee - Check Dimension Details

6.1.9   Test 9 - Compare Checksum With SQL Source

Now let's move on to our next dimension - dimCustomer. In automating the testing of this dimension, we will learn how we can compare the Sum of column Checksums of source and target tables where the data from the staging table is sourced via SQL rather than a table. In order to do this, we need to add two new general functions to our Utility.java file.

GetTableChecksumSourceSQL - Gets the Sum of Checksum of columns of a table sourced via SQL		
Input Parameters	*dbName*	Name of the database
	sourcSQL	Source table SQL
	resultColumns	List of columns for which we want Sum of Checksum
Return Value	*Checksum*	Returns a list of Sum of Checksum of specified columns

CompareChecksumsSourceSQL - Compares the Sum of Checksum of columns of a table (sourced via SQL) with another table and reports the outcome		
Input Parameters	*sourcDBName*	Name of the source database
	sourcSQL	Source SQL
	sourceColumnsList	List of columns in the source table
	targetDBName	Name of the target database
	targetTblName	Name of the target table
	ignoreTargetCol	List of columns to be ignored from the target table
	targetClause	Clause to be applied to the target table
Return Value	*void*	Returns nothing

Add Listing 6.14 code to the Utility.java file.

Listing 6.14: Utility.java - New functions

```
1  public static List<String> ←
       ↪ GetTableChecksumSourceSQL(String dbName, String ←
       ↪ sourcSQL, List<String> resultColumns)
2  {
3     Utility.log.info("GetTableChecksumSourceSQL... ");
4
5     List<String> myChksum = new ArrayList<String>();
6
7     try
8     {
9        for(int j=0; j<resultColumns.size();j++)
10       {
11          Connection conn1;
12          Class.forName("com.microsoft.sqlserver.jdbc. ←
                ↪ SQLServerDriver");
13
```

```
14        conn1 = DriverManager.getConnection(dbName, ←
              ↪ Environment.DB_USERID, Environment.DB_PWD);
15
16        Utility.log.info("Going for column...."+ ←
              ↪ resultColumns.get(j));
17        Statement statement1 = conn1.createStatement();
18        String queryString1 = "with stage as (" + ←
              ↪ Config.newLine;
19        queryString1 += sourcSQL + Config.newLine;
20        queryString1 += ")select ←
              ↪ Sum(Cast(CHECKSUM(CAST(ISNULL(" + ←
              ↪ resultColumns.get(j) + "," + Config.MY_NULL ←
              ↪ + ") as varchar(max))) as Decimal(32,0))) ←
              ↪ as MySum from stage" + Config.newLine;;
21        queryString1 += "" + Config.newLine;
22
23        Utility.log.info("SQL is: " + queryString1);
24        ResultSet rs1 = ←
              ↪ statement1.executeQuery(queryString1);
25
26        while (rs1.next())
27        {
28            myChksum.add(resultColumns.get(j) + ": " + ←
                  ↪ rs1.getString("MySum"));
29        }
30      }
31    } catch (Exception e)
32    {
33      e.printStackTrace();
34      Utility.ReportExpectedVsActual("Exception occurred" ←
              ↪ + e.getMessage(), "Failing test");
35    }
36
37    return myChksum;
38 }
39
40 public static void CompareChecksumsSourceSQL(String ←
       ↪ sourcDBName, String sourceSQL, List<String> ←
       ↪ sourceColumnsList, String targetDBName, String ←
       ↪ targetSchemaName, String targetTblName, String ←
       ↪ ignoreTargetCol, String targetClause)
41 {
42    Utility.log.info("targetTblName: " + targetTblName);
43
44    List<String> expChksum = new ArrayList<String>();
```

```
45    List<String> actChksum = new ArrayList<String>();
46
47    expChksum = ↵
          ↪ Utility.GetTableChecksumSourceSQL(sourcDBName, ↵
          ↪ sourceSQL, sourceColumnsList);
48    actChksum = Utility.GetTableChecksum(targetDBName, ↵
          ↪ targetSchemaName, targetTblName, ↵
          ↪ ignoreTargetCol, targetClause);
49
50    Utility.ReportExpectedVsActual("Column Count: " + ↵
          ↪ String.valueOf(expChksum.size()), "Column Count: ↵
          ↪ " + String.valueOf(actChksum.size()));
51
52    for(int g=0; g<expChksum.size();g++)
53    {
54        Utility.ReportExpectedVsActual(expChksum.get(g), ↵
              ↪ actChksum.get(g));
55    }
56 }
```

Line 9: Loop through the list of columns for which we want the Sum of Checksum.

Line 19: Construct the SQL query.

Line 47: Get the Sum of Checksum of the source table via SQL.

Line 48: Get the Sum of Checksum of the target table.

Line 54: Compare the Sum of Checksum and report the result.

Now create a new test dimCustomer and add the code from Listing 6.15 to it.

Listing 6.15: Code for dimCustomer

```
1  package autoDW;
2
3  import java.sql.Connection;
4  import java.sql.DriverManager;
5  import java.sql.ResultSet;
6  import java.sql.Statement;
7  import java.util.ArrayList;
8  import java.util.Arrays;
9  import java.util.List;
10
11 import org.junit.AfterClass;
12 import org.junit.Before;
13 import org.junit.FixMethodOrder;
14 import org.junit.runners.MethodSorters;
```

```
15  import org.junit.Rule;
16  import org.junit.Test;
17  import org.junit.rules.TestName;
18
19  @FixMethodOrder(MethodSorters.NAME_ASCENDING)
20
21  public class dimCustomer {
22      @Rule public TestName name = new TestName();
23
24      public String sourceQueryString;
25
26      public String colmNames = ↵
              ↪ "CustomerID,LastName,FirstName,Title,DisplayName, ↵
              ↪ DateOfBirth,Address,City,County,Postcode,Country, ↵
              ↪ Phone,Fax,Region";
27      public List<String> ColmList = ↵
              ↪ Arrays.asList(colmNames.split(","));
28
29      @Before
30      public void setUp() throws Exception {
31          Config.TestResult = Config.PASS;
32
33          sourceQueryString = "SELECT ↵
              ↪ [CustomerID],[LastName],[FirstName],[Title]"+ ↵
              ↪ Config.newLine;
34          sourceQueryString += "        , Rtrim(Ltrim([Title] + ↵
              ↪ ' ' + [FirstName] + ' ' + [LastName])) AS ↵
              ↪ [DisplayName]"+ Config.newLine;
35          sourceQueryString += "          ↵
              ↪ ,[DateOfBirth],[Address]"+ Config.newLine;
36          sourceQueryString += "          ↵
              ↪ ,[City],[County],[Postcode],[Country], ↵
              ↪ [Phone],[Fax],"+ Config.newLine;
37          sourceQueryString += "        CASE WHEN ↵
              ↪ UPPER(LEFT([Postcode],2)) Between 'A' and 'G' ↵
              ↪ THEN 'North' "+ Config.newLine;
38          sourceQueryString += "          WHEN ↵
              ↪ UPPER(LEFT([Postcode],2)) Between 'H' and 'N' ↵
              ↪ THEN 'South'"+ Config.newLine;
39          sourceQueryString += "          WHEN ↵
              ↪ UPPER(LEFT([Postcode],2)) Between 'O' and 'R' ↵
              ↪ THEN 'East'"+ Config.newLine;
40          sourceQueryString += "          WHEN ↵
              ↪ UPPER(LEFT([Postcode],2)) Between 'S' and 'Z' ↵
              ↪ THEN 'West'"+ Config.newLine;
```

```
41   sourceQueryString += "              ELSE 'Unknown' "+ ↵
        ↪ Config.newLine;
42   sourceQueryString += "            END AS [Region]"+ ↵
        ↪ Config.newLine;
43   sourceQueryString += "FROM [dbo].[Customers]";
44
45   Utility.log.info("Source SQL is: " + ↵
        ↪ sourceQueryString);
46   }
47
48   @BeforeClass
49   public static void setUpBeforeClass() throws ↵
        ↪ Exception {
50     Utility.SetupSummaryFile(Utility.GetName(Thread. ↵
        ↪ currentThread().getStackTrace()[1]. ↵
        ↪ getClassName()));
51   }
52
53   @AfterClass
54   public static void tearDownAfterClass() throws ↵
        ↪ Exception {
55     Utility.SaveLogWithSummary(Utility.GetName( ↵
        ↪ Thread.currentThread().getStackTrace()[1]. ↵
        ↪ getClassName()));
56   }
57
58   @Test
59   public void _05_test_CheckForEmptySourceTables() {
60       Utility.log.info("***********  Starting Test: " + ↵
        ↪ name.getMethodName());
61
62       Utility.CheckForEmptyTable(Environment.DB_OPS_STAGING, ↵
        ↪ "dbo", "Customers");
63       Utility.ReportResultWithSummary(name.getMethodName());
64   }
65
66   @Test
67   public void _10_test_CheckForEmptyTargetTables() {
68       Utility.log.info("***********  Starting Test: " + ↵
        ↪ name.getMethodName());
69
70       Utility.CheckForEmptyTable(Environment.DB_OPS_DWS, ↵
        ↪ "dbo", "dimCustomer");
71       Utility.ReportResultWithSummary(name.getMethodName());
72   }
```

```
73
74      @Test
75      public void _15_test_CheckForUniqueKey() {
76          Utility.log.info("***********   Starting Test: " + ←
                 ↪ name.getMethodName());
77
78          Utility.CheckForUniqueKey(Environment.DB_OPS_DWS, ←
                 ↪ "dbo", "dimCustomer", "CustomerID");
79
80          Utility.ReportResultWithSummary(name.getMethodName());
81      }
82
83      @Test
84      public void _20_test_CheckForNullValues() {
85          Utility.log.info("***********   Starting Test: " + ←
                 ↪ name.getMethodName());
86
87          Utility.CheckForNullValues(Environment.DB_OPS_DWS, ←
                 ↪ "dbo", "dimCustomer", "", "CustomerKey <> -1");
88
89          Utility.ReportResult();
90      }
91
92      @Test
93      public void _25_test_CheckTableRecoundCounts() {
94          Utility.log.info("***********   Starting Test: " + ←
                 ↪ name.getMethodName());
95
96          Utility.CompareCountOfRecordsWIthCondition( ←
                 ↪ Environment.DB_OPS_STAGING, "dbo", ←
                 ↪ "Customers", Environment.DB_OPS_DWS, "dbo", ←
                 ↪ "dimCustomer", "CustomerKey <> -1");
97          Utility.ReportResult();
98      }
99
100     @Test
101     public void _30_test_CheckTableChecksums() {
102         Utility.log.info("***********   Starting Test: " + ←
                 ↪ name.getMethodName());
103
104         Utility.CompareChecksumsSourceSQL( ←
                 ↪ Environment.DB_OPS_STAGING, sourceQueryString, ←
                 ↪ ColmList, Environment.DB_OPS_DWS, "dbo", ←
                 ↪ "dimCustomer", "CustomerKey,DateCreated", ←
                 ↪ "CustomerKey <> -1");
```

```
105        Utility.ReportResultWithSummary(name.getMethodName());
106    }
107
108    @Test
109    public void _35_test_CheckForUnknownRecord() {
110        Utility.log.info("************    Starting Test: " + ↵
            ↪ name.getMethodName());
111
112        List<String> resultExpCustomerID = new ↵
            ↪ ArrayList<String>();
113        List<String> resultActCustomerID = new ↵
            ↪ ArrayList<String>();
114        List<String> resultExpLastName = new ↵
            ↪ ArrayList<String>();
115        List<String> resultActLastName = new ↵
            ↪ ArrayList<String>();
116        List<String> resultExpFirstName = new ↵
            ↪ ArrayList<String>();
117        List<String> resultActFirstName = new ↵
            ↪ ArrayList<String>();
118        List<String> resultExpTitle = new ArrayList<String>();
119        List<String> resultActTitle = new ArrayList<String>();
120        List<String> resultExpDisplayName = new ↵
            ↪ ArrayList<String>();
121        List<String> resultActDisplayName = new ↵
            ↪ ArrayList<String>();
122        List<String> resultExpDateOfBirth = new ↵
            ↪ ArrayList<String>();
123        List<String> resultActDateOfBirth = new ↵
            ↪ ArrayList<String>();
124        List<String> resultExpAddress = new ↵
            ↪ ArrayList<String>();
125        List<String> resultActAddress = new ↵
            ↪ ArrayList<String>();
126        List<String> resultExpCity = new ArrayList<String>();
127        List<String> resultActCity = new ArrayList<String>();
128        List<String> resultExpCounty = new ↵
            ↪ ArrayList<String>();
129        List<String> resultActCounty = new ↵
            ↪ ArrayList<String>();
130        List<String> resultExpPostcode = new ↵
            ↪ ArrayList<String>();
131        List<String> resultActPostcode = new ↵
            ↪ ArrayList<String>();
132        List<String> resultExpCountry = new ↵
```

```
                  ↪ ArrayList<String>();
133      List<String> resultActCountry = new ←
                  ↪ ArrayList<String>();
134      List<String> resultExpPhone = new ArrayList<String>();
135      List<String> resultActPhone = new ArrayList<String>();
136      List<String> resultExpFax = new ArrayList<String>();
137      List<String> resultActFax = new ArrayList<String>();
138      List<String> resultExpRegion = new ←
                  ↪ ArrayList<String>();
139      List<String> resultActRegion = new ←
                  ↪ ArrayList<String>();
140
141      //Find Expected Result from Data Mapping document
142      resultExpCustomerID.add("CustomerID ==> -1");
143      resultExpLastName.add("LastName ==> Unknown");
144      resultExpFirstName.add("FirstName ==> Unknown");
145      resultExpTitle.add("Title ==> Unknown");
146      resultExpDisplayName.add("DisplayName ==> Unknown");
147      resultExpDateOfBirth.add("DateOfBirth ==> null");
148      resultExpAddress.add("Address ==> Unknown");
149      resultExpCity.add("City ==> Unknown");
150      resultExpCounty.add("County ==> Unknown");
151      resultExpPostcode.add("Postcode ==> Unknown");
152      resultExpCountry.add("Country ==> Unknown");
153      resultExpPhone.add("Phone ==> Unknown");
154      resultExpFax.add("Fax ==> Unknown");
155      resultExpRegion.add("Region ==> Unknown");
156
157      //Find Actual Result
158      try
159      {
160          Class.forName("com.microsoft.sqlserver.jdbc. ←
                  ↪ SQLServerDriver");
161          Connection conn = DriverManager.getConnection( ←
                  ↪ Environment.DB_OPS_DWS, ←
                  ↪ Environment.DB_USERID, Environment.DB_PWD);
162          Utility.log.info("DB connected..." + ←
                  ↪ Environment.DB_OPS_DWS);
163          Statement statement = conn.createStatement();
164          String queryString = "Select " + colmNames + ←
                  ↪ Config.newLine;
165          queryString += "From dbo.dimCustomer" + ←
                  ↪ Config.newLine;
166          queryString += "Where CustomerKey = -1" + ←
                  ↪ Config.newLine;
```

```
167         queryString += "Order by CustomerID";
168
169         Utility.log.info("SQL is: " + queryString);
170         ResultSet rs = statement.executeQuery(queryString);
171         while (rs.next())
172         {
173             resultActCustomerID.add("CustomerID ==> " + ↵
                    ↪ rs.getString("CustomerID"));
174             resultActLastName.add("LastName ==> " + ↵
                    ↪ rs.getString("LastName"));
175             resultActFirstName.add("FirstName ==> " + ↵
                    ↪ rs.getString("FirstName"));
176             resultActTitle.add("Title ==> " + ↵
                    ↪ rs.getString("Title"));
177             resultActDisplayName.add("DisplayName ==> " + ↵
                    ↪ rs.getString("DisplayName"));
178             resultActDateOfBirth.add("DateOfBirth ==> " + ↵
                    ↪ rs.getString("DateOfBirth"));
179             resultActAddress.add("Address ==> " + ↵
                    ↪ rs.getString("Address"));
180             resultActCity.add("City ==> " + ↵
                    ↪ rs.getString("City"));
181             resultActCounty.add("County ==> " + ↵
                    ↪ rs.getString("County"));
182             resultActPostcode.add("Postcode ==> " + ↵
                    ↪ rs.getString("Postcode"));
183             resultActCountry.add("Country ==> " + ↵
                    ↪ rs.getString("Country"));
184             resultActPhone.add("Phone ==> " + ↵
                    ↪ rs.getString("Phone"));
185             resultActFax.add("Fax ==> " + ↵
                    ↪ rs.getString("Fax"));
186             resultActRegion.add("Region ==> " + ↵
                    ↪ rs.getString("Region"));
187         }
188     } catch (Exception e)
189     {
190         e.printStackTrace();
191         Utility.ReportExpectedVsActual("Exception ↵
                ↪ occurred. " + e.getMessage(), "Failing test");
192     }
193
194     Utility.log.info("Verifying CustomerID.....");
195     if (resultExpCustomerID.size() != ↵
            ↪ resultActCustomerID.size())
```

```
196        {
197                Utility.log.error("Size mismatch ←
                   ↪ CustomerID....");
198                Utility.ReportExpectedVsActual( ←
                   ↪ String.valueOf(resultExpCustomerID.size()), ←
                   ↪ String.valueOf(resultActCustomerID.size()));
199        }
200
201        for(int j=0; j<resultExpCustomerID.size();j++){
202                Utility.ReportExpectedVsActual( ←
                   ↪ resultExpCustomerID.get(j), ←
                   ↪ resultActCustomerID.get(j));
203            }
204
205        Utility.log.info("Verifying LastName.....");
206        if (resultExpLastName.size() != ←
           ↪ resultActLastName.size())
207        {
208                Utility.log.error("Size mismatch LastName....");
209                Utility.ReportExpectedVsActual( ←
                   ↪ String.valueOf(resultExpLastName.size()), ←
                   ↪ String.valueOf(resultActLastName.size()));
210        }
211
212        for(int j=0; j<resultExpLastName.size();j++){
213                Utility.ReportExpectedVsActual( ←
                   ↪ resultExpLastName.get(j), ←
                   ↪ resultActLastName.get(j));
214            }
215
216        Utility.log.info("Verifying FirstName.....");
217        if (resultExpFirstName.size() != ←
           ↪ resultActFirstName.size())
218        {
219                Utility.log.error("Size mismatch ←
                   ↪ FirstName....");
220                Utility.ReportExpectedVsActual ←
                   ↪ (String.valueOf(resultExpFirstName.size()), ←
                   ↪ String.valueOf(resultActFirstName.size()));
221        }
222
223        for(int j=0; j<resultExpFirstName.size();j++){
224                Utility.ReportExpectedVsActual( ←
                   ↪ resultExpFirstName.get(j), ←
                   ↪ resultActFirstName.get(j));
```

```
225                    }
226
227        Utility.log.info("Verifying Title.....");
228        if (resultExpTitle.size() != resultActTitle.size())
229        {
230                Utility.log.error("Size mismatch Title....");
231                Utility.ReportExpectedVsActual ↵
                      ↪ (String.valueOf(resultExpTitle.size()), ↵
                      ↪ String.valueOf(resultActTitle.size()));
232        }
233
234        for(int j=0; j<resultExpTitle.size();j++){
235                Utility.ReportExpectedVsActual( ↵
                      ↪ resultExpTitle.get(j), ↵
                      ↪ resultActTitle.get(j));
236                }
237
238        Utility.log.info("Verifying DisplayName.....");
239        if (resultExpDisplayName.size() != ↵
              ↪ resultActDisplayName.size())
240        {
241                Utility.log.error("Size mismatch ↵
                      ↪ DisplayName....");
242                Utility.ReportExpectedVsActual( ↵
                      ↪ String.valueOf(resultExpDisplayName.size()), ↵
                      ↪ String.valueOf(resultActDisplayName.size()));
243        }
244
245        for(int j=0; j<resultExpDisplayName.size();j++){
246                Utility.ReportExpectedVsActual( ↵
                      ↪ resultExpDisplayName.get(j), ↵
                      ↪ resultActDisplayName.get(j));
247                }
248
249        Utility.log.info("Verifying DateOfBirth.....");
250        if (resultExpDateOfBirth.size() != ↵
              ↪ resultActDateOfBirth.size())
251        {
252                Utility.log.error("Size mismatch ↵
                      ↪ DateOfBirth....");
253                Utility.ReportExpectedVsActual( ↵
                      ↪ String.valueOf(resultExpDateOfBirth.size()), ↵
                      ↪ String.valueOf(resultActDateOfBirth.size()));
254        }
255
```

```
256     for(int j=0; j<resultExpDateOfBirth.size();j++){
257             Utility.ReportExpectedVsActual( ←
                ↪ resultExpDateOfBirth.get(j), ←
                ↪ resultActDateOfBirth.get(j));
258             }
259
260     Utility.log.info("Verifying Address.....");
261     if (resultExpAddress.size() != ←
            ↪ resultActAddress.size())
262     {
263             Utility.log.error("Size mismatch Address....");
264             Utility.ReportExpectedVsActual( ←
                ↪ String.valueOf(resultExpAddress.size()), ←
                ↪ String.valueOf(resultActAddress.size()));
265     }
266
267     for(int j=0; j<resultExpAddress.size();j++){
268             Utility.ReportExpectedVsActual( ←
                ↪ resultExpAddress.get(j), ←
                ↪ resultActAddress.get(j));
269             }
270
271     Utility.log.info("Verifying City.....");
272     if (resultExpCity.size() != resultActCity.size())
273     {
274             Utility.log.error("Size mismatch City....");
275             Utility.ReportExpectedVsActual( ←
                ↪ String.valueOf(resultExpCity.size()), ←
                ↪ String.valueOf(resultActCity.size()));
276     }
277
278     for(int j=0; j<resultExpCity.size();j++){
279             Utility.ReportExpectedVsActual( ←
                ↪ resultExpCity.get(j), ←
                ↪ resultActCity.get(j));
280             }
281
282     Utility.log.info("Verifying County.....");
283     if (resultExpCounty.size() != resultActCounty.size())
284     {
285             Utility.log.error("Size mismatch County....");
286             Utility.ReportExpectedVsActual( ←
                ↪ String.valueOf(resultExpCounty.size()), ←
                ↪ String.valueOf(resultActCounty.size()));
287     }
```

```
288
289     for(int j=0; j<resultExpCounty.size();j++){
290             Utility.ReportExpectedVsActual( ←
                ↪ resultExpCounty.get(j), ←
                ↪ resultActCounty.get(j));
291             }
292
293     Utility.log.info("Verifying Postcode.....");
294     if (resultExpPostcode.size() != ←
            ↪ resultActPostcode.size())
295     {
296             Utility.log.error("Size mismatch Postcode....");
297             Utility.ReportExpectedVsActual( ←
                ↪ String.valueOf(resultExpPostcode.size()), ←
                ↪ String.valueOf(resultActPostcode.size()));
298     }
299
300     for(int j=0; j<resultExpPostcode.size();j++){
301             Utility.ReportExpectedVsActual( ←
                ↪ resultExpPostcode.get(j), ←
                ↪ resultActPostcode.get(j));
302             }
303
304     Utility.log.info("Verifying Country.....");
305     if (resultExpCountry.size() != ←
            ↪ resultActCountry.size())
306     {
307             Utility.log.error("Size mismatch Country....");
308             Utility.ReportExpectedVsActual( ←
                ↪ String.valueOf(resultExpCountry.size()), ←
                ↪ String.valueOf(resultActCountry.size()));
309     }
310
311     for(int j=0; j<resultExpCountry.size();j++){
312             Utility.ReportExpectedVsActual( ←
                ↪ resultExpCountry.get(j), ←
                ↪ resultActCountry.get(j));
313             }
314
315     Utility.log.info("Verifying Phone.....");
316     if (resultExpPhone.size() != resultActPhone.size())
317     {
318             Utility.log.error("Size mismatch Phone....");
319             Utility.ReportExpectedVsActual( ←
                ↪ String.valueOf(resultExpPhone.size()), ←
```

```
                          ↪ String.valueOf(resultActPhone.size()));
320        }
321
322        for(int j=0; j<resultExpPhone.size();j++){
323                Utility.ReportExpectedVsActual( ↩
                     ↪ resultExpPhone.get(j), ↩
                     ↪ resultActPhone.get(j));
324                }
325
326        Utility.log.info("Verifying Fax.....");
327        if (resultExpFax.size() != resultActFax.size())
328        {
329                Utility.log.error("Size mismatch Fax....");
330                Utility.ReportExpectedVsActual( ↩
                     ↪ String.valueOf(resultExpFax.size()), ↩
                     ↪ String.valueOf(resultActFax.size()));
331        }
332
333        for(int j=0; j<resultExpFax.size();j++){
334                Utility.ReportExpectedVsActual( ↩
                     ↪ resultExpFax.get(j), resultActFax.get(j));
335                }
336
337        Utility.log.info("Verifying Region.....");
338        if (resultExpRegion.size() != resultActRegion.size())
339        {
340                Utility.log.error("Size mismatch Region....");
341                Utility.ReportExpectedVsActual( ↩
                     ↪ String.valueOf(resultExpRegion.size()), ↩
                     ↪ String.valueOf(resultActRegion.size()));
342        }
343
344        for(int j=0; j<resultExpRegion.size();j++){
345                Utility.ReportExpectedVsActual( ↩
                     ↪ resultExpRegion.get(j), ↩
                     ↪ resultActRegion.get(j));
346                }
347
348        Utility.ReportResultWithSummary(name.getMethodName());
349    }
350
351    @Test
352    public void _40_test_CheckCustomerDetails() {
353        Utility.log.info("***********   Starting Test: " + ↩
                ↪ name.getMethodName());
```

```
354
355         List<String> resultExpCustomerID = new ←
              ↪ ArrayList<String>();
356         List<String> resultActCustomerID = new ←
              ↪ ArrayList<String>();
357         List<String> resultExpLastName = new ←
              ↪ ArrayList<String>();
358         List<String> resultActLastName = new ←
              ↪ ArrayList<String>();
359         List<String> resultExpFirstName = new ←
              ↪ ArrayList<String>();
360         List<String> resultActFirstName = new ←
              ↪ ArrayList<String>();
361         List<String> resultExpTitle = new ArrayList<String>();
362         List<String> resultActTitle = new ArrayList<String>();
363         List<String> resultExpDisplayName = new ←
              ↪ ArrayList<String>();
364         List<String> resultActDisplayName = new ←
              ↪ ArrayList<String>();
365         List<String> resultExpDateOfBirth = new ←
              ↪ ArrayList<String>();
366         List<String> resultActDateOfBirth = new ←
              ↪ ArrayList<String>();
367         List<String> resultExpAddress = new ←
              ↪ ArrayList<String>();
368         List<String> resultActAddress = new ←
              ↪ ArrayList<String>();
369         List<String> resultExpCity = new ArrayList<String>();
370         List<String> resultActCity = new ArrayList<String>();
371         List<String> resultExpCounty = new ←
              ↪ ArrayList<String>();
372         List<String> resultActCounty = new ←
              ↪ ArrayList<String>();
373         List<String> resultExpPostcode = new ←
              ↪ ArrayList<String>();
374         List<String> resultActPostcode = new ←
              ↪ ArrayList<String>();
375         List<String> resultExpCountry = new ←
              ↪ ArrayList<String>();
376         List<String> resultActCountry = new ←
              ↪ ArrayList<String>();
377         List<String> resultExpPhone = new ArrayList<String>();
378         List<String> resultActPhone = new ArrayList<String>();
379         List<String> resultExpFax = new ArrayList<String>();
380         List<String> resultActFax = new ArrayList<String>();
```

```
381        List<String> resultExpRegion = new ←
               ↪ ArrayList<String>();
382        List<String> resultActRegion = new ←
               ↪ ArrayList<String>();
383
384        //Find Expected Result
385        try
386        {
387            Class.forName("com.microsoft.sqlserver.jdbc. ←
                   ↪ SQLServerDriver");
388            Connection conn = DriverManager.getConnection( ←
                   ↪ Environment.DB_OPS_STAGING, ←
                   ↪ Environment.DB_USERID, Environment.DB_PWD);
389            Utility.log.info("DB connected..." + ←
                   ↪ Environment.DB_OPS_STAGING);
390            Statement statement = conn.createStatement();
391
392            String queryString = sourceQueryString + ←
                   ↪ Config.newLine;
393            queryString += "Order by CustomerID";
394
395            Utility.log.info("SQL is: " + queryString);
396
397            ResultSet rs = statement.executeQuery(queryString);
398
399            while (rs.next())
400            {
401                resultExpCustomerID.add("CustomerID ==> " + ←
                       ↪ rs.getString("CustomerID"));
402                resultExpLastName.add("LastName ==> " + ←
                       ↪ rs.getString("LastName"));
403                resultExpFirstName.add("FirstName ==> " + ←
                       ↪ rs.getString("FirstName"));
404                resultExpTitle.add("Title ==> " + ←
                       ↪ rs.getString("Title"));
405                resultExpDisplayName.add("DisplayName ==> " + ←
                       ↪ rs.getString("DisplayName"));
406                resultExpDateOfBirth.add("DateOfBirth ==> " + ←
                       ↪ rs.getString("DateOfBirth"));
407                resultExpAddress.add("Address ==> " + ←
                       ↪ rs.getString("Address"));
408                resultExpCity.add("City ==> " + ←
                       ↪ rs.getString("City"));
409                resultExpCounty.add("County ==> " + ←
                       ↪ rs.getString("County"));
```

```
410        resultExpPostcode.add("Postcode ==> " + ↵
             ↪ rs.getString("Postcode"));
411        resultExpCountry.add("Country ==> " + ↵
             ↪ rs.getString("Country"));
412        resultExpPhone.add("Phone ==> " + ↵
             ↪ rs.getString("Phone"));
413        resultExpFax.add("Fax ==> " + ↵
             ↪ rs.getString("Fax"));
414        resultExpRegion.add("Region ==> " + ↵
             ↪ rs.getString("Region"));
415      }
416   } catch (Exception e)
417   {
418      e.printStackTrace();
419      Utility.ReportExpectedVsActual("Exception ↵
             ↪ occurred. " + e.getMessage(), "Failing test");
420   }
421
422   //Find Actual Result
423   try
424   {
425      Class.forName("com.microsoft.sqlserver.jdbc. ↵
             ↪ SQLServerDriver");
426      Connection conn = DriverManager.getConnection( ↵
             ↪ Environment.DB_OPS_DWS, ↵
             ↪ Environment.DB_USERID, Environment.DB_PWD);
427      Utility.log.info("DB connected..." + ↵
             ↪ Environment.DB_OPS_DWS);
428      Statement statement = conn.createStatement();
429      String queryString = "Select " + colmNames + ↵
             ↪ Config.newLine;
430      queryString += "From dbo.dimCustomer" + ↵
             ↪ Config.newLine;
431      queryString += "Where CustomerKey <> -1" + ↵
             ↪ Config.newLine;
432      queryString += "Order by CustomerID";
433
434      Utility.log.info("SQL is: " + queryString);
435      ResultSet rs = statement.executeQuery(queryString);
436      while (rs.next())
437      {
438         resultActCustomerID.add("CustomerID ==> " + ↵
                ↪ rs.getString("CustomerID"));
439         resultActLastName.add("LastName ==> " + ↵
                ↪ rs.getString("LastName"));
```

```
440         resultActFirstName.add("FirstName ==> " + ←
               ↪ rs.getString("FirstName"));
441         resultActTitle.add("Title ==> " + ←
               ↪ rs.getString("Title"));
442         resultActDisplayName.add("DisplayName ==> " + ←
               ↪ rs.getString("DisplayName"));
443         resultActDateOfBirth.add("DateOfBirth ==> " + ←
               ↪ rs.getString("DateOfBirth"));
444         resultActAddress.add("Address ==> " + ←
               ↪ rs.getString("Address"));
445         resultActCity.add("City ==> " + ←
               ↪ rs.getString("City"));
446         resultActCounty.add("County ==> " + ←
               ↪ rs.getString("County"));
447         resultActPostcode.add("Postcode ==> " + ←
               ↪ rs.getString("Postcode"));
448         resultActCountry.add("Country ==> " + ←
               ↪ rs.getString("Country"));
449         resultActPhone.add("Phone ==> " + ←
               ↪ rs.getString("Phone"));
450         resultActFax.add("Fax ==> " + ←
               ↪ rs.getString("Fax"));
451         resultActRegion.add("Region ==> " + ←
               ↪ rs.getString("Region"));
452      }
453   } catch (Exception e)
454   {
455      e.printStackTrace();
456      Utility.ReportExpectedVsActual("Exception ←
               ↪ occurred. " + e.getMessage(), "Failing test");
457   }
458
459   Utility.log.info("Verifying CustomerID.....");
460   if (resultExpCustomerID.size() != ←
           ↪ resultActCustomerID.size())
461   {
462         Utility.log.error("Size mismatch ←
               ↪ CustomerID....");
463         Utility.ReportExpectedVsActual( ←
               ↪ String.valueOf(resultExpCustomerID.size()), ←
               ↪ String.valueOf(resultActCustomerID.size()));
464   }
465
466   for(int j=0; j<resultExpCustomerID.size();j++){
467         Utility.ReportExpectedVsActual( ←
```

```
                    ↪ resultExpCustomerID.get(j), ↵
                    ↪ resultActCustomerID.get(j));
468             }
469
470     Utility.log.info("Verifying LastName.....");
471     if (resultExpLastName.size() != ↵
            ↪ resultActLastName.size())
472     {
473             Utility.log.error("Size mismatch LastName....");
474             Utility.ReportExpectedVsActual( ↵
                    ↪ String.valueOf(resultExpLastName.size()), ↵
                    ↪ String.valueOf(resultActLastName.size()));
475     }
476
477     for(int j=0; j<resultExpLastName.size();j++){
478             Utility.ReportExpectedVsActual( ↵
                    ↪ resultExpLastName.get(j), ↵
                    ↪ resultActLastName.get(j));
479             }
480
481     Utility.log.info("Verifying FirstName.....");
482     if (resultExpFirstName.size() != ↵
            ↪ resultActFirstName.size())
483     {
484             Utility.log.error("Size mismatch ↵
                    ↪ FirstName....");
485             Utility.ReportExpectedVsActual( ↵
                    ↪ String.valueOf(resultExpFirstName.size()), ↵
                    ↪ String.valueOf(resultActFirstName.size()));
486     }
487
488     for(int j=0; j<resultExpFirstName.size();j++){
489             Utility.ReportExpectedVsActual( ↵
                    ↪ resultExpFirstName.get(j), ↵
                    ↪ resultActFirstName.get(j));
490             }
491
492     Utility.log.info("Verifying Title.....");
493     if (resultExpTitle.size() != resultActTitle.size())
494     {
495             Utility.log.error("Size mismatch Title....");
496             Utility.ReportExpectedVsActual( ↵
                    ↪ String.valueOf(resultExpTitle.size()), ↵
                    ↪ String.valueOf(resultActTitle.size()));
497     }
```

```
498
499     for(int j=0; j<resultExpTitle.size();j++){
500             Utility.ReportExpectedVsActual( ↵
                    ↪ resultExpTitle.get(j), ↵
                    ↪ resultActTitle.get(j));
501             }
502
503     Utility.log.info("Verifying DisplayName.....");
504     if (resultExpDisplayName.size() != ↵
           ↪ resultActDisplayName.size())
505     {
506             Utility.log.error("Size mismatch ↵
                    ↪ DisplayName....");
507             Utility.ReportExpectedVsActual( ↵
                    ↪ String.valueOf(resultExpDisplayName.size()), ↵
                    ↪ String.valueOf(resultActDisplayName.size()));
508     }
509
510     for(int j=0; j<resultExpDisplayName.size();j++){
511             Utility.ReportExpectedVsActual( ↵
                    ↪ resultExpDisplayName.get(j), ↵
                    ↪ resultActDisplayName.get(j));
512             }
513
514     Utility.log.info("Verifying DateOfBirth.....");
515     if (resultExpDateOfBirth.size() != ↵
           ↪ resultActDateOfBirth.size())
516     {
517             Utility.log.error("Size mismatch ↵
                    ↪ DateOfBirth....");
518             Utility.ReportExpectedVsActual( ↵
                    ↪ String.valueOf(resultExpDateOfBirth.size()), ↵
                    ↪ String.valueOf(resultActDateOfBirth.size()));
519     }
520
521     for(int j=0; j<resultExpDateOfBirth.size();j++){
522             Utility.ReportExpectedVsActual( ↵
                    ↪ resultExpDateOfBirth.get(j), ↵
                    ↪ resultActDateOfBirth.get(j));
523             }
524
525     Utility.log.info("Verifying Address.....");
526     if (resultExpAddress.size() != ↵
           ↪ resultActAddress.size())
527     {
```

```
528                     Utility.log.error("Size mismatch Address....");
529                     Utility.ReportExpectedVsActual( ↩
                            ↪ String.valueOf(resultExpAddress.size()), ↩
                            ↪ String.valueOf(resultActAddress.size()));
530             }
531
532             for(int j=0; j<resultExpAddress.size();j++){
533                     Utility.ReportExpectedVsActual( ↩
                            ↪ resultExpAddress.get(j), ↩
                            ↪ resultActAddress.get(j));
534                     }
535
536             Utility.log.info("Verifying City.....");
537             if (resultExpCity.size() != resultActCity.size())
538             {
539                     Utility.log.error("Size mismatch City....");
540                     Utility.ReportExpectedVsActual( ↩
                            ↪ String.valueOf(resultExpCity.size()), ↩
                            ↪ String.valueOf(resultActCity.size()));
541             }
542
543             for(int j=0; j<resultExpCity.size();j++){
544                     Utility.ReportExpectedVsActual( ↩
                            ↪ resultExpCity.get(j), ↩
                            ↪ resultActCity.get(j));
545                     }
546
547             Utility.log.info("Verifying County.....");
548             if (resultExpCounty.size() != resultActCounty.size())
549             {
550                     Utility.log.error("Size mismatch County....");
551                     Utility.ReportExpectedVsActual( ↩
                            ↪ String.valueOf(resultExpCounty.size()), ↩
                            ↪ String.valueOf(resultActCounty.size()));
552             }
553
554             for(int j=0; j<resultExpCounty.size();j++){
555                     Utility.ReportExpectedVsActual( ↩
                            ↪ resultExpCounty.get(j), ↩
                            ↪ resultActCounty.get(j));
556                     }
557
558             Utility.log.info("Verifying Postcode.....");
559             if (resultExpPostcode.size() != ↩
                    ↪ resultActPostcode.size())
```

```
560              {
561                      Utility.log.error("Size mismatch Postcode....");
562                      Utility.ReportExpectedVsActual( ↵
                              ↪ String.valueOf(resultExpPostcode.size()), ↵
                              ↪ String.valueOf(resultActPostcode.size()));
563              }
564
565              for(int j=0; j<resultExpPostcode.size();j++){
566                      Utility.ReportExpectedVsActual( ↵
                              ↪ resultExpPostcode.get(j), ↵
                              ↪ resultActPostcode.get(j));
567                      }
568
569              Utility.log.info("Verifying Country.....");
570              if (resultExpCountry.size() != ↵
                      ↪ resultActCountry.size())
571              {
572                      Utility.log.error("Size mismatch Country....");
573                      Utility.ReportExpectedVsActual( ↵
                              ↪ String.valueOf(resultExpCountry.size()), ↵
                              ↪ String.valueOf(resultActCountry.size()));
574              }
575
576              for(int j=0; j<resultExpCountry.size();j++){
577                      Utility.ReportExpectedVsActual( ↵
                              ↪ resultExpCountry.get(j), ↵
                              ↪ resultActCountry.get(j));
578                      }
579
580              Utility.log.info("Verifying Phone.....");
581              if (resultExpPhone.size() != resultActPhone.size())
582              {
583                      Utility.log.error("Size mismatch Phone....");
584                      Utility.ReportExpectedVsActual( ↵
                              ↪ String.valueOf(resultExpPhone.size()), ↵
                              ↪ String.valueOf(resultActPhone.size()));
585              }
586
587              for(int j=0; j<resultExpPhone.size();j++){
588                      Utility.ReportExpectedVsActual( ↵
                              ↪ resultExpPhone.get(j), ↵
                              ↪ resultActPhone.get(j));
589                      }
590
591              Utility.log.info("Verifying Fax.....");
```

```
592        if (resultExpFax.size() != resultActFax.size())
593        {
594                Utility.log.error("Size mismatch Fax....");
595                Utility.ReportExpectedVsActual( ↵
                    ↪ String.valueOf(resultExpFax.size()), ↵
                    ↪ String.valueOf(resultActFax.size()));
596        }
597
598        for(int j=0; j<resultExpFax.size();j++){
599                Utility.ReportExpectedVsActual( ↵
                    ↪ resultExpFax.get(j), resultActFax.get(j));
600                }
601
602        Utility.log.info("Verifying Region.....");
603        if (resultExpRegion.size() != resultActRegion.size())
604        {
605                Utility.log.error("Size mismatch Region....");
606                Utility.ReportExpectedVsActual( ↵
                    ↪ String.valueOf(resultExpRegion.size()), ↵
                    ↪ String.valueOf(resultActRegion.size()));
607        }
608
609        for(int j=0; j<resultExpRegion.size();j++){
610                Utility.ReportExpectedVsActual( ↵
                    ↪ resultExpRegion.get(j), ↵
                    ↪ resultActRegion.get(j));
611                }
612
613        Utility.ReportResultWithSummary(name.getMethodName());
614    }
615 }
```

Line 26: String to hold column names separated by comma.

Line 27: Convert comma delimited string to a List.

Line 33 - 43: Construct source query string based on the Data Mapping document.

Line 104 and 392: Note the use of sourceQueryString.

Figure 6.10 shows the Result Summary file of dimCustomer test execution.

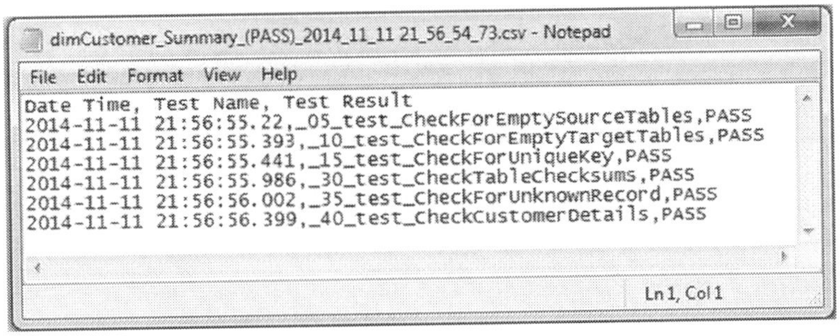

Figure 6.10: Result Summary - dimCustomer

6.1.10 Test 10 - Dimension Details Random

Now let's automate the testing of dimProduct which will expand your knowledge. Test _40_test_CheckProductDetails_Random in Listing 6.16 verifies that the field level details of all the records (other than 'Unknown') in the dimension table are as per the Data Mapping document once transferred from the staging area to the dimensional table. However, in this case the test verifies a random set of rows rather than all rows. This is useful where there are too many rows to check and you want to verify a selected subset only e.g. to verify 10,000 records from a table with 5 million rows. Retrieving and verifying different rows each time the test is executed, provides additional data coverage.

Listing 6.16: Code for dimProduct

```
1  package autoDW;
2
3  import java.sql.Connection;
4  import java.sql.DriverManager;
5  import java.sql.ResultSet;
6  import java.sql.Statement;
7  import java.util.ArrayList;
8  import java.util.Arrays;
9  import java.util.List;
10
11 import org.junit.AfterClass;
12 import org.junit.Before;
13 import org.junit.BeforeClass;
14 import org.junit.FixMethodOrder;
15 import org.junit.runners.MethodSorters;
16 import org.junit.Rule;
17 import org.junit.Test;
18 import org.junit.rules.TestName;
19
20 @FixMethodOrder(MethodSorters.NAME_ASCENDING)
21 public class dimProduct {
```

```
22    @Rule public TestName name = new TestName();
23
24    public String sourceQueryString;
25
26    public String colmNames = ↵
          ↪ "ProductID,ProductType,ProductName,UnitPrice, ↵
          ↪ UnitsInStock,UnitsOnOrder,ReorderLevel,Discontinued";
27    public List<String> ColmList = ↵
          ↪ Arrays.asList(colmNames.split(","));
28
29    @Before
30    public void setUp() throws Exception {
31        Config.TestResult = Config.PASS;
32
33        sourceQueryString = "SELECT [ProductID],"+ ↵
              ↪ Config.newLine;
34        sourceQueryString += "        CASE WHEN [ProductID] <= ↵
              ↪ 50 THEN 'Domenstic' "+ Config.newLine;
35        sourceQueryString += "            WHEN [ProductID] ↵
              ↪ Between 50 and 75 THEN 'Commercial' "+ ↵
              ↪ Config.newLine;
36        sourceQueryString += "            WHEN [ProductID] > ↵
              ↪ 75 THEN 'Other' "+ Config.newLine;
37        sourceQueryString += "            ELSE 'Unknown' "+ ↵
              ↪ Config.newLine;
38        sourceQueryString += "        END AS [ProductType],"+ ↵
              ↪ Config.newLine;
39        sourceQueryString += "        ↵
              ↪ [ProductName],[UnitPrice],[UnitsInStock],"+ ↵
              ↪ Config.newLine;
40        sourceQueryString += "        ↵
              ↪ [UnitsOnOrder],[ReorderLevel],"+ Config.newLine;
41        sourceQueryString += "        CASE [Discontinued] "+ ↵
              ↪ Config.newLine;
42        sourceQueryString += "            WHEN 1 THEN 'Yes' ↵
              ↪ "+ Config.newLine;
43        sourceQueryString += "            WHEN 0 THEN 'No' "+ ↵
              ↪ Config.newLine;
44        sourceQueryString += "            ELSE 'Unknown' "+ ↵
              ↪ Config.newLine;
45        sourceQueryString += "        END AS [Discontinued]"+ ↵
              ↪ Config.newLine;
46        sourceQueryString += "FROM [dbo].[Products]";
47
48        Utility.log.info("Source SQL is: " + ↵
```

```
              ↪ sourceQueryString);
49      }
50
51      @BeforeClass
52      public static void setUpBeforeClass() throws ↵
            ↪ Exception {
53          Utility.SetupSummaryFile(Utility.GetName(Thread. ↵
               ↪ currentThread().getStackTrace()[1]. ↵
               ↪ getClassName()));
54      }
55
56      @AfterClass
57      public static void tearDownAfterClass() throws ↵
            ↪ Exception {
58          Utility.SaveLogWithSummary(Utility.GetName(Thread. ↵
               ↪ currentThread().getStackTrace()[1]. ↵
               ↪ getClassName()));
59      }
60
61      @Test
62      public void _05_test_CheckForEmptySourceTables() {
63          Utility.log.info("***********    Starting Test: " + ↵
               ↪ name.getMethodName());
64
65          Utility.CheckForEmptyTable(Environment.DB_OPS_STAGING, ↵
               ↪ "dbo", "Products");
66
67          Utility.ReportResultWithSummary(name.getMethodName());
68      }
69
70      @Test
71      public void _10_test_CheckForEmptyTargetTables() {
72          Utility.log.info("***********    Starting Test: " + ↵
               ↪ name.getMethodName());
73
74          Utility.CheckForEmptyTable(Environment.DB_OPS_DWS, ↵
               ↪ "dbo", "dimProduct");
75
76          Utility.ReportResultWithSummary(name.getMethodName());
77      }
78
79      @Test
80      public void _15_test_CheckForUniqueKey() {
81          Utility.log.info("***********    Starting Test: " + ↵
               ↪ name.getMethodName());
```

```
82
83        Utility.CheckForUniqueKey(Environment.DB_OPS_DWS, ↵
             ↪ "dbo", "dimProduct", "ProductID");
84
85        Utility.ReportResultWithSummary(name.getMethodName());
86     }
87
88     @Test
89     public void _20_test_CheckForNullValues() {
90        Utility.log.info("***********   Starting Test: " + ↵
             ↪ name.getMethodName());
91
92        Utility.CheckForNullValues(Environment.DB_OPS_DWS, ↵
             ↪ "dbo", "dimProduct", "", "ProductKey <> -1");
93
94        Utility.ReportResultWithSummary(name.getMethodName());
95     }
96
97     @Test
98     public void _25_test_CheckTableRecoundCounts() {
99        Utility.log.info("***********   Starting Test: " + ↵
             ↪ name.getMethodName());
100
101       Utility.CompareCountOfRecordsWIthCondition( ↵
             ↪ Environment.DB_OPS_STAGING, "dbo", "Products", ↵
             ↪ Environment.DB_OPS_DWS, "dbo", "dimProduct", ↵
             ↪ "ProductKey <> -1");
102
103       Utility.ReportResultWithSummary(name.getMethodName());
104    }
105
106    @Test
107    public void _30_test_CheckTableChecksums() {
108       Utility.log.info("***********   Starting Test: " + ↵
             ↪ name.getMethodName());
109
110       Utility.CompareChecksumsSourceSQL( ↵
             ↪ Environment.DB_OPS_STAGING, sourceQueryString, ↵
             ↪ ColmList, Environment.DB_OPS_DWS, "dbo", ↵
             ↪ "dimProduct", "ProductKey,DateCreated", ↵
             ↪ "ProductKey <> -1");
111
112       Utility.ReportResultWithSummary(name.getMethodName());
113    }
114
```

```
115    @Test
116    public void _35_test_CheckForUnknownRecord() {
117      Utility.log.info("************   Starting Test: " + ↵
            ↪ name.getMethodName());
118
119      List<String> resultExpProductID = new ↵
            ↪ ArrayList<String>();
120      List<String> resultExpProductType = new ↵
            ↪ ArrayList<String>();
121      List<String> resultExpProductName = new ↵
            ↪ ArrayList<String>();
122      List<String> resultExpUnitPrice = new ↵
            ↪ ArrayList<String>();
123      List<String> resultExpUnitsInStock = new ↵
            ↪ ArrayList<String>();
124      List<String> resultExpUnitsOnOrder = new ↵
            ↪ ArrayList<String>();
125      List<String> resultExpReorderLevel = new ↵
            ↪ ArrayList<String>();
126      List<String> resultExpDiscontinued = new ↵
            ↪ ArrayList<String>();
127
128      //Find Expected Result from Data Mapping document
129      resultExpProductID.add("ProductID ==> -1");
130      resultExpProductType.add("ProductType ==> Unknown");
131      resultExpProductName.add("ProductName ==> Unknown");
132      resultExpUnitPrice.add("UnitPrice ==> -1.0000");
133      resultExpUnitsInStock.add("UnitsInStock ==> -1");
134      resultExpUnitsOnOrder.add("UnitsOnOrder ==> -1");
135      resultExpReorderLevel.add("ReorderLevel ==> -1");
136      resultExpDiscontinued.add("Discontinued ==> Unknown");
137
138      //Find Actual Result
139      try
140      {
141        List<String> resultActProductID = new ↵
              ↪ ArrayList<String>();
142        List<String> resultActProductType = new ↵
              ↪ ArrayList<String>();
143        List<String> resultActProductName = new ↵
              ↪ ArrayList<String>();
144        List<String> resultActUnitPrice = new ↵
              ↪ ArrayList<String>();
145        List<String> resultActUnitsInStock = new ↵
              ↪ ArrayList<String>();
```

```
146        List<String> resultActUnitsOnOrder = new ↵
              ↪ ArrayList<String>();
147        List<String> resultActReorderLevel = new ↵
              ↪ ArrayList<String>();
148        List<String> resultActDiscontinued = new ↵
              ↪ ArrayList<String>();
149
150        Class.forName("com.microsoft.sqlserver.jdbc. ↵
              ↪ SQLServerDriver");
151        Connection conn = DriverManager.getConnection( ↵
              ↪ Environment.DB_OPS_DWS, ↵
              ↪ Environment.DB_USERID, Environment.DB_PWD);
152        Utility.log.info("DB connected..." + ↵
              ↪ Environment.DB_OPS_DWS);
153        Statement statement = conn.createStatement();
154        String queryString = "select " + colmNames + ↵
              ↪ Config.newLine;
155        queryString += "from dbo.dimProduct" + ↵
              ↪ Config.newLine;
156        queryString += "Where ProductID = -1";
157
158        Utility.log.info("SQL is: " + queryString);
159
160        ResultSet rs = statement.executeQuery(queryString);
161
162        while (rs.next())
163        {
164            resultActProductID.add("ProductID ==> " + ↵
                  ↪ rs.getString("ProductID"));
165            resultActProductType.add("ProductType ==> " + ↵
                  ↪ rs.getString("ProductType"));
166            resultActProductName.add("ProductName ==> " + ↵
                  ↪ rs.getString("ProductName"));
167            resultActUnitPrice.add("UnitPrice ==> " + ↵
                  ↪ rs.getString("UnitPrice"));
168            resultActUnitsInStock.add("UnitsInStock ==> " ↵
                  ↪ + rs.getString("UnitsInStock"));
169            resultActUnitsOnOrder.add("UnitsOnOrder ==> " ↵
                  ↪ + rs.getString("UnitsOnOrder"));
170            resultActReorderLevel.add("ReorderLevel ==> " ↵
                  ↪ + rs.getString("ReorderLevel"));
171            resultActDiscontinued.add("Discontinued ==> " ↵
                  ↪ + rs.getString("Discontinued"));
172        }
173
```

```
174          for(int j=0; j<resultActProductID.size();j++)
175          {
176              Utility.ReportExpectedVsActual( ↵
                     ↪ resultExpProductID.get(j), ↵
                     ↪ resultActProductID.get(0));
177              Utility.ReportExpectedVsActual( ↵
                     ↪ resultExpProductType.get(j), ↵
                     ↪ resultActProductType.get(0));
178              Utility.ReportExpectedVsActual( ↵
                     ↪ resultExpProductName.get(j), ↵
                     ↪ resultActProductName.get(0));
179              Utility.ReportExpectedVsActual( ↵
                     ↪ resultExpUnitPrice.get(j), ↵
                     ↪ resultActUnitPrice.get(0));
180              Utility.ReportExpectedVsActual( ↵
                     ↪ resultExpUnitsInStock.get(j), ↵
                     ↪ resultActUnitsInStock.get(0));
181              Utility.ReportExpectedVsActual( ↵
                     ↪ resultExpUnitsOnOrder.get(j), ↵
                     ↪ resultActUnitsOnOrder.get(0));
182              Utility.ReportExpectedVsActual( ↵
                     ↪ resultExpReorderLevel.get(j), ↵
                     ↪ resultActReorderLevel.get(0));
183              Utility.ReportExpectedVsActual( ↵
                     ↪ resultExpDiscontinued.get(j), ↵
                     ↪ resultActDiscontinued.get(0));
184          }
185
186      } catch (Exception e)
187      {
188          e.printStackTrace();
189          Utility.ReportExpectedVsActual("Exception ↵
                 ↪ occurred. " + e.getMessage(), "Failing test");
190      }
191
192      Utility.ReportResultWithSummary(name.getMethodName());
193  }
194
195  @Test
196  public void _40_test_CheckProductDetails_Random() {
197      Utility.log.info("***********   Starting Test: " + ↵
                 ↪ name.getMethodName());
198
199      CheckProductDetails("", 20);
200      Utility.ReportResultWithSummary(name.getMethodName());
```

```
201        }
202
203        public void CheckProductDetails(String prodID, int ←
             ↪ howMany) {
204          Utility.log.info("***********   Starting Test: " + ←
             ↪ name.getMethodName());
205
206          List<String> resultExpProductID = new ←
             ↪ ArrayList<String>();
207          List<String> resultExpProductType = new ←
             ↪ ArrayList<String>();
208          List<String> resultExpProductName = new ←
             ↪ ArrayList<String>();
209          List<String> resultExpUnitPrice = new ←
             ↪ ArrayList<String>();
210          List<String> resultExpUnitsInStock = new ←
             ↪ ArrayList<String>();
211          List<String> resultExpUnitsOnOrder = new ←
             ↪ ArrayList<String>();
212          List<String> resultExpReorderLevel = new ←
             ↪ ArrayList<String>();
213          List<String> resultExpDiscontinued = new ←
             ↪ ArrayList<String>();
214
215          //Find Expected Result
216          try
217          {
218              Class.forName("com.microsoft.sqlserver.jdbc. ←
                 ↪ SQLServerDriver");
219              Connection conn = DriverManager.getConnection( ←
                 ↪ Environment.DB_OPS_STAGING, ←
                 ↪ Environment.DB_USERID, Environment.DB_PWD);
220              Utility.log.info("DB connected..." + ←
                 ↪ Environment.DB_OPS_STAGING);
221              Statement statement = conn.createStatement();
222              String queryString = "with stage as (" + ←
                 ↪ Config.newLine;
223              queryString += sourceQueryString + Config.newLine;
224
225              if (!prodID.equals("")) {
226              {
227                  Utility.log.info("Going for specific ←
                     ↪ ProductID: " + prodID);
228                  queryString += ") select TOP 1 " + colmNames ←
                     ↪ + " from stage"  + Config.newLine;
```

```
229          queryString += "Where ProductID = " + prodID;
230       }
231       else {
232       {
233          queryString += ") select TOP " + howMany + " ↵
                 ↪ " + colmNames + " from stage" + ↵
                 ↪ Config.newLine;
234          queryString += "Order by NEWID()"; {
235       }
236
237       Utility.log.info("SQL is: " + queryString);
238
239       ResultSet rs = statement.executeQuery(queryString);
240
241       while (rs.next())
242       {
243          resultExpProductID.add(rs.getString("ProductID"));
244          resultExpProductType.add("ProductType ==> " + ↵
                 ↪ rs.getString("ProductType"));
245          resultExpProductName.add("ProductName ==> " + ↵
                 ↪ rs.getString("ProductName"));
246          resultExpUnitPrice.add("UnitPrice ==> " + ↵
                 ↪ rs.getString("UnitPrice"));
247          resultExpUnitsInStock.add("UnitsInStock ==> " ↵
                 ↪ + rs.getString("UnitsInStock"));
248          resultExpUnitsOnOrder.add("UnitsOnOrder ==> " ↵
                 ↪ + rs.getString("UnitsOnOrder"));
249          resultExpReorderLevel.add("ReorderLevel ==> " ↵
                 ↪ + rs.getString("ReorderLevel"));
250          resultExpDiscontinued.add("Discontinued ==> " ↵
                 ↪ + rs.getString("Discontinued"));
251       }
252    } catch (Exception e)
253    {
254       e.printStackTrace();
255       Utility.ReportExpectedVsActual("Exception ↵
                 ↪ occurred. " + e.getMessage(), "Failing test");
256    }
257
258    if (resultExpProductID.size() != howMany)
259       Utility.ReportExpectedVsActual("Something wrong ↵
                 ↪ as " + howMany + " records not found", ↵
                 ↪ "Failing test");
260
261    for(int j=0; j<howMany;j++)
```

```
262              {
263                    Utility.log.info("Row....." + j + "           ↵
                       ↪ ProductID....." + resultExpProductID.get(j) );
264
265                  //Find Actual Result
266                  try
267                  {
268                      List<String> resultActProductID = new ↵
                         ↪ ArrayList<String>();
269                      List<String> resultActProductType = new ↵
                         ↪ ArrayList<String>();
270                      List<String> resultActProductName = new ↵
                         ↪ ArrayList<String>();
271                      List<String> resultActUnitPrice = new ↵
                         ↪ ArrayList<String>();
272                      List<String> resultActUnitsInStock = new ↵
                         ↪ ArrayList<String>();
273                      List<String> resultActUnitsOnOrder = new ↵
                         ↪ ArrayList<String>();
274                      List<String> resultActReorderLevel = new ↵
                         ↪ ArrayList<String>();
275                      List<String> resultActDiscontinued = new ↵
                         ↪ ArrayList<String>();
276
277                      Class.forName("com.microsoft.sqlserver.jdbc. ↵
                         ↪ SQLServerDriver");
278                      Connection conn = ↵
                         ↪ DriverManager.getConnection( ↵
                         ↪ Environment.DB_OPS_DWS, ↵
                         ↪ Environment.DB_USERID, Environment.DB_PWD);
279                      Utility.log.info("DB connected..." + ↵
                         ↪ Environment.DB_OPS_DWS);
280                      Statement statement = conn.createStatement();
281                      String queryString = "select " + colmNames + ↵
                         ↪ Config.newLine;
282                      queryString += "from dbo.dimProduct" + ↵
                         ↪ Config.newLine;
283                      queryString += "Where ProductID = " + ↵
                         ↪ resultExpProductID.get(j);
284
285                      Utility.log.info("SQL is: " + queryString);
286
287                      ResultSet rs = ↵
                         ↪ statement.executeQuery(queryString);
288
```

```
289            while (rs.next())
290            {
291                resultActProductID.add(rs.getString("ProductID"));
292                resultActProductType.add("ProductType ==> ↩
                   ↪ " + rs.getString("ProductType"));
293                resultActProductName.add("ProductName ==> ↩
                   ↪ " + rs.getString("ProductName"));
294                resultActUnitPrice.add("UnitPrice ==> " + ↩
                   ↪ rs.getString("UnitPrice"));
295                resultActUnitsInStock.add("UnitsInStock ↩
                   ↪ ==> " + rs.getString("UnitsInStock"));
296                resultActUnitsOnOrder.add("UnitsOnOrder ↩
                   ↪ ==> " + rs.getString("UnitsOnOrder"));
297                resultActReorderLevel.add("ReorderLevel ↩
                   ↪ ==> " + rs.getString("ReorderLevel"));
298                resultActDiscontinued.add("Discontinued ↩
                   ↪ ==> " + rs.getString("Discontinued"));
299            }
300
301            Utility.ReportExpectedVsActual( ↩
                   ↪ resultExpProductID.get(j), ↩
                   ↪ resultActProductID.get(0));
302            Utility.ReportExpectedVsActual( ↩
                   ↪ resultExpProductType.get(j), ↩
                   ↪ resultActProductType.get(0));
303            Utility.ReportExpectedVsActual( ↩
                   ↪ resultExpProductName.get(j), ↩
                   ↪ resultActProductName.get(0));
304            Utility.ReportExpectedVsActual( ↩
                   ↪ resultExpUnitPrice.get(j), ↩
                   ↪ resultActUnitPrice.get(0));
305            Utility.ReportExpectedVsActual( ↩
                   ↪ resultExpUnitsInStock.get(j), ↩
                   ↪ resultActUnitsInStock.get(0));
306            Utility.ReportExpectedVsActual( ↩
                   ↪ resultExpUnitsOnOrder.get(j), ↩
                   ↪ resultActUnitsOnOrder.get(0));
307            Utility.ReportExpectedVsActual( ↩
                   ↪ resultExpReorderLevel.get(j), ↩
                   ↪ resultActReorderLevel.get(0));
308            Utility.ReportExpectedVsActual( ↩
                   ↪ resultExpDiscontinued.get(j), ↩
                   ↪ resultActDiscontinued.get(0));
309        } catch (Exception e) {
310            e.printStackTrace();
```

```
311          Utility.ReportExpectedVsActual("Exception ←
               ↪ occurred. " + e.getMessage(), "Failing ←
               ↪ test");
312          }
313       }
314    }
315 }
```

Line 199: Call function 'CheckProductDetails' to check the product details.

Line 203: Parameter 'prodID' - provide a valid value if you want to check details of a specific 'ProductID' otherwise leave blank. Parameter 'howMany' - number of records to be checked randomly.

Line 225: If 'ProductID' was specified then use it in the selection criteria.

Line 231: Otherwise pick 'Top <n>' records specified by the parameter 'howMany'.

Line 234: Note the 'Order by NEWID()' statement that selects different records each time the SQL Query is executed.

Line 258: Report an error if you cannot find the specified number of records.

6.1.11   Test 11 - Dimension Details Specific

During your testing you may come across a specific 'ProductID' that fails and you may want to retest this 'ProductID' in the regression testing after fixes have been made to the system code. In this situation I always create a separate test for these specific records because the previous test may or may not select the failed records(s) because of the random selection method used. We have already defined a parameter 'prodID' in the function 'CheckProductDetails' to verify specific values. Remember to set the other parameter 'howMany' value to '1' when using a specific 'ProductID' as shown in the Listing 6.17.

Listing 6.17: Code for _45_test_CheckProductDetails_Specific

```
1 @Test
2 public void _45_test_CheckProductDetails_Specific() {
3    Utility.log.info("***********   Starting Test: " + ←
        ↪ name.getMethodName());
4
5    CheckProductDetails("7", 1);
6    Utility.ReportResultWithSummary(name.getMethodName());
7 }
```

Line 5: Call the function with a specific 'ProductID'.

Figure 6.11 shows the Result Summary file of dimProduct test execution.

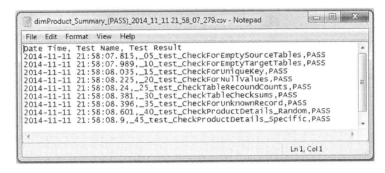

Figure 6.11: Result Summary - dimProduct

Ok, it is now time to automate the testing of dimYesNo. For this dimension, we assumed that the data is loaded into it via static text rather than from a table in the source database. Listing 6.18 shows the coding needed for dimYesNo.

Listing 6.18: Code for dimYesNo.java

```
1  package autoDW;
2
3  import java.sql.Connection;
4  import java.sql.DriverManager;
5  import java.sql.ResultSet;
6  import java.sql.Statement;
7  import java.util.ArrayList;
8  import java.util.List;
9
10 import org.junit.AfterClass;
11 import org.junit.Before;
12 import org.junit.BeforeClass;
13 import org.junit.FixMethodOrder;
14 import org.junit.runners.MethodSorters;
15 import org.junit.Rule;
16 import org.junit.Test;
17 import org.junit.rules.TestName;
18
19 @FixMethodOrder(MethodSorters.NAME_ASCENDING)
20
21 public class dimYesNo
22 {
23     @Rule public TestName name = new TestName();
24
25     @BeforeClass
```

```
26    public static void setUpBeforeClass() throws Exception
27    {
28           Utility.SetupSummaryFile(Utility.GetName( ←
                ↪ Thread.currentThread().getStackTrace()[1]. ←
                ↪ getClassName()));
29    }
30
31    @Before
32    public void setUp() throws Exception
33    {
34        Config.TestResult = Config.PASS;
35    }
36
37    @AfterClass
38    public static void tearDownAfterClass() throws Exception
39    {
40        Utility.SaveLogWithSummary(Utility.GetName( ←
                ↪ Thread.currentThread().getStackTrace()[1]. ←
                ↪ getClassName()));
41    }
42
43    @Test
44    public void _10_test_CheckForEmptyTargetTables()
45    {
46        Utility.log.info("***********    Starting Test: " + ←
                ↪ name.getMethodName());
47
48        Utility.CheckForEmptyTable(Environment.DB_OPS_DWS, ←
                ↪ "dbo", "dimYesNo");
49        Utility.ReportResultWithSummary(name.getMethodName());
50    }
51
52    @Test
53    public void _15_test_CheckForUniqueKey()
54    {
55        Utility.log.info("***********    Starting Test: " + ←
                ↪ name.getMethodName());
56
57        Utility.CheckForUniqueKey(Environment.DB_OPS_DWS, ←
                ↪ "dbo", "dimYesNo", "YesNoID");
58        Utility.ReportResultWithSummary(name.getMethodName());
59    }
60
61    @Test
62    public void _20_test_CheckForNullValues()
```

```
63    {
64        Utility.log.info("***********    Starting Test: " + ←
              ↪ name.getMethodName());
65
66        Utility.CheckForNullValues(Environment.DB_OPS_DWS, ←
              ↪ "dbo", "dimYesNo", "", "");
67        Utility.ReportResultWithSummary(name.getMethodName());
68    }
69
70    @Test
71    public void _25_test_CheckTableRecoundCounts()
72    {
73        Utility.log.info("***********    Starting Test: " + ←
              ↪ name.getMethodName());
74
75        int expCount = 3; //Yes, No and Unknown
76        int actCount = 0;
77
78        actCount = Utility.GetCountOfRecords( ←
              ↪ Environment.DB_OPS_DWS, "dbo", "dimYesNo");
79        Utility.ReportExpectedVsActual( ←
              ↪ String.valueOf(expCount), ←
              ↪ String.valueOf(actCount));
80        Utility.ReportResultWithSummary(name.getMethodName());
81    }
82
83    @Test
84    public void _30_test_CheckYesNoDetails()
85    {
86        Utility.log.info("***********    Starting Test: " + ←
              ↪ name.getMethodName());
87
88        List<String> resultExpYesNoID = new ←
              ↪ ArrayList<String>();
89        List<String> resultActYesNoID = new ←
              ↪ ArrayList<String>();
90        List<String> resultExpYesNoDescription = new ←
              ↪ ArrayList<String>();
91        List<String> resultActYesNoDescription = new ←
              ↪ ArrayList<String>();
92
93        //Expected Result
94        resultExpYesNoID.add("-1");
95        resultExpYesNoID.add("1");
96        resultExpYesNoID.add("2");
```

```
97
98      resultExpYesNoDescription.add("Unknown");
99      resultExpYesNoDescription.add("Yes");
100     resultExpYesNoDescription.add("No");
101
102     //Find Actual Result
103     try
104     {
105         Class.forName("com.microsoft.sqlserver.jdbc. ↵
                ↪ SQLServerDriver");
106         Connection conn = DriverManager.getConnection( ↵
                ↪ Environment.DB_OPS_DWS, ↵
                ↪ Environment.DB_USERID, Environment.DB_PWD);
107         Utility.log.info("DB connected..." + ↵
                ↪ Environment.DB_OPS_DWS);
108         Statement statement = conn.createStatement();
109
110         String queryString = "select YesNoID, ↵
                ↪ YesNoDescription From dbo.dimYesNo order by ↵
                ↪ YesNoKey ";
111
112         Utility.log.info("SQL is: " + queryString);
113         ResultSet rs = statement.executeQuery(queryString);
114         while (rs.next())
115         {
116             resultActYesNoID.add(rs.getString("YesNoID"));
117             resultActYesNoDescription.add(rs.getString( ↵
                    ↪ "YesNoDescription"));
118         }
119     } catch (Exception e)
120     {
121         e.printStackTrace();
122         Utility.ReportExpectedVsActual("Exception ↵
                ↪ occurred. " + e.getMessage(), "Failing test");
123     }
124
125     Utility.log.info("Verifying YesNoID.....");
126     if (resultExpYesNoID.size() != ↵
            ↪ resultActYesNoID.size())
127     {
128         Utility.log.error("YesNoID Size mismatch");
129         Utility.ReportExpectedVsActual( ↵
                ↪ String.valueOf(resultExpYesNoID.size()), ↵
                ↪ String.valueOf(resultActYesNoID.size()));
130     }
```

```
131
132     for(int j=0; j<resultExpYesNoID.size();j++){
133         Utility.ReportExpectedVsActual( ↵
                ↪ resultExpYesNoID.get(j), ↵
                ↪ resultActYesNoID.get(j));
134     }
135
136     Utility.log.info("Verifying YesNoDescription.....");
137     if (resultExpYesNoDescription.size() != ↵
            ↪ resultActYesNoDescription.size())
138     {
139         Utility.log.error("YesNoDescription Size ↵
                ↪ mismatch");
140         Utility.ReportExpectedVsActual( ↵
                ↪ String.valueOf(resultExpYesNoDescription. ↵
                ↪ size()), ↵
                ↪ String.valueOf(resultActYesNoDescription. ↵
                ↪ size()));
141     }
142
143     for(int j=0; j<resultExpYesNoDescription.size(); j++){
144         Utility.ReportExpectedVsActual( ↵
                ↪ resultExpYesNoDescription.get(j), ↵
                ↪ resultActYesNoDescription.get(j));
145     }
146
147     Utility.ReportResultWithSummary(name.getMethodName());
148     }
149 }
```

Line 94 - 100: Build the lists from static data. Ensure that the order used is the same as that used to fetch data from the dimension table.

Figure 6.12 shows the Result Summary file of dimYesNo test execution.

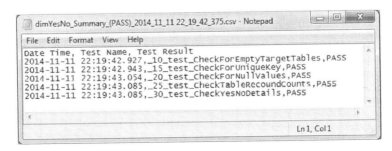

Figure 6.12: Result Summary - dimYesNo

Now let's automate dimDate. For this we will need one more generic function in our Utility.java file.

CheckForUniqueKeyIgnoreNulls - Checks for the 'Unique Key' in a table but ignores its Null values		
Input Parameters	*dbName*	Name of the database
	schemaName	Name of the schema
	tblName	Name of the table to be checked
	uniqueKeyName	Unique Key to be checked
Return Value	*void*	Returns nothing

Listing 6.19: Utility.java - Code for CheckForUniqueKeyIgnoreNulls

```
1  public static void CheckForUniqueKeyIgnoreNulls( String ↵
     ↪ dbName, String schemaName, String tblName, String ↵
     ↪ uniqueKeyName)
2  {
3      Utility.log.info("CheckForUniqueKey - tblName: " + ↵
         ↪ tblName);
4      int exp, act;
5      String sql = "select count(distinct " + uniqueKeyName ↵
         ↪ + ") from " + schemaName + "." + tblName + " ↵
         ↪ Where " + uniqueKeyName + " is not null";
6      String sql1 = "select count(*) from " + schemaName + ↵
         ↪ "." + tblName + " Where " + uniqueKeyName + " is ↵
         ↪ not null";
7
8      exp = Utility.GetCountOfDistinctRecordsSourceSQL ↵
         ↪ (dbName, sql);
9      act = Utility.GetCountOfDistinctRecordsSourceSQL ↵
         ↪ (dbName, sql1);
10
11     Utility.ReportExpectedVsActual(String.valueOf(exp), ↵
         ↪ String.valueOf(act));
12 }
```

Line 5 and 6: Include 'not null' condition in the 'where' clause.

Listing 6.20 shows the code for dimDate.

Listing 6.20: Code for dimDate

```
1  package autoDW;
```

```
2
3   import java.sql.Connection;
4   import java.sql.DriverManager;
5   import java.sql.ResultSet;
6   import java.sql.Statement;
7   import java.util.ArrayList;
8   import java.util.List;
9
10  import org.junit.AfterClass;
11  import org.junit.Before;
12  import org.junit.BeforeClass;
13  import org.junit.FixMethodOrder;
14  import org.junit.runners.MethodSorters;
15  import org.junit.Rule;
16  import org.junit.Test;
17  import org.junit.rules.TestName;
18
19  @FixMethodOrder(MethodSorters.NAME_ASCENDING)
20
21  public class dimDate
22  {
23      @Rule public TestName name = new TestName();
24
25      private String strtDate = "1985-01-01";
26      private String endDate = "2014-08-31";
27
28      @BeforeClass
29      public static void setUpBeforeClass() throws Exception
30      {
31          Utility.SetupSummaryFile(Utility.GetName( ↵
                ↪ Thread.currentThread().getStackTrace()[1]. ↵
                ↪ getClassName()));
32      }
33
34      @Before
35      public void setUp() throws Exception
36      {
37          Config.TestResult = Config.PASS;
38      }
39
40      @AfterClass
41      public static void tearDownAfterClass() throws Exception
42      {
43          Utility.SaveLogWithSummary(Utility.GetName( ↵
                ↪ Thread.currentThread().getStackTrace()[1]. ↵
```

```
              ↪ getClassName()));
44      }
45
46      @Test
47      public void _10_test_CheckForEmptyTargetTables()
48      {
49          Utility.log.info("***********    Starting Test: " + ↩
              ↪ name.getMethodName());
50
51          Utility.CheckForEmptyTable(Environment.DB_OPS_DWS, ↩
              ↪ "dbo", "dimDate");
52          Utility.ReportResultWithSummary(name.getMethodName());
53      }
54
55      @Test
56      public void _15_test_CheckForUniqueKey()
57      {
58          Utility.log.info("***********    Starting Test: " + ↩
              ↪ name.getMethodName());
59
60          Utility.CheckForUniqueKeyIgnoreNulls( ↩
              ↪ Environment.DB_OPS_DWS, "dbo", "dimDate", ↩
              ↪ "FullDate");
61
62          Utility.ReportResultWithSummary(name.getMethodName());
63      }
64
65      @Test
66      public void _20_test_CheckForNullValues()
67      {
68          Utility.log.info("***********    Starting Test: " + ↩
              ↪ name.getMethodName());
69
70          Utility.CheckForNullValues(Environment.DB_OPS_DWS, ↩
              ↪ "dbo", "dimDate", "", "DateKey <> -1");
71
72          Utility.ReportResultWithSummary(name.getMethodName());
73      }
74
75      @Test
76      public void _25_test_CheckTableRecoundCounts()
77      {
78          Utility.log.info("***********    Starting Test: " + ↩
              ↪ name.getMethodName());
79
```

```
80      String exp = "Expected Initialised";
81      String act = "Actual Initialised";
82
83      try
84      {
85          Class.forName("com.microsoft.sqlserver.jdbc. ↵
              ↪ SQLServerDriver");
86          Connection conn = DriverManager.getConnection( ↵
              ↪ Environment.DB_OPS_DWS, ↵
              ↪ Environment.DB_USERID, Environment.DB_PWD);
87          Utility.log.info("DB connected.." + ↵
              ↪ Environment.DB_OPS_DWS);
88          Statement statement = conn.createStatement();
89          String queryString = "SELECT DATEDIFF(day, ↵
              ↪ Cast('" + strtDate + "' as date), Cast('" + ↵
              ↪ endDate + "' as date)) +1";
90          Utility.log.info("SQL is: " + queryString);
91          ResultSet rs = statement.executeQuery(queryString);
92          while (rs.next())
93          {
94              exp = rs.getString(1);
95          }
96      } catch (Exception e)
97      {
98          e.printStackTrace();
99          Utility.ReportExpectedVsActual("Exception ↵
              ↪ occurred. " + e.getMessage(), "Failing test");
100     }
101
102     try
103     {
104         Class.forName("com.microsoft.sqlserver.jdbc. ↵
              ↪ SQLServerDriver");
105         Connection conn = DriverManager.getConnection( ↵
              ↪ Environment.DB_OPS_DWS, ↵
              ↪ Environment.DB_USERID, Environment.DB_PWD);
106         Utility.log.info("DB connected.." + ↵
              ↪ Environment.DB_OPS_DWS);
107         Statement statement = conn.createStatement();
108         String queryString = "select COUNT(*) from ↵
              ↪ dbo.dimDate where DateKey <> -1";
109         Utility.log.info("SQL is: " + queryString);
110         ResultSet rs = statement.executeQuery(queryString);
111         while (rs.next())
112         {
```

```
113              act = rs.getString(1);
114          }
115      } catch (Exception e)
116      {
117          e.printStackTrace();
118          Utility.ReportExpectedVsActual("Exception ↵
              ↪ occurred. " + e.getMessage(), "Failing test");
119      }
120
121      Utility.ReportExpectedVsActual(exp, act);
122      Utility.ReportResultWithSummary(name.getMethodName());
123  }
124
125  @Test
126  public void _35_test_CheckForUnknownRecord()
127  {
128      Utility.log.info("************    Starting Test: " + ↵
              ↪ name.getMethodName());
129
130      List<String> resultExpFullDate = new ↵
              ↪ ArrayList<String>();
131      List<String> resultActFullDate = new ↵
              ↪ ArrayList<String>();
132      List<String> resultExpQuarter = new ↵
              ↪ ArrayList<String>();
133      List<String> resultActQuarter = new ↵
              ↪ ArrayList<String>();
134      List<String> resultExpQuarterName = new ↵
              ↪ ArrayList<String>();
135      List<String> resultActQuarterName = new ↵
              ↪ ArrayList<String>();
136      List<String> resultExpYear = new ArrayList<String>();
137      List<String> resultActYear = new ArrayList<String>();
138      List<String> resultExpDayNumber = new ↵
              ↪ ArrayList<String>();
139      List<String> resultActDayNumber = new ↵
              ↪ ArrayList<String>();
140      List<String> resultExpWeekNumber = new ↵
              ↪ ArrayList<String>();
141      List<String> resultActWeekNumber = new ↵
              ↪ ArrayList<String>();
142      List<String> resultExpMonth = new ArrayList<String>();
143      List<String> resultActMonth = new ArrayList<String>();
144      List<String> resultExpMonthName = new ↵
              ↪ ArrayList<String>();
```

```
145     List<String> resultActMonthName = new ↵
          ↪ ArrayList<String>();
146     List<String> resultExpMonthShortName = new ↵
          ↪ ArrayList<String>();
147     List<String> resultActMonthShortName = new ↵
          ↪ ArrayList<String>();
148     List<String> resultExpDayofWeek = new ↵
          ↪ ArrayList<String>();
149     List<String> resultActDayofWeek = new ↵
          ↪ ArrayList<String>();
150     List<String> resultExpDayofWeekName = new ↵
          ↪ ArrayList<String>();
151     List<String> resultActDayofWeekName = new ↵
          ↪ ArrayList<String>();
152     List<String> resultExpDayofWeekShortName = new ↵
          ↪ ArrayList<String>();
153     List<String> resultActDayofWeekShortName = new ↵
          ↪ ArrayList<String>();
154
155     //Find Expected Result from Data Mapping document
156     resultExpFullDate.add("FullDate ==> null");
157     resultExpQuarter.add("Quarter ==> -1");
158     resultExpQuarterName.add("QuarterName ==> Unknown");
159     resultExpYear.add("Year ==> -1");
160     resultExpDayNumber.add("DayNumber ==> -1");
161     resultExpWeekNumber.add("WeekNumber ==> -1");
162     resultExpMonth.add("Month ==> -1");
163     resultExpMonthName.add("MonthName ==> Unknown");
164     resultExpMonthShortName.add("MonthShortName ==> ↵
          ↪ Unknown");
165     resultExpDayofWeek.add("DayofWeek ==> -1");
166     resultExpDayofWeekName.add("DayofWeekName ==> ↵
          ↪ Unknown");
167     resultExpDayofWeekShortName.add("DayofWeekShortName ↵
          ↪ ==> Unknown");
168
169     //Find Actual Result
170     try
171     {
172         Class.forName("com.microsoft.sqlserver.jdbc. ↵
              ↪ SQLServerDriver");
173         Connection conn = DriverManager.getConnection( ↵
              ↪ Environment.DB_OPS_DWS, ↵
              ↪ Environment.DB_USERID, Environment.DB_PWD);
```

```
174        Utility.log.info("DB connected..." + ←
               ↪ Environment.DB_OPS_DWS);
175        Statement statement = conn.createStatement();
176        String queryString = "Select FullDate, Quarter, ←
               ↪ QuarterName, Year, DayNumber," + ←
               ↪ Config.newLine;
177        queryString += "WeekNumber, Month, MonthName, ←
               ↪ MonthShortName, DayofWeek, DayofWeekName, ←
               ↪ DayofWeekShortName" + Config.newLine;
178        queryString += "From dbo.dimDate" + Config.newLine;
179        queryString += "Where DateKey = -1";
180
181        Utility.log.info("SQL is: " + queryString);
182        ResultSet rs = statement.executeQuery(queryString);
183        while (rs.next())
184        {
185            resultActFullDate.add("FullDate ==> " + ←
                   ↪ rs.getString("FullDate"));
186            resultActQuarter.add("Quarter ==> " + ←
                   ↪ rs.getString("Quarter"));
187            resultActQuarterName.add("QuarterName ==> " + ←
                   ↪ rs.getString("QuarterName"));
188            resultActYear.add("Year ==> " + ←
                   ↪ rs.getString("Year"));
189            resultActDayNumber.add("DayNumber ==> " + ←
                   ↪ rs.getString("DayNumber"));
190            resultActWeekNumber.add("WeekNumber ==> " + ←
                   ↪ rs.getString("WeekNumber"));
191            resultActMonth.add("Month ==> " + ←
                   ↪ rs.getString("Month"));
192            resultActMonthName.add("MonthName ==> " + ←
                   ↪ rs.getString("MonthName"));
193            resultActMonthShortName.add("MonthShortName ←
                   ↪ ==> " + rs.getString("MonthShortName"));
194            resultActDayofWeek.add("DayofWeek ==> " + ←
                   ↪ rs.getString("DayofWeek"));
195            resultActDayofWeekName.add("DayofWeekName ==> ←
                   ↪ " + rs.getString("DayofWeekName"));
196            resultActDayofWeekShortName.add( ←
                   ↪ "DayofWeekShortName ==> " + ←
                   ↪ rs.getString("DayofWeekShortName"));
197        }
198    } catch (Exception e)
199    {
200        e.printStackTrace();
```

```
201         Utility.ReportExpectedVsActual("Exception ←
                ↪ occurred. " + e.getMessage(), "Failing test");
202         }
203
204         Utility.log.info("Verifying FullDate.....");
205         if (resultExpFullDate.size() != ←
                ↪ resultActFullDate.size())
206         {
207             Utility.log.error("Size mismatch FullDate....");
208             Utility.ReportExpectedVsActual( ←
                    ↪ String.valueOf(resultExpFullDate.size()), ←
                    ↪ String.valueOf(resultActFullDate.size()));
209         }
210
211         for(int j=0; j<resultExpFullDate.size();j++)
212         {
213             Utility.ReportExpectedVsActual( ←
                    ↪ resultExpFullDate.get(j), ←
                    ↪ resultActFullDate.get(j));
214         }
215
216         Utility.log.info("Verifying Quarter.....");
217         if (resultExpQuarter.size() != ←
                ↪ resultActQuarter.size())
218         {
219             Utility.log.error("Size mismatch Quarter....");
220             Utility.ReportExpectedVsActual( ←
                    ↪ String.valueOf(resultExpQuarter.size()), ←
                    ↪ String.valueOf(resultActQuarter.size()));
221         }
222
223         for(int j=0; j<resultExpQuarter.size();j++)
224         {
225             Utility.ReportExpectedVsActual( ←
                    ↪ resultExpQuarter.get(j), ←
                    ↪ resultActQuarter.get(j));
226         }
227
228         Utility.log.info("Verifying QuarterName.....");
229         if (resultExpQuarterName.size() != ←
                ↪ resultActQuarterName.size())
230         {
231             Utility.log.error("Size mismatch QuarterName....");
232             Utility.ReportExpectedVsActual( ←
                    ↪ String.valueOf(resultExpQuarterName.size()), ←
```

```
                    ↪ String.valueOf(resultActQuarterName.size()));
233         }
234
235         for(int j=0; j<resultExpQuarterName.size();j++)
236         {
237             Utility.ReportExpectedVsActual( ↵
                    ↪ resultExpQuarterName.get(j), ↵
                    ↪ resultActQuarterName.get(j));
238         }
239
240         Utility.log.info("Verifying Year.....");
241         if (resultExpYear.size() != resultActYear.size())
242         {
243             Utility.log.error("Size mismatch Year....");
244             Utility.ReportExpectedVsActual( ↵
                    ↪ String.valueOf(resultExpYear.size()), ↵
                    ↪ String.valueOf(resultActYear.size()));
245         }
246
247         for(int j=0; j<resultExpYear.size();j++)
248         {
249             Utility.ReportExpectedVsActual( ↵
                    ↪ resultExpYear.get(j), resultActYear.get(j));
250         }
251
252         Utility.log.info("Verifying DayNumber.....");
253         if (resultExpDayNumber.size() != ↵
                ↪ resultActDayNumber.size())
254         {
255             Utility.log.error("Size mismatch DayNumber....");
256             Utility.ReportExpectedVsActual( ↵
                    ↪ String.valueOf(resultExpDayNumber.size()), ↵
                    ↪ String.valueOf(resultActDayNumber.size()));
257         }
258
259         for(int j=0; j<resultExpDayNumber.size();j++)
260         {
261             Utility.ReportExpectedVsActual( ↵
                    ↪ resultExpDayNumber.get(j), ↵
                    ↪ resultActDayNumber.get(j));
262         }
263
264         Utility.log.info("Verifying WeekNumber.....");
265         if (resultExpWeekNumber.size() != ↵
                ↪ resultActWeekNumber.size())
```

```
266         {
267             Utility.log.error("Size mismatch WeekNumber....");
268             Utility.ReportExpectedVsActual( ↵
                    ↪ String.valueOf(resultExpWeekNumber.size()), ↵
                    ↪ String.valueOf(resultActWeekNumber.size()));
269         }
270
271         for(int j=0; j<resultExpWeekNumber.size();j++)
272         {
273             Utility.ReportExpectedVsActual( ↵
                    ↪ resultExpWeekNumber.get(j), ↵
                    ↪ resultActWeekNumber.get(j));
274         }
275
276         Utility.log.info("Verifying Month.....");
277         if (resultExpMonth.size() != resultActMonth.size())
278         {
279             Utility.log.error("Size mismatch Month....");
280             Utility.ReportExpectedVsActual( ↵
                    ↪ String.valueOf(resultExpMonth.size()), ↵
                    ↪ String.valueOf(resultActMonth.size()));
281         }
282
283         for(int j=0; j<resultExpMonth.size();j++)
284         {
285             Utility.ReportExpectedVsActual( ↵
                    ↪ resultExpMonth.get(j), resultActMonth.get(j));
286         }
287
288         Utility.log.info("Verifying MonthName.....");
289         if (resultExpMonthName.size() != ↵
                ↪ resultActMonthName.size())
290         {
291             Utility.log.error("Size mismatch MonthName....");
292             Utility.ReportExpectedVsActual( ↵
                    ↪ String.valueOf(resultExpMonthName.size()), ↵
                    ↪ String.valueOf(resultActMonthName.size()));
293         }
294
295         for(int j=0; j<resultExpMonthName.size();j++)
296         {
297             Utility.ReportExpectedVsActual( ↵
                    ↪ resultExpMonthName.get(j), ↵
                    ↪ resultActMonthName.get(j));
298         }
```

```
299
300        Utility.log.info("Verifying MonthShortName.....");
301        if (resultExpMonthShortName.size() != ↵
           ↪ resultActMonthShortName.size())
302        {
303            Utility.log.error("Size mismatch ↵
               ↪ MonthShortName....");
304            Utility.ReportExpectedVsActual( ↵
               ↪ String.valueOf(resultExpMonthShortName. ↵
               ↪ size()), ↵
               ↪ String.valueOf(resultActMonthShortName. ↵
               ↪ size()));
305        }
306
307        for(int j=0; j<resultExpMonthShortName.size();j++)
308        {
309            Utility.ReportExpectedVsActual( ↵
               ↪ resultExpMonthShortName.get(j), ↵
               ↪ resultActMonthShortName.get(j));
310        }
311
312        Utility.log.info("Verifying DayofWeek.....");
313        if (resultExpDayofWeek.size() != ↵
           ↪ resultActDayofWeek.size())
314        {
315            Utility.log.error("Size mismatch DayofWeek....");
316            Utility.ReportExpectedVsActual( ↵
               ↪ String.valueOf(resultExpDayofWeek.size()), ↵
               ↪ String.valueOf(resultActDayofWeek.size()));
317        }
318
319        for(int j=0; j<resultExpDayofWeek.size();j++)
320        {
321            Utility.ReportExpectedVsActual( ↵
               ↪ resultExpDayofWeek.get(j), ↵
               ↪ resultActDayofWeek.get(j));
322        }
323
324        Utility.log.info("Verifying DayofWeekName.....");
325        if (resultExpDayofWeekName.size() != ↵
           ↪ resultActDayofWeekName.size())
326        {
327            Utility.log.error("Size mismatch ↵
               ↪ DayofWeekName....");
```

```
328          Utility.ReportExpectedVsActual( ←
                 ↪ String.valueOf(resultExpDayofWeekName.size()), ←
                 ↪ String.valueOf(resultActDayofWeekName.size()));
329      }
330
331      for(int j=0; j<resultExpDayofWeekName.size();j++)
332      {
333          Utility.ReportExpectedVsActual( ←
                 ↪ resultExpDayofWeekName.get(j), ←
                 ↪ resultActDayofWeekName.get(j));
334      }
335
336      Utility.log.info("Verifying DayofWeekShortName.....");
337      if (resultExpDayofWeekShortName.size() != ←
             ↪ resultActDayofWeekShortName.size())
338      {
339          Utility.log.error("Size mismatch ←
                 ↪ DayofWeekShortName....");
340          Utility.ReportExpectedVsActual( ←
                 ↪ String.valueOf(resultExpDayofWeekShortName. ←
                 ↪ size()), ←
                 ↪ String.valueOf(resultActDayofWeekShortName. ←
                 ↪ size()));
341      }
342
343      for(int j=0; j<resultExpDayofWeekShortName.size();j++)
344      {
345          Utility.ReportExpectedVsActual( ←
                 ↪ resultExpDayofWeekShortName.get(j), ←
                 ↪ resultActDayofWeekShortName.get(j));
346      }
347
348      Utility.ReportResultWithSummary(name.getMethodName());
349  }
350
351  @Test
352  public void _40_test_CheckDateDetails()
353  {
354      Utility.log.info("************   Starting Test: " + ←
             ↪ name.getMethodName());
355
356      List<String> resultExpFullDate = new ←
             ↪ ArrayList<String>();
357      List<String> resultActFullDate = new ←
             ↪ ArrayList<String>();
```

```
358     List<String> resultExpQuarter = new ↩
              ↪ ArrayList<String>();
359     List<String> resultActQuarter = new ↩
              ↪ ArrayList<String>();
360     List<String> resultExpQuarterName = new ↩
              ↪ ArrayList<String>();
361     List<String> resultActQuarterName = new ↩
              ↪ ArrayList<String>();
362     List<String> resultExpYear = new ArrayList<String>();
363     List<String> resultActYear = new ArrayList<String>();
364     List<String> resultExpDayNumber = new ↩
              ↪ ArrayList<String>();
365     List<String> resultActDayNumber = new ↩
              ↪ ArrayList<String>();
366     List<String> resultExpWeekNumber = new ↩
              ↪ ArrayList<String>();
367     List<String> resultActWeekNumber = new ↩
              ↪ ArrayList<String>();
368     List<String> resultExpMonth = new ArrayList<String>();
369     List<String> resultActMonth = new ArrayList<String>();
370     List<String> resultExpMonthName = new ↩
              ↪ ArrayList<String>();
371     List<String> resultActMonthName = new ↩
              ↪ ArrayList<String>();
372     List<String> resultExpMonthShortName = new ↩
              ↪ ArrayList<String>();
373     List<String> resultActMonthShortName = new ↩
              ↪ ArrayList<String>();
374     List<String> resultExpDayofWeek = new ↩
              ↪ ArrayList<String>();
375     List<String> resultActDayofWeek = new ↩
              ↪ ArrayList<String>();
376     List<String> resultExpDayofWeekName = new ↩
              ↪ ArrayList<String>();
377     List<String> resultActDayofWeekName = new ↩
              ↪ ArrayList<String>();
378     List<String> resultExpDayofWeekShortName = new ↩
              ↪ ArrayList<String>();
379     List<String> resultActDayofWeekShortName = new ↩
              ↪ ArrayList<String>();
380
381     //Find Expected Result
382     try
383     {
```

```
384    Class.forName("com.microsoft.sqlserver.jdbc. ↵
           ↳ SQLServerDriver");
385    Connection conn = DriverManager.getConnection( ↵
           ↳ Environment.DB_OPS_STAGING, ↵
           ↳ Environment.DB_USERID, Environment.DB_PWD);
386    Utility.log.info("DB connected..." + ↵
           ↳ Environment.DB_OPS_STAGING);
387    Statement statement = conn.createStatement();
388
389    String queryString = "DECLARE @StartDate DATE = ↵
           ↳ '" + strtDate +"';" + Config.newLine;
390    queryString += "DECLARE @EndDate DATE = '" + ↵
           ↳ endDate +"';" + Config.newLine;
391    queryString += "WITH Stage AS" + Config.newLine;
392    queryString += "(" + Config.newLine;
393    queryString += "SELECT CAST(@StartDate AS ↵
           ↳ DATETIME) MyDate" + Config.newLine;
394    queryString += "UNION ALL" + Config.newLine;
395    queryString += "SELECT MyDate + 1" + ↵
           ↳ Config.newLine;
396    queryString += "FROM Stage" + Config.newLine;
397    queryString += "WHERE MyDate + 1 <= @EndDate" + ↵
           ↳ Config.newLine;
398    queryString += ")" + Config.newLine;
399    queryString += "SELECT ↵
           ↳ CAST(CONVERT(CHAR(8),CAST(MyDate AS ↵
           ↳ DATETIME),112) AS INT) AS DateKey" + ↵
           ↳ Config.newLine;
400    queryString += ", MyDate" + Config.newLine;
401    queryString += ",Case " + Config.newLine;
402    queryString += "  When MONTH(MyDate) Between 1 ↵
           ↳ and 3 Then 1 " + Config.newLine;
403    queryString += "  When MONTH(MyDate) Between 4 ↵
           ↳ and 6 Then 2 " + Config.newLine;
404    queryString += "  When MONTH(MyDate) Between 7 ↵
           ↳ and 9 Then 3" + Config.newLine;
405    queryString += "  When MONTH(MyDate) Between 10 ↵
           ↳ and 12 Then 4" + Config.newLine;
406    queryString += "End As [Quarter]" + Config.newLine;
407    queryString += ",Case " + Config.newLine;
408    queryString += "  When MONTH(MyDate) Between 1 ↵
           ↳ and 3 Then 'Quarter 1'" + Config.newLine;
409    queryString += "  When MONTH(MyDate) Between 4 ↵
           ↳ and 6 Then 'Quarter 2'" + Config.newLine;
```

```
410    queryString += "   When MONTH(MyDate) Between 7 ↵
         ↪ and 9 Then 'Quarter 3'" + Config.newLine;
411    queryString += "   When MONTH(MyDate) Between 10 ↵
         ↪ and 12 Then 'Quarter 4'" + Config.newLine;
412    queryString += "End As QuarterName" + ↵
         ↪ Config.newLine;
413    queryString += ", YEAR(MyDate) AS [Year]" + ↵
         ↪ Config.newLine;
414    queryString += ", DATEPART(dy, MyDate) AS ↵
         ↪ DayNumber" + Config.newLine;
415    queryString += ", DATEPART(wk, MyDate) AS ↵
         ↪ WeekNumber" + Config.newLine;
416    queryString += ", MONTH(MyDate) AS [Month]" + ↵
         ↪ Config.newLine;
417    queryString += ", DATENAME(mm, MyDate) AS ↵
         ↪ [MonthName]" + Config.newLine;
418    queryString += ", CONVERT(VARCHAR(3), ↵
         ↪ DATENAME(MONTH, MyDate), 100) AS ↵
         ↪ MonthShortName" + Config.newLine;
419    queryString += ", DAY(MyDate) AS DayOfWeek" + ↵
         ↪ Config.newLine;
420    queryString += ", DATENAME(dw, MyDate) AS ↵
         ↪ DayOfWeekName" + Config.newLine;
421    queryString += ", CONVERT(VARCHAR(3), ↵
         ↪ DATENAME(dw, MyDate)) AS ↵
         ↪ DayOfWeekShortName" + Config.newLine;
422    queryString += "FROM Stage" + Config.newLine;
423    queryString += "OPTION (MAXRECURSION 0)";
424
425    Utility.log.info("SQL is: " + queryString);
426
427    ResultSet rs = statement.executeQuery(queryString);
428
429    while (rs.next())
430    {
431       resultExpFullDate.add("FullDate ==> " + ↵
            ↪ rs.getString("MyDate").substring(0, 10));
432       resultExpQuarter.add("Quarter ==> " + ↵
            ↪ rs.getString("Quarter"));
433       resultExpQuarterName.add("QuarterName ==> " + ↵
            ↪ rs.getString("QuarterName"));
434       resultExpYear.add("Year ==> " + ↵
            ↪ rs.getString("Year"));
435       resultExpDayNumber.add("DayNumber ==> " + ↵
            ↪ rs.getString("DayNumber"));
```

```
436        resultExpWeekNumber.add("WeekNumber ==> " + ↩
              ↪ rs.getString("WeekNumber"));
437        resultExpMonth.add("Month ==> " + ↩
              ↪ rs.getString("Month"));
438        resultExpMonthName.add("MonthName ==> " + ↩
              ↪ rs.getString("MonthName"));
439        resultExpMonthShortName.add("MonthShortName ↩
              ↪ ==> " + rs.getString("MonthShortName"));
440        resultExpDayofWeek.add("DayofWeek ==> " + ↩
              ↪ rs.getString("DayofWeek"));
441        resultExpDayofWeekName.add("DayofWeekName ==> ↩
              ↪ " + rs.getString("DayofWeekName"));
442        resultExpDayofWeekShortName.add( ↩
              ↪ "DayofWeekShortName ==> " + ↩
              ↪ rs.getString("DayofWeekShortName"));
443      }
444    } catch (Exception e)
445    {
446        e.printStackTrace();
447        Utility.ReportExpectedVsActual("Exception ↩
              ↪ occurred. " + e.getMessage(), "Failing test");
448    }
449
450    //Find Actual Result
451    try
452    {
453        Class.forName("com.microsoft.sqlserver.jdbc. ↩
              ↪ SQLServerDriver");
454        Connection conn = DriverManager.getConnection( ↩
              ↪ Environment.DB_OPS_DWS, ↩
              ↪ Environment.DB_USERID, Environment.DB_PWD);
455        Utility.log.info("DB connected..." + ↩
              ↪ Environment.DB_OPS_DWS);
456        Statement statement = conn.createStatement();
457        String queryString = "Select FullDate, Quarter, ↩
              ↪ QuarterName, Year, DayNumber," + ↩
              ↪ Config.newLine;
458        queryString += "WeekNumber, Month, MonthName, ↩
              ↪ MonthShortName, DayofWeek, DayofWeekName, ↩
              ↪ DayofWeekShortName" + Config.newLine;
459        queryString += "From dbo.dimDate" + Config.newLine;
460        queryString += "Where DateKey <> -1" + ↩
              ↪ Config.newLine;
461        queryString += "Order by DateKey";
462
```

```
463        Utility.log.info("SQL is: " + queryString);
464        ResultSet rs = statement.executeQuery(queryString);
465        while (rs.next())
466        {
467            resultActFullDate.add("FullDate ==> " + ↵
                  ↪ rs.getString("FullDate"));
468            resultActQuarter.add("Quarter ==> " + ↵
                  ↪ rs.getString("Quarter"));
469            resultActQuarterName.add("QuarterName ==> " + ↵
                  ↪ rs.getString("QuarterName"));
470            resultActYear.add("Year ==> " + ↵
                  ↪ rs.getString("Year"));
471            resultActDayNumber.add("DayNumber ==> " + ↵
                  ↪ rs.getString("DayNumber"));
472            resultActWeekNumber.add("WeekNumber ==> " + ↵
                  ↪ rs.getString("WeekNumber"));
473            resultActMonth.add("Month ==> " + ↵
                  ↪ rs.getString("Month"));
474            resultActMonthName.add("MonthName ==> " + ↵
                  ↪ rs.getString("MonthName"));
475            resultActMonthShortName.add("MonthShortName ↵
                  ↪ ==> " + rs.getString("MonthShortName"));
476            resultActDayofWeek.add("DayofWeek ==> " + ↵
                  ↪ rs.getString("DayofWeek"));
477            resultActDayofWeekName.add("DayofWeekName ==> ↵
                  ↪ " + rs.getString("DayofWeekName"));
478            resultActDayofWeekShortName.add( ↵
                  ↪ "DayofWeekShortName ==> " + ↵
                  ↪ rs.getString("DayofWeekShortName"));
479        }
480    } catch (Exception e)
481    {
482        e.printStackTrace();
483        Utility.ReportExpectedVsActual("Exception ↵
              ↪ occurred. " + e.getMessage(), "Failing test");
484    }
485
486    Utility.log.info("Verifying FullDate.....");
487    if (resultExpFullDate.size() != ↵
          ↪ resultActFullDate.size())
488    {
489        Utility.log.error("Size mismatch FullDate....");
490        Utility.ReportExpectedVsActual( ↵
              ↪ String.valueOf(resultExpFullDate.size()), ↵
              ↪ String.valueOf(resultActFullDate.size()));
```

```
491         }
492
493         for(int j=0; j<resultExpFullDate.size();j++)
494         {
495             Utility.ReportExpectedVsActual( ←
                    ↪ resultExpFullDate.get(j), ←
                    ↪ resultActFullDate.get(j));
496         }
497
498         Utility.log.info("Verifying Quarter.....");
499         if (resultExpQuarter.size() != ←
                ↪ resultActQuarter.size())
500         {
501             Utility.log.error("Size mismatch Quarter....");
502             Utility.ReportExpectedVsActual( ←
                    ↪ String.valueOf(resultExpQuarter.size()), ←
                    ↪ String.valueOf(resultActQuarter.size()));
503         }
504
505         for(int j=0; j<resultExpQuarter.size();j++)
506         {
507             Utility.ReportExpectedVsActual( ←
                    ↪ resultExpQuarter.get(j), ←
                    ↪ resultActQuarter.get(j));
508         }
509
510         Utility.log.info("Verifying QuarterName.....");
511         if (resultExpQuarterName.size() != ←
                ↪ resultActQuarterName.size())
512         {
513             Utility.log.error("Size mismatch QuarterName....");
514             Utility.ReportExpectedVsActual( ←
                    ↪ String.valueOf(resultExpQuarterName.size()), ←
                    ↪ String.valueOf(resultActQuarterName.size()));
515         }
516
517         for(int j=0; j<resultExpQuarterName.size();j++)
518         {
519             Utility.ReportExpectedVsActual( ←
                    ↪ resultExpQuarterName.get(j), ←
                    ↪ resultActQuarterName.get(j));
520         }
521
522         Utility.log.info("Verifying Year.....");
523         if (resultExpYear.size() != resultActYear.size())
```

```
524            {
525                Utility.log.error("Size mismatch Year....");
526                Utility.ReportExpectedVsActual( ←
                       ↪ String.valueOf(resultExpYear.size()), ←
                       ↪ String.valueOf(resultActYear.size()));
527            }
528
529        for(int j=0; j<resultExpYear.size();j++)
530        {
531            Utility.ReportExpectedVsActual( ←
                   ↪ resultExpYear.get(j), resultActYear.get(j));
532        }
533
534        Utility.log.info("Verifying DayNumber.....");
535        if (resultExpDayNumber.size() != ←
               ↪ resultActDayNumber.size())
536        {
537            Utility.log.error("Size mismatch DayNumber....");
538            Utility.ReportExpectedVsActual( ←
                   ↪ String.valueOf(resultExpDayNumber.size()), ←
                   ↪ String.valueOf(resultActDayNumber.size()));
539        }
540
541        for(int j=0; j<resultExpDayNumber.size();j++)
542        {
543            Utility.ReportExpectedVsActual( ←
                   ↪ resultExpDayNumber.get(j), ←
                   ↪ resultActDayNumber.get(j));
544        }
545
546        Utility.log.info("Verifying WeekNumber.....");
547        if (resultExpWeekNumber.size() != ←
               ↪ resultActWeekNumber.size())
548        {
549            Utility.log.error("Size mismatch WeekNumber....");
550            Utility.ReportExpectedVsActual( ←
                   ↪ String.valueOf(resultExpWeekNumber.size()), ←
                   ↪ String.valueOf(resultActWeekNumber.size()));
551        }
552
553        for(int j=0; j<resultExpWeekNumber.size();j++)
554        {
555            Utility.ReportExpectedVsActual( ←
                   ↪ resultExpWeekNumber.get(j), ←
                   ↪ resultActWeekNumber.get(j));
```

```
556         }
557
558         Utility.log.info("Verifying Month.....");
559         if (resultExpMonth.size() != resultActMonth.size())
560         {
561             Utility.log.error("Size mismatch Month....");
562             Utility.ReportExpectedVsActual( ←
                    ↪ String.valueOf(resultExpMonth.size()), ←
                    ↪ String.valueOf(resultActMonth.size()));
563         }
564
565         for(int j=0; j<resultExpMonth.size();j++)
566         {
567             Utility.ReportExpectedVsActual( ←
                    ↪ resultExpMonth.get(j), resultActMonth.get(j));
568         }
569
570         Utility.log.info("Verifying MonthName.....");
571         if (resultExpMonthName.size() != ←
                ↪ resultActMonthName.size())
572         {
573             Utility.log.error("Size mismatch MonthName....");
574             Utility.ReportExpectedVsActual( ←
                    ↪ String.valueOf(resultExpMonthName.size()), ←
                    ↪ String.valueOf(resultActMonthName.size()));
575         }
576
577         for(int j=0; j<resultExpMonthName.size();j++)
578         {
579             Utility.ReportExpectedVsActual( ←
                    ↪ resultExpMonthName.get(j), ←
                    ↪ resultActMonthName.get(j));
580         }
581
582         Utility.log.info("Verifying MonthShortName.....");
583         if (resultExpMonthShortName.size() != ←
                ↪ resultActMonthShortName.size())
584         {
585             Utility.log.error("Size mismatch ←
                    ↪ MonthShortName....");
586             Utility.ReportExpectedVsActual( ←
                    ↪ String.valueOf(resultExpMonthShortName. ←
                    ↪ size()), ←
                    ↪ String.valueOf(resultActMonthShortName. ←
                    ↪ size()));
```

```
587        }
588
589        for(int j=0; j<resultExpMonthShortName.size();j++)
590        {
591            Utility.ReportExpectedVsActual( ↵
                    ↪ resultExpMonthShortName.get(j), ↵
                    ↪ resultActMonthShortName.get(j));
592        }
593
594        Utility.log.info("Verifying DayofWeek.....");
595        if (resultExpDayofWeek.size() != ↵
                ↪ resultActDayofWeek.size())
596        {
597            Utility.log.error("Size mismatch DayofWeek....");
598            Utility.ReportExpectedVsActual( ↵
                    ↪ String.valueOf(resultExpDayofWeek.size()), ↵
                    ↪ String.valueOf(resultActDayofWeek.size()));
599        }
600
601        for(int j=0; j<resultExpDayofWeek.size();j++)
602        {
603            Utility.ReportExpectedVsActual( ↵
                    ↪ resultExpDayofWeek.get(j), ↵
                    ↪ resultActDayofWeek.get(j));
604        }
605
606        Utility.log.info("Verifying DayofWeekName.....");
607        if (resultExpDayofWeekName.size() != ↵
                ↪ resultActDayofWeekName.size())
608        {
609            Utility.log.error("Size mismatch ↵
                    ↪ DayofWeekName....");
610            Utility.ReportExpectedVsActual ↵
                    ↪ (String.valueOf(resultExpDayofWeekName.size()), ↵
                    ↪ String.valueOf(resultActDayofWeekName.size()));
611        }
612
613        for(int j=0; j<resultExpDayofWeekName.size();j++)
614        {
615            Utility.ReportExpectedVsActual( ↵
                    ↪ resultExpDayofWeekName.get(j), ↵
                    ↪ resultActDayofWeekName.get(j));
616        }
617
618        Utility.log.info("Verifying DayofWeekShortName.....");
```

```
619    if (resultExpDayofWeekShortName.size() != ←
         ↪ resultActDayofWeekShortName.size())
620    {
621        Utility.log.error("Size mismatch ←
             ↪ DayofWeekShortName....");
622        Utility.ReportExpectedVsActual( ←
             ↪ String.valueOf(resultExpDayofWeekShortName. ←
             ↪ size()), ←
             ↪ String.valueOf(resultActDayofWeekShortName. ←
             ↪ size()));
623    }
624
625    for(int j=0; j<resultExpDayofWeekShortName.size();j++)
626    {
627        Utility.ReportExpectedVsActual( ←
             ↪ resultExpDayofWeekShortName.get(j), ←
             ↪ resultActDayofWeekShortName.get(j));
628    }
629
630    Utility.ReportResultWithSummary(name.getMethodName());
631  }
632 }
```

Line 25: Change the start date based on your dimension load script.

Line 26: Change the end date based on your dimension load script.

Line 89: SQL Query to retrieve the number of days between the start date and end date for Expected Result.

Line 108: SQL Query to get the number of records in the dimension table for the Actual Result.

Line 389 - 423: Construct the Expected Result SQL Query.

Figure 6.13 shows the Result Summary file of dimDate test execution.

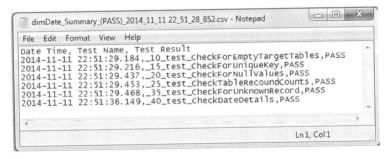

Figure 6.13: Result Summary - dimDate

Now let's automate the testing of dimPriceMatch. We will need to define two more generic functions in the Utility.java file.

GetCountOfRecordsSourceSQL - Gets a count of records where source is a SQL Query rather than a table		
Input Parameters	*dbName*	Name of the database
	sourceSQL	Source SQL
Return Value	*count*	Returns a count of records in the sourceSQL

CompareCountOfRecordsSourceSQLWIthCondition - Compares count of records between a source SQL and a target table with condition		
Input Parameters	*sourcDBName*	Name of the source database
	sourcSQL	SQL Query to be executed on the source database
	targetDBName	Name of the target database
	targetSchemaName	Name of the target schema
	targetTblName	Name of the target table
	condition	Condition to be applied to the target table
Return Value	*void*	Returns nothing

Listing 6.21: Utility.java - additional functions

```
1  public static int GetCountOfRecordsSourceSQL( String ↵
      ↳ dbName, String sourceSQL)
2  {
3      int count = -99;
4
5      try
6      {
7          Connection conn;
8          Class.forName("com.microsoft.sqlserver.jdbc. ↵
             ↳ SQLServerDriver");
9
10         conn = DriverManager.getConnection(dbName, ↵
             ↳ Environment.DB_USERID, Environment.DB_PWD);
11
12         Utility.log.info("DB connected: " + dbName);
13         Statement statement = conn.createStatement();
14
```

```
15    String queryString = "with stage as (" + ←
          ↪ Config.newLine;
16    queryString += sourceSQL + Config.newLine;
17    queryString += ") select COUNT(*) from stage";
18
19    Utility.log.info("SQL is: " + queryString);
20
21    ResultSet rs = statement.executeQuery(queryString);
22
23    while (rs.next())
24    {
25        count= rs.getInt(1);
26    }
27  } catch (Exception e)
28  {
29      e.printStackTrace();
30      Utility.ReportExpectedVsActual("Exception occurred" ←
          ↪ + e.getMessage(), "Failing test");
31  }
32
33    return count;
34 }
35
36 public static void ←
      ↪ CompareCountOfRecordsSourceSQLWIthCondition( String ←
      ↪ sourcDBName, String sourceSQL, String targetDBName, ←
      ↪ String targetSchemaName, String targetTblName, ←
      ↪ String condition)
37 {
38    Utility.log.info("targetTblName: " + targetTblName);
39    int exp, act;
40
41    exp = Utility.GetCountOfRecordsSourceSQL(sourcDBName, ←
          ↪ sourceSQL);
42    act = Utility.GetCountOfRecordsWithCondition( ←
          ↪ targetDBName, targetSchemaName, targetTblName, ←
          ↪ condition);
43
44    Utility.ReportExpectedVsActual(String.valueOf(exp), ←
          ↪ String.valueOf(act));
45 }
```

Line 16: Use the provided SQL Query to get a count of records.
Line 41: Get the expected count with SQL Query executed on the source database.
Line 42: Get the actual count from the target table with condition applied.

Listing 6.22 shows the code for dimPriceMatch.

```java
1  package autoDW;
2
3  import java.sql.Connection;
4  import java.sql.DriverManager;
5  import java.sql.ResultSet;
6  import java.sql.Statement;
7  import java.util.ArrayList;
8  import java.util.Arrays;
9  import java.util.List;
10
11 import org.junit.AfterClass;
12 import org.junit.Before;
13 import org.junit.BeforeClass;
14 import org.junit.FixMethodOrder;
15 import org.junit.runners.MethodSorters;
16 import org.junit.Rule;
17 import org.junit.Test;
18 import org.junit.rules.TestName;
19
20 @FixMethodOrder(MethodSorters.NAME_ASCENDING)
21
22 public class dimPriceMatch
23 {
24     @Rule public TestName name = new TestName();
25
26     public String sourceQueryString;
27
28     public String colmNames = "PriceMatchDescription";
29     public List<String> ColmList = ↵
          ↪ Arrays.asList(colmNames.split(","));
30
31     @BeforeClass
32     public static void setUpBeforeClass() throws Exception
33     {
34         Utility.SetupSummaryFile(Utility.GetName( ↵
              ↪ Thread.currentThread().getStackTrace()[1]. ↵
              ↪ getClassName()));
35     }
36
```

```
37    @Before
38    public void setUp() throws Exception
39    {
40        Config.TestResult = Config.PASS;
41
42        sourceQueryString = "SELECT Distinct PriceMatch as ↵
              ↪ PriceMatchDescription"+ Config.newLine;
43        sourceQueryString += "FROM [dbo].[OrderDetails]" + ↵
              ↪ Config.newLine;
44        sourceQueryString += "Where PriceMatch is not NULL";
45
46        Utility.log.info("Source SQL is: " + ↵
              ↪ sourceQueryString);
47    }
48
49    @AfterClass
50    public static void tearDownAfterClass() throws Exception
51    {
52        Utility.SaveLogWithSummary(Utility.GetName( ↵
              ↪ Thread.currentThread().getStackTrace()[1]. ↵
              ↪ getClassName()));
53    }
54
55    @Test
56    public void _05_test_CheckForEmptySourceTables()
57    {
58        Utility.log.info("***********    Starting Test: " + ↵
              ↪ name.getMethodName());
59
60        Utility.CheckForEmptyTable(Environment.DB_OPS_STAGING, ↵
              ↪ "dbo", "OrderDetails");
61
62        Utility.ReportResultWithSummary(name.getMethodName());
63    }
64
65    @Test
66    public void _10_test_CheckForEmptyTargetTables()
67    {
68        Utility.log.info("***********    Starting Test: " + ↵
              ↪ name.getMethodName());
69
70        Utility.CheckForEmptyTable(Environment.DB_OPS_DWS, ↵
              ↪ "dbo", "dimPriceMatch");
71
72        Utility.ReportResultWithSummary(name.getMethodName());
```

```
73          }
74
75          @Test
76          public void _15_test_CheckForUniqueKey()
77          {
78              Utility.log.info("************    Starting Test: " + ←
                ↪ name.getMethodName());
79
80              Utility.CheckForUniqueKey(Environment.DB_OPS_DWS, ←
                ↪ "dbo", "dimPriceMatch", "PriceMatchDescription");
81
82              Utility.ReportResultWithSummary(name.getMethodName());
83          }
84
85          @Test
86          public void _20_test_CheckForNullValues()
87          {
88              Utility.log.info("************    Starting Test: " + ←
                ↪ name.getMethodName());
89
90              Utility.CheckForNullValues(Environment.DB_OPS_DWS, ←
                ↪ "dbo", "dimPriceMatch", "", "PriceMatchKey <> ←
                ↪ -1");
91
92              Utility.ReportResultWithSummary(name.getMethodName());
93          }
94
95          @Test
96          public void _25_test_CheckTableRecoundCounts()
97          {
98              Utility.log.info("************    Starting Test: " + ←
                ↪ name.getMethodName());
99
100             Utility.CompareCountOfRecordsSourceSQLWIthCondition( ←
                ↪ Environment.DB_OPS_STAGING, sourceQueryString, ←
                ↪ Environment.DB_OPS_DWS, "dbo", ←
                ↪ "dimPriceMatch", "PriceMatchKey <> -1");
101
102             Utility.ReportResultWithSummary(name.getMethodName());
103         }
104
105         @Test
106         public void _30_test_CheckTableChecksums()
107         {
```

```
108        Utility.log.info("***********    Starting Test: " + ↵
               ↪ name.getMethodName());

109
110        Utility.CompareChecksumsSourceSQL( ↵
               ↪ Environment.DB_OPS_STAGING, sourceQueryString, ↵
               ↪ ColmList, Environment.DB_OPS_DWS, "dbo", ↵
               ↪ "dimPriceMatch", "PriceMatchKey,DateCreated", ↵
               ↪ "PriceMatchKey <> -1");

111
112        Utility.ReportResultWithSummary(name.getMethodName());
113     }

114
115     @Test
116     public void _35_test_CheckForUnknownRecord()
117     {
118        Utility.log.info("***********    Starting Test: " + ↵
               ↪ name.getMethodName());

119
120        List<String> resultExpPriceMatchDescription = new ↵
               ↪ ArrayList<String>();
121        List<String> resultActPriceMatchDescription = new ↵
               ↪ ArrayList<String>();

122
123        resultExpPriceMatchDescription.add( ↵
               ↪ "PriceMatchDescription ==> Unknown");

124
125        //Find Actual Result
126        try
127        {
128            Class.forName("com.microsoft.sqlserver.jdbc. ↵
                   ↪ SQLServerDriver");
129            Connection conn = DriverManager.getConnection( ↵
                   ↪ Environment.DB_OPS_DWS, ↵
                   ↪ Environment.DB_USERID, Environment.DB_PWD);
130            Utility.log.info("DB connected..." + ↵
                   ↪ Environment.DB_OPS_DWS);
131            Statement statement = conn.createStatement();
132            String queryString = "Select " + colmNames + ↵
                   ↪ Config.newLine;
133            queryString += "From dbo.dimPriceMatch" + ↵
                   ↪ Config.newLine;
134            queryString += "Where PriceMatchKey = -1";
135
136            Utility.log.info("SQL is: " + queryString);
137            ResultSet rs = statement.executeQuery(queryString);
```

```
138          while (rs.next())
139          {
140              resultActPriceMatchDescription.add( ↵
                     ↪ "PriceMatchDescription ==> " + ↵
                     ↪ rs.getString("PriceMatchDescription"));
141          }
142      } catch (Exception e)
143      {
144          e.printStackTrace();
145          Utility.ReportExpectedVsActual("Exception ↵
                 ↪ occurred. " + e.getMessage(), "Failing test");
146      }
147
148      Utility.log.info("Verifying ↵
                 ↪ PriceMatchDescription.....");
149      if (resultExpPriceMatchDescription.size() != ↵
                 ↪ resultActPriceMatchDescription.size())
150      {
151          Utility.log.error("Size mismatch ↵
                 ↪ PriceMatchDescription....");
152          Utility.ReportExpectedVsActual( String.valueOf( ↵
                 ↪ resultExpPriceMatchDescription.size()), ↵
                 ↪ String.valueOf( ↵
                 ↪ resultActPriceMatchDescription.size()));
153      }
154
155      for(int j=0; ↵
                 ↪ j<resultExpPriceMatchDescription.size();j++)
156      {
157          Utility.ReportExpectedVsActual( ↵
                 ↪ resultExpPriceMatchDescription.get(j), ↵
                 ↪ resultActPriceMatchDescription.get(j));
158      }
159
160      Utility.ReportResultWithSummary(name.getMethodName());
161  }
162
163  @Test
164  public void _40_test_CheckPriceMatchDetails()
165  {
166      Utility.log.info("***********   Starting Test: " + ↵
                 ↪ name.getMethodName());
167
168      List<String> resultExpPriceMatchDescription = new ↵
                 ↪ ArrayList<String>();
```

```
169     List<String> resultActPriceMatchDescription = new ↵
          ↪ ArrayList<String>();
170
171     //Find Expected Result
172     try
173     {
174         Class.forName("com.microsoft.sqlserver.jdbc. ↵
              ↪ SQLServerDriver");
175         Connection conn = DriverManager.getConnection( ↵
              ↪ Environment.DB_OPS_STAGING, ↵
              ↪ Environment.DB_USERID, Environment.DB_PWD);
176         Utility.log.info("DB connected..." + ↵
              ↪ Environment.DB_OPS_STAGING);
177         Statement statement = conn.createStatement();
178
179         String queryString = sourceQueryString + ↵
              ↪ Config.newLine;
180         queryString += "Order by PriceMatchDescription";
181
182         Utility.log.info("SQL is: " + queryString);
183
184         ResultSet rs = statement.executeQuery(queryString);
185
186         while (rs.next())
187         {
188             resultExpPriceMatchDescription.add( ↵
                  ↪ "PriceMatchDescription ==> " + ↵
                  ↪ rs.getString("PriceMatchDescription"));
189         }
190     } catch (Exception e)
191     {
192         e.printStackTrace();
193         Utility.ReportExpectedVsActual("Exception ↵
              ↪ occurred. " + e.getMessage(), "Failing test");
194     }
195
196     //Find Actual Result
197     try
198     {
199         Class.forName("com.microsoft.sqlserver.jdbc. ↵
              ↪ SQLServerDriver");
200         Connection conn = DriverManager.getConnection( ↵
              ↪ Environment.DB_OPS_DWS, ↵
              ↪ Environment.DB_USERID, Environment.DB_PWD);
```

```
201        Utility.log.info("DB connected..." + ↵
              ↪ Environment.DB_OPS_DWS);
202        Statement statement = conn.createStatement();
203        String queryString = "Select " + colmNames + ↵
              ↪ Config.newLine;
204        queryString += "From dbo.dimPriceMatch" + ↵
              ↪ Config.newLine;
205        queryString += "Where PriceMatchKey <> -1" + ↵
              ↪ Config.newLine;
206        queryString += "Order by PriceMatchDescription";
207
208        Utility.log.info("SQL is: " + queryString);
209        ResultSet rs = statement.executeQuery(queryString);
210        while (rs.next())
211        {
212            resultActPriceMatchDescription.add( ↵
                  ↪ "PriceMatchDescription ==> " + ↵
                  ↪ rs.getString("PriceMatchDescription"));
213        }
214     } catch (Exception e)
215     {
216        e.printStackTrace();
217        Utility.ReportExpectedVsActual("Exception ↵
              ↪ occurred. " + e.getMessage(), "Failing test");
218     }
219
220     Utility.log.info("Verifying ↵
           ↪ PriceMatchDescription.....");
221     if (resultExpPriceMatchDescription.size() != ↵
           ↪ resultActPriceMatchDescription.size())
222     {
223        Utility.log.error("Size mismatch ↵
              ↪ PriceMatchDescription....");
224        Utility.ReportExpectedVsActual( String.valueOf( ↵
              ↪ resultExpPriceMatchDescription.size()), ↵
              ↪ String.valueOf( ↵
              ↪ resultActPriceMatchDescription.size()));
225     }
226
227     for(int j=0; ↵
           ↪ j<resultExpPriceMatchDescription.size();j++){
228        Utility.ReportExpectedVsActual( ↵
              ↪ resultExpPriceMatchDescription.get(j), ↵
              ↪ resultActPriceMatchDescription.get(j));
229     }
```

```
230
231        Utility.ReportResultWithSummary(name.getMethodName());
232    }
233 }
```

Line 42: Construct source SQL Query based on the Data Mapping document.

Figure 6.14 shows the Result Summary file of dimPriceMatch test execution.

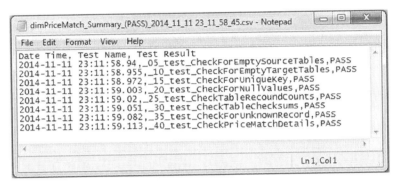

Figure 6.14: Result Summary - dimPriceMatch

6.2   Automating Fact Tables

Ok, let's move on to automate the testing of our fact table - factSales. To begin we will add a new declaration to the Config.java file which we will need.

Listing 6.23: Code for Config.java

```
1 public static final String UNKNOWN_STRING = "Unknown";
```

Now let's define three new generic functions in the Utility.java file.

GetTableChecksumSpecificCols - Gets the Sum of Checksum of specific columns of a table		
Input Parameters	*dbName*	Name of the database
	dbSchema	Name of the schema
	tblName	Name of the table
	resultColumns	Column list for which we want Checksum
	targetClause	Clause to be applied
Return Value	*Checksum*	Returns a list of the Sum of Checksum of specified columns of the table

CompareChecksumsSourceSQLSpecificCols - Compares the Sum of Checksum of specific columns sourced via SQL with another table and reports the outcome		
Input Parameters	*sourcDBName*	Name of the source database
	sourcSQL	Source SQL
	sourceColumnsList	Source column list
	targetDBName	Name of the target database
	targetTblName	Name of the target table
	ignoreTargetCol	Ignore columns from the target table
	targetClause	Condition to be applied to the target table
Return Value	*void*	Returns nothing

CheckForUniqueKeyMultipleCols - Checks for the 'Unique Key' made up of multiple columns and reports the outcome		
Input Parameters	*dbName*	Name of the database
	dbSchema	Name of the schema
	tblName	Name of the table
	uniqueKeyCols	Unique Key Columns
Return Value	*void*	Returns nothing

Listing 6.24: Utility.java - Code for additional functions

```
1  public static List<String> GetTableChecksumSpecificCols( ↵
       ↪ String dbName, String dbSchema, String tblName, ↵
       ↪ List<String> resultColumns, String targetClause)
2  {
3      Utility.log.info("GetTableChecksumSpecificCols... ");
4
5      List<String> myChksum = new ArrayList<String>();
6
7      try
8      {
9          for(int j=0; j<resultColumns.size();j++)
10         {
11             Connection conn1;
12             Class.forName("com.microsoft.sqlserver.jdbc. ↵
                   ↪ SQLServerDriver");
13
14             conn1 = DriverManager.getConnection(dbName, ↵
                   ↪ Environment.DB_USERID, Environment.DB_PWD);
15
```

```
16        Utility.log.info("Going for column...."+ ←
              ↪ resultColumns.get(j));
17        Statement statement1 = conn1.createStatement();
18        String queryString1 = "Select ←
              ↪ Sum(Cast(CHECKSUM(CAST(ISNULL(" + ←
              ↪ resultColumns.get(j) + "," + Config.MY_NULL ←
              ↪ + ") as varchar(max))) as Decimal(32,0))) ←
              ↪ as MySum from "  + dbSchema + "." + tblName ;
19
20        if (!targetClause.equals(""))
21            queryString1 += " Where " + targetClause;
22
23        Utility.log.info("SQL is: " + queryString1);
24        ResultSet rs1 = ←
              ↪ statement1.executeQuery(queryString1);
25
26        while (rs1.next())
27        {
28            myChksum.add(resultColumns.get(j) + ": " + ←
                  ↪ rs1.getString("MySum"));
29        }
30     }
31  } catch (Exception e)
32  {
33     e.printStackTrace();
34     Utility.ReportExpectedVsActual("Exception occurred" ←
              ↪ + e.getMessage(), "Failing test");
35  }
36  return myChksum;
37 }
38
39 public static void ←
       ↪ CompareChecksumsSourceSQLSpecificCols(String ←
       ↪ sourcDBName, String sourceSQL, List<String> ←
       ↪ sourceColumnsList, String targetDBName, String ←
       ↪ targetSchemaName, String targetTblName, String ←
       ↪ ignoreTargetCol, String targetClause)
40 {
41    Utility.log.info("targetTblName: " + targetTblName);
42
43    List<String> expChksum = new ArrayList<String>();
44    List<String> actChksum = new ArrayList<String>();
45
46    expChksum = ←
          ↪ Utility.GetTableChecksumSourceSQL(sourcDBName, ←
```

```
47          ↪ sourceSQL, sourceColumnsList);
47      actChksum = ←
            ↪ Utility.GetTableChecksumSpecificCols(targetDBName, ←
            ↪ targetSchemaName, targetTblName, ←
            ↪ sourceColumnsList, targetClause);
48
49      Utility.ReportExpectedVsActual("Column Count: " + ←
            ↪ String.valueOf(expChksum.size()), "Column Count: ←
            ↪ " + String.valueOf(actChksum.size()));
50
51      for(int g=0; g<expChksum.size();g++)
52      {
53          Utility.ReportExpectedVsActual(expChksum.get(g), ←
                ↪ actChksum.get(g));
54      }
55  }
56
57  public static void CheckForUniqueKeyMultipleCols(String ←
        ↪ dbName, String schemaName, String tblName, String ←
        ↪ uniqueKeyCols)
58  {
59      Utility.log.info("CheckForUniqueKeyMultipleCols - ←
            ↪ tblName: " + tblName);
60      int exp, act;
61      String sql = "Select count (*) From (select distinct " ←
            ↪ + uniqueKeyCols + " from " + schemaName + "." + ←
            ↪ tblName + " ) g";
62
63      exp = ←
            ↪ Utility.GetCountOfDistinctRecordsSourceSQL(dbName, ←
            ↪ sql);
64      act = Utility.GetCountOfRecords(dbName, schemaName, ←
            ↪ tblName);
65
66      Utility.ReportExpectedVsActual(String.valueOf(exp), ←
            ↪ String.valueOf(act));
67  }
```

Line 9: Loop through specific columns list.

Line 20: Add the condition if specified.

Line 46: Get the expected Sum of Checksum from the 'sourceSQL'.

Line 47: Get the actual Sum of Checksum for the same columns from the target table.

Line 61: Construct the SQL query for unique columns.

6.2.1 Tests 1 - 8 Fact Table

Create a new test factSales.java and add the code in Listing 6.25 to it.

Listing 6.25: Code for factSales.java Tests 1-8

```java
1  package autoDW;
2
3  import java.util.Arrays;
4  import java.util.List;
5
6  import org.junit.AfterClass;
7  import org.junit.Before;
8  import org.junit.BeforeClass;
9  import org.junit.FixMethodOrder;
10 import org.junit.runners.MethodSorters;
11 import org.junit.Rule;
12 import org.junit.Test;
13 import org.junit.rules.TestName;
14
15 @FixMethodOrder(MethodSorters.NAME_ASCENDING)
16
17 public class factSales {
18     @Rule public TestName name = new TestName();
19
20     public String sourceQueryString;
21
22     public String colmNames = ↵
           ↪ "DataSource,OrderID,UnitPrice,Quantity,Discount";
23     public List<String> ColmList = ↵
           ↪ Arrays.asList(colmNames.split(","));
24
25     @BeforeClass
26     public static void setUpBeforeClass() throws Exception {
27         Utility.SetupSummaryFile(Utility.GetName(Thread. ↵
             ↪ currentThread().getStackTrace()[1]. ↵
             ↪ getClassName()));
28     }
29
30     @Before
31     public void setUp() throws Exception {
32         Config.TestResult = Config.PASS;
33
34         sourceQueryString = "SELECT"+ Config.newLine;
```

```
35     sourceQueryString += "            'Table Order' as ↵
       ↪ DataSource, o.OrderID" + Config.newLine;
36     sourceQueryString += "           ,o.CustomerID, ↵
       ↪ od.ProductID, o.EmployeeID,o.OrderDate, ↵
       ↪ o.DispatchDate" + Config.newLine;
37     sourceQueryString += "           ,ISNULL(od.PriceMatch, ↵
       ↪ '" + Config.UNKNOWN_STRING +"') As PriceMatch" ↵
       ↪ + Config.newLine;
38     sourceQueryString += "           ,od.UnitPrice, ↵
       ↪ od.Quantity, od.Discount, od.GiftWrap" + ↵
       ↪ Config.newLine;
39     sourceQueryString += "FROM [dbo].[Orders] o" + ↵
       ↪ Config.newLine;
40     sourceQueryString += "INNER JOIN ↵
       ↪ [dbo].[OrderDetails] od on od.[OrderID] = ↵
       ↪ o.[OrderID]";
41
42     Utility.log.info("Source SQL is: " + ↵
       ↪ sourceQueryString);
43   }
44
45   @AfterClass
46   public static void tearDownAfterClass() throws ↵
     ↪ Exception {
47     Utility.SaveLogWithSummary(Utility.GetName(Thread. ↵
       ↪ currentThread().getStackTrace()[1]. ↵
       ↪ getClassName()));
48   }
49
50   @Test
51   public void _05_test_CheckForEmptySourceTables() {
52     Utility.log.info("***********  Starting Test: " + ↵
       ↪ name.getMethodName());
53
54     Utility.CheckForEmptyTable(Environment.DB_OPS_STAGING, ↵
       ↪ "dbo", "Orders");
55     Utility.CheckForEmptyTable(Environment.DB_OPS_STAGING, ↵
       ↪ "dbo", "OrderDetails");
56     Utility.ReportResultWithSummary(name.getMethodName());
57   }
58
59   @Test
60   public void _10_test_CheckForEmptyTargetTables() {
61     Utility.log.info("***********  Starting Test: " + ↵
       ↪ name.getMethodName());
```

```
62
63        Utility.CheckForEmptyTable(Environment.DB_OPS_DWS, ←
             ↪ "dbo", "factSales");
64        Utility.ReportResultWithSummary(name.getMethodName());
65    }
66
67    @Test
68    public void _15_test_CheckForUniqueKey() {
69        Utility.log.info("***********  Starting Test: " + ←
             ↪ name.getMethodName());
70
71        Utility.CheckForUniqueKeyMultipleCols( ←
             ↪ Environment.DB_OPS_DWS, "dbo", "factSales", ←
             ↪ "DataSource,OrderID,ProductKey");
72        Utility.ReportResultWithSummary(name.getMethodName());
73    }
74
75    @Test
76    public void _20_test_CheckForNullValues() {
77        Utility.log.info("***********  Starting Test: " + ←
             ↪ name.getMethodName());
78
79        Utility.CheckForNullValues(Environment.DB_OPS_DWS, ←
             ↪ "dbo", "factSales", "", "");
80        Utility.ReportResultWithSummary(name.getMethodName());
81    }
82
83    @Test
84    public void _25_test_CheckTableRecoundCounts() {
85        Utility.log.info("***********  Starting Test: " + ←
             ↪ name.getMethodName());
86
87        Utility.CompareCountOfRecordsSourceSQLWIthCondition( ←
             ↪ Environment.DB_OPS_STAGING, sourceQueryString, ←
             ↪ Environment.DB_OPS_DWS, "dbo", "factSales", ←
             ↪ "DataSource = 'Table Order'");
88        Utility.ReportResultWithSummary(name.getMethodName());
89    }
90
91    @Test
92    public void _30_test_CheckTableChecksums() {
93        Utility.log.info("***********  Starting Test: " + ←
             ↪ name.getMethodName());
94
95        Utility.CompareChecksumsSourceSQLSpecificCols( ←
```

```
        ↪ Environment.DB_OPS_STAGING, sourceQueryString, ←
        ↪ ColmList, Environment.DB_OPS_DWS, "dbo", ←
        ↪ "factSales", "factSalesKey,DateCreated", ←
        ↪ "DataSource = 'Table Order'");
96      Utility.ReportResultWithSummary(name.getMethodName());
97    }
98
99    @Test
100   public void _40_test_CheckSalesDetails_Random() {
101     Utility.log.info("***********    Starting Test: " + ←
        ↪ name.getMethodName());
102
103     Utility.CheckSalesDetails(sourceQueryString, "Table ←
        ↪ Order", 0, 0, 10);
104     Utility.ReportResultWithSummary(name.getMethodName());
105   }
106
107   @Test
108   public void _45_test_CheckSalesDetails_Specific() {
109     Utility.log.info("***********    Starting Test: " + ←
        ↪ name.getMethodName());
110
111     Utility.CheckSalesDetails(sourceQueryString, "Table ←
        ↪ Order", 4, 33, 1);
112     Utility.ReportResultWithSummary(name.getMethodName());
113   }
114 }
```

Line 103 and 111: Note the parameter value "Table Order" as we know in this case we are comparing data sourced from the 'Order' table. We will see more options for this parameter when we get data from other sources in a later chapter.

Don't execute these tests yet as we still need to define our function 'CheckSalesDetails'. We will add this to our Utility.java file instead of the factSales.java so that we can use it in other tests (as we will see in the later chapters).

CheckSalesDetails - Verifies sales details in the fact table and reports the outcome		
Input Parameters	*sourceQueryString*	SQL Query for the source recordset
	dataSource	Source of data which populated this row in the fact table
	orderID	OrderID to be verified
	productID	ProductID to be verified
Return Value	*void*	Returns nothing

```
1  public static void CheckSalesDetails(String ←
       ↪ sourceQueryString, String dataSource, int orderID, ←
       ↪ int productID, int howMany)
2  {
3          Utility.log.info("CheckSalesDetails....");
4
5          List<String> resultExpDataSource = new ←
              ↪ ArrayList<String>();
6          List<String> resultExpOrderID = new ←
              ↪ ArrayList<String>();
7          List<String> resultExpProductID = new ←
              ↪ ArrayList<String>();
8          List<String> resultExpCustomerID = new ←
              ↪ ArrayList<String>();
9          List<String> resultExpEmployeeID = new ←
              ↪ ArrayList<String>();
10         List<String> resultExpOrderDate = new ←
              ↪ ArrayList<String>();
11         List<String> resultExpDispatchDate = new ←
              ↪ ArrayList<String>();
12         List<String> resultExpPriceMatch = new ←
              ↪ ArrayList<String>();
13         List<String> resultExpUnitPrice = new ←
              ↪ ArrayList<String>();
14         List<String> resultExpQuantity = new ←
              ↪ ArrayList<String>();
15         List<String> resultExpDiscount = new ←
              ↪ ArrayList<String>();
16         List<String> resultExpGiftWrap = new ←
              ↪ ArrayList<String>();
17
18         List<String> resultSaveDataSource = new ←
              ↪ ArrayList<String>();
19         List<String> resultSaveOrderID = new ←
              ↪ ArrayList<String>();
20         List<String> resultSaveProductID = new ←
              ↪ ArrayList<String>();
21
22     //Find Expected Result
23     try
24     {
```

```
25    Class.forName("com.microsoft.sqlserver.jdbc. ↵
          ↪ SQLServerDriver");
26    Connection conn = DriverManager.getConnection( ↵
          ↪ Environment.DB_OPS_STAGING, ↵
          ↪ Environment.DB_USERID, Environment.DB_PWD);
27    Utility.log.info("DB connected..." + ↵
          ↪ Environment.DB_OPS_STAGING);
28    Statement statement = conn.createStatement();
29    String queryString = "with stage as (" + ↵
          ↪ Config.newLine;
30    queryString += sourceQueryString + Config.newLine;
31
32    if (orderID != 0)
33    {
34        Utility.log.info("Going for specific DataSource: ↵
              ↪ " + dataSource + "  orderID: " + orderID + ↵
              ↪ "  productID: " + productID);
35        queryString += ") select TOP 1 * from stage" + ↵
              ↪ Config.newLine;
36        queryString += "Where DataSource = '" + ↵
              ↪ dataSource + "'" + Config.newLine;
37        queryString += "And OrderID = " + orderID + ↵
              ↪ Config.newLine;
38        queryString += "And ProductID = " + productID;
39    }
40    else
41    {
42        queryString += ") Select TOP " + howMany + ↵
              ↪ Config.newLine;
43        queryString += "DataSource, OrderID, ProductID, ↵
              ↪ CustomerID, EmployeeID," + Config.newLine;
44        queryString += "OrderDate, DispatchDate, ↵
              ↪ PriceMatch," + Config.newLine;
45        queryString += "UnitPrice, Quantity, Discount, ↵
              ↪ GiftWrap" + Config.newLine;
46        queryString += "From stage" + Config.newLine;
47        queryString += "Order by NEWID()";
48    }
49
50    Utility.log.info("SQL is: " + queryString);
51
52    ResultSet rs = statement.executeQuery(queryString);
53
54    while (rs.next())
55    {
```

```
56          //Save for later use
57          resultSaveDataSource.add(rs.getString("DataSource"));
58          resultSaveOrderID.add(rs.getString("OrderID"));
59          resultSaveProductID.add(rs.getString("ProductID"));
60
61          resultExpDataSource.add("DataSource ==> " + ↵
               ↪ rs.getString("DataSource"));
62          resultExpOrderID.add("OrderID ==> " + ↵
               ↪ rs.getString("OrderID"));
63          resultExpProductID.add("ProductID ==> " + ↵
               ↪ rs.getString("ProductID"));
64          resultExpCustomerID.add("CustomerID ==> " + ↵
               ↪ rs.getString("CustomerID"));
65          resultExpEmployeeID.add("EmployeeID ==> " + ↵
               ↪ rs.getString("EmployeeID"));
66          resultExpOrderDate.add("OrderDate ==> " + ↵
               ↪ rs.getString("OrderDate").substring(0, 10));
67          resultExpDispatchDate.add("DispatchDate ==> " + ↵
               ↪ rs.getString("DispatchDate").substring(0, ↵
               ↪ 10));
68          resultExpPriceMatch.add("PriceMatch ==> " + ↵
               ↪ rs.getString("PriceMatch"));
69          resultExpUnitPrice.add("UnitPrice ==> " + ↵
               ↪ rs.getString("UnitPrice"));
70          resultExpQuantity.add("Quantity ==> " + ↵
               ↪ rs.getString("Quantity"));
71          resultExpDiscount.add("Discount ==> " + ↵
               ↪ rs.getString("Discount"));
72          resultExpGiftWrap.add("GiftWrap ==> " + ↵
               ↪ rs.getString("GiftWrap"));
73      }
74  } catch (Exception e)
75  {
76      e.printStackTrace();
77      Utility.ReportExpectedVsActual("Exception occurred. ↵
           ↪ " + e.getMessage(), "Failing test");
78  }
79
80  if (resultExpDataSource.size()==0)
81      Utility.ReportExpectedVsActual("Something wrong as ↵
           ↪ no data found", "Failing test");
82
83  for(int j=0; j<howMany;j++)
84  {
```

```
85    Utility.log.info("Row....." + j + "          ↵
         ↪ DataSource....." + resultExpDataSource.get(j) );
86
87    //Find Actual Result
88    try
89    {
90        List<String> resultActDataSource = new ↵
             ↪ ArrayList<String>();
91        List<String> resultActOrderID = new ↵
             ↪ ArrayList<String>();
92        List<String> resultActProductID = new ↵
             ↪ ArrayList<String>();
93        List<String> resultActCustomerID = new ↵
             ↪ ArrayList<String>();
94        List<String> resultActEmployeeID = new ↵
             ↪ ArrayList<String>();
95        List<String> resultActOrderDate = new ↵
             ↪ ArrayList<String>();
96        List<String> resultActDispatchDate = new ↵
             ↪ ArrayList<String>();
97        List<String> resultActPriceMatch = new ↵
             ↪ ArrayList<String>();
98        List<String> resultActUnitPrice = new ↵
             ↪ ArrayList<String>();
99        List<String> resultActQuantity = new ↵
             ↪ ArrayList<String>();
100       List<String> resultActDiscount = new ↵
             ↪ ArrayList<String>();
101       List<String> resultActGiftWrap = new ↵
             ↪ ArrayList<String>();
102
103       Class.forName("com.microsoft.sqlserver.jdbc. ↵
             ↪ SQLServerDriver");
104       Connection conn = DriverManager.getConnection( ↵
             ↪ Environment.DB_OPS_DWS, ↵
             ↪ Environment.DB_USERID, Environment.DB_PWD);
105       Utility.log.info("DB connected..." + ↵
             ↪ Environment.DB_OPS_DWS);
106       Statement statement = conn.createStatement();
107       String queryString = "SELECT DataSource " + ↵
             ↪ Config.newLine;
108       queryString += "          ,s.OrderID, c.CustomerID, ↵
             ↪ p.ProductID, e.EmployeeID" + Config.newLine;
109       queryString += "          ,dtOrd.FullDate As ↵
             ↪ OrderDate, dtShp.FullDate As DispatchDate" ↵
```

```
                     ↪ + Config.newLine;
110      queryString += "          ,pm.PriceMatchDescription ↩
                     ↪ As PriceMatch, s.UnitPrice" + Config.newLine;
111      queryString += "          ,s.Quantity ,s.Discount, ↩
                     ↪ yn.YesNoDescription As GiftWrap" + ↩
                     ↪ Config.newLine;
112      queryString += "FROM [dbo].[factSales] s" + ↩
                     ↪ Config.newLine;
113      queryString += "LEFT JOIN [dbo].[dimCustomer] c ↩
                     ↪ on c.CustomerKey = s.CustomerKey " + ↩
                     ↪ Config.newLine;
114      queryString += "LEFT JOIN [dbo].[dimProduct] p ↩
                     ↪ on p.ProductKey = s.ProductKey" + ↩
                     ↪ Config.newLine;
115      queryString += "LEFT JOIN [dbo].[dimEmployee] e ↩
                     ↪ on e.EmployeeKey = s.EmployeeKey" + ↩
                     ↪ Config.newLine;
116      queryString += "LEFT JOIN [dbo].[dimDate] dtOrd ↩
                     ↪ on dtOrd.DateKey = s.OrderDateKey" + ↩
                     ↪ Config.newLine;
117      queryString += "LEFT JOIN [dbo].[dimDate] dtShp ↩
                     ↪ on dtShp.DateKey = s.DispatchDateKey" + ↩
                     ↪ Config.newLine;
118      queryString += "LEFT JOIN [dbo].[dimYesNo] yn on ↩
                     ↪ yn.YesNoKey = s.GiftWrapYesNoKey" + ↩
                     ↪ Config.newLine;
119      queryString += "LEFT JOIN [dbo].[dimPriceMatch] ↩
                     ↪ pm on pm.PriceMatchKey = s.PriceMatchKey" + ↩
                     ↪ Config.newLine;
120      queryString += "Where DataSource = '" + ↩
                     ↪ resultSaveDataSource.get(j) + "'" + ↩
                     ↪ Config.newLine;
121      queryString += "And OrderID = " + ↩
                     ↪ resultSaveOrderID.get(j) + Config.newLine;
122      queryString += "And ProductID = " + ↩
                     ↪ resultSaveProductID.get(j);
123
124      Utility.log.info("SQL is: " + queryString);
125
126      ResultSet rs = statement.executeQuery(queryString);
127
128      while (rs.next())
129      {
130          resultActDataSource.add("DataSource ==> " + ↩
                     ↪ rs.getString("DataSource"));
```

```
131        resultActOrderID.add("OrderID ==> " + ↵
              ↪ rs.getString("OrderID"));
132        resultActProductID.add("ProductID ==> " + ↵
              ↪ rs.getString("ProductID"));
133        resultActCustomerID.add("CustomerID ==> " + ↵
              ↪ rs.getString("CustomerID"));
134        resultActEmployeeID.add("EmployeeID ==> " + ↵
              ↪ rs.getString("EmployeeID"));
135        resultActOrderDate.add("OrderDate ==> " + ↵
              ↪ rs.getString("OrderDate"));
136        resultActDispatchDate.add("DispatchDate ==> " ↵
              ↪ + rs.getString("DispatchDate"));
137        resultActPriceMatch.add("PriceMatch ==> " + ↵
              ↪ rs.getString("PriceMatch"));
138        resultActUnitPrice.add("UnitPrice ==> " + ↵
              ↪ rs.getString("UnitPrice"));
139        resultActQuantity.add("Quantity ==> " + ↵
              ↪ rs.getString("Quantity"));
140        resultActDiscount.add("Discount ==> " + ↵
              ↪ rs.getString("Discount"));
141        resultActGiftWrap.add("GiftWrap ==> " + ↵
              ↪ rs.getString("GiftWrap"));
142      }
143
144      Utility.ReportExpectedVsActual( ↵
              ↪ resultExpDataSource.get(j), ↵
              ↪ resultActDataSource.get(0));
145      Utility.ReportExpectedVsActual( ↵
              ↪ resultExpOrderID.get(j), ↵
              ↪ resultActOrderID.get(0));
146      Utility.ReportExpectedVsActual( ↵
              ↪ resultExpProductID.get(j), ↵
              ↪ resultActProductID.get(0));
147      Utility.ReportExpectedVsActual( ↵
              ↪ resultExpCustomerID.get(j), ↵
              ↪ resultActCustomerID.get(0));
148      Utility.ReportExpectedVsActual( ↵
              ↪ resultExpEmployeeID.get(j), ↵
              ↪ resultActEmployeeID.get(0));
149      Utility.ReportExpectedVsActual( ↵
              ↪ resultExpOrderDate.get(j), ↵
              ↪ resultActOrderDate.get(0));
150      Utility.ReportExpectedVsActual( ↵
              ↪ resultExpDispatchDate.get(j), ↵
              ↪ resultActDispatchDate.get(0));
```

```
151        Utility.ReportExpectedVsActual( ↵
           ↪ resultExpPriceMatch.get(j), ↵
           ↪ resultActPriceMatch.get(0));
152        Utility.ReportExpectedVsActual( ↵
           ↪ resultExpUnitPrice.get(j), ↵
           ↪ resultActUnitPrice.get(0));
153        Utility.ReportExpectedVsActual( ↵
           ↪ resultExpQuantity.get(j), ↵
           ↪ resultActQuantity.get(0));
154        Utility.ReportExpectedVsActual( ↵
           ↪ resultExpDiscount.get(j), ↵
           ↪ resultActDiscount.get(0));
155        Utility.ReportExpectedVsActual( ↵
           ↪ resultExpGiftWrap.get(j), ↵
           ↪ resultActGiftWrap.get(0));
156      } catch (Exception e)
157      {
158        e.printStackTrace();
159        Utility.ReportExpectedVsActual("Exception ↵
           ↪ occurred. " + e.getMessage(), "Failing test");
160      }
161    }
162 }
```

Line 120 - 122: Use saved values to fetch record.

Now you should be able to execute the fact tests we have written so far. Figure 6.15 shows the Result Summary file of the factSales test execution.

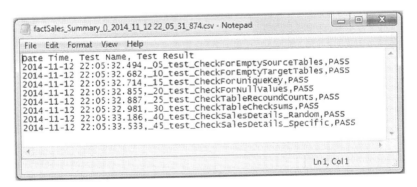

Figure 6.15: Result Summary - factSales Tests 1 to 8

6.2.2   Test 9 - Orphaned Keys

The fact table contains several keys that point to various dimension tables in the data warehouse. This test checks that none of the keys in the fact table are orphaned i.e.

store a key value that doesn't exist in the dimension table.

First of all let's add a new function ReportOrphanedKeys to our Utility.java file.

ReportOrphanedKeys - Reports if there are any orphaned keys in the fact table		
Input Parameters	*dbName*	Name of the database
	tblFact	Fact table name
	colFact	Fact column name
	tblDim	Dimension table name
	colDim	Dimension column name
	ignoreFactKeyValue	Keys to be ignored in the fact table
Return Value	*true or false*	Returns true if the fact table contains orphaned values

Listing 6.27: Utility.java - Code for ReportOrphanedKeys

```
1  public static boolean ReportOrphanedKeys(String dbName,
       String tblFact, String colFact, String tblDim,
       String colDim, String ignoreFactKeyValue)
2  {
3      Utility.log.info("ReportOrphanedKeys for... " +
          tblFact + " to " + tblDim);
4
5      List<String> myVals = new ArrayList<String>();
6
7      boolean res = true;
8
9      try
10     {
11         Connection conn1;
12         Class.forName("com.microsoft.sqlserver.jdbc.
              SQLServerDriver");
13
14         conn1 = DriverManager.getConnection(dbName,
              Environment.DB_USERID, Environment.DB_PWD);
15
16         Statement statement1 = conn1.createStatement();
17         String queryString1 = "Select distinct ft." +
              colFact + " as vals From " + tblFact + " ft" +
              Config.newLine;
18         queryString1 += "FULL OUTER JOIN " + tblDim + " dm
              ON " + "ft." + colFact + " = dm." + colDim +
```

```
                        ↪ Config.newLine;
19          queryString1 += "Where dm." + colDim + " is NULL ";
20
21          if (!ignoreFactKeyValue.equals(""))
22              queryString1 += "and ft." + colFact + " <> " + ↩
                    ↪ ignoreFactKeyValue;
23
24          Utility.log.info("SQL is: " + queryString1);
25          ResultSet rs1 = statement1.executeQuery(queryString1);
26
27          while (rs1.next())
28          {
29              myVals.add(rs1.getString("vals"));
30          }
31
32          if (myVals.size() != 0)
33          {
34              Utility.log.error("Reporting Orphaned values in ↩
                    ↪ " + tblFact + " to " + tblDim);
35
36              for(int j=0; j<myVals.size();j++)
37              {
38                  Utility.log.error(colDim + ": " + ↩
                        ↪ myVals.get(j));
39              }
40
41              Utility.ReportExpectedVsActual("No Orphaned ↩
                    ↪ values", "Orphaned values. Failing test");
42              res = true;
43          }
44          else
45          {
46              Utility.ReportExpectedVsActual("No Orphaned ↩
                    ↪ values", "No Orphaned values");
47              res = false;
48          }
49      } catch (Exception e)
50      {
51          e.printStackTrace();
52          Utility.ReportExpectedVsActual("Exception occurred" ↩
                ↪ + e.getMessage(), "Failing test");
53      }
54
55      return res;
56 }
```

Line 17: Construct the SQL Query to get orphaned keys.
Line 21: If provided, add condition to ignore keys.
Line 32: If exist, report orphaned keys.
Line 44: Report success otherwise.

Now add a new test to the factSales.java file as shown in Listing 6.28.

Listing 6.28: Code for _50_test_OrphanedFactKeys

```
1  @Test
2  public void _50_test_OrphanedFactKeys()
3  {
4      Utility.log.info("***********   Starting Test: " +
           name.getMethodName());
5
6      Utility.ReportOrphanedKeys(Environment.DB_OPS_DWS,
           "dbo.factSales", "CustomerKey",
           "dbo.dimCustomer", "CustomerKey", "");
7      Utility.ReportOrphanedKeys(Environment.DB_OPS_DWS,
           "dbo.factSales", "ProductKey", "dbo.dimProduct",
           "ProductKey", "");
8      Utility.ReportOrphanedKeys(Environment.DB_OPS_DWS,
           "dbo.factSales", "EmployeeKey",
           "dbo.dimEmployee", "EmployeeKey", "");
9      Utility.ReportOrphanedKeys(Environment.DB_OPS_DWS,
           "dbo.factSales", "OrderDateKey", "dbo.dimDate",
           "DateKey", "");
10     Utility.ReportOrphanedKeys(Environment.DB_OPS_DWS,
           "dbo.factSales", "DispatchDateKey",
           "dbo.dimDate", "DateKey", "");
11     Utility.ReportOrphanedKeys(Environment.DB_OPS_DWS,
           "dbo.factSales", "PriceMatchKey",
           "dbo.dimPriceMatch", "PriceMatchKey", "");
12     Utility.ReportOrphanedKeys(Environment.DB_OPS_DWS,
           "dbo.factSales", "GiftWrapYesNoKey",
           "dbo.dimYesNo", "YesNoKey", "");
13
14     Utility.ReportResultWithSummary(name.getMethodName());
15 }
```

Line 6 - 12: Call 'ReportOrphanedKeys' function for each reference to the dimension table as per the Data Mapping document.

Automated Data Warehouse Testing

Execute the test and you will see a Console output as shown in Figure 6.16.

```
Problems @ Javadoc Declaration Console
<terminated> Rerun autoDW.factSales._50_test_OrphanedFactKeys [JUnit] C:\Program Files\Java\jre7\bin\javaw.exe (20 Feb 2015 09:12:29)
09:12:31.176 [main] INFO  MyLogger - ReportOrphanedKeys for... dbo.factSales to dbo.dimPriceMatch
09:12:31.185 [main] INFO  MyLogger - SQL is: Select distinct ft.PriceMatchKey as vals From dbo.factSales ft
FULL OUTER JOIN dbo.dimPriceMatch dm ON ft.PriceMatchKey = dm.PriceMatchKey
Where dm.PriceMatchKey is NULL
09:12:31.191 [main] INFO  MyLogger - [Expected:] No Orphaned values    [Actual:] No Orphaned values    [Step Passed]
09:12:31.191 [main] INFO  MyLogger - ReportOrphanedKeys for... dbo.factSales to dbo.dimYesNo
09:12:31.198 [main] INFO  MyLogger - SQL is: Select distinct ft.GiftWrapYesNoKey as vals From dbo.factSales ft
FULL OUTER JOIN dbo.dimYesNo dm ON ft.GiftWrapYesNoKey = dm.YesNoKey
Where dm.YesNoKey is NULL
09:12:31.202 [main] INFO  MyLogger - [Expected:] No Orphaned values    [Actual:] No Orphaned values    [Step Passed]
09:12:31.202 [main] INFO  MyLogger - Reporting result....
09:12:31.203 [main] INFO  MyLogger - Test Passed.
09:12:31.206 [main] INFO  MyLogger - Result File: factSales_(PASS)_2015_02_20 09_12_31_206.csv
```

Figure 6.16: Console Output - factSales - Check For Orphaned Keys

6.2.3 Test 10 - Check If All Values Unknown

This is a test that checks to see if all the values in a column in the fact table point to the 'Unknown Key'. This test is useful if something has gone wrong in the data transformation and all the values in the fact table for a particular column map to the 'Unknown Key'. So how do we do it?

First of all we need to add a new function 'ReportIfAllTableColumnUnknown' to our Utility.java file.

ReportIfAllTableColumnUnknown - Reports if all the values of a column point to the 'Unknown Key'		
Input Parameters	dbName	Name of the database
	dbSchema	Name of the schema
	tblName	Name of the table
	ignoreColumn	Columns to be ignored
	targetClause	Condition to be applied
Return Value	void	Returns nothing

Listing 6.29: Utility.java Code for ReportIfAllTableColumnUnknown

```
1  public static void ReportIfAllTableColumnUnknown(String ↵
       ↪ dbName, String dbSchema, String tblName, String ↵
       ↪ ignoreColumn, String targetClause)
2  {
3      Utility.log.info("ReportIfAllTableColumn_Unknown... ");
4
```

Chapter 6   251

```
5     List<String> resultColumns = new ArrayList<String>();
6     List<String> resultColumnsDataType = new ↵
        ↪ ArrayList<String>();
7
8     List<String> ignoreColmList = ↵
        ↪ Arrays.asList(ignoreColumn.split(","));
9
10    try
11    {
12        Connection conn;
13        Class.forName("com.microsoft.sqlserver.jdbc. ↵
            ↪ SQLServerDriver");
14
15        conn = DriverManager.getConnection(dbName, ↵
            ↪ Environment.DB_USERID, Environment.DB_PWD);
16
17        Utility.log.info("DB connected: " + dbName);
18        Statement statement = conn.createStatement();
19        String queryString = "select COLUMN_NAME, DATA_TYPE ↵
            ↪ from information_schema.columns where ↵
            ↪ table_name = '" + tblName + "'";
20
21        //Utility.log.info("SQL is: " + queryString);
22        ResultSet rs = statement.executeQuery(queryString);
23
24        while (rs.next())
25        {
26            if (ignoreColmList.contains( ↵
                ↪ rs.getString("COLUMN_NAME")))
27                Utility.log.info("**** Ignoring column **** : ↵
                    ↪ " + rs.getString("COLUMN_NAME"));
28            else
29            {
30                if (rs.getString("DATA_TYPE").equals("int") | ↵
                    ↪ rs.getString("DATA_TYPE").equals("varchar"))
31                {
32                    resultColumns.add(rs.getString( ↵
                        ↪ "COLUMN_NAME"));
33                    resultColumnsDataType.add(rs.getString( ↵
                        ↪ "DATA_TYPE"));
34                }
35                else
36                    Utility.log.info("**** Skipping column ↵
                        ↪ **** : " + ↵
                        ↪ rs.getString("COLUMN_NAME") + "  Data ↵
```

```
                                    ↪ Type: " + rs.getString("DATA_TYPE"));
37        }
38     }
39
40     if (resultColumns.size()== 0)
41     {
42         Utility.ReportExpectedVsActual("Something wrong ↵
                ↪ as no data found", "Failing test");
43     }
44
45     for(int j=0; j<resultColumns.size();j++)
46     {
47         String tmp = "";
48         Connection conn1;
49         Class.forName("com.microsoft.sqlserver.jdbc. ↵
                ↪ SQLServerDriver");
50
51         conn1 = DriverManager.getConnection(dbName, ↵
                ↪ Environment.DB_USERID, Environment.DB_PWD);
52
53         Statement statement1 = conn1.createStatement();
54         String queryString1 = "select Count(*) as ↵
                ↪ CountUnknown from "  + dbSchema + "." + ↵
                ↪ tblName ;
55         if (resultColumnsDataType.get(j).equals("int"))
56         {
57             queryString1 += " Where " + ↵
                    ↪ resultColumns.get(j) + " = -1";
58             tmp =  " = -1";
59         }
60         else if (resultColumnsDataType.get(j). ↵
                ↪ equals("varchar"))
61         {
62             queryString1 += " Where " + ↵
                    ↪ resultColumns.get(j) + " = 'Unknown'";
63             tmp =  " = 'Unknown'";
64         }
65
66         if (!targetClause.equals(""))
67             queryString1 += " And " + targetClause;
68
69         Utility.log.info("SQL is: " + queryString1);
70         ResultSet rs1 = ↵
                ↪ statement1.executeQuery(queryString1);
71
```

```
72          int cntUnknown = -9;
73          int cntAll = -9;
74
75          while (rs1.next())
76          {
77              cntUnknown = rs1.getInt("CountUnknown");
78          }
79
80          queryString1 = "select Count(*) as CountAll from ↵
                ↪ "  + dbSchema + "." + tblName ;
81
82          if (!targetClause.equals(""))
83              queryString1 += "Where " + targetClause;
84
85          Utility.log.info("SQL is: " + queryString1);
86          rs1 = statement1.executeQuery(queryString1);
87
88          while (rs1.next())
89          {
90              cntAll = rs1.getInt("CountAll");
91          }
92
93          if (cntAll == cntUnknown)
94              Utility.ReportExpectedVsActual("Seems all ↵
                    ↪ values Unknown (-1): " + ↵
                    ↪ resultColumns.get(j), "Failing test");
95          else
96              Utility.log.info("Column OK: " + ↵
                    ↪ resultColumns.get(j) + "    Value ↵
                    ↪ checked: " + tmp);
97      }
98  } catch (Exception e)
99  {
100     e.printStackTrace();
101     Utility.ReportExpectedVsActual("Exception occurred" ↵
            ↪ + e.getMessage(), "Failing test");
102 }
103 }
```

Line 8: Convert comma separated string of 'columns to be ignored' to a list.
Line 19: Get column name and data type from the information_schema.
Line 26: Ignore the column if it is in the ignore list.
Line 30: If data type is int or varchar then add it to the list.
Line 55: If data type is int then check if it equals -1.
Line 60: If data type is varchar then check if it equals 'Unknown'.

Line 66: If provided, add any additional clause.

Line 77: Get count of unknowns.

Line 90: Get count of all records.

Line 93: If count of unknowns equals the count of all records then report an error.

Now add a new test to the factSales.java file as shown in Listing 6.30.

Listing 6.30: factSales.java - Code for _55_test_IfAllColumnUnknown

```
1  @Test
2  public void _55_test_IfAllColumnUnknown() {
3      Utility.log.info("***********   Starting Test: " + ←
             ↪ name.getMethodName());
4
5      Utility.ReportIfAllTableColumnUnknown( ←
             ↪ Environment.DB_OPS_DWS, "dbo", "factSales", ←
             ↪ "factSalesKey,DataSource,OrderID, ←
             ↪ UnitPrice,Quantity,Discount", "");
6
7      Utility.ReportResultWithSummary(name.getMethodName());
8  }
```

Execute the test and you will see a Console output as shown in Figure 6.17.

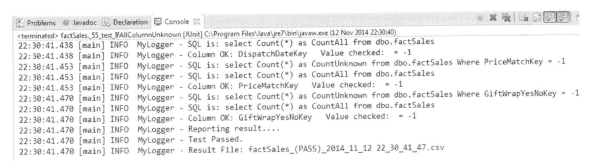

Figure 6.17: Console Output - factSales - Check If All Column Unknown

6.2.4 Test 11 - Comparing Group By Counts

Fact tables are typically very large and in a previous section we saw how to retrieve and verify a random set of records. To provide us with more confidence in our automated testing we can include this new test that compares counts by grouping records in the source and target tables. In our case, let's compare the counts between the source and target tables when we group them by 'ProductID'. Here is how we do it.

Add a new test to the factSales.java file as shown in Listing 6.31.

Listing 6.31: Code for _60_test_TableRecoundCountsByProductID

```
1   import java.sql.Connection;
2   import java.sql.DriverManager;
3   import java.sql.ResultSet;
4   import java.sql.Statement;
5   import java.util.ArrayList;
6
7   @Test
8   public void _60_test_TableRecoundCountsByProductID()
9   {
10      Utility.log.info("***********   Starting Test: " + ↵
        ↪ name.getMethodName());
11
12      List<String> resultExpProductIDCount = new ↵
        ↪ ArrayList<String>();
13      List<String> resultActProductIDCount = new ↵
        ↪ ArrayList<String>();
14
15      //Find Expected Result1
16      try
17      {
18          Class.forName("com.microsoft.sqlserver.jdbc. ↵
            ↪ SQLServerDriver");
19          Connection conn = DriverManager.getConnection( ↵
            ↪ Environment.DB_OPS_STAGING, ↵
            ↪ Environment.DB_USERID, Environment.DB_PWD);
20          Utility.log.info("DB connected..." + ↵
            ↪ Environment.DB_OPS_STAGING);
21          Statement statement = conn.createStatement();
22
23          String queryString = "with stage as (" + ↵
            ↪ Config.newLine;
24          queryString += sourceQueryString + Config.newLine;
25          queryString += ") select ProductID, COUNT(*) as ↵
            ↪ Kount ";
26          queryString += "from stage " + Config.newLine;
27          queryString += "Group by ProductID" + ↵
            ↪ Config.newLine;
28          queryString += "Order by ProductID";
29
30          Utility.log.info("SQL is: " + queryString);
```

```
31
32      ResultSet rs = statement.executeQuery(queryString);
33
34      while (rs.next())
35      {
36          resultExpProductIDCount.add("ProductID: " + ↵
            ↪ rs.getString("ProductID") + "     Count: " + ↵
            ↪ rs.getString("Kount"));
37      }
38  } catch (Exception e)
39  {
40      e.printStackTrace();
41      Utility.ReportExpectedVsActual("Exception occurred. ↵
        ↪ " + e.getMessage(), "Failing test");
42  }
43
44  //Find Actual Result
45  try
46  {
47      Class.forName("com.microsoft.sqlserver.jdbc. ↵
        ↪ SQLServerDriver");
48      Connection conn = DriverManager.getConnection( ↵
        ↪ Environment.DB_OPS_DWS, Environment.DB_USERID, ↵
        ↪ Environment.DB_PWD);
49      Utility.log.info("DB connected..." + ↵
        ↪ Environment.DB_OPS_DWS);
50      Statement statement = conn.createStatement();
51
52      String queryString = "SELECT ProductID, COUNT(*) as ↵
        ↪ Kount" + Config.newLine;
53      queryString += "FROM [dbo].[factSales] ft" + ↵
        ↪ Config.newLine;
54      queryString += "Left Join dbo.dimProduct pd on ↵
        ↪ pd.ProductKey = ft.ProductKey " + Config.newLine;
55      queryString += "where DataSource = 'Table Order' " ↵
        ↪ + Config.newLine;
56      queryString += "Group by ProductID " + ↵
        ↪ Config.newLine;
57      queryString += "Order by ProductID";
58
59      Utility.log.info("SQL is: " + queryString);
60      ResultSet rs = statement.executeQuery(queryString);
61      while (rs.next())
62      {
63          resultActProductIDCount.add("ProductID: " + ↵
```

```
        ↪ rs.getString("ProductID") + "    Count: " + ↵
        ↪ rs.getString("Kount"));
64        }
65     } catch (Exception e)
66     {
67        e.printStackTrace();
68        Utility.ReportExpectedVsActual("Exception occurred. ↵
           ↪ " + e.getMessage(), "Failing test");
69     }
70
71     Utility.log.info("Verifying Counts.....");
72     if (resultExpProductIDCount.size() != ↵
        ↪ resultActProductIDCount.size())
73     {
74        Utility.log.error("ProductIDCount Size mismatch");
75        Utility.ReportExpectedVsActual( ↵
           ↪ String.valueOf(resultExpProductIDCount.size()), ↵
           ↪ String.valueOf(resultActProductIDCount.size()));
76     }
77
78     for(int j=0; j<resultExpProductIDCount.size();j++)
79     {
80        Utility.ReportExpectedVsActual( ↵
           ↪ resultExpProductIDCount.get(j), ↵
           ↪ resultActProductIDCount.get(j));
81     }
82
83     Utility.ReportResultWithSummary(name.getMethodName());
84 }
```

Line 27: Get expected counts grouped by 'ProductID'.
Line 56: Get actual counts grouped by 'ProductID'.
Line 80: Compare expected and actual counts and report the outcome.

Execute the test and you will see a Console output as shown in 6.18

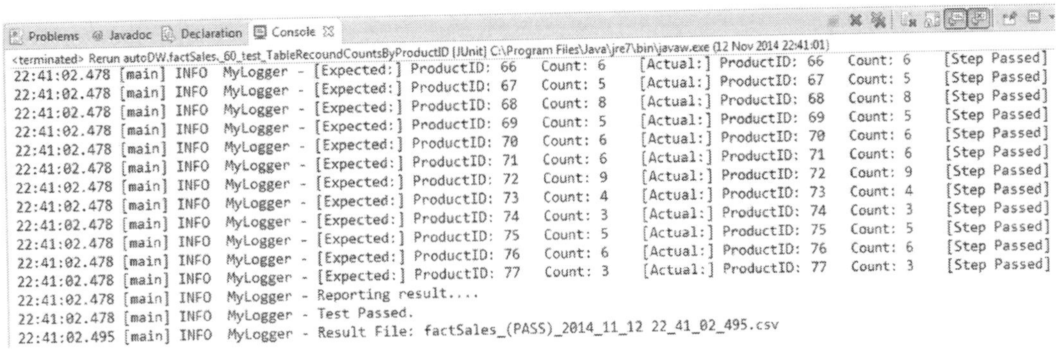

Figure 6.18: Console Output - factSales - Comparing Group By Counts

You can create similar tests that compare counts grouped by EmployeeID, OrderDate etc.

6.3 Test Runner

In the earlier chapters we learnt how to execute an individual test (by right clicking on the test and then selecting Run As ⇒ JUnit), or execute all the tests in a class (by right clicking on the class and then selecting Run As ⇒ JUnit). However, sometimes you may need to execute a group of tests in a class e.g. you want to execute all the tests that verify sales figures. This requirement is more likely when you are testing fact tables where you have a lot of tests in a class and you want to execute them in groups rather than executing them individually or all at once. Alternatively you might want to run a number of tests together e.g. sanity tests.

Let's say in our example that we want to execute tests _40_test_CheckSalesDetails_- Random and _45_test_CheckSalesDetails_Specific together. So how do we do it? We need to create an 'Interface'.

- Create a new interface by right clicking the 'src' folder and selecting New ⇒ Interface

- Type autoDWInterfaces in the 'Package' edit box as shown in Figure 6.19

- Type ifactSales in the 'Name' edit box

- Click the Finish button

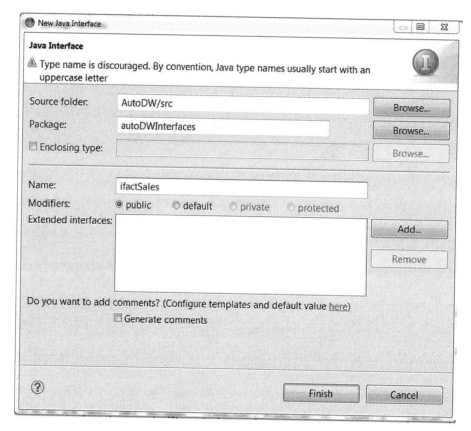

Figure 6.19: Adding New Interface

You will see that Listing 6.32 code has been added to the ifactSales.java file. Leave it as it is.

Listing 6.32: Code for ifactSales.java

```
1  package autoDWInterfaces;
2
3  public interface ifactSales {
4
5  }
```

Now add two new import statements to the factSales.java file as shown in Listing 6.33 to support the additional functionality.

Listing 6.33: Code for factSales.java

```
1  import org.junit.experimental.categories.Category;
2  import autoDWInterfaces.ifactSales;
```

Before each test you want to execute as a group in the factSales.java file, add a statement
'@Category(ifactSales.class)'. In our case, we want to execute tests _40_test_Check-
SalesDetails_Random and _45_test_CheckSalesDetails_Specific together as a group. The
updated code with these new statements is shown in Listing 6.34.

Listing 6.34: Code for factSales.java

```
1  @Category ( ifactSales . class )
2  @Test
3  public void _40_test_CheckSalesDetails_Random ()
4  {
5      Utility . log . info ("************    Starting Test: " + ←
          ↪ name . getMethodName ());
6
7      Utility . CheckSalesDetails ( sourceQueryString , "Table ←
          ↪ Order", 0, 0, 10);
8
9      Utility . ReportResultWithSummary ( name . getMethodName ());
10 }
11
12 @Category ( ifactSales . class )
13 @Test
14 public void _45_test_CheckSalesDetails_Specific ()
15 {
16     Utility . log . info ("************    Starting Test: " + ←
          ↪ name . getMethodName ());
17
18     Utility . CheckSalesDetails ( sourceQueryString , "Table ←
          ↪ Order", 4, 33, 1);
19
20     Utility . ReportResultWithSummary ( name . getMethodName ());
21 }
```

Line 1 and 12: Add statements to define categories.

Now add a new JUnit test class testRunner.java as shown in Figure 6.20.

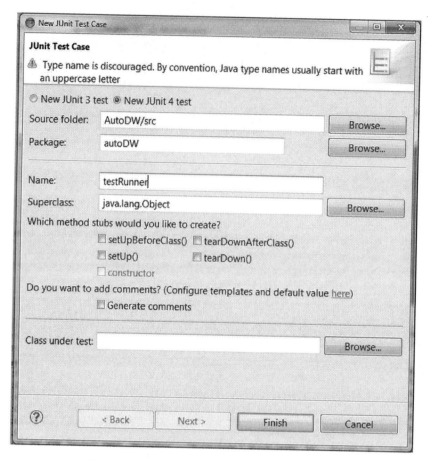

Figure 6.20: Adding testRunner.java

Add Listing 6.35 code to the testRunner.java file.

Listing 6.35: Code for testRunner.java

```
1  package autoDW;
2
3  import org.junit.experimental.categories.Categories;
4  import org.junit.experimental.categories.Categories. ↵
       ↪ IncludeCategory;
5  import org.junit.runner.RunWith;
6  import org.junit.runners.Suite.SuiteClasses;
7  import autoDWInterfaces.ifactSales;
8
9  @RunWith(Categories.class)
10 @IncludeCategory(ifactSales.class)
11 @SuiteClasses({factSales.class})
12
13 public class testRunner {
14
```

Line 9: Instructs JUnit to invoke the class it references to run the tests in that class.
Line 10: Categories runner runs the classes and methods that are annotated with the category given with the @IncludeCategory.
Line 11: The SuiteClasses specifies the classes to be run when a class annotated with @RunWith is executed (in our case Categories.class).

Right click on testRunner and select Run As ⇒ Junit Test. You will see that tests _40_-test_CheckSalesDetails_Random and _45_test_CheckSalesDetails_Specific are executed. Figure 6.21 shows the Result Summary file of the test execution.

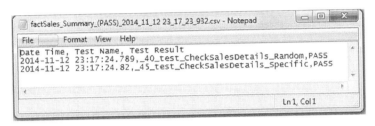

Figure 6.21: Test Runner in Action

Similarly you can create other test categories to execute them as a suite.

6.4   Automation Framework - Adding More Features

Before we end this chapter, let's add some more features to our Automation Framework. So here we go...

6.4.1   Logging System Version

In a fast moving development environment you may end up getting one build a day for testing. As you repeatedly perform the automated testing, one thing is for certain, you will produce too many log files.

Usually every system build released to a QA team has a version number. I have found it very useful to log the version number of the system under test as part of the test results. This is particularly helpful when you are investigating issues and during an audit. How you determine this version number will depend upon the practice used in your organisation - it might be held in a table or a file or some other means. In our example a table exists in both the staging and data warehouse schemas called 'VersionInfo'. We assume that the table gets updated with the latest release number as new builds are deployed into the test environment. So let's see how we can log the version number as part of our test results.

First of all let's add the following two new functions to the Utility.java file:

GetVersion - Gets the latest version number of the database		
Input Parameters	*dbName*	Name of the database
Return Value	*Version Number*	Latest version number of the database

LogInfo - Logs useful information		
Input Parameters	*none*	No parameters
Return Value	*void*	Returns nothing

Listing 6.36: Utility.java - Code for GetVersion

```
1  public static String GetVersion(String dbName)
2  {
3      String ver = "";
4
5      try
6      {
7          Class.forName("com.microsoft.sqlserver.jdbc. ←
              ↪ SQLServerDriver");
8          Connection conn = ←
              ↪ DriverManager.getConnection(dbName, ←
              ↪ Environment.DB_USERID, Environment.DB_PWD);
9          Statement statement = conn.createStatement();
10         String queryString = "Select Top 1 ReleaseVersion ←
              ↪ from dbo.VersionInfo Order By DateCreated Desc";
11         ResultSet rs = statement.executeQuery(queryString);
12         while (rs.next())
13         {
14             ver= rs.getString(1);
15         }
16     } catch (Exception e)
17     {
18         e.printStackTrace();
19         Utility.ReportExpectedVsActual("Exception occurred" ←
              ↪ + e.getMessage() , "Failing test");
20     }
21
22     return ver;
23 }
24
25 public static void LogInfo()
26 {
```

```
27    Utility.log.info("OPS_STG " + ↵
          ↪ Environment.DB_OPS_STAGING + " Version number: " ↵
          ↪ + GetVersion(Environment.DB_OPS_STAGING));
28    Utility.log.info("OPS_DWS " + Environment.DB_OPS_DWS + ↵
          ↪ " Version number: " + ↵
          ↪ GetVersion(Environment.DB_OPS_DWS));
29  }
```

Line 10: Get the latest version number from the table.
Line 22: Return version number.
Line 27: Get the latest version number of the Staging Database.
Line 28: Get the latest version number of the Data Warehouse.

Now update the factSales @Before setup code as shown in Figure 6.37.

Listing 6.37: Updated code for factSales @Before setup

```
1  @Before
2  public void setUp() throws Exception
3  {
4      Config.TestResult = Config.PASS;
5      Utility.LogInfo();
6
7      sourceQueryString = "SELECT"+ Config.newLine;
8      sourceQueryString += "          'Table Order' as ↵
          ↪ DataSource, o.OrderID" + Config.newLine;
9      sourceQueryString += "          ,o.CustomerID, ↵
          ↪ od.ProductID, o.EmployeeID,o.OrderDate, ↵
          ↪ o.DispatchDate" + Config.newLine;
10     sourceQueryString += "          ,ISNULL(od.PriceMatch, '" ↵
          ↪ + Config.UNKNOWN_STRING +"') As PriceMatch" + ↵
          ↪ Config.newLine;
11     sourceQueryString += "          ,od.UnitPrice, ↵
          ↪ od.Quantity, od.Discount, od.GiftWrap" + ↵
          ↪ Config.newLine;
12     sourceQueryString += "FROM [dbo].[Orders] o" + ↵
          ↪ Config.newLine;
13     sourceQueryString += "INNER JOIN [dbo].[OrderDetails] ↵
          ↪ od on od.[OrderID] = o.[OrderID]";
14
15     Utility.log.info("Source SQL is: " + sourceQueryString);
16  }
```

Line 5: Call to 'LogInfo' function when each test starts.

Now every time you execute a test, the version number from both the source and the data warehouse tables will be logged as shown in Figure 6.22.

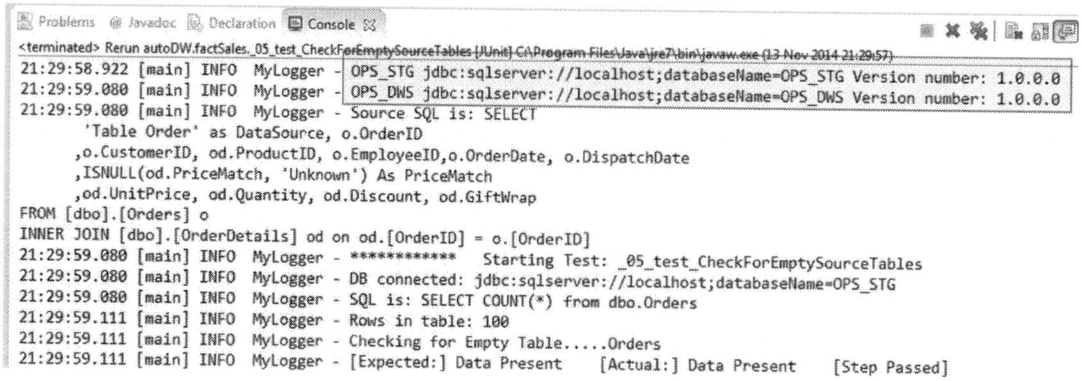

Figure 6.22: Logging System Version

6.4.2 Test Step Failure Threshold

Let us consider a scenario where you are executing a long test with many test steps. The current Automation Framework will execute all of the steps and only report any failures at the end. Sometimes you may want to fail the test as soon as the first failure occurs. On the other hand, you may want to continue the test execution until you reach a predefined threshold of test step failures. So let's see how we can achieve this.

First of all, let's add some new declarations to the Config.java file as shown in Listing 6.38.

Listing 6.38: Code for Config.java

```
1 public static final int STEP_PASS = 0;
2 public static final int STEP_FAIL = 1;
3 public static final int STEP_FAIL_THRESHOLD = 3;
```

Line 1: Integer value of a Passed step.
Line 2: Integer value of a Failed step.
Line 3: Test step failure threshold of 3 means when the test encounters 3 failures then it will stop executing further.

Now add a new function to the Utility.java file.

CheckFailureThreshold - Checks for the failure threshold; if reached fails the test		
Input Parameters	*count*	Current count of failures
Return Value	*void*	Returns nothing

Listing 6.39: Utility.java - code for CheckFailureThreshold

```java
1  public static void CheckFailureThreshold(int cnt)
2  {
3      if (cnt >= Config.STEP_FAIL_THRESHOLD)
4      {
5          log.error("Test Step Failure Threshold reached.... ↵
              ↪ Failing Test.");
6          assertFalse(true);
7      }
8  }
```

Line 3: If current failure count reaches configured threshold fail the test.

Let's update our existing function 'ReportExpectedVsActual' as follows:

Listing 6.40: Utility.java - updated code for ReportExpectedVsActual

```java
1  public static int ReportExpectedVsActual(String exp, ↵
       ↪ String act)
2  {
3      exp = exp.trim();
4      act = act.trim();
5
6      if (exp.equals(act))
7      {
8          log.info("[Expected:] " + exp + "    [Actual:] " + ↵
              ↪ act + "    [Step Passed]");
9          return Config.STEP_PASS;
10     }
11     else
12     {
13         log.error("[Expected:] " + exp + "    [Actual:] " + ↵
              ↪ act + "    [Step FAILED]");
14         Config.TestResult = Config.FAIL;
15         Config.OverAllTestResult = Config.FAIL;
16         return Config.STEP_FAIL;
17     }
```

18 }

Line 1: Return an int instead of void.
Line 9: Return Config.STEP_PASS if step passes.
Line 16: Return Config.STEP_FAIL if step fails.

Update the function 'LogInfo' code as shown in Listing 6.41.

Listing 6.41: Utility.java - updated code for LogInfo

```
1 public static void LogInfo()
2 {
3    Utility.log.info("OPS_STG " + ↵
        ↪ Environment.DB_OPS_STAGING + " Version number: " ↵
        ↪ + GetVersion(Environment.DB_OPS_STAGING));
4    Utility.log.info("OPS_DWS " + Environment.DB_OPS_DWS + ↵
        ↪ " Version number: " + ↵
        ↪ GetVersion(Environment.DB_OPS_DWS));
5    Utility.log.info("Test Step Failure Threshold: " + ↵
        ↪ Config.STEP_FAIL_THRESHOLD);
6 }
```

Line 5: Log the test step failure threshold value.

Now update the function 'CheckSalesDetails' as shown in Listing 6.42.

Listing 6.42: Utility.java - updated code for CheckSalesDetails

```
1 public static void CheckSalesDetails(String ↵
     ↪ sourceQueryString, String dataSource, int orderID, ↵
     ↪ int productID, int howMany)
2 {
3    Utility.log.info("CheckSalesDetails....");
4    int failedTimes = 0;
5
6    List<String> resultExpDataSource = new ↵
        ↪ ArrayList<String>();
7    List<String> resultExpOrderID = new ArrayList<String>();
8    List<String> resultExpProductID = new ↵
        ↪ ArrayList<String>();
9    List<String> resultExpCustomerID = new ↵
        ↪ ArrayList<String>();
```

```
10    List<String> resultExpEmployeeID = new ←
         ↪ ArrayList<String>();
11    List<String> resultExpOrderDate = new ←
         ↪ ArrayList<String>();
12    List<String> resultExpDispatchDate = new ←
         ↪ ArrayList<String>();
13    List<String> resultExpPriceMatch = new ←
         ↪ ArrayList<String>();
14    List<String> resultExpUnitPrice = new ←
         ↪ ArrayList<String>();
15    List<String> resultExpQuantity = new ArrayList<String>();
16    List<String> resultExpDiscount = new ArrayList<String>();
17    List<String> resultExpGiftWrap = new ArrayList<String>();
18
19    List<String> resultSaveDataSource = new ←
         ↪ ArrayList<String>();
20    List<String> resultSaveOrderID = new ArrayList<String>();
21    List<String> resultSaveProductID = new ←
         ↪ ArrayList<String>();
22
23    //Find Expected Result
24    try
25    {
26        Class.forName("com.microsoft.sqlserver.jdbc. ←
             ↪ SQLServerDriver");
27        Connection conn = DriverManager.getConnection( ←
             ↪ Environment.DB_OPS_STAGING, ←
             ↪ Environment.DB_USERID, Environment.DB_PWD);
28        Utility.log.info("DB connected..." + ←
             ↪ Environment.DB_OPS_STAGING);
29        Statement statement = conn.createStatement();
30        String queryString = "with stage as (" + ←
             ↪ Config.newLine;
31        queryString += sourceQueryString + Config.newLine;
32
33        if (orderID != 0)
34        {
35            Utility.log.info("Going for specific DataSource: ←
                 ↪ " + dataSource + "  orderID: " + orderID + ←
                 ↪ "  productID: " + productID);
36            queryString += ") select TOP 1 * from stage" + ←
                 ↪ Config.newLine;
37            queryString += "Where DataSource = '" + ←
                 ↪ dataSource + "'" + Config.newLine;
38            queryString += "And OrderID = " + orderID + ←
```

```
                          ↪ Config.newLine;
39          queryString += "And ProductID = " + productID;
40        }
41      else
42      {
43          queryString += ") Select TOP " + howMany + ↵
                          ↪ Config.newLine;
44          queryString += "DataSource, OrderID, ProductID, ↵
                          ↪ CustomerID, EmployeeID," + Config.newLine;
45          queryString += "OrderDate, DispatchDate, ↵
                          ↪ PriceMatch," + Config.newLine;
46          queryString += "UnitPrice, Quantity, Discount, ↵
                          ↪ GiftWrap" + Config.newLine;
47          queryString += "From stage" + Config.newLine;
48          queryString += "Order by NEWID()";
49      }
50
51      Utility.log.info("SQL is: " + queryString);
52
53      ResultSet rs = statement.executeQuery(queryString);
54
55      while (rs.next())
56      {
57        //Save for later use
58        resultSaveDataSource.add(rs.getString("DataSource"));
59        resultSaveOrderID.add(rs.getString("OrderID"));
60        resultSaveProductID.add(rs.getString("ProductID"));
61
62        resultExpDataSource.add("DataSource ==> " + ↵
                          ↪ rs.getString("DataSource"));
63        resultExpOrderID.add("OrderID ==> " + ↵
                          ↪ rs.getString("OrderID"));
64        resultExpProductID.add("ProductID ==> " + ↵
                          ↪ rs.getString("ProductID"));
65        resultExpCustomerID.add("CustomerID ==> " + ↵
                          ↪ rs.getString("CustomerID"));
66        resultExpEmployeeID.add("EmployeeID ==> " + ↵
                          ↪ rs.getString("EmployeeID"));
67        resultExpOrderDate.add("OrderDate ==> " + ↵
                          ↪ rs.getString("OrderDate").substring(0, 10));
68        resultExpDispatchDate.add("DispatchDate ==> " + ↵
                          ↪ rs.getString("DispatchDate"). substring(0, ↵
                          ↪ 10));
69        resultExpPriceMatch.add("PriceMatch ==> " + ↵
                          ↪ rs.getString("PriceMatch"));
```

```
70      resultExpUnitPrice.add("UnitPrice ==> " + ↵
          ↪ rs.getString("UnitPrice"));
71      resultExpQuantity.add("Quantity ==> " + ↵
          ↪ rs.getString("Quantity"));
72      resultExpDiscount.add("Discount ==> " + ↵
          ↪ rs.getString("Discount"));
73      resultExpGiftWrap.add("GiftWrap ==> " + ↵
          ↪ rs.getString("GiftWrap"));
74      }
75  } catch (Exception e)
76  {
77      e.printStackTrace();
78      Utility.ReportExpectedVsActual("Exception occurred. ↵
          ↪ " + e.getMessage(), "Failing test");
79  }
80
81  if (resultExpDataSource.size()==0)
82      Utility.ReportExpectedVsActual("Something wrong as ↵
          ↪ no data found", "Failing test");
83
84  for(int j=0; j<howMany;j++)
85  {
86      Utility.log.info("Row....." + j + "           ↵
          ↪ DataSource....." + resultExpDataSource.get(j) );
87
88      //Find Actual Result
89      try
90      {
91          List<String> resultActDataSource = new ↵
              ↪ ArrayList<String>();
92          List<String> resultActOrderID = new ↵
              ↪ ArrayList<String>();
93          List<String> resultActProductID = new ↵
              ↪ ArrayList<String>();
94          List<String> resultActCustomerID = new ↵
              ↪ ArrayList<String>();
95          List<String> resultActEmployeeID = new ↵
              ↪ ArrayList<String>();
96          List<String> resultActOrderDate = new ↵
              ↪ ArrayList<String>();
97          List<String> resultActDispatchDate = new ↵
              ↪ ArrayList<String>();
98          List<String> resultActPriceMatch = new ↵
              ↪ ArrayList<String>();
99          List<String> resultActUnitPrice = new ↵
```

```
                    ↪ ArrayList<String>();
100       List<String> resultActQuantity = new ↵
                    ↪ ArrayList<String>();
101       List<String> resultActDiscount = new ↵
                    ↪ ArrayList<String>();
102       List<String> resultActGiftWrap = new ↵
                    ↪ ArrayList<String>();
103
104       Class.forName("com.microsoft.sqlserver.jdbc. ↵
                    ↪ SQLServerDriver");
105       Connection conn = DriverManager.getConnection( ↵
                    ↪ Environment.DB_OPS_DWS, ↵
                    ↪ Environment.DB_USERID, Environment.DB_PWD);
106       Utility.log.info("DB connected..." + ↵
                    ↪ Environment.DB_OPS_DWS);
107       Statement statement = conn.createStatement();
108
109       String queryString = "SELECT DataSource " + ↵
                    ↪ Config.newLine;
110       queryString += "          ,s.OrderID, c.CustomerID, ↵
                    ↪ p.ProductID, e.EmployeeID" + Config.newLine;
111       queryString += "          ,dtOrd.FullDate As ↵
                    ↪ OrderDate, dtShp.FullDate As DispatchDate" ↵
                    ↪ + Config.newLine;
112       queryString += "          ,pm.PriceMatchDescription ↵
                    ↪ As PriceMatch, s.UnitPrice" + Config.newLine;
113       queryString += "          ,s.Quantity ,s.Discount, ↵
                    ↪ yn.YesNoDescription As GiftWrap" + ↵
                    ↪ Config.newLine;
114       queryString += "FROM [dbo].[factSales] s" + ↵
                    ↪ Config.newLine;
115       queryString += "LEFT JOIN [dbo].[dimCustomer] c ↵
                    ↪ on c.CustomerKey = s.CustomerKey " + ↵
                    ↪ Config.newLine;
116       queryString += "LEFT JOIN [dbo].[dimProduct] p ↵
                    ↪ on p.ProductKey = s.ProductKey" + ↵
                    ↪ Config.newLine;
117       queryString += "LEFT JOIN [dbo].[dimEmployee] e ↵
                    ↪ on e.EmployeeKey = s.EmployeeKey" + ↵
                    ↪ Config.newLine;
118       queryString += "LEFT JOIN [dbo].[dimDate] dtOrd ↵
                    ↪ on dtOrd.DateKey = s.OrderDateKey" + ↵
                    ↪ Config.newLine;
119       queryString += "LEFT JOIN [dbo].[dimDate] dtShp ↵
                    ↪ on dtShp.DateKey = s.DispatchDateKey" + ↵
```

```
                     ↪ Config.newLine;
120      queryString += "LEFT JOIN [dbo].[dimYesNo] yn on ↵
                     ↪ yn.YesNoKey = s.GiftWrapYesNoKey" + ↵
                     ↪ Config.newLine;
121      queryString += "LEFT JOIN [dbo].[dimPriceMatch] ↵
                     ↪ pm on pm.PriceMatchKey = s.PriceMatchKey" + ↵
                     ↪ Config.newLine;
122      queryString += "Where DataSource = '" + ↵
                     ↪ resultSaveDataSource.get(j) + "'" + ↵
                     ↪ Config.newLine;
123      queryString += "And OrderID = " + ↵
                     ↪ resultSaveOrderID.get(j) + Config.newLine;
124      queryString += "And ProductID = " + ↵
                     ↪ resultSaveProductID.get(j);
125
126      Utility.log.info("SQL is: " + queryString);
127
128      ResultSet rs = statement.executeQuery(queryString);
129
130      while (rs.next())
131      {
132          resultActDataSource.add("DataSource ==> " + ↵
                     ↪ rs.getString("DataSource"));
133          resultActOrderID.add("OrderID ==> " + ↵
                     ↪ rs.getString("OrderID"));
134          resultActProductID.add("ProductID ==> " + ↵
                     ↪ rs.getString("ProductID"));
135          resultActCustomerID.add("CustomerID ==> " + ↵
                     ↪ rs.getString("CustomerID"));
136          resultActEmployeeID.add("EmployeeID ==> " + ↵
                     ↪ rs.getString("EmployeeID"));
137          resultActOrderDate.add("OrderDate ==> " + ↵
                     ↪ rs.getString("OrderDate"));
138          resultActDispatchDate.add("DispatchDate ==> " ↵
                     ↪ + rs.getString("DispatchDate"));
139          resultActPriceMatch.add("PriceMatch ==> " + ↵
                     ↪ rs.getString("PriceMatch"));
140          resultActUnitPrice.add("UnitPrice ==> " + ↵
                     ↪ rs.getString("UnitPrice"));
141          resultActQuantity.add("Quantity ==> " + ↵
                     ↪ rs.getString("Quantity"));
142          resultActDiscount.add("Discount ==> " + ↵
                     ↪ rs.getString("Discount"));
143          resultActGiftWrap.add("GiftWrap ==> " + ↵
                     ↪ rs.getString("GiftWrap"));
```

```
144          }
145
146          failedTimes += Utility.ReportExpectedVsActual( ↵
             ↪ resultExpDataSource.get(j), ↵
             ↪ resultActDataSource.get(0));
147          CheckFailureThreshold(failedTimes);
148          failedTimes += Utility.ReportExpectedVsActual( ↵
             ↪ resultExpOrderID.get(j), ↵
             ↪ resultActOrderID.get(0));
149          CheckFailureThreshold(failedTimes);
150          failedTimes += Utility.ReportExpectedVsActual( ↵
             ↪ resultExpProductID.get(j), ↵
             ↪ resultActProductID.get(0));
151          CheckFailureThreshold(failedTimes);
152          failedTimes += Utility.ReportExpectedVsActual( ↵
             ↪ resultExpCustomerID.get(j), ↵
             ↪ resultActCustomerID.get(0));
153          CheckFailureThreshold(failedTimes);
154          CheckFailureThreshold(failedTimes);
155          failedTimes += Utility.ReportExpectedVsActual( ↵
             ↪ resultExpEmployeeID.get(j), ↵
             ↪ resultActEmployeeID.get(0));
156          CheckFailureThreshold(failedTimes);
157          failedTimes += Utility.ReportExpectedVsActual( ↵
             ↪ resultExpOrderDate.get(j), ↵
             ↪ resultActOrderDate.get(0));
158          CheckFailureThreshold(failedTimes);
159          failedTimes += Utility.ReportExpectedVsActual( ↵
             ↪ resultExpDispatchDate.get(j), ↵
             ↪ resultActDispatchDate.get(0));
160          CheckFailureThreshold(failedTimes);
161          failedTimes += Utility.ReportExpectedVsActual( ↵
             ↪ resultExpPriceMatch.get(j), ↵
             ↪ resultActPriceMatch.get(0));
162          CheckFailureThreshold(failedTimes);
163          failedTimes += Utility.ReportExpectedVsActual( ↵
             ↪ resultExpUnitPrice.get(j), ↵
             ↪ resultActUnitPrice.get(0));
164          CheckFailureThreshold(failedTimes);
165          failedTimes += Utility.ReportExpectedVsActual( ↵
             ↪ resultExpQuantity.get(j), ↵
             ↪ resultActQuantity.get(0));
166          CheckFailureThreshold(failedTimes);
167          failedTimes += Utility.ReportExpectedVsActual( ↵
             ↪ resultExpDiscount.get(j), ↵
```

```
                      ↪ resultActDiscount.get(0));
168             CheckFailureThreshold(failedTimes);
169             failedTimes += Utility.ReportExpectedVsActual( ↩
                      ↪ resultExpGiftWrap.get(j), ↩
                      ↪ resultActGiftWrap.get(0));
170             CheckFailureThreshold(failedTimes);
171
172       } catch (Exception e)
173       {
174           e.printStackTrace();
175           Utility.ReportExpectedVsActual("Exception ↩
                  ↪ occurred. " + e.getMessage(), "Failing test");
176       }
177   }
178 }
```

Line 4: Initialise variable 'failedTimes' to hold the value of the number of times the test step has failed.

Line 146: Increment the value of variable 'failedTimes' for each failed test step. Remember that the function 'ReportExpectedVsActual' returns zero for passed steps.

Line 147: Check if the failure count has reached the threshold by passing its current value to the 'CheckFailureThreshold' function.

So wherever you want to check the failure threshold, increment the failure count by the returned value of function 'ReportExpectedVsActual' and then call the generic function 'CheckFailureThreshold'.

6.4.3   Log Failed Test Steps Only

The Automation Framework uses the generic function 'ReportExpectedVsActual' to compare the expected and actual values and then reports the outcome. If your test script is performing a lot of comparisons, your log file may become very large. In that case you may want to log expected vs. actual comparisons only if there is a failure. In other words, we don't want to log the passed steps . We need to add a new configuration parameter that determines whether the framework should log all comparisons or only failures, as shown in Listing 6.43.

Listing 6.43: Code for Config.java

```
1 public static final boolean logAllCompare = false;
```

Line 1: A false value will log failures only.

Now modify function 'ReportExpectedVsActual' as shown in Listing 6.44.

Listing 6.44: Utility.java - updated code for ReportExpectedVsActual

```
1  public static int ReportExpectedVsActual(String exp, ↵
      ↪ String act)
2  {
3     exp = exp.trim();
4     act = act.trim();
5
6     if (exp.equals(act))
7     {
8        if (Config.logAllCompare)
9        {
10          log.info("[Expected:] " + exp + "     [Actual:] " ↵
             ↪ + act + "     [Step Passed]");
11       }
12       return Config.STEP_PASS;
13    }
14    else
15    {
16       log.error("[Expected:] " + exp + "     [Actual:] " + ↵
          ↪ act + "     [Step FAILED]");
17       Config.TestResult = Config.FAIL;
18       Config.OverAllTestResult = Config.FAIL;
19       return Config.STEP_FAIL;
20    }
21 }
```

Line 8: Log a passed step if Config.logAllCompare is 'true'.

Execute test _60_test_TableRecoundCountsByProductID from factSales.java. You will see that none of the passed comparison steps are logged.

You may now want to change logAllCompare flag's value to 'true' so that it logs all the comparisons.

6.4.4 Comparing Decimal Numbers

As a general rule, we can confidently use the 'ReportExpectedVsActual' function to report the outcome of test steps where the parameters are passed as strings. However when we are comparing two decimal numbers (passed as strings) the function may report unnecessary failures. For example, if the values being compared are held in a different number of decimal places or if the difference between them is 'insignificant', the function will still report them as failures because it does an exact comparison. Also, if the decimal values of the expected result differ from the actual result because of the way the calculations are performed in the programming language used. In this situation you may want to ignore any minor difference between the Expected and Actual Result e.g. if the Expected Result is 1418.055556 and the Actual Result calculated by the application is 1418.0555. You may want to ignore the difference of 0.000056 when reporting the result and pass the test step. So here is how we do it.

First of all, add a new configuration parameter to the Config.java file as shown in Listing 6.45.

Listing 6.45: Code for Config.java

```
1  public static final double IGNORE_DIFF_THRESHOLD =
       0.0001;
```

Line 1: Ignore difference of 0.0001 between the Expected and the Actual Result.

Now add a new function to the Utility.java file as shown in Listing 6.46.

Listing 6.46: Utility.java - Code for ReportExpectedVsActualWithThreshold

```
1  public static int ReportExpectedVsActualWithThreshold(
       String exp, String act)
2  {
3      exp = exp.trim();
4      act = act.trim();
5
6      Double expDbl, actDbl;
7
8      String expFormatted = String.format("%.4f",
           Double.parseDouble(exp));
9      String actFormatted = String.format("%.4f",
           Double.parseDouble(act));
10
11     expDbl = Double.parseDouble(expFormatted);
12     actDbl = Double.parseDouble(actFormatted);
13
14     if (expFormatted.equals(actFormatted))
15     {
16         log.info("[Expected:] " + exp + "    [Actual:] " +
               act + "    [Step Passed]");
17
18         return Config.STEP_PASS;
```

```
19      }
20      else if (Math.abs(actDbl - expDbl) <= ↵
           ↪ Config.IGNORE_DIFF_THRESHOLD)
21      {
22          log.info("Ignored minor difference of " + ↵
               ↪ String.format( "%.4f", (actDbl - expDbl) ) + " ↵
               ↪ between expDbl = " + expDbl + " and actDbl = " ↵
               ↪ + actDbl);
23          log.info("Original [Expected:] " + exp + "    ↵
               ↪ Original [Actual:] " + act + "      [Step ↵
               ↪ Passed]");
24
25          return Config.STEP_PASS;
26      }
27      else
28      {
29          log.error("[Expected:] " + exp + "      [Actual:] " + ↵
               ↪ act + "     [Step FAILED]");
30          log.info("Difference of " + String.format( "%.4f", ↵
               ↪ (actDbl - expDbl) ) + " between expDbl = " + ↵
               ↪ expDbl + " and actDbl = " + actDbl);
31
32          Config.TestResult = Config.FAIL;
33          Config.OverAllTestResult = Config.FAIL;
34
35          return Config.STEP_FAIL;
36      }
37  }
```

Line 8 and 9: Format expected and actual values to the same precision.

Line 11 and 12: Convert expected and actual values to 'double' format.

Line 14: First of all, check if formatted values are equal.

Line 20: Now check if 'double' values are equal after ignoring the threshold difference. Also log additional information.

Line 29: Otherwise report failure and log additional information.

Add a new test to factSales.java file as shown in Listing 6.47.

Listing 6.47: factSales.java - Code for _90_test_CompareDecimalNumbers

```
1  @Test
2  public void _90_test_CompareDecimalNumbers()
3  {
4      Utility.log.info("***********     Starting Test: " + ↵
```

```
            ↪  name.getMethodName());
5
6       Utility.ReportExpectedVsActualWithThreshold( ↩
            ↪ "1418.055556", "1418.0555");
7
8       Utility.ReportResultWithSummary(name.getMethodName());
9  }
```

Line 6: Call 'ReportExpectedVsActualWithThreshold' with values "1418.055556" and "1418.0555". The test should pass after ignoring the difference.

Execute the test _90_test_CompareDecimalNumbers and you will see a Console output as shown in 6.23.

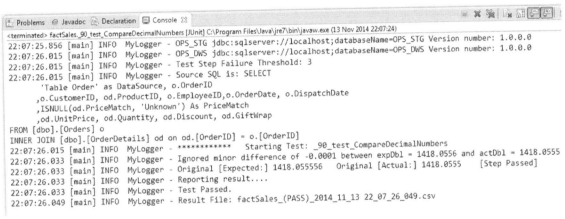

Figure 6.23: Console output - Comparing Decimal Numbers

Chapter 7

Automating Other Data Sources

Automating Other Data Sources

In this chapter, we will learn how to:

- *Automate the testing of data sourced from a CSV file*

- *Automate the testing of data sourced from an Excel file*

So let's get on with it...

DATA can be fed into the data warehouse from a variety of sources. Each data source may have its own method of extracting and storing data. In the earlier chapters, all of the data was sourced from database tables. Let's now automate the testing of some of the other data sources.

7.1   Data Source - CSV File

The data for the warehouse may come from a number of heterogeneous sources and one of the most commonly used source is a CSV file. This section explains how to automate the testing of this type of data source. Let us consider the scenario where our data warehouse receives a daily sales transaction file 'SalesTransactions.CSV' in the following format:

```
OrderID, CustomerID, ProductID, EmployeeID, OrderDate, DispatchDate,
PriceMatch, UnitPrice, Quantity, Discount, GiftWrap
```

Appendix A has a listing of the sample 'SalesTransactions.CSV' file. You may have a date and timestamp in the file name but for simplicity let's assume we just have the file name with CSV extension.

☞   In the real world, loading the 'SalesTransactions.CSV' data into the warehouse would usually be performed via an ETL job as shown in Figure 1.1. The data might first go into a staging table and then be loaded into the fact table, or the ETL job might load it directly into the fact table.

For our automated testing, we need to mimic something similar so that we have some data for our testing. In order to do this, we will create a temporary table in the staging area and load 'SalesTransactions.CSV' data into it. Listing 7.1 contains the code to achieve this. We will then use Listing 7.2 code to populate the fact table. This will ensure that the fact table is populated with the test data.

Listing 7.1: Creating and Loading Temp Table

```
1  USE [OPS_STG]
2  GO
3
4  IF OBJECT_ID('[dbo].[tmpDailyTxn]') IS NOT NULL
5     BEGIN
6        DROP TABLE [dbo].[tmpDailyTxn]
7     END
8  Go
9
10 SET ANSI_NULLS ON
11 GO
12
13 SET QUOTED_IDENTIFIER ON
14 GO
15
16 SET DATEFORMAT dmy;
17 GO
18
19 CREATE TABLE [dbo].[tmpDailyTxn](
20    [OrderID] [int] NOT NULL,
21    [CustomerID] [nchar](5) NOT NULL,
22    [ProductID] [int] NOT NULL,
23    [EmployeeID] [int] NULL,
24    [OrderDate] [datetime] NULL,
25    [DispatchDate] [datetime] NULL,
26    [PriceMatch] [nvarchar](50) NULL,
27    [UnitPrice] [money] NOT NULL,
28    [Quantity] [smallint] NOT NULL,
29    [Discount] [real] NOT NULL,
30    [GiftWrap] [nchar](5) NULL,
31 ) ON [PRIMARY]
32 GO
33
34 BULK INSERT dbo.tmpDailyTxn FROM ↵
```

```
   ↪ 'C:/Workspace/TestData/SalesTransactions.csv' WITH ↩
   ↪ (FIRSTROW = 2, FIELDTERMINATOR = ',', ROWTERMINATOR ↩
   ↪ = '\n')
35 GO
```

Line 4: Drop the temporary table if it already exists.
Line 19: Create the temporary table.
Line 34: Load data into the temporary table from CSV file.

Listing 7.2: CSV Source - Loading Fact Table

```
1  ALTER TABLE [OPS_DWS].[dbo].[factSales] DROP CONSTRAINT ↩
       ↪ [FK_factSales_Customer]
2  ALTER TABLE [OPS_DWS].[dbo].[factSales] DROP CONSTRAINT ↩
       ↪ [FK_factSales_Product]
3  ALTER TABLE [OPS_DWS].[dbo].[factSales] DROP CONSTRAINT ↩
       ↪ [FK_factSales_Employee]
4  ALTER TABLE [OPS_DWS].[dbo].[factSales] DROP CONSTRAINT ↩
       ↪ [FK_factSales_OrderDate]
5  ALTER TABLE [OPS_DWS].[dbo].[factSales] DROP CONSTRAINT ↩
       ↪ [FK_factSales_DispatchDate]
6  ALTER TABLE [OPS_DWS].[dbo].[factSales] DROP CONSTRAINT ↩
       ↪ [FK_factSales_GiftWrapYesNoKey]
7  ALTER TABLE [OPS_DWS].[dbo].[factSales] DROP CONSTRAINT ↩
       ↪ [FK_factSales_PriceMatch]
8  GO
9
10 Delete FROM [OPS_DWS].[dbo].[factSales]
11 where [DataSource] = 'SalesTransactions.csv'
12 GO
13
14 INSERT INTO [OPS_DWS].[dbo].[factSales]
15 SELECT 'SalesTransactions.csv'
16        ,o.[OrderID]
17        ,ISNULL(c.CustomerKey, -1) CustomerKey
18        ,ISNULL(p.ProductKey, -1)  ProductKey
19        ,ISNULL(e.EmployeeKey, -1) EmployeeKey
20        ,ISNULL(dtOrd.DateKey, -1) OrderDateKey
21        ,ISNULL(dtShp.DateKey, -1) DispatchDateKey
22        ,ISNULL(pm.PriceMatchKey, -1) PriceMatchKey
23        ,o.UnitPrice
24        ,o.Quantity
25        ,o.Discount
26        ,ISNULL(yn.YesNoKey, -1) GiftWrapYesNoKey
```

```
27          ,GETDATE()
28  FROM [OPS_STG].[dbo].[tmpDailyTxn] o
29  LEFT JOIN [OPS_DWS].[dbo].[dimCustomer] c on c.CustomerID ←
    ↪ = o.CustomerID
30  LEFT JOIN [OPS_DWS].[dbo].[dimProduct] p on p.ProductID = ←
    ↪ o.ProductID
31  LEFT JOIN [OPS_DWS].[dbo].[dimEmployee] e on e.EmployeeID ←
    ↪ = o.EmployeeID
32  LEFT JOIN [OPS_DWS].[dbo].[dimDate] dtOrd on ←
    ↪ dtOrd.FullDate = o.OrderDate
33  LEFT JOIN [OPS_DWS].[dbo].[dimDate] dtShp on ←
    ↪ dtShp.FullDate = o.DispatchDate
34  LEFT JOIN [OPS_DWS].[dbo].[dimYesNo] yn on ←
    ↪ yn.YesNoDescription = o.GiftWrap
35  LEFT JOIN [OPS_DWS].[dbo].[dimPriceMatch] pm on ←
    ↪ pm.[PriceMatchDescription] = o.PriceMatch
36  GO
37
38  ALTER TABLE [OPS_DWS].[dbo].[factSales] WITH NOCHECK ADD ←
    ↪ CONSTRAINT [FK_factSales_Customer] FOREIGN ←
    ↪ KEY([CustomerKey])
39  REFERENCES [OPS_DWS].[dbo].[dimCustomer] ([CustomerKey])
40  ALTER TABLE [OPS_DWS].[dbo].[factSales] CHECK CONSTRAINT ←
    ↪ [FK_factSales_Customer]
41  ALTER TABLE [OPS_DWS].[dbo].[factSales] WITH NOCHECK ADD ←
    ↪ CONSTRAINT [FK_factSales_Product] FOREIGN ←
    ↪ KEY([ProductKey])
42  REFERENCES [OPS_DWS].[dbo].[dimProduct] ([ProductKey])
43  ALTER TABLE [OPS_DWS].[dbo].[factSales] CHECK CONSTRAINT ←
    ↪ [FK_factSales_Product]
44  ALTER TABLE [OPS_DWS].[dbo].[factSales] WITH NOCHECK ADD ←
    ↪ CONSTRAINT [FK_factSales_Employee] FOREIGN ←
    ↪ KEY([EmployeeKey])
45  REFERENCES [OPS_DWS].[dbo].[dimEmployee] ([EmployeeKey])
46  ALTER TABLE [OPS_DWS].[dbo].[factSales] CHECK CONSTRAINT ←
    ↪ [FK_factSales_Employee]
47  ALTER TABLE [OPS_DWS].[dbo].[factSales] WITH NOCHECK ADD ←
    ↪ CONSTRAINT [FK_factSales_OrderDate] FOREIGN ←
    ↪ KEY([OrderDateKey])
48  REFERENCES [OPS_DWS].[dbo].[dimDate] ([DateKey])
49  ALTER TABLE [OPS_DWS].[dbo].[factSales] CHECK CONSTRAINT ←
    ↪ [FK_factSales_OrderDate]
50  ALTER TABLE [OPS_DWS].[dbo].[factSales] WITH NOCHECK ADD ←
    ↪ CONSTRAINT [FK_factSales_DispatchDate] FOREIGN ←
    ↪ KEY([DispatchDateKey])
```

```
51 REFERENCES [OPS_DWS].[dbo].[dimDate] ([DateKey])
52 ALTER TABLE [OPS_DWS].[dbo].[factSales] CHECK CONSTRAINT ↵
     ↳ [FK_factSales_DispatchDate]
53 ALTER TABLE [OPS_DWS].[dbo].[factSales]  WITH NOCHECK ADD ↵
     ↳ CONSTRAINT [FK_factSales_GiftWrapYesNoKey] FOREIGN ↵
     ↳ KEY([GiftWrapYesNoKey])
54 REFERENCES [OPS_DWS].[dbo].[dimYesNo] ([YesNoKey])
55 ALTER TABLE [OPS_DWS].[dbo].[factSales] CHECK CONSTRAINT ↵
     ↳ [FK_factSales_GiftWrapYesNoKey]
56 ALTER TABLE [OPS_DWS].[dbo].[factSales]  WITH NOCHECK ADD ↵
     ↳ CONSTRAINT [FK_factSales_PriceMatch] FOREIGN ↵
     ↳ KEY([PriceMatchKey])
57 REFERENCES [OPS_DWS].[dbo].[dimPriceMatch] ([PriceMatchKey])
58 ALTER TABLE [OPS_DWS].[dbo].[factSales] CHECK CONSTRAINT ↵
     ↳ [FK_factSales_PriceMatch]
59 GO
```

In order to automate the testing of CSV data sources, our test strategy will be to use a temporary table in the staging area. We will automatically load this temporary table with the CSV data file before we start executing our tests and then use the temporary table to verify the fact table load. We will reuse the temporary table 'tmpDailyTxn' created earlier in Listing 7.1 for this purpose.

So let's get on with automating our tests. First of all, define a new parameter in the Config.java file as shown in Listing 7.3.

Listing 7.3: Code for Config.java

```
1 public static final String DATAFILE_LOCATION = ↵
     ↳ "C:/Workspace/TestData/";
```

Line 1: Location of the data files on the workstation. This location will be used for CSV, XLSX and XLS data file uploads.

Now add a new function to the Utility.java file.

LoadTempTable - Loads the temporary table with a CSV file		
Input Parameters	*dbName*	Name of the database
	tmpTable	Name of the temporary table to be loaded
	serverPathFile	Path and name of the file to be loaded
Return Value	*void*	Returns nothing

Listing 7.4: Code for LoadTempTable

```
1  public static void LoadTempTable(String dbName, String ←
       ↪ tmpTable, String serverPathFile)
2  {
3      Utility.log.info("LoadTempTable... " + serverPathFile);
4
5      try
6      {
7          Connection conn1;
8          Class.forName("com.microsoft.sqlserver.jdbc. ←
               ↪ SQLServerDriver");
9
10         conn1 = DriverManager.getConnection(dbName, ←
               ↪ Environment.DB_USERID, Environment.DB_PWD);
11
12         Statement statement1 = conn1.createStatement();
13
14         String queryString1 = "SET DATEFORMAT dmy" + ←
               ↪ Config.newLine;
15         queryString1 += ";" + Config.newLine;
16         queryString1 += "Truncate Table " + tmpTable + ←
               ↪ Config.newLine;
17         queryString1 += ";" + Config.newLine;
18         queryString1 += "BULK INSERT " + tmpTable + " FROM ←
               ↪ '" + serverPathFile + "' WITH (FIRSTROW = 2, ←
               ↪ FIELDTERMINATOR = ',', ROWTERMINATOR = '\\n')" ←
               ↪ + Config.newLine;
19         queryString1 += ";" + Config.newLine;
20
21         Utility.log.info("SQL is: " + queryString1);
22
23         statement1.execute(queryString1);
24     } catch (Exception e)
25     {
26         e.printStackTrace();
27         Utility.ReportExpectedVsActual("Exception occurred" ←
               ↪ + e.getMessage(), "Failing test");
28     }
29  }
```

Line 14: Set date format to day/month/year.
Line 16: Truncate table for any existing data.
Line 18: First row is a header row so start with row 2, file is comma separated and the

rows are terminated by the Enter key.

Now add a new test sourceDataCSV as shown in Listing 7.5.

Listing 7.5: Code for sourceDataCSV.java

```java
1  package autoDW;
2
3  import java.util.Arrays;
4  import java.util.List;
5
6  import org.junit.AfterClass;
7  import org.junit.Before;
8  import org.junit.BeforeClass;
9  import org.junit.FixMethodOrder;
10 import org.junit.runners.MethodSorters;
11 import org.junit.Rule;
12 import org.junit.Test;
13 import org.junit.rules.TestName;
14
15 @FixMethodOrder(MethodSorters.NAME_ASCENDING)
16
17 public class sourceDataCSV {
18     @Rule public TestName name = new TestName();
19     public String sourceQueryString;
20
21     public String colmNames = ↵
         ↪ "DataSource,OrderID,UnitPrice,Quantity,Discount";
22     public List<String> ColmList = ↵
         ↪ Arrays.asList(colmNames.split(","));
23
24     public static String sourceFileName = ↵
         ↪ "SalesTransactions.csv";
25
26     @BeforeClass
27     public static void setUpBeforeClass() throws Exception {
28         Utility.log.info("@BeforeClass- setUp");
29         Utility.SetupSummaryFile(Utility.GetName( ↵
             ↪ Thread.currentThread().getStackTrace()[1]. ↵
             ↪ getClassName()));
30         Utility.LoadTempTable(Environment.DB_OPS_STAGING, ↵
             ↪ "dbo.tmpDailyTxn", Config.DATAFILE_LOCATION + ↵
             ↪ sourceFileName);
31     }
```

```
32
33    @Before
34    public void setUp() throws Exception {
35        Config.TestResult = Config.PASS;
36
37        sourceQueryString = "SELECT"+ Config.newLine;
38        sourceQueryString += "          '" + sourceFileName + ↵
              ↪ "' as DataSource" + Config.newLine;
39        sourceQueryString += "         ,OrderID, CustomerID, ↵
              ↪ ProductID, EmployeeID " + Config.newLine;
40        sourceQueryString += "         ,OrderDate, ↵
              ↪ DispatchDate " + Config.newLine;
41        sourceQueryString += "         ,ISNULL(PriceMatch, '" ↵
              ↪ + Config.UNKNOWN_STRING +"') As PriceMatch" + ↵
              ↪ Config.newLine;
42        sourceQueryString += "         ,UnitPrice, Quantity, ↵
              ↪ Discount, GiftWrap" + Config.newLine;
43        sourceQueryString += "FROM [dbo].[tmpDailyTxn]";
44
45        Utility.log.info("Source SQL is: " + ↵
              ↪ sourceQueryString);
46    }
47
48    @AfterClass
49    public static void tearDownAfterClass() throws ↵
          ↪ Exception {
50        Utility.SaveLogWithSummary(Utility.GetName( ↵
              ↪ Thread.currentThread().getStackTrace()[1]. ↵
              ↪ getClassName()));
51    }
52
53    @Test
54    public void _05_test_CheckForEmptySourceTables() {
55        Utility.log.info("***********  Starting Test: " + ↵
              ↪ name.getMethodName());
56
57        Utility.CheckForEmptyTable( ↵
              ↪ Environment.DB_OPS_STAGING, "dbo", ↵
              ↪ "tmpDailyTxn");
58        Utility.ReportResultWithSummary(name.getMethodName());
59    }
60
61    @Test
62    public void _10_test_CheckForEmptyTargetTables() {
63        Utility.log.info("***********  Starting Test: " + ↵
```

```
64
65          Utility.CheckForEmptyTable(Environment.DB_OPS_DWS, ↩
               ↪ "dbo", "factSales");
66          Utility.ReportResultWithSummary(name.getMethodName());
67      }
68
69      @Test
70      public void _15_test_CheckForUniqueKey() {
71          Utility.log.info("************   Starting Test: " + ↩
               ↪ name.getMethodName());
72
73          Utility.CheckForUniqueKeyMultipleCols( ↩
               ↪ Environment.DB_OPS_DWS, "dbo", "factSales", ↩
               ↪ "DataSource,OrderID,ProductKey");
74          Utility.ReportResultWithSummary(name.getMethodName());
75      }
76
77      @Test
78      public void _20_test_CheckForNullValues() {
79          Utility.log.info("************   Starting Test: " + ↩
               ↪ name.getMethodName());
80
81          Utility.CheckForNullValues(Environment.DB_OPS_DWS, ↩
               ↪ "dbo", "factSales", "", "");
82          Utility.ReportResultWithSummary(name.getMethodName());
83      }
84
85      @Test
86      public void _30_test_CheckTableChecksums() {
87          Utility.log.info("************   Starting Test: " + ↩
               ↪ name.getMethodName());
88
89          Utility.CompareChecksumsSourceSQLSpecificCols( ↩
               ↪ Environment.DB_OPS_STAGING, sourceQueryString, ↩
               ↪ ColmList, Environment.DB_OPS_DWS, "dbo", ↩
               ↪ "factSales", "factSalesKey,DateCreated", ↩
               ↪ "DataSource = '" + sourceFileName + "'");
90          Utility.ReportResultWithSummary(name.getMethodName());
91      }
92
93      @Test
94      public void _40_test_CheckSalesDetails_Random() {
95          Utility.log.info("************   Starting Test: " + ↩
               ↪ name.getMethodName());
```

```
96
97        Utility.CheckSalesDetails(sourceQueryString, ↩
              ↪ sourceFileName, 0, 0, 10);
98        Utility.ReportResultWithSummary(name.getMethodName());
99    }
100
101   @Test
102   public void _45_test_CheckSalesDetails_Specific() {
103       Utility.log.info("***********   Starting Test: " + ↩
              ↪ name.getMethodName());
104
105       Utility.CheckSalesDetails(sourceQueryString, ↩
              ↪ sourceFileName, 32, 10, 1);
106       Utility.ReportResultWithSummary(name.getMethodName());
107    }
108 }
```

Line 24: Specify the source CSV file name. You may want to have a file name with a date and timestamp if dealing with multiple files.

Line 30: Load the temporary table 'tmpDailyTxn' with the CSV file.

Line 43: Note that the source uses temporary table 'tmpDailyTxn'.

Line 97 and 105: Note the parameter 'dataSource' of function 'CheckSalesDetails' which is "SalesTransactions.csv" in this case.

Execute all the tests and you will see a Summary Result file as shown in Figure 7.1.

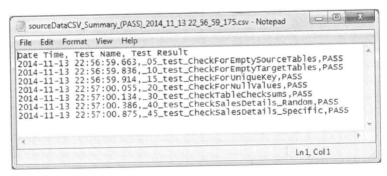

Figure 7.1: Summary File - CSV Data Source

7.2 Data Source - Excel File

Let's now consider the scenario where our data warehouse receives a daily sales transaction file in the Excel format. This section illustrates how you can automate the testing of this type of source. We will automate two Excel formats – XLSX and XLS (Excel 97 – 2003).

First of all let's add the required references to our Automation Framework.

- Right click on the 'src' folder select Build Path ⇒ Configure Build Path

- Go to Libraries and click on 'Add External JARs'

- Select 'poi-3.10.1-20140818.jar', 'poi-ooxml-3.10.1-20140818.jar' and 'poi-ooxml-schemas-3.10.1-20140818.jar' as shown in Figure 7.2. Remember we extracted the files in 'C:\poi-3.10.1' folder

- Press the Open button

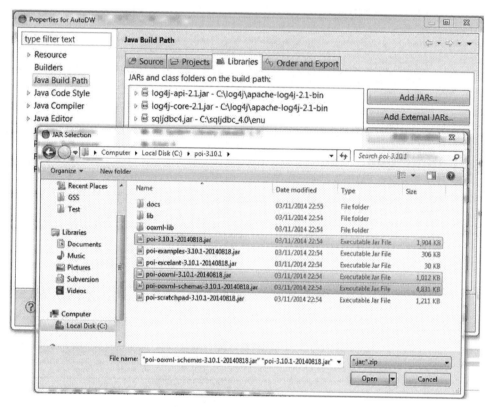

Figure 7.2: Adding Poi Jars

- Now add 'dom4j-1.6.1.jar' and 'xmlbeans-2.3.0.jar' from folder 'C:\poi-3.10.1\ooxml-lib' as shown in Figure 7.3

- Press the Open button and then the OK button

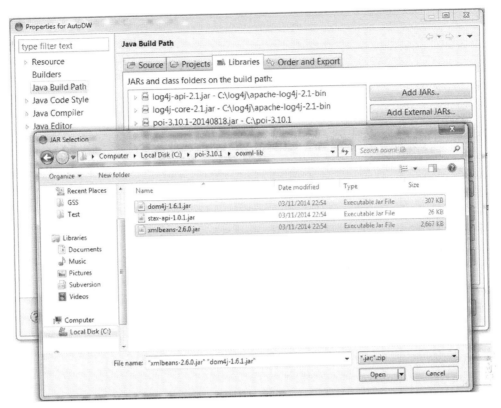

Figure 7.3: Adding More Poi Jars

7.2.1 XLSX Format

Appendix A has a listing of the sample 'SalesTransactions.XLSX' file. Make sure that the data file is sorted in ascending order by 'OrderID' and then by 'ProductID' which is the order the data is fetched from the target (fact) table.

In the real world, loading of 'SalesTransactions.XLSX' data into the warehouse would usually be performed via an ETL job as shown in Figure 1.1. The data might first go into a staging table and then be loaded into the fact table, or the ETL job might load it directly into the fact table.

For our automated testing, we need to mimic something similar so that we have some data for our testing. In order to do so, you will need to save the 'SalesTransactions.XLSX' file as 'XLSX.CSV' [use Excel option 'Save As', select 'Save as type:' option 'CSV(Comma delimited)(*.csv)']. Now use Listing 7.6 code to load the 'XLSX.CSV' file into the temporary table 'tmpDailyTxn' and finally load the fact table. This will ensure that the fact table is populated with the test data. Note the reuse of temp table 'tmpDailyTxn'.

Listing 7.6: XLSX Source - Loading Fact Table

```
1  SET DATEFORMAT dmy;
```

```
 2  GO
 3
 4  Truncate Table [OPS_STG].dbo.tmpDailyTxn
 5  GO
 6
 7  BULK INSERT [OPS_STG].dbo.tmpDailyTxn FROM ↵
    ↪ 'C:/Workspace/TestData/XLSX.csv'  WITH (FIRSTROW = ↵
    ↪ 2, FIELDTERMINATOR = ',', ROWTERMINATOR = '\n')
 8  GO
 9
10  ALTER TABLE [OPS_DWS].[dbo].[factSales] DROP CONSTRAINT ↵
    ↪ [FK_factSales_Customer]
11  ALTER TABLE [OPS_DWS].[dbo].[factSales] DROP CONSTRAINT ↵
    ↪ [FK_factSales_Product]
12  ALTER TABLE [OPS_DWS].[dbo].[factSales] DROP CONSTRAINT ↵
    ↪ [FK_factSales_Employee]
13  ALTER TABLE [OPS_DWS].[dbo].[factSales] DROP CONSTRAINT ↵
    ↪ [FK_factSales_OrderDate]
14  ALTER TABLE [OPS_DWS].[dbo].[factSales] DROP CONSTRAINT ↵
    ↪ [FK_factSales_DispatchDate]
15  ALTER TABLE [OPS_DWS].[dbo].[factSales] DROP CONSTRAINT ↵
    ↪ [FK_factSales_GiftWrapYesNoKey]
16  ALTER TABLE [OPS_DWS].[dbo].[factSales] DROP CONSTRAINT ↵
    ↪ [FK_factSales_PriceMatch]
17  GO
18
19  delete FROM [OPS_DWS].[dbo].[factSales]
20  where [DataSource] = 'SalesTransactions.xlsx'
21  GO
22  INSERT INTO [OPS_DWS].[dbo].[factSales]
23  SELECT 'SalesTransactions.xlsx'
24      ,o.[OrderID]
25      , ISNULL(c.CustomerKey, -1) CustomerKey
26      , ISNULL(p.ProductKey, -1)  ProductKey
27      , ISNULL(e.EmployeeKey, -1) EmployeeKey
28      , ISNULL(dtOrd.DateKey, -1) OrderDateKey
29      , ISNULL(dtShp.DateKey, -1) DispatchDateKey
30      , ISNULL(pm.PriceMatchKey, -1) PriceMatchKey
31      ,o.UnitPrice
32      ,o.Quantity
33      ,o.Discount
34      , ISNULL(yn.YesNoKey, -1) GiftWrapYesNoKey
35      ,GETDATE()
36  FROM [OPS_STG].[dbo].[tmpDailyTxn] o
37  LEFT JOIN [OPS_DWS].[dbo].[dimCustomer] c on c.CustomerID ↵
```

```
          ↪ = o.CustomerID
38 LEFT JOIN [OPS_DWS].[dbo].[dimProduct] p on p.ProductID = ↵
          ↪ o.ProductID
39 LEFT JOIN [OPS_DWS].[dbo].[dimEmployee] e on e.EmployeeID ↵
          ↪ = o.EmployeeID
40 LEFT JOIN [OPS_DWS].[dbo].[dimDate] dtOrd on ↵
          ↪ dtOrd.FullDate = o.OrderDate
41 LEFT JOIN [OPS_DWS].[dbo].[dimDate] dtShp on ↵
          ↪ dtShp.FullDate = o.DispatchDate
42 LEFT JOIN [OPS_DWS].[dbo].[dimYesNo] yn on ↵
          ↪ yn.YesNoDescription = o.GiftWrap
43 LEFT JOIN [OPS_DWS].[dbo].[dimPriceMatch] pm on ↵
          ↪ pm.[PriceMatchDescription] = o.PriceMatch
44 GO
45
46 ALTER TABLE [OPS_DWS].[dbo].[factSales] WITH NOCHECK ADD ↵
          ↪ CONSTRAINT [FK_factSales_Customer] FOREIGN ↵
          ↪ KEY([CustomerKey])
47 REFERENCES [OPS_DWS].[dbo].[dimCustomer] ([CustomerKey])
48 ALTER TABLE [OPS_DWS].[dbo].[factSales] CHECK CONSTRAINT ↵
          ↪ [FK_factSales_Customer]
49 ALTER TABLE [OPS_DWS].[dbo].[factSales] WITH NOCHECK ADD ↵
          ↪ CONSTRAINT [FK_factSales_Product] FOREIGN ↵
          ↪ KEY([ProductKey])
50 REFERENCES [OPS_DWS].[dbo].[dimProduct] ([ProductKey])
51 ALTER TABLE [OPS_DWS].[dbo].[factSales] CHECK CONSTRAINT ↵
          ↪ [FK_factSales_Product]
52 ALTER TABLE [OPS_DWS].[dbo].[factSales] WITH NOCHECK ADD ↵
          ↪ CONSTRAINT [FK_factSales_Employee] FOREIGN ↵
          ↪ KEY([EmployeeKey])
53 REFERENCES [OPS_DWS].[dbo].[dimEmployee] ([EmployeeKey])
54 ALTER TABLE [OPS_DWS].[dbo].[factSales] CHECK CONSTRAINT ↵
          ↪ [FK_factSales_Employee]
55 ALTER TABLE [OPS_DWS].[dbo].[factSales] WITH NOCHECK ADD ↵
          ↪ CONSTRAINT [FK_factSales_OrderDate] FOREIGN ↵
          ↪ KEY([OrderDateKey])
56 REFERENCES [OPS_DWS].[dbo].[dimDate] ([DateKey])
57 ALTER TABLE [OPS_DWS].[dbo].[factSales] CHECK CONSTRAINT ↵
          ↪ [FK_factSales_OrderDate]
58 ALTER TABLE [OPS_DWS].[dbo].[factSales] WITH NOCHECK ADD ↵
          ↪ CONSTRAINT [FK_factSales_DispatchDate] FOREIGN ↵
          ↪ KEY([DispatchDateKey])
59 REFERENCES [OPS_DWS].[dbo].[dimDate] ([DateKey])
60 ALTER TABLE [OPS_DWS].[dbo].[factSales] CHECK CONSTRAINT ↵
          ↪ [FK_factSales_DispatchDate]
```

```
61  ALTER  TABLE  [OPS_DWS].[dbo].[factSales]  WITH NOCHECK  ADD ↵
        ↳  CONSTRAINT [FK_factSales_GiftWrapYesNoKey]  FOREIGN ↵
        ↳ KEY([GiftWrapYesNoKey])
62  REFERENCES  [OPS_DWS].[dbo].[dimYesNo]  ([YesNoKey])
63  ALTER  TABLE  [OPS_DWS].[dbo].[factSales]  CHECK  CONSTRAINT ↵
        ↳ [FK_factSales_GiftWrapYesNoKey]
64  ALTER  TABLE  [OPS_DWS].[dbo].[factSales]  WITH  NOCHECK  ADD ↵
        ↳  CONSTRAINT [FK_factSales_PriceMatch]  FOREIGN ↵
        ↳ KEY([PriceMatchKey])
65  REFERENCES  [OPS_DWS].[dbo].[dimPriceMatch]  ([PriceMatchKey])
66  ALTER  TABLE  [OPS_DWS].[dbo].[factSales]  CHECK  CONSTRAINT ↵
        ↳ [FK_factSales_PriceMatch]
67  GO
```

So let's get on with automating our tests. Add the following new function to the
Utility.java file.

GetSpreadSheetXLSX - Gets data from a file which is in the XLSX format		
Input Parameters	*pathName*	Path and name of the input XLSX file
	sheetNumber	Sheet number of the XLSX file to read
Return Value	*Spreadsheet Data*	Returns the spreadsheet data in a two dimensional array

Listing 7.7: Utility.java - Code for GetSpreadSheetXLSX

```
1  import org.apache.poi.ss.usermodel.Cell;
2  import org.apache.poi.ss.usermodel.Row;
3  import org.apache.poi.xssf.usermodel.XSSFCell;
4  import org.apache.poi.xssf.usermodel.XSSFRow;
5  import org.apache.poi.xssf.usermodel.XSSFSheet;
6  import org.apache.poi.xssf.usermodel.XSSFWorkbook;
7
8  import java.io.InputStream;
9  import java.util.Iterator;
10 import java.io.FileInputStream;
11 import java.io.IOException;
12
13 public static String[][] GetSpreadSheetXLSX(String ↵
       ↳ pathName, int sheetNumber) throws IOException
14 {
15     Utility.log.info("GetSpreadSheetXLSX....... File: " + ↵
```

```
             ↪ pathName + "        Sheet: " + sheetNumber);
16
17      String[][] ssData = {};
18
19      try
20      {
21          InputStream ExcelFileToRead = new ←
                ↪ FileInputStream(pathName);
22          XSSFWorkbook  workbk = new ←
                ↪ XSSFWorkbook(ExcelFileToRead);
23
24          XSSFSheet sheet = workbk.getSheetAt(sheetNumber);
25          Utility.log.info("SHEET Name: " + ←
                ↪ sheet.getSheetName());
26
27          XSSFRow row;
28          XSSFCell cell;
29
30          int rr=0, cc=0;
31
32          rr = sheet.getLastRowNum() + 2;
33
34          cc = 12;
35
36          ssData = new String[rr][cc];
37
38          Iterator<Row> rows = sheet.rowIterator();
39
40          Utility.log.info("Last Row is: " + rr);
41
42          while (rows.hasNext())
43          {
44              row=(XSSFRow) rows.next();
45              Iterator<Cell> cells = row.cellIterator();
46
47              while (cells.hasNext())
48              {
49                  cell=(XSSFCell) cells.next();
50
51                  if (cell.getCellType() == ←
                        ↪ XSSFCell.CELL_TYPE_STRING)
52                  {
53                      Utility.log.info("Row: " + ←
                            ↪ (cell.getRowIndex() + 1) + "    Col: ←
                            ↪ " + (cell.getColumnIndex() + 1) + " ←
```

```
54                    " + cell.getStringCellValue() + " ");
                    ssData[cell.getRowIndex() +
                     1][cell.getColumnIndex() + 1] =
                     cell.getStringCellValue();
55                }
56            else if(cell.getCellType() ==
                XSSFCell.CELL_TYPE_NUMERIC)
57            {
58                Utility.log.info("Row: " +
                   (cell.getRowIndex() + 1) + "     Col:
                   " + (cell.getColumnIndex() + 1) + "
                   " + cell.getNumericCellValue() +" ");
59                ssData[cell.getRowIndex() +
                   1][cell.getColumnIndex() + 1] =
                   String.valueOf(
                   cell.getNumericCellValue());
60            }
61            else
62            {
63                Utility.log.info("Row: " +
                   (cell.getRowIndex() + 1) + "     Col:
                   " + (cell.getColumnIndex() + 1) + "
                   *** I M HERE *** Cell Type: " +
                   cell.getCellType());
64            }
65        }
66      }
67    }
68    catch (Exception e)
69    {
70        e.printStackTrace();
71        Utility.ReportExpectedVsActual("Exception occurred"
            + e.getMessage() , "Failing test");
72    }
73
74    return ssData;
75 }
```

Line 1 - 11: Additional imports needed to support functionality.
Line 17: Declare two dimensional string array to store data.
Line 25: Log the worksheet name.
Line 32: Variable 'rr' is the row index. To make things easier to reference, we will make ssData[1][1] our first element (instead of ssData[0][0]) which will save the spreadsheet data for row=1 and column=1 so we add two extras in the row index - one for starting with row 1 and the other for getRowIndex which starts with zero.

Line 34: Variable 'cc' is the column index with value of 12 - to cover for 11 columns and one extra as our first data element is ssData[1][1] instead of ssData[0][0].
Line 36: Redefine array based on data rows and columns in the spreadsheet.
Line 51: Deal with string cell type.
Line 53: Log the cell value.
Line 54: Save the cell value in the two dimensional array.
Line 56: Deal with numeric cell type.
Line 61: Deal with other cell types.
Line 74: Return the data array.

Add another generic function 'ExcelDateParse' to the Utility.java file.

ExcelDateParse - Converts Excel date format to a defined date format		
Input Parameters	*ExcelDate*	Date in Excel format
Return Value	*Date*	Returns date in yyyy-MM-dd format

Listing 7.8: Utility.java - Code for ExcelDateParse

```
1  import java.util.Date;
2  import java.text.SimpleDateFormat;
3
4  public static String ExcelDateParse(String ExcelDate)
5  {
6      double dt = Double.parseDouble(ExcelDate);
7
8      Date jdt = org.apache.poi.ss.usermodel.DateUtil.
            getJavaDate(dt);
9
10     SimpleDateFormat myDateFormat = new
            SimpleDateFormat("yyyy-MM-dd");
11     String date = myDateFormat.format(jdt);
12
13     return date;
14 }
```

Line 6: Parse the Excel date in string format to a double value.
Line 8: Get java date of the double value.
Line 10: Define the new date format we need.
Line 11: Convert to the required date format.

Let's add another generic function 'CheckSalesDetailsSourceArray' to the Utility.java file.

CheckSalesDetailsSourceArray - Checks the sales detail in fact table with a two dimensional array which contains data from the Excel file		
Input Parameters	*expFileData*	Excel file data for the Expected Result in a two dimensional array
Input Parameters	*dataSource*	Source of the data
Return Value	*void*	Returns nothing

Listing 7.9: Utility.java - Code for CheckSalesDetailsSourceArray

```java
1  public static void CheckSalesDetailsSourceArray( ←
       ↪ String[][] expFileData, String dataSource)
2  {
3      Utility.log.info("CheckSalesDetailsSourceArray....");
4
5      List<String> resultActDataSource = new ←
           ↪ ArrayList<String>();
6      List<String> resultActOrderID = new ArrayList<String>();
7      List<String> resultActProductID = new ←
           ↪ ArrayList<String>();
8      List<String> resultActCustomerID = new ←
           ↪ ArrayList<String>();
9      List<String> resultActEmployeeID = new ←
           ↪ ArrayList<String>();
10     List<String> resultActOrderDate = new ←
           ↪ ArrayList<String>();
11     List<String> resultActDispatchDate = new ←
           ↪ ArrayList<String>();
12     List<String> resultActPriceMatch = new ←
           ↪ ArrayList<String>();
13     List<String> resultActUnitPrice = new ←
           ↪ ArrayList<String>();
14     List<String> resultActQuantity = new ArrayList<String>();
15     List<String> resultActDiscount = new ArrayList<String>();
16     List<String> resultActGiftWrap = new ArrayList<String>();
17
18     //Find Actual Result
19     try
20     {
21         Class.forName("com.microsoft.sqlserver.jdbc. ←
               ↪ SQLServerDriver");
22         Connection conn = DriverManager.getConnection( ←
               ↪ Environment.DB_OPS_DWS, Environment.DB_USERID, ←
               ↪ Environment.DB_PWD);
```

```
23    Utility.log.info("DB connected..." + ←
          ↪ Environment.DB_OPS_DWS);
24    Statement statement = conn.createStatement();
25
26    String queryString = "SELECT DataSource " + ←
          ↪ Config.newLine;
27    queryString += "          ,s.OrderID, c.CustomerID, ←
          ↪ p.ProductID, e.EmployeeID" + Config.newLine;
28    queryString += "          ,dtOrd.FullDate As OrderDate, ←
          ↪ dtShp.FullDate As DispatchDate" + Config.newLine;
29    queryString += "          ,pm.PriceMatchDescription As ←
          ↪ PriceMatch, s.UnitPrice" + Config.newLine;
30    queryString += "          ,s.Quantity ,s.Discount, ←
          ↪ yn.YesNoDescription As GiftWrap" + ←
          ↪ Config.newLine;
31    queryString += "FROM [dbo].[factSales] s" + ←
          ↪ Config.newLine;
32    queryString += "LEFT JOIN [dbo].[dimCustomer] c on ←
          ↪ c.CustomerKey = s.CustomerKey " + Config.newLine;
33    queryString += "LEFT JOIN [dbo].[dimProduct] p on ←
          ↪ p.ProductKey = s.ProductKey" + Config.newLine;
34    queryString += "LEFT JOIN [dbo].[dimEmployee] e on ←
          ↪ e.EmployeeKey = s.EmployeeKey" + Config.newLine;
35    queryString += "LEFT JOIN [dbo].[dimDate] dtOrd on ←
          ↪ dtOrd.DateKey = s.OrderDateKey" + Config.newLine;
36    queryString += "LEFT JOIN [dbo].[dimDate] dtShp on ←
          ↪ dtShp.DateKey = s.DispatchDateKey" + ←
          ↪ Config.newLine;
37    queryString += "LEFT JOIN [dbo].[dimYesNo] yn on ←
          ↪ yn.YesNoKey = s.GiftWrapYesNoKey" + ←
          ↪ Config.newLine;
38    queryString += "LEFT JOIN [dbo].[dimPriceMatch] pm ←
          ↪ on pm.PriceMatchKey = s.PriceMatchKey" + ←
          ↪ Config.newLine;
39    queryString += "Where DataSource = '" + dataSource ←
          ↪ + "'" + Config.newLine;
40    queryString += "Order by OrderID, ProductID ";
41
42    Utility.log.info("SQL is: " + queryString);
43
44    ResultSet rs = statement.executeQuery(queryString);
45
46    while (rs.next())
47    {
48        resultActDataSource.add("DataSource ==> " + ←
```

```
                            ↪ rs.getString("DataSource"));
49          resultActOrderID.add("OrderID ==> " + ↩
                            ↪ rs.getString("OrderID"));
50          resultActProductID.add("ProductID ==> " + ↩
                            ↪ rs.getString("ProductID"));
51          resultActCustomerID.add("CustomerID ==> " + ↩
                            ↪ rs.getString("CustomerID"));
52          resultActEmployeeID.add("EmployeeID ==> " + ↩
                            ↪ rs.getString("EmployeeID"));
53          resultActOrderDate.add("OrderDate ==> " + ↩
                            ↪ rs.getString("OrderDate"));
54          resultActDispatchDate.add("DispatchDate ==> " + ↩
                            ↪ rs.getString("DispatchDate"));
55          resultActPriceMatch.add("PriceMatch ==> " + ↩
                            ↪ rs.getString("PriceMatch"));
56          resultActUnitPrice.add("UnitPrice ==> " + ↩
                            ↪ rs.getString("UnitPrice"));
57          resultActQuantity.add("Quantity ==> " + ↩
                            ↪ rs.getString("Quantity"));
58          resultActDiscount.add("Discount ==> " + ↩
                            ↪ rs.getString("Discount"));
59          resultActGiftWrap.add("GiftWrap ==> " + ↩
                            ↪ rs.getString("GiftWrap"));
60      }
61  } catch (Exception e)
62  {
63      e.printStackTrace();
64      Utility.ReportExpectedVsActual("Exception occurred. ↩
            ↪ " + e.getMessage(), "Failing test");
65  }
66
67  for(int j=2; j <= expFileData.length-1; j++)
68  {
69      Utility.log.info("Row....." + j + "          ↩
            ↪ DataSource....." + dataSource );
70
71      Utility.ReportExpectedVsActual("DataSource ==> " + ↩
            ↪ dataSource, resultActDataSource.get(j-2));
72      Utility.ReportExpectedVsActual("OrderID ==> " + ↩
            ↪ String.valueOf((int)Double.parseDouble( ↩
            ↪ expFileData[j][1])), ↩
            ↪ resultActOrderID.get(j-2));
73      Utility.ReportExpectedVsActual("ProductID ==> " + ↩
            ↪ String.valueOf((int)Double.parseDouble( ↩
            ↪ expFileData[j][3])), ↩
```

```
                    ↪ resultActProductID.get(j-2));
74          Utility.ReportExpectedVsActual("CustomerID ==> " + ↵
                    ↪ expFileData[j][2], resultActCustomerID.get(j-2));
75          Utility.ReportExpectedVsActual("EmployeeID ==> " + ↵
                    ↪ String.valueOf((int)Double.parseDouble( ↵
                    ↪ expFileData[j][4])), ↵
                    ↪ resultActEmployeeID.get(j-2));
76          Utility.ReportExpectedVsActual("OrderDate ==> " + ↵
                    ↪ Utility.ExcelDateParse( expFileData[j][5]), ↵
                    ↪ resultActOrderDate.get(j-2));
77          Utility.ReportExpectedVsActual("DispatchDate ==> " ↵
                    ↪ + Utility.ExcelDateParse( expFileData[j][6]), ↵
                    ↪ resultActDispatchDate.get(j-2));
78
79          if (expFileData[j][7] == null)
80              Utility.ReportExpectedVsActual("PriceMatch ==> ↵
                    ↪ Unknown", resultActPriceMatch.get(j-2));
81          else
82              Utility.ReportExpectedVsActual("PriceMatch ==> " ↵
                    ↪ + expFileData[j][7], ↵
                    ↪ resultActPriceMatch.get(j-2));
83
84          Utility.ReportExpectedVsActual("UnitPrice ==> " + ↵
                    ↪ String.format("%.4f", ↵
                    ↪ Double.parseDouble(expFileData[j][8])), ↵
                    ↪ resultActUnitPrice.get(j-2));
85          Utility.ReportExpectedVsActual("Quantity ==> " + ↵
                    ↪ String.valueOf((int)Double.parseDouble( ↵
                    ↪ expFileData[j][9])), resultActQuantity.get(j-2));
86          Utility.ReportExpectedVsActual("Discount ==> " + ↵
                    ↪ expFileData[j][10], resultActDiscount.get(j-2));
87          Utility.ReportExpectedVsActual("GiftWrap ==> " + ↵
                    ↪ expFileData[j][11], resultActGiftWrap.get(j-2));
88      }
89  }
```

Line 67: Start with row number two as the first row is a header.

Line 71: Note the comparison with the (j-2)th element. First iteration of the loop i.e. j=2 will be compared with the first element of List 'resultActDataSource'.

Line 72: Cast 'OrderID' to integer and then convert to a string for comparison.

Line 76 and 77: Call to 'ExcelDateParse' function for conversion to the desired date format.

Line 79: If the expected 'PriceMatch' value is null then compare with the 'Unknown' string.

Now add a new test sourceDataXLSX.java as shown in Listing 7.10.

Listing 7.10: Code for sourceDataXLSX.java

```
1  package autoDW;
2
3  import java.io.IOException;
4  import org.junit.rules.TestName;
5  import org.junit.AfterClass;
6  import org.junit.Before;
7  import org.junit.BeforeClass;
8  import org.junit.FixMethodOrder;
9  import org.junit.Rule;
10 import org.junit.Test;
11 import org.junit.runners.MethodSorters;
12
13 @FixMethodOrder(MethodSorters.NAME_ASCENDING)
14 public class sourceDataXLSX
15 {
16     @Rule public TestName name = new TestName();
17
18     static String sourceFileName =    ↵
          ↪ "SalesTransactions.xlsx";
19     static String[][] expFileData;
20
21     @BeforeClass
22     public static void setUpBeforeClass() throws Exception
23     {
24         Utility.SetupSummaryFile(Utility.GetName(Thread. ↵
              ↪ currentThread().getStackTrace()[1]. ↵
              ↪ getClassName()));
25         expFileData = Utility.GetSpreadSheetXLSX( ↵
              ↪ Config.DATAFILE_LOCATION + sourceFileName, 0);
26     }
27
28     @Before
29     public void setUp() throws Exception
30     {
31         Config.TestResult = Config.PASS;
32     }
33
34     @AfterClass
35     public static void tearDownAfterClass() throws Exception
36     {
37         Utility.SaveLogWithSummary(Utility.GetName(Thread. ↵
```

```
           ↪ currentThread().getStackTrace()[1]. ←
           ↪ getClassName()));
38    }
39
40    @Test
41    public void _05_test_CheckForEmptySourceXLSX() throws ←
          ↪ IOException
42    {
43        Utility.log.info("***********   Starting Test: " + ←
              ↪ name.getMethodName());
44
45        Utility.log.info("expFileInfo Row Size: " + ←
              ↪ expFileData.length);
46        Utility.log.info("expFileInfo Col Size: " + ←
              ↪ expFileData[0].length);
47
48        if(expFileData.length > 0 & expFileData[0].length > 0)
49            Utility.ReportExpectedVsActual("Data exists in " ←
                  ↪ + sourceFileName, "Data exists in " + ←
                  ↪ sourceFileName);
50        else
51            Utility.ReportExpectedVsActual("No Data exists ←
                  ↪ in " + sourceFileName, "Failing test");
52
53        Utility.ReportResultWithSummary(name.getMethodName());
54    }
55
56    @Test
57    public void _10_test_CheckForEmptyTargetTables()
58    {
59        Utility.log.info("***********   Starting Test: " + ←
              ↪ name.getMethodName());
60
61        Utility.CheckForEmptyTable(Environment.DB_OPS_DWS, ←
              ↪ "dbo", "factSales");
62        Utility.ReportResultWithSummary(name.getMethodName());
63    }
64
65    @Test
66    public void _15_test_CheckForUniqueKey()
67    {
68        Utility.log.info("***********   Starting Test: " + ←
              ↪ name.getMethodName());
69
70        Utility.CheckForUniqueKeyMultipleCols( ←
```

```
              ↪ Environment.DB_OPS_DWS, "dbo", "factSales", ←
              ↪ "DataSource,OrderID,ProductKey");
71            Utility.ReportResultWithSummary(name.getMethodName());
72        }
73
74        @Test
75        public void _20_test_CheckForNullValues()
76        {
77            Utility.log.info("***********   Starting Test: " + ←
              ↪ name.getMethodName());
78
79            Utility.CheckForNullValues(Environment.DB_OPS_DWS, ←
              ↪ "dbo", "factSales", "", "");
80            Utility.ReportResultWithSummary(name.getMethodName());
81        }
82
83        @Test
84        public void _40_test_CheckSalesDetails()
85        {
86            Utility.log.info("***********   Starting Test: " + ←
              ↪ name.getMethodName());
87
88            Utility.CheckSalesDetailsSourceArray(expFileData, ←
              ↪ sourceFileName);
89            Utility.ReportResultWithSummary(name.getMethodName());
90        }
91  }
```

Line 18: Specify the source XLSX file name. You may want to have a file name with a date and timestamp if dealing with multiple files.

Line 25: Read XLSX source file data.

Line 88: Note the parameter 'dataSource' of function 'CheckSalesDetailsSourceArray' which in this case is "SalesTransactions.xlsx".

Execute the tests and you will see a Summary Result file as shown in the Figure 7.4.

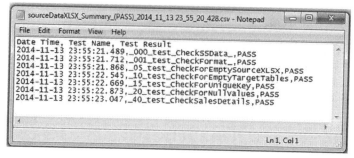

Figure 7.4: Summary File - XLSX Data Source

7.2.2   XLS Format

Appendix A has a listing of the sample 'SalesTransactions.XLS' file. Make sure that the data is sorted in ascending order by 'OrderID' and then by 'ProductID' which is the order the data is fetched from the target (fact) table.

☞   In the real world, loading the 'SalesTransactions.XLS' data into the warehouse would usually be performed via an ETL job as shown in Figure 1.1. The data might first go into a staging table and then be loaded into the fact table, or the ETL job might load it directly into the fact table.

For our automated testing, we need to mimic something similar so that we have some data for our testing. In order to do this, you need to save the 'SalesTransactions.XLS' as 'XLS.CSV' [use Excel option 'Save As', select 'Save as type:' option 'CSV(Comma delimited)(*.csv)']. Now use Listing 7.11 code to load the 'XLS.CSV' file into the temporary table 'tmpDailyTxn' and finally load the fact table. This will ensure that the fact table is populated with the test data. Note the reuse of temp table 'tmpDailyTxn'.

Listing 7.11: XLS Source - Loading Fact Table

```
1  SET DATEFORMAT dmy;
2  GO
3
4  Truncate Table [OPS_STG].dbo.tmpDailyTxn
5  GO
6
7  BULK INSERT [OPS_STG].dbo.tmpDailyTxn FROM ↵
       ↪ 'C:/Workspace/TestData/XLS.csv' WITH (FIRSTROW = 2, ↵
       ↪ FIELDTERMINATOR = ',', ROWTERMINATOR = '\n')
8  GO
9
10 ALTER TABLE [OPS_DWS].[dbo].[factSales] DROP CONSTRAINT ↵
       ↪ [FK_factSales_Customer]
11 ALTER TABLE [OPS_DWS].[dbo].[factSales] DROP CONSTRAINT ↵
       ↪ [FK_factSales_Product]
12 ALTER TABLE [OPS_DWS].[dbo].[factSales] DROP CONSTRAINT ↵
       ↪ [FK_factSales_Employee]
13 ALTER TABLE [OPS_DWS].[dbo].[factSales] DROP CONSTRAINT ↵
       ↪ [FK_factSales_OrderDate]
14 ALTER TABLE [OPS_DWS].[dbo].[factSales] DROP CONSTRAINT ↵
       ↪ [FK_factSales_DispatchDate]
15 ALTER TABLE [OPS_DWS].[dbo].[factSales] DROP CONSTRAINT ↵
       ↪ [FK_factSales_GiftWrapYesNoKey]
16 ALTER TABLE [OPS_DWS].[dbo].[factSales] DROP CONSTRAINT ↵
```

```
        ↪ [FK_factSales_PriceMatch]
17  GO
18
19  delete FROM [OPS_DWS].[dbo].[factSales]
20  where [DataSource] = 'SalesTransactions.xls'
21  GO
22  INSERT INTO [OPS_DWS].[dbo].[factSales]
23  SELECT 'SalesTransactions.xls'
24         ,o.[OrderID]
25         ,ISNULL(c.CustomerKey, -1)  CustomerKey
26         ,ISNULL(p.ProductKey, -1)   ProductKey
27         ,ISNULL(e.EmployeeKey, -1)  EmployeeKey
28         ,ISNULL(dtOrd.DateKey, -1)  OrderDateKey
29         ,ISNULL(dtShp.DateKey, -1)  DispatchDateKey
30         ,ISNULL(pm.PriceMatchKey, -1) PriceMatchKey
31         ,o.UnitPrice
32         ,o.Quantity
33         ,o.Discount
34         ,ISNULL(yn.YesNoKey, -1) GiftWrapYesNoKey
35         ,GETDATE()
36  FROM [OPS_STG].[dbo].[tmpDailyTxn] o
37  LEFT JOIN [OPS_DWS].[dbo].[dimCustomer] c on c.CustomerID ↵
        ↪ = o.CustomerID
38  LEFT JOIN [OPS_DWS].[dbo].[dimProduct] p on p.ProductID = ↵
        ↪ o.ProductID
39  LEFT JOIN [OPS_DWS].[dbo].[dimEmployee] e on e.EmployeeID ↵
        ↪ = o.EmployeeID
40  LEFT JOIN [OPS_DWS].[dbo].[dimDate] dtOrd on ↵
        ↪ dtOrd.FullDate = o.OrderDate
41  LEFT JOIN [OPS_DWS].[dbo].[dimDate] dtShp on ↵
        ↪ dtShp.FullDate = o.DispatchDate
42  LEFT JOIN [OPS_DWS].[dbo].[dimYesNo] yn on ↵
        ↪ yn.YesNoDescription = o.GiftWrap
43  LEFT JOIN [OPS_DWS].[dbo].[dimPriceMatch] pm on ↵
        ↪ pm.[PriceMatchDescription] = o.PriceMatch
44  GO
45
46  ALTER TABLE [OPS_DWS].[dbo].[factSales]  WITH NOCHECK ADD ↵
        ↪  CONSTRAINT [FK_factSales_Customer] FOREIGN ↵
        ↪ KEY([CustomerKey])
47  REFERENCES [OPS_DWS].[dbo].[dimCustomer] ([CustomerKey])
48  ALTER TABLE [OPS_DWS].[dbo].[factSales] CHECK CONSTRAINT ↵
        ↪ [FK_factSales_Customer]
49  ALTER TABLE [OPS_DWS].[dbo].[factSales]  WITH NOCHECK ADD ↵
        ↪  CONSTRAINT [FK_factSales_Product] FOREIGN ↵
```

```
       ↪ KEY([ProductKey])
50  REFERENCES [OPS_DWS].[dbo].[dimProduct] ([ProductKey])
51  ALTER TABLE [OPS_DWS].[dbo].[factSales] CHECK CONSTRAINT ↩
       ↪ [FK_factSales_Product]
52  ALTER TABLE [OPS_DWS].[dbo].[factSales]  WITH NOCHECK ADD ↩
       ↪  CONSTRAINT [FK_factSales_Employee] FOREIGN ↩
       ↪ KEY([EmployeeKey])
53  REFERENCES [OPS_DWS].[dbo].[dimEmployee] ([EmployeeKey])
54  ALTER TABLE [OPS_DWS].[dbo].[factSales] CHECK CONSTRAINT ↩
       ↪ [FK_factSales_Employee]
55  ALTER TABLE [OPS_DWS].[dbo].[factSales]  WITH NOCHECK ADD ↩
       ↪  CONSTRAINT [FK_factSales_OrderDate] FOREIGN ↩
       ↪ KEY([OrderDateKey])
56  REFERENCES [OPS_DWS].[dbo].[dimDate] ([DateKey])
57  ALTER TABLE [OPS_DWS].[dbo].[factSales] CHECK CONSTRAINT ↩
       ↪ [FK_factSales_OrderDate]
58  ALTER TABLE [OPS_DWS].[dbo].[factSales]  WITH NOCHECK ADD ↩
       ↪  CONSTRAINT [FK_factSales_DispatchDate] FOREIGN ↩
       ↪ KEY([DispatchDateKey])
59  REFERENCES [OPS_DWS].[dbo].[dimDate] ([DateKey])
60  ALTER TABLE [OPS_DWS].[dbo].[factSales] CHECK CONSTRAINT ↩
       ↪ [FK_factSales_DispatchDate]
61  ALTER TABLE [OPS_DWS].[dbo].[factSales]  WITH NOCHECK ADD ↩
       ↪  CONSTRAINT [FK_factSales_GiftWrapYesNoKey] FOREIGN ↩
       ↪ KEY([GiftWrapYesNoKey])
62  REFERENCES [OPS_DWS].[dbo].[dimYesNo] ([YesNoKey])
63  ALTER TABLE [OPS_DWS].[dbo].[factSales] CHECK CONSTRAINT ↩
       ↪ [FK_factSales_GiftWrapYesNoKey]
64  ALTER TABLE [OPS_DWS].[dbo].[factSales]  WITH NOCHECK ADD ↩
       ↪  CONSTRAINT [FK_factSales_PriceMatch] FOREIGN ↩
       ↪ KEY([PriceMatchKey])
65  REFERENCES [OPS_DWS].[dbo].[dimPriceMatch] ([PriceMatchKey])
66  ALTER TABLE [OPS_DWS].[dbo].[factSales] CHECK CONSTRAINT ↩
       ↪ [FK_factSales_PriceMatch]
67  GO
```

So let's get on with automating our tests. Add the following new function to the Utility.java file.

GetSpreadSheetXLS - Gets data from a file which is in the XLS format		
Input Parameters	*pathName*	Path and name of the input XLS file
	sheetNumber	Sheet number of the XLS to read
Return Value	*Spreadsheet Data*	Returns the spreadsheet data in a two dimensional array

Listing 7.12: Utility.java - code for GetSpreadSheetXLS

```java
1  import org.apache.poi.hssf.usermodel.HSSFCell;
2  import org.apache.poi.hssf.usermodel.HSSFRow;
3  import org.apache.poi.hssf.usermodel.HSSFSheet;
4  import org.apache.poi.hssf.usermodel.HSSFWorkbook;
5
6  public static String[][] GetSpreadSheetXLS(String ↵
       ↪ pathName, int sheetNumber) throws IOException
7  {
8      Utility.log.info("GetSpreadSheetXLS...... File: " + ↵
           ↪ pathName + "        Sheet: " + sheetNumber);
9
10     String[][] ssData = {};
11
12     try
13     {
14         InputStream ExcelFileToRead = new ↵
               ↪ FileInputStream(pathName);
15         HSSFWorkbook workbook = new ↵
               ↪ HSSFWorkbook(ExcelFileToRead);
16
17         HSSFSheet sheet=workbook.getSheetAt(sheetNumber);
18         Utility.log.info("SHEET Name: " + ↵
               ↪ sheet.getSheetName());
19         HSSFRow row;
20         HSSFCell cell;
21
22         int rr=0, cc=0;
23
24         rr = sheet.getLastRowNum() + 2;
25
26         cc = 12;
27
28         ssData = new String[rr][cc];
29
30         Iterator<Row> rows = sheet.rowIterator();
```

```
31
32      Utility.log.info("getLastRowNum: " + ↵
          ↪ sheet.getLastRowNum());
33
34      while (rows.hasNext())
35      {
36          row=(HSSFRow) rows.next();
37          Iterator<Cell> cells = row.cellIterator();
38
39          while (cells.hasNext())
40          {
41              cell=(HSSFCell) cells.next();
42
43              if (cell.getCellType() == ↵
                  ↪ HSSFCell.CELL_TYPE_STRING)
44              {
45                  Utility.log.info("Row: " + ↵
                      ↪ (cell.getRowIndex() + 1) + "    Col: ↵
                      ↪ " + (cell.getColumnIndex() + 1) + "  ↵
                      ↪ " + cell.getStringCellValue()+" ");
46                  ssData[cell.getRowIndex() + ↵
                      ↪ 1][cell.getColumnIndex() + 1] = ↵
                      ↪ cell.getStringCellValue();
47              }
48              else if(cell.getCellType() == ↵
                  ↪ HSSFCell.CELL_TYPE_NUMERIC)
49              {
50                  Utility.log.info("Row: " + ↵
                      ↪ (cell.getRowIndex() + 1) + "    Col: ↵
                      ↪ " + (cell.getColumnIndex() + 1) + "  ↵
                      ↪ " + cell.getNumericCellValue()+" ");
51                  ssData[cell.getRowIndex() + ↵
                      ↪ 1][cell.getColumnIndex() + 1] = ↵
                      ↪ String.valueOf( ↵
                      ↪ cell.getNumericCellValue());
52              }
53              else
54              {
55                  Utility.log.info("Row: " + ↵
                      ↪ (cell.getRowIndex() + 1) + "    Col: ↵
                      ↪ " + (cell.getColumnIndex() + 1) + "   " ↵
                      ↪ *** I M HERE *** Cell Type: " + ↵
                      ↪ cell.getCellType());
56              }
57          }
```

```
58          }
59      }
60      catch (Exception e)
61      {
62          e.printStackTrace();
63          Utility.ReportExpectedVsActual("Exception occurred" ↵
               ↪ + e.getMessage() , "Failing test");
64      }
65
66      return ssData;
67  }
```

Line 1 - 4: Additional imports needed to support functionality.

Line 10: Declare two dimensional string array to store data.

Line 18: Log the worksheet name.

Line 24: Variable 'rr' is the row index. To make things easier to reference, we will make ssData[1][1] our first element (instead of ssData[0][0]) which will save the spreadsheet data for row=1 and column=1 so we add two extras in the row index - one for starting with row 1 and the other for getRowIndex which starts with zero.

Line 26: Variable 'cc' is the column index with value of 12 - to cover for 11 columns and one extra as our first data element is ssData[1][1] instead of ssData[0][0].

Line 28: Redefine array based on data rows and columns in the spreadsheet.

Line 43: Deal with string cell type.

Line 45: Log the cell value.

Line 46: Save the cell value in the two dimensional array.

Line 48: Deal with numeric cell type.

Line 53: Deal with other cell types.

Line 66: Return the data array.

Now add a new test sourceDataXLS.java.

Listing 7.13: Code for sourceDataXLS.java

```
1  package autoDW;
2
3  import java.io.IOException;
4  import org.junit.rules.TestName;
5  import org.junit.AfterClass;
6  import org.junit.Before;
7  import org.junit.BeforeClass;
8  import org.junit.FixMethodOrder;
9  import org.junit.Rule;
10 import org.junit.Test;
11 import org.junit.runners.MethodSorters;
```

```
12
13  @FixMethodOrder(MethodSorters.NAME_ASCENDING)
14  public class sourceDataXLS
15  {
16      @Rule public TestName name = new TestName();
17
18      static String sourceFileName =      ↵
            ↪ "SalesTransactions.xls";
19      static String[][] expFileData;
20
21      @BeforeClass
22      public static void setUpBeforeClass() throws Exception
23      {
24          Utility.SetupSummaryFile(Utility.GetName ↵
                ↪ (Thread.currentThread().getStackTrace()[1]. ↵
                ↪ getClassName()));
25          expFileData = Utility.GetSpreadSheetXLS( ↵
                ↪ Config.DATAFILE_LOCATION + sourceFileName, 0);
26      }
27
28      @Before
29      public void setUp() throws Exception
30      {
31          Config.TestResult = Config.PASS;
32      }
33
34      @AfterClass
35      public static void tearDownAfterClass() throws Exception
36      {
37          Utility.SaveLogWithSummary(Utility.GetName(Thread. ↵
                ↪ currentThread().getStackTrace()[1]. ↵
                ↪ getClassName()));
38      }
39
40      @Test
41      public void _05_test_CheckForEmptySourcexls() throws ↵
            ↪ IOException
42      {
43          Utility.log.info("************   Starting Test: " + ↵
                ↪ name.getMethodName());
44
45          Utility.log.info("expFileInfo Row Size: " + ↵
                ↪ expFileData.length);
46          Utility.log.info("expFileInfo Col Size: " + ↵
                ↪ expFileData[0].length);
```

```
47
48      if(expFileData.length > 0 & expFileData[0].length > 0)
49          Utility.ReportExpectedVsActual("Data exists in " ↵
              ↳ + sourceFileName, "Data exists in " + ↵
              ↳ sourceFileName);
50      else
51          Utility.ReportExpectedVsActual("No Data exists ↵
              ↳ in " + sourceFileName, "Failing test");
52
53      Utility.ReportResultWithSummary(name.getMethodName());
54  }
55
56  @Test
57  public void _10_test_CheckForEmptyTargetTables()
58  {
59      Utility.log.info("***********   Starting Test: " + ↵
          ↳ name.getMethodName());
60
61      Utility.CheckForEmptyTable(Environment.DB_OPS_DWS, ↵
          ↳ "dbo", "factSales");
62
63      Utility.ReportResultWithSummary(name.getMethodName());
64  }
65
66  @Test
67  public void _15_test_CheckForUniqueKey()
68  {
69      Utility.log.info("***********   Starting Test: " + ↵
          ↳ name.getMethodName());
70
71      Utility.CheckForUniqueKeyMultipleCols( ↵
          ↳ Environment.DB_OPS_DWS, "dbo", "factSales", ↵
          ↳ "DataSource,OrderID,ProductKey");
72
73      Utility.ReportResultWithSummary(name.getMethodName());
74  }
75
76  @Test
77  public void _20_test_CheckForNullValues()
78  {
79      Utility.log.info("***********   Starting Test: " + ↵
          ↳ name.getMethodName());
80
81      Utility.CheckForNullValues(Environment.DB_OPS_DWS, ↵
          ↳ "dbo", "factSales", "", "");
```

Automated Data Warehouse Testing

```
82
83      Utility.ReportResultWithSummary(name.getMethodName());
84   }
85
86   @Test
87   public void _40_test_CheckSalesDetails()
88   {
89      Utility.log.info("***********   Starting Test: " + ↵
           ↪ name.getMethodName());
90
91      Utility.CheckSalesDetailsSourceArray(expFileData, ↵
           ↪ sourceFileName);
92
93      Utility.ReportResultWithSummary(name.getMethodName());
94   }
95 }
```

Line 18: Specify the source XLS file name. You may want to have a file name with a date and timestamp if dealing with multiple files.

Line 25: Read XLS source file data.

Line 91: Note the parameter 'dataSource' of function 'CheckSalesDetailsSourceArray' which in this case is "SalesTransactions.xls".

Execute the tests and you will see a Summary Result file as shown in Figure 7.5.

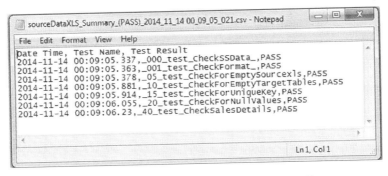

Figure 7.5: Summary File - XLS Data Source

Chapter 7   315

Chapter 8

Automated HTML Test Report

Automated HTML Test Report

In this chapter, we will learn how to:

- *Generate the Build.xml file and use it to execute tests*

- *Create an automatic archive of test reports*

So let's get on with it. . .

Test reporting is one of the many important tasks carried out by testers. Usually, in an automated testing environment, a lot of test results are produced in a short span of time and everyone wants to see a consolidated view of the testing with the ability to drill down to a detail level. In earlier chapters, we saw how our Automation Framework can generate test summary and detail reports in a CSV format. In this chapter, we will see how we can generate well formatted HTML reports. We will also look at how to execute a number of test files at once e.g. to execute all the dimYesNo and dimCustomer tests together. So let's continue.

First things first, let's make sure that the environment variable JAVA_HOME on your workstation is pointing to the JDK folder. The JDK on my workstation was installed in folder 'C:\Program Files\Java\jdk1.7.0_40' so the JAVA_HOME environment variable was set as follows:

```
JAVA_HOME=C:\Program Files\Java\jdk1.7.0_40
```

If you are using a Windows 7 workstation, here is how to set this environment variable:

- Type 'Control Panel\System and Security\System' in Windows Explorer and press the Enter key.

- Click on 'Advanced system settings'.

- Click 'Environment Variables...'

- Under user variables ensure JAVA_HOME is defined and check that it points to the JDK installation folder. If not, click on the 'Edit...' button to change the location as shown in Figure 8.1.

- If JAVA_HOME is not defined then click 'New...' and create the new environment variable.

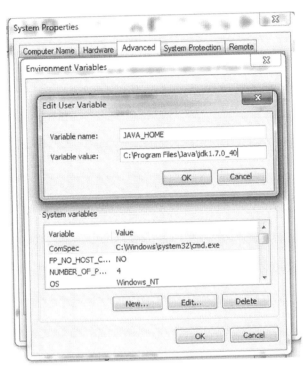

Figure 8.1: Environment Variable: JAVA_HOME

You can also check the value of environment variables as follows:

- Click on the Start button and select Run...

- Type CMD and then press OK.

- Type SET on the command prompt and press the Enter key. You can now check the value set for the environment variable JAVA_HOME.

8.1 Generating Build.XML

Let's now create the Build.XML file that defines the compiling and packaging targets.

- Right click on AutoDW in the 'Package Explorer' and select 'Export...'

- In the Export window select 'General ⇒ Ant Buildfiles' as shown in Figure 8.2.

- Press the Next button.

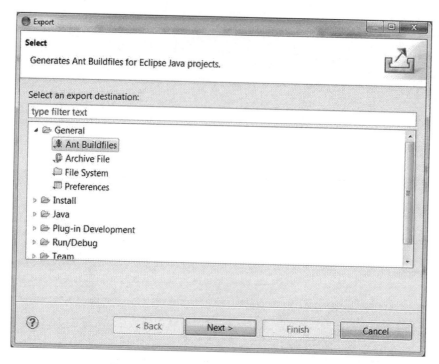

Figure 8.2: Select Ant Buildfiles

On the next window tick AutoDW project and click Finish as shown in Figure 8.3.

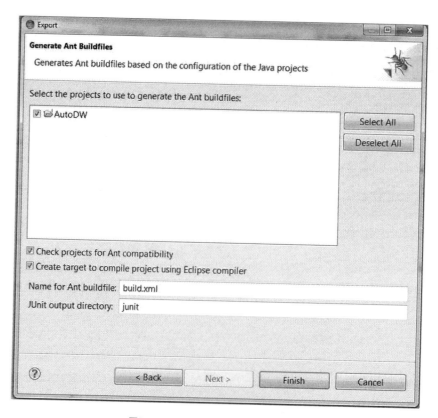

Figure 8.3: Select Project

Now in the 'Package Explorer' window you will see a new file 'build.xml'. If you don't see this file, right click on the AutoDW in the 'Package Explorer' and select 'Refresh' or press F5 and you should now be able to see the 'build.xml' file.

8.2   Executing Tests Via Build.XML

Let's see how to execute our tests using 'build.xml'. Right click on the 'build.xml' file and select Run As ⇒ Ant Build... You will see the 'Edit Configuration' window. Click on the 'Targets' tab. Tick the targets build, dimYesNo, factSales, junitreport in the selection box as shown in Figure 8.4.

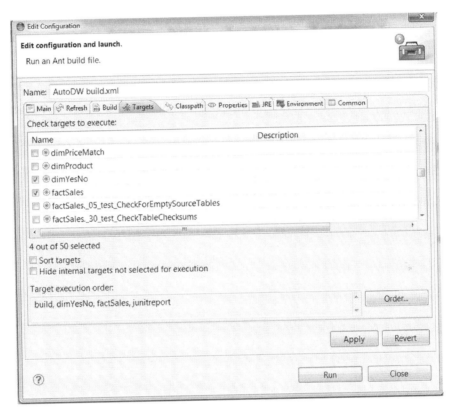

Figure 8.4: Select Targets For Execution

Before we proceed further, I want to highlight two important features on this window that you may need in the future.

Firstly, the 'Sort targets' check box which, when selected, will sort the targets alphabetically. This helps you to easily find the location of your tests.

Secondly, the 'Hide internal targets not selected for execution' feature which, when selected, hides the unnecessary targets and gives you all the selected targets as shown in Figure 8.5.

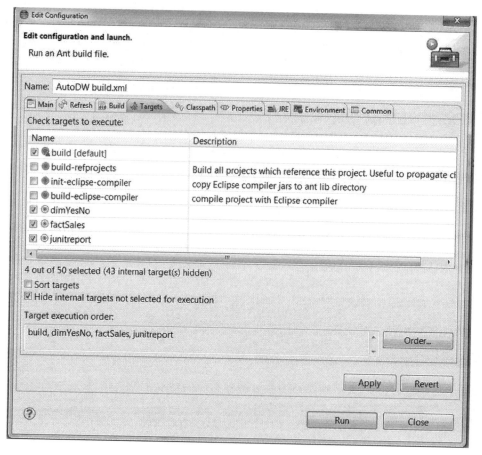

Figure 8.5: Hide Internal Targets

Make sure that the 'Target execution order' at the bottom frame is ⇒ build, dimYesNo, factSales, junitreport. If not then you can order the execution by clicking on the 'Order...' button which displays the dialog shown in Figure 8.6.

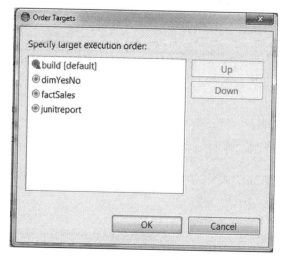

Figure 8.6: Ordering Target Execution

To re-order, just select an item and then click 'Up' or 'Down' button to order the execution. Press the 'OK' button.

Make sure that the 'Targets' tab now looks like as shown in Figure 8.7:

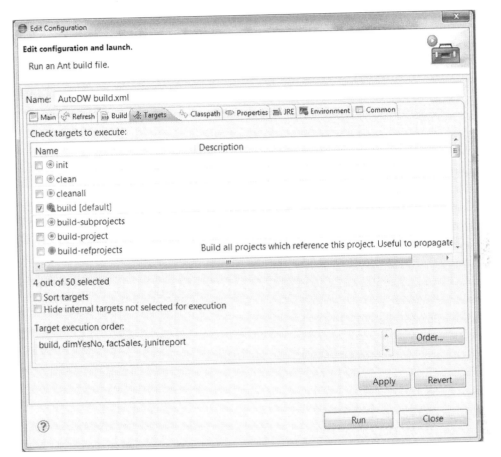

Figure 8.7: Final Target Execution Order

On the 'Edit Configuration' window click the 'JRE' tab and make sure that the option 'Run in the same JRE as workspace' is selected as shown in Figure 8.8.

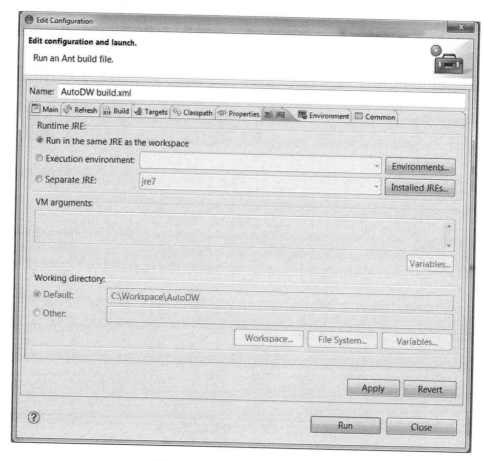

Figure 8.8: Runtime JRE

We are now all set to execute our chosen tests. Just click on the 'Run' button. You should be able to see the test execution progress in the Console. If the Console is not displayed, select Window ⇒ Show View ⇒ Console. In the Console window you may see an error message as shown in Figure 8.9

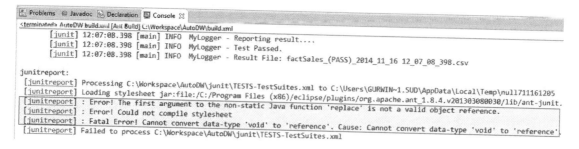

Figure 8.9: JUnit Report Error

Frankly speaking, it took me a while to understand why this was happening! It seemed like a bug with the Ant 1.8.4 distributed in the Eclipse version I was using. The solution for this was to download Ant 1.9.1 (https://archive.apache.org/dist/ant/binaries/). Extract it to folder 'C:\apache-ant-1.9.1'. Now in Eclipse go to Window ⇒

Preferences click on the 'Ant Home...' button, navigate to 'C:\apache-ant-1.9.1' folder and click OK and then OK as shown in Figure 8.10.

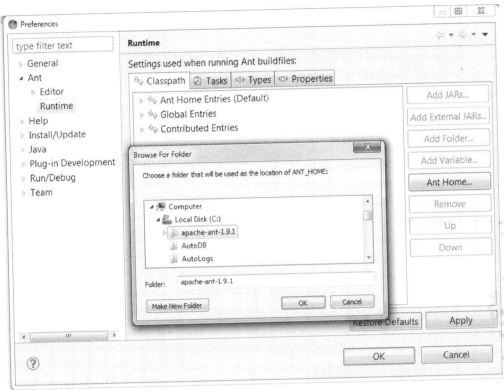

Figure 8.10: Setting Ant Home

Now right click on the Build.XML file and select Run As ⇒ Ant Build... and then click on the Run button. This time you should see a Console window similar to Figure 8.11.

```
Problems  @ Javadoc  Declaration  Console
<terminated> AutoDW build.xml [Ant Build] C:\Workspace\AutoDW\build.xml
    [junit]       ,o.CustomerID, od.ProductID,o.OrderDate, o.DispatchDate
    [junit]       ,ISNULL(od.PriceMatch, 'Unknown') As PriceMatch
    [junit]       ,od.UnitPrice, od.Quantity, od.Discount, od.GiftWrap
    [junit] FROM [dbo].[Orders] o
    [junit] INNER JOIN [dbo].[OrderDetails] od on od.[OrderID] = o.[OrderID]
    [junit] 15:18:03.773 [main] INFO  MyLogger - ***********  Starting Test: _90_test_CompareDecimalNumbers
    [junit] 15:18:03.773 [main] INFO  MyLogger - Ignored minor difference of -0.0001 between expDbl = 1418.0556 a
    [junit] 15:18:03.773 [main] INFO  MyLogger - Original [Expected:] 1418.055556   Original [Actual:] 1418.0555
    [junit] 15:18:03.773 [main] INFO  MyLogger - Reporting result....
    [junit] 15:18:03.773 [main] INFO  MyLogger - Test Passed.
    [junit] 15:18:03.773 [main] INFO  MyLogger - Result File: factSales_(PASS)_2014_11_16 15_18_03_773.csv

junitreport:
  [junitreport] Processing C:\Workspace\AutoDW\junit\TESTS-TestSuites.xml to C:\Users\GURWIN~1.SUD\AppData\Local\Temp'
  [junitreport] Loading stylesheet jar:file:C:/apache-ant-1.9.1/lib/ant-junit.jar!/org/apache/tools/ant/taskdefs/opti
  [junitreport] Transform time: 126ms
  [junitreport] Deleting: C:\Users\GURWIN~1.SUD\AppData\Local\Temp\null11298961665
BUILD SUCCESSFUL
Total time: 5 seconds
```

Figure 8.11: Console Output - HTML Report

Go to 'C:\Workspace\AutoDW\junit' in your Windows Explorer and you will find a set of files as shown in Figure 8.12.

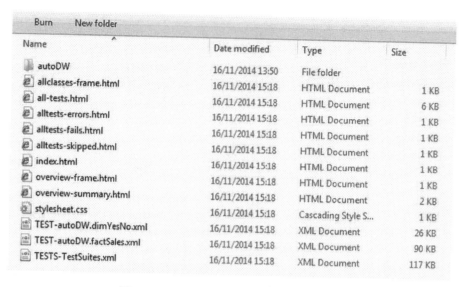

Figure 8.12: HTML Report Files

Double click on the index.html file. Depending on the default internet browser on your workstation, you will see a browser window similar to Figure 8.13.

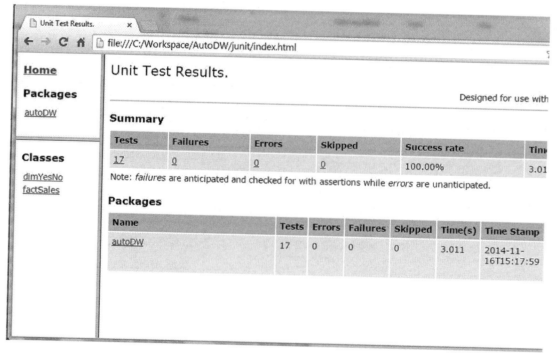

Figure 8.13: HTML Report Index Page

Hurray! You have successfully created an HTML report of the test run. The summary at the top identifies the total number of tests executed, the number of tests failed (due to assertions) and how many tests produced unanticipated errors (e.g. had exceptions) during execution. This is a drill down report which means you can click on any hot link and it will take you to the details. If you want to see all the failures, just click on the link and it will take you there.

As we don't have any failures, click on Tests link (17 in our case) to display the window as shown in Figure 8.14

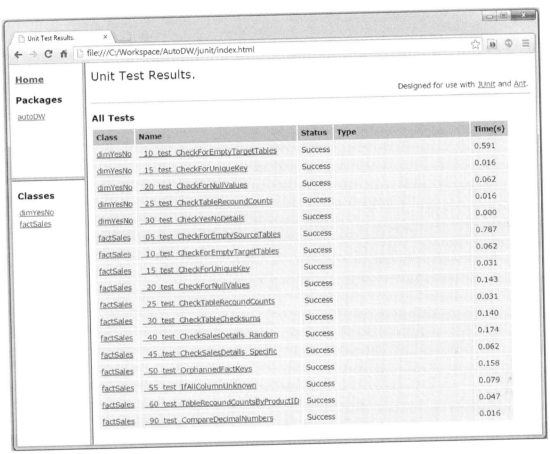

Figure 8.14: HTML Report Details Page

In order to return to the summary screen, just click on the Home link on the top left corner. If you want see the results of a particular test e.g. dimYesNo click on its link in the left hand side pane to see a window as shown in Figure 8.15. At the top pane it shows a summary of tests in dimYesNo e.g. total, errors, failures and other statistics.

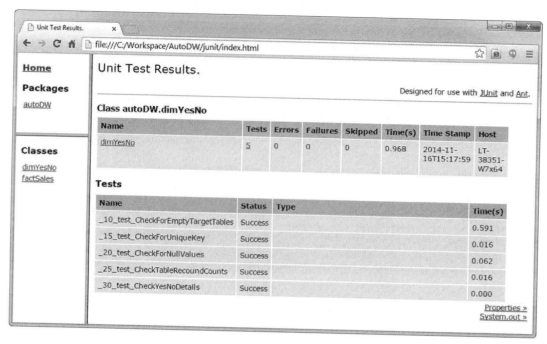

Figure 8.15: HTML Report dimYesNo

At the bottom pane, it displays the status of each test along with the time it took to execute. Click on the 'System.out' link at the bottom right of the browser window. You will see a window similar to Figure 8.16 that displays all the information we get in the CSV test result file!

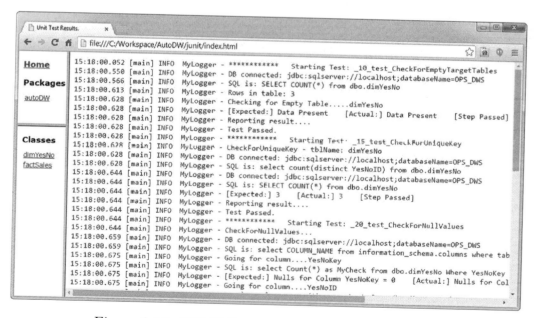

Figure 8.16: HTML Report dimYesNo - System.out

8.3 Archiving HTML Test Results

Ok, we have now seen how our Automation Framework can generate an HTML report at the end of test execution. However, each time you execute the tests in this manner, any previous HTML files are overwritten, so we need the Automation Framework to save a copy of the HTML test results at the end of test execution.

We will write a separate routine to create a zip file of the junit folder at the end of test execution and save it with a date and timestamp for easy reference.

First off all let's define a new function in the Utility.java file.

MyWait - Wait for a specified number of seconds		
Input Parameters	*secs*	Wait time in seconds
Return Value	*void*	Returns nothing

Listing 8.1: Utility.Java - code for MyWait

```
1  public static void MyWait(int secs)
2  {
3     try
4     {
5        Utility.log.info("Waiting..." + secs + " secs.");
6        Thread.sleep(secs * 1000);
7     }
8     catch(InterruptedException ex)
9     {
10       Thread.currentThread().interrupt();
11    }
12 }
```

Line 6 - Call to 'Thread.sleep' causes the current thread to suspend execution for the specified number of milliseconds.

Now let's add a new test 'SaveHTMLLogs' to autoDW (within 'Package Explorer', right click on the folder name 'src' and select New ⇒ Other.... Select JUnit Test Case). Add Listing 8.2 code to it.

Listing 8.2: Code for SaveHTMLLogs.java

```
1  package autoDW;
2
```

```
3   import java.io.BufferedReader;
4   import java.io.IOException;
5   import java.io.InputStreamReader;
6   import org.junit.rules.TestName;
7   import org.junit.FixMethodOrder;
8   import org.junit.Rule;
9   import org.junit.Test;
10  import org.junit.runners.MethodSorters;
11
12  @FixMethodOrder(MethodSorters.NAME_ASCENDING)
13  public class SaveHTMLLogs
14  {
15      @Rule public TestName name = new TestName();
16
17      @Test
18      public void test_SaveHTMLLogs()
19      {
20          Utility.log.info("***********  Starting Test: " + ↵
                ↪ name.getMethodName());
21
22          String sourcePath = ↵
                ↪ getClass().getResource("").getPath();
23
24          sourcePath = sourcePath.replace("/bin/autoDW/", ↵
                ↪ "");
25
26          sourcePath = sourcePath.substring(1);
27
28          Utility.log.info("Class Path: " + sourcePath);
29
30          //breathing space for html report to be finished
31          Utility.MyWait(3);
32
33          try
34          {
35              Process p = Runtime.getRuntime().exec("cmd /C" + ↵
                    ↪ sourcePath + "/SaveHTMLLogs.bat");
36
37              BufferedReader in = new BufferedReader(new ↵
                    ↪ InputStreamReader(p.getInputStream()));
38
39              String line = null;
40              while ((line = in.readLine()) != null)
41              {
42                  Utility.log.info(line);
```

```
43              }
44          }
45          catch (IOException e)
46          {
47              e.printStackTrace();
48          }
49      }
50 }
```

Line 22 - Get the class path which is '/C:/Workspace/AutoDW/bin/autoDW/'.
Line 24 - Remove occurrence of '/bin/autoDW/' which yields '/C:/Workspace/AutoDW'.
Line 26 - Get substring from the first position which yields 'C:/Workspace/AutoDW'.
Line 31 - To be on the safe side, wait 3 seconds for the report generation to finish.
Line 35 - Execute batch file 'SaveHTMLLogs.bat' to create the archive file.
Line 37 - Read the command window output.
Line 42 - Log each line in the logger.

Now create a batch file 'SaveHTMLLogs.bat' in folder 'C:\Workspace\AutoDW' with the code shown in Listing 8.3.

Listing 8.3: Code for SaveHTMLLogs.bat

```
1 "C:\Program Files\7-Zip\7z.exe" a ↵
    ↪ C:\Workspace\AutoDW\htmllogs\TestResult.zip ↵
    ↪ C:\Workspace\AutoDW\junit\* -ssw
2 ren C:\Workspace\AutoDW\htmllogs\TestResult.zip ↵
    ↪ TestResult_%date:~0,2%%date:~3,2%%date:~6,4%_%time:~0, ↵
    ↪ 2%%time:~3,2%.zip
```

Line 1 - Create a 'TestResult.zip' file of the contents in 'junit' folder. Flag -ssw allows for the compressing of locked files, if there are any.
Line 2 - Rename 'TestResult.zip' file to include a date and timestamp.

Now right click on the SaveHTMLLogs and then select Run As ⇒ JUnit Test. You will see a Console output as shown in Figure 8.17.

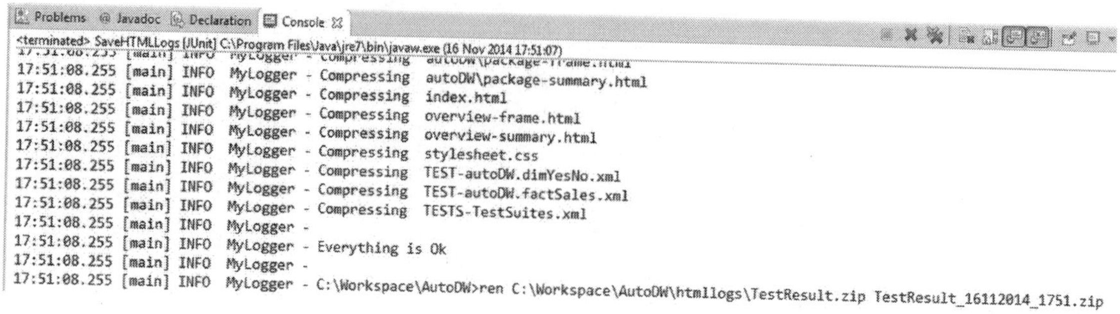

Figure 8.17: Console Output - Save HTML Logs

Now let's add another test 'CleanupPreviousHTMLLogs' to AutoDW (Within 'Package Explorer', right click on the folder name 'src' and select New ⇒ Other.... Select JUnit Test Case). Add Listing 8.4 code to it.

Listing 8.4: Code for CleanupPreviousHTMLLogs.java

```
1  package autoDW;
2
3  import java.io.BufferedReader;
4  import java.io.IOException;
5  import java.io.InputStreamReader;
6  import org.junit.rules.TestName;
7  import org.junit.FixMethodOrder;
8  import org.junit.Rule;
9  import org.junit.Test;
10 import org.junit.runners.MethodSorters;
11
12 @FixMethodOrder(MethodSorters.NAME_ASCENDING)
13 public class CleanupPreviousHTMLLogs
14 {
15     @Rule public TestName name = new TestName();
16
17     @Test
18     public void CleanUpPreviousLogs()
19     {
20         Utility.log.info("***********    Starting Test: " + ↵
             ↪ name.getMethodName());
21
22         String sourcePath = ↵
             ↪ getClass().getResource("").getPath();
23
24         sourcePath = sourcePath.replace("/bin/autoDW/", ↵
             ↪ "");
25
```

```
26        sourcePath = sourcePath.substring(1);
27
28        Utility.log.info("Class Path: " + sourcePath);
29
30        try
31        {
32            Process p = Runtime.getRuntime().exec("cmd /C" + ↵
                  ↪ sourcePath + ↵
                  ↪ "/CleanupPreviousHTMLLogs.Bat");
33
34            BufferedReader in = new BufferedReader( new ↵
                  ↪ InputStreamReader(p.getInputStream()));
35
36            String line = null;
37            while ((line = in.readLine()) != null)
38            {
39                Utility.log.info(line);
40            }
41        }
42        catch (IOException e)
43        {
44            e.printStackTrace();
45        }
46    }
47 }
```

Line 22 - Get the class path which is '/C:/Workspace/AutoDW/bin/autoDW/'.
Line 24 - Remove occurrence of '/bin/autoDW/' which yields '/C:/Workspace/AutoDW'.
Line 26 - Get substring from the first position which yields 'C:/Workspace/AutoDW'.
Line 32 - Execute the batch file 'CleanupPreviousHTMLLogs.Bat' to clean-up previous logs.
Line 34 - Read the command window output.
Line 39 - Log each line in the logger.

Now create a batch file 'CleanupPreviousHTMLLogs.bat' in the folder 'C:\Workspace\AutoDW' with the code as shown in Listing 8.5.

Listing 8.5: Code for CleanupPreviousHTMLLogs.Bat

```
1 rd/s/q C:\Workspace\AutoDW\junit
2 Echo Folder junit deleted
```

Line 1 - Delete the contents of 'junit' folder.
Line 2 - Echo the folder deletion message.

Now right click on the CleanupPreviousHTMLLogs and then select Run As ⇒ JUnit Test. You will see a Console output as shown in Figure 8.18.

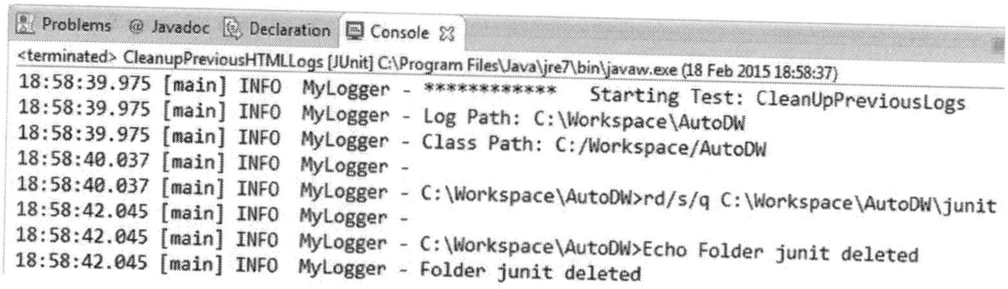

Figure 8.18: Console Output - Clean-up HTML Logs

Create a new folder 'htmllogs' in 'C:\Workspace\AutoDW' (right click in the right pane of Windows Explorer and select New ⇒ Folder and type htmllogs).

Now we need to regenerate the build.xml file so that newly generated tests are included in the targets.

- Right click on AutoDW in the 'Package Explorer' and select 'Export...'.

- In the Export window select 'Ant Buildfiles' and press the Next button.

- On the next window tick the AutoDW project and click Finish.

- Right click on the Build.xml file and select 'Refresh'. This will ensure that the latest files are loaded in the workspace including 'CleanupPreviousHTMLLogs' and 'SaveHTMLLogs' tests.

Now right click on the 'Build.xml' file and select Run As ⇒ Ant Build... Select targets 'CleanupPreviousHTMLLogs' and 'SaveHTMLLogs'. Note that targets build, dimYesNo, factSales, junitreport should already be selected. If not, select them all again.

Now click on the 'Order...' button. Make sure the order is as shown in the Figure 8.19. Use Up/Down buttons as necessary to move the items around.

Chapter 8

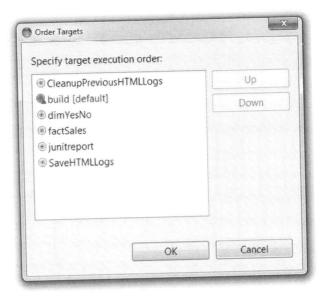

Figure 8.19: Ordering Targets

Press the OK button.

Make sure that the 'Edit Configuration' window now shows the 'Target execution order:' as CleanupPreviousHTMLLogs, build, dimYesNo, factSales, junitreport, SaveHTML-Logs. Click on the Run button.

This time when the execution finishes, the Automation Framework will also create a backup of the test results in the 'htmllogs' folder as shown in Figure 8.20.

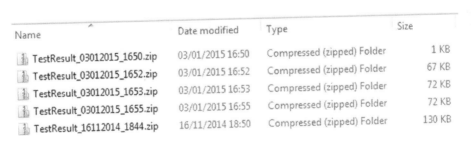

Figure 8.20: Archival Zip File

If you want to look at the results later, just right click on the zip file, select 7-Zip ⇒ and then Extract to '<<folder name\>>' as shown in Figure 8.21.

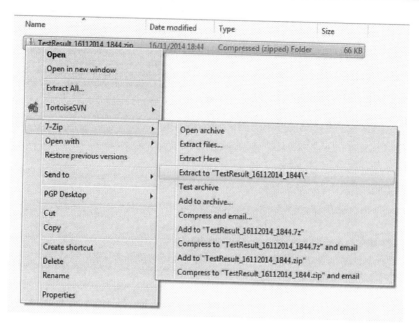

Figure 8.21: Extracting Results From Archival Zip File

To clean up the previous logs and create an archive of HTML report, make sure you include 'CleanupPreviousHTMLLogs' as your first target and 'SaveHTMLLogs' as your last target in the execution order.

Chapter 9

Final Thoughts

Final Thoughts

In this chapter, we will learn about:

- *Data profiling*

- *Automating data profiling tests*

So let's get on with it...

SINCE I started writing this book one topic has remained in the back of my mind which I intend to cover now.

9.1 Data Profiling

Data profiling is an analysis of the source system's data to clarify its characteristics e.g. how data is structured, the contents, how the data relates to other data items, the derivation rules etc. Data profiling is an important step undertaken by data warehouse architects and designers in order to understand the quality and overall nature of the underlying operational source system's data. In general this task is performed by data warehouse architects and designers via a tool. It will be very useful if testers can highlight any anomalies that may exist in the source system data, for example:

- Source table 'Products' contains zero 'UnitPrice' for some items

- Table 'OrderDetails' has a 'Discount' of 150% on an item

- A customer's age is 200 years!

If this data doesn't adhere to the business rules specified in the Data Mapping document then the data may be deemed invalid and the business analyst will need to devise rules to transform these data items based on the organisation's needs.

As a tester, you may want to automate some of the important Data Profiling tests. For our sample data warehouse, let's automate the following data profiling scenarios:

- Records in 'Products' table having zero 'UnitPrice'.

- Table 'OrderDetails' has a 'Discount' more than 50%.

- Table 'Order' has 'OrderDate' in future.

Create a new test dataProfiling and add Listing 9.1 code to it.

Listing 9.1: Code for dataProfiling

```
1  package autoDW;
2
3  import org.junit.AfterClass;
4  import org.junit.Before;
5  import org.junit.BeforeClass;
6  import org.junit.FixMethodOrder;
7  import org.junit.runners.MethodSorters;
8  import org.junit.Rule;
9  import org.junit.Test;
10 import org.junit.rules.TestName;
11
12 @FixMethodOrder(MethodSorters.NAME_ASCENDING)
13 public class dataProfiling
14 {
15     @Rule public TestName name = new TestName();
16
17     @BeforeClass
18     public static void setUpBeforeClass() throws Exception {
19         Utility.SetupSummaryFile(Utility.GetName(Thread. ↵
           ↪ currentThread().getStackTrace()[1]. ↵
           ↪ getClassName()));
20     }
21
22     @Before
23     public void setUp() throws Exception {
24         Config.TestResult = Config.PASS;
25     }
26
27     @AfterClass
28     public static void tearDownAfterClass() throws ↵
           ↪ Exception {
29         Utility.SaveLogWithSummary(Utility.GetName(Thread. ↵
           ↪ currentThread().getStackTrace()[1]. ↵
           ↪ getClassName()));
30     }
```

```
31
32      @Test
33      public void _10_test_ProductsWithZeroUnitPrice()
34      {
35          Utility.log.info("************    Starting Test: " + ↵
                ↪ name.getMethodName());
36
37          int count = Utility.GetCountOfRecordsWithCondition( ↵
                ↪ Environment.DB_OPS_SOURCE, "dbo", "Products", ↵
                ↪ "UnitPrice = 0");
38
39          Utility.ReportExpectedVsActual("0", ↵
                ↪ String.valueOf(count));
40
41          Utility.ReportResultWithSummary(name.getMethodName());
42      }
43
44      @Test
45      public void ↵
            ↪ _20_test_OrderDetailsWithMoreThan50PercentDiscount()
46      {
47          Utility.log.info("************    Starting Test: " + ↵
                ↪ name.getMethodName());
48
49          int count = Utility.GetCountOfRecordsWithCondition( ↵
                ↪ Environment.DB_OPS_SOURCE, "dbo", ↵
                ↪ "OrderDetails", "Discount > 0.5");
50
51          Utility.ReportExpectedVsActual("0", ↵
                ↪ String.valueOf(count));
52
53          Utility.ReportResultWithSummary(name.getMethodName());
54      }
55
56      @Test
57      public void _30_test_OrderWithFutureOrderDate()
58      {
59          Utility.log.info("************    Starting Test: " + ↵
                ↪ name.getMethodName());
60
61          int count = Utility.GetCountOfRecordsWithCondition( ↵
                ↪ Environment.DB_OPS_SOURCE, "dbo", "Orders", " ↵
                ↪ OrderDate > GETDATE()");
62
```

```
63        Utility.ReportExpectedVsActual("0", ↵
            ↪ String.valueOf(count));

64
65        Utility.ReportResultWithSummary(name.getMethodName());
66    }
67 }
```

Line 37, 49 and 61: Specify the conditions to check for profiling.

Line 39, 51 and 63: Note the expected count is zero.

Execute the test and you will see a Console output as shown in Figure 9.1.

Figure 9.1: Console Output Data Profiling Tests

Similarly you can create tests based on the requirements you are testing.

Hopefully, now that you have learnt about automating the testing of our sample data warehouse, you are feeling extremely comfortable using this Automation Framework and are now confident enough to be able to apply it to a number of different data warehouse systems.

Happy automated testing!

Appendices

A.1   Test Data - Products Table

Column Header
ProductID,ProductName,UnitPrice,UnitsInStock,UnitsOnOrder,
ReorderLevel,Discontinued

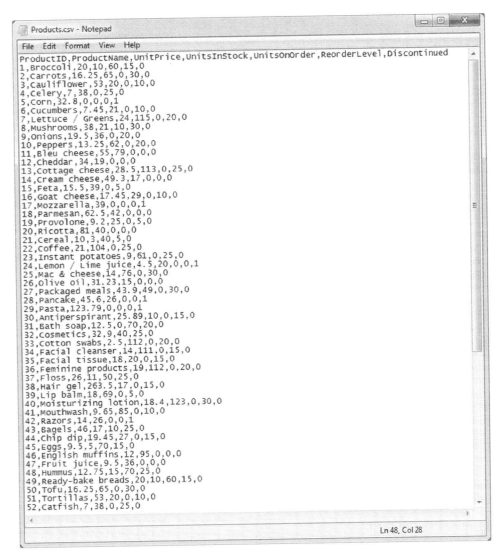

Figure A.1: Products.CSV

A.2 Test Data - Employees Table

Column Header

`EmployeeID,LastName,FirstName,Title,BirthDate,Adress,City,County,PostalCode,Country,HomePhone`

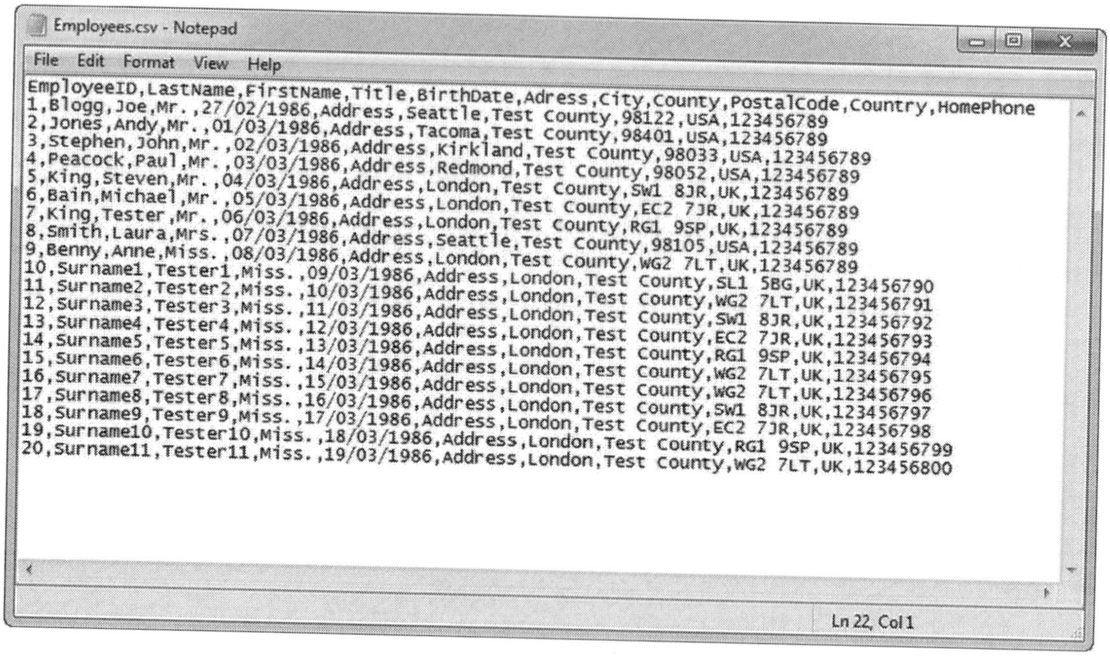

```
EmployeeID,LastName,FirstName,Title,BirthDate,Adress,City,County,PostalCode,Country,HomePhone
1,Blogg,Joe,Mr.,27/02/1986,Address,Seattle,Test County,98122,USA,123456789
2,Jones,Andy,Mr.,01/03/1986,Address,Tacoma,Test County,98401,USA,123456789
3,Stephen,John,Mr.,02/03/1986,Address,Kirkland,Test County,98033,USA,123456789
4,Peacock,Paul,Mr.,03/03/1986,Address,Redmond,Test County,98052,USA,123456789
5,King,Steven,Mr.,04/03/1986,Address,London,Test County,SW1 8JR,UK,123456789
6,Bain,Michael,Mr.,05/03/1986,Address,London,Test County,EC2 7JR,UK,123456789
7,King,Tester,Mr.,06/03/1986,Address,London,Test County,RG1 9SP,UK,123456789
8,Smith,Laura,Mrs.,07/03/1986,Address,Seattle,Test County,98105,USA,123456789
9,Benny,Anne,Miss.,08/03/1986,Address,London,Test County,WG2 7LT,UK,123456789
10,Surname1,Tester1,Miss.,09/03/1986,Address,London,Test County,SL1 5BG,UK,123456790
11,Surname2,Tester2,Miss.,10/03/1986,Address,London,Test County,WG2 7LT,UK,123456791
12,Surname3,Tester3,Miss.,11/03/1986,Address,London,Test County,SW1 8JR,UK,123456792
13,Surname4,Tester4,Miss.,12/03/1986,Address,London,Test County,EC2 7JR,UK,123456793
14,Surname5,Tester5,Miss.,13/03/1986,Address,London,Test County,RG1 9SP,UK,123456794
15,Surname6,Tester6,Miss.,14/03/1986,Address,London,Test County,WG2 7LT,UK,123456795
16,Surname7,Tester7,Miss.,15/03/1986,Address,London,Test County,WG2 7LT,UK,123456796
17,Surname8,Tester8,Miss.,16/03/1986,Address,London,Test County,SW1 8JR,UK,123456797
18,Surname9,Tester9,Miss.,17/03/1986,Address,London,Test County,EC2 7JR,UK,123456798
19,Surname10,Tester10,Miss.,18/03/1986,Address,London,Test County,RG1 9SP,UK,123456799
20,Surname11,Tester11,Miss.,19/03/1986,Address,London,Test County,WG2 7LT,UK,123456800
```


Figure A.2: Employees.CSV

A.3 Test Data - Customers Table

Column Header

`CustomerID,LastName,FirstName,Title,DateOfBirth,Address,City,County,`
`PostalCode,Country,Phone,Fax`

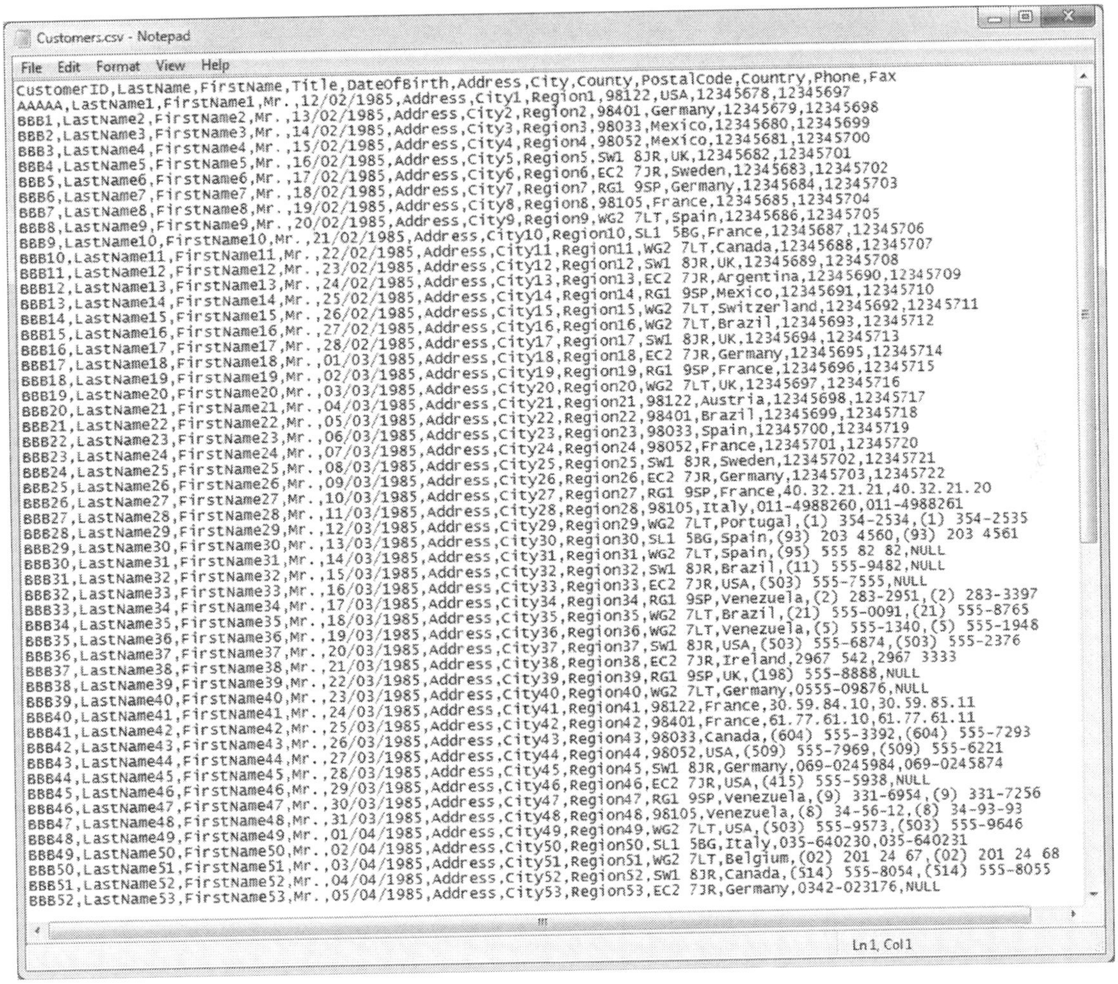

```
Customers.csv - Notepad
File Edit Format View Help
CustomerID,LastName,FirstName,Title,DateofBirth,Address,City,County,PostalCode,Country,Phone,Fax
AAAAA,LastName1,FirstName1,Mr.,12/02/1985,Address,City1,Region1,98122,USA,12345678,12345697
BBB1,LastName2,FirstName2,Mr.,13/02/1985,Address,City2,Region2,98401,Germany,12345679,12345698
BBB2,LastName3,FirstName3,Mr.,14/02/1985,Address,City3,Region3,98033,Mexico,12345680,12345699
BBB3,LastName4,FirstName4,Mr.,15/02/1985,Address,City4,Region4,98052,Mexico,12345681,12345700
BBB4,LastName5,FirstName5,Mr.,16/02/1985,Address,City5,Region5,SW1 8JR,UK,12345682,12345701
BBB5,LastName6,FirstName6,Mr.,17/02/1985,Address,City6,Region6,EC2 7JR,Sweden,12345683,12345702
BBB6,LastName7,FirstName7,Mr.,18/02/1985,Address,City7,Region7,RG1 9SP,Germany,12345684,12345703
BBB7,LastName8,FirstName8,Mr.,19/02/1985,Address,City8,Region8,98105,France,12345685,12345704
BBB8,LastName9,FirstName9,Mr.,20/02/1985,Address,City9,Region9,WG2 7LT,Spain,12345686,12345705
BBB9,LastName10,FirstName10,Mr.,21/02/1985,Address,City10,Region10,SL1 5BG,France,12345687,12345706
BBB10,LastName11,FirstName11,Mr.,22/02/1985,Address,City11,Region11,WG2 7LT,Canada,12345688,12345707
BBB11,LastName12,FirstName12,Mr.,23/02/1985,Address,City12,Region12,SW1 8JR,UK,12345689,12345708
BBB12,LastName13,FirstName13,Mr.,24/02/1985,Address,City13,Region13,EC2 7JR,Argentina,12345690,12345709
BBB13,LastName14,FirstName14,Mr.,25/02/1985,Address,City14,Region14,RG1 9SP,Mexico,12345691,12345710
BBB14,LastName15,FirstName15,Mr.,26/02/1985,Address,City15,Region15,WG2 7LT,Switzerland,12345692,12345711
BBB15,LastName16,FirstName16,Mr.,27/02/1985,Address,City16,Region16,WG2 7LT,Brazil,12345693,12345712
BBB16,LastName17,FirstName17,Mr.,28/02/1985,Address,City17,Region17,SW1 8JR,UK,12345694,12345713
BBB17,LastName18,FirstName18,Mr.,01/03/1985,Address,City18,Region18,EC2 7JR,Germany,12345695,12345714
BBB18,LastName19,FirstName19,Mr.,02/03/1985,Address,City19,Region19,RG1 9SP,France,12345696,12345715
BBB19,LastName20,FirstName20,Mr.,03/03/1985,Address,City20,Region20,WG2 7LT,UK,12345697,12345716
BBB20,LastName21,FirstName21,Mr.,04/03/1985,Address,City21,Region21,98122,Austria,12345698,12345717
BBB21,LastName22,FirstName22,Mr.,05/03/1985,Address,City22,Region22,98401,Brazil,12345699,12345718
BBB22,LastName23,FirstName23,Mr.,06/03/1985,Address,City23,Region23,98033,Spain,12345700,12345719
BBB23,LastName24,FirstName24,Mr.,07/03/1985,Address,City24,Region24,98052,France,12345701,12345720
BBB24,LastName25,FirstName25,Mr.,08/03/1985,Address,City25,Region25,SW1 8JR,Sweden,12345702,12345721
BBB25,LastName26,FirstName26,Mr.,09/03/1985,Address,City26,Region26,EC2 7JR,Germany,12345703,12345722
BBB26,LastName27,FirstName27,Mr.,10/03/1985,Address,City27,Region27,RG1 9SP,France,40.32.21.21,40.32.21.20
BBB27,LastName28,FirstName28,Mr.,11/03/1985,Address,City28,Region28,98105,Italy,011-4988260,011-4988261
BBB28,LastName29,FirstName29,Mr.,12/03/1985,Address,City29,Region29,WG2 7LT,Portugal,(1) 354-2534,(1) 354-2535
BBB29,LastName30,FirstName30,Mr.,13/03/1985,Address,City30,Region30,SL1 5BG,Spain,(93) 203 4560,(93) 203 4561
BBB30,LastName31,FirstName31,Mr.,14/03/1985,Address,City31,Region31,WG2 7LT,Spain,(95) 555 82 82,NULL
BBB31,LastName32,FirstName32,Mr.,15/03/1985,Address,City32,Region32,SW1 8JR,Brazil,(11) 555-9482,NULL
BBB32,LastName33,FirstName33,Mr.,16/03/1985,Address,City33,Region33,EC2 7JR,USA,(503) 555-7555,NULL
BBB33,LastName34,FirstName34,Mr.,17/03/1985,Address,City34,Region34,RG1 9SP,Venezuela,(2) 283-2951,(2) 283-3397
BBB34,LastName35,FirstName35,Mr.,18/03/1985,Address,City35,Region35,WG2 7LT,Brazil,(21) 555-0091,(21) 555-8765
BBB35,LastName36,FirstName36,Mr.,19/03/1985,Address,City36,Region36,WG2 7LT,Venezuela,(5) 555-1340,(5) 555-1948
BBB36,LastName37,FirstName37,Mr.,20/03/1985,Address,City37,Region37,SW1 8JR,USA,(503) 555-6874,(503) 555-2376
BBB37,LastName38,FirstName38,Mr.,21/03/1985,Address,City38,Region38,EC2 7JR,Ireland,2967 542,2967 3333
BBB38,LastName39,FirstName39,Mr.,22/03/1985,Address,City39,Region39,RG1 9SP,UK,(198) 555-8888,NULL
BBB39,LastName40,FirstName40,Mr.,23/03/1985,Address,City40,Region40,WG2 7LT,Germany,0555-09876,NULL
BBB40,LastName41,FirstName41,Mr.,24/03/1985,Address,City41,Region41,98122,France,30.59.84.10,30.59.85.11
BBB41,LastName42,FirstName42,Mr.,25/03/1985,Address,City42,Region42,98401,France,61.77.61.10,61.77.61.11
BBB42,LastName43,FirstName43,Mr.,26/03/1985,Address,City43,Region43,98033,Canada,(604) 555-3392,(604) 555-7293
BBB43,LastName44,FirstName44,Mr.,27/03/1985,Address,City44,Region44,98052,USA,(509) 555-7969,(509) 555-6221
BBB44,LastName45,FirstName45,Mr.,28/03/1985,Address,City45,Region45,SW1 8JR,Germany,069-0245984,069-0245874
BBB45,LastName46,FirstName46,Mr.,29/03/1985,Address,City46,Region46,EC2 7JR,USA,(415) 555-5938,NULL
BBB46,LastName47,FirstName47,Mr.,30/03/1985,Address,City47,Region47,RG1 9SP,Venezuela,(9) 331-6954,(9) 331-7256
BBB47,LastName48,FirstName48,Mr.,31/03/1985,Address,City48,Region48,98105,Venezuela,(8) 34-56-12,(8) 34-93-93
BBB48,LastName49,FirstName49,Mr.,01/04/1985,Address,City49,Region49,WG2 7LT,USA,(503) 555-9573,(503) 555-9646
BBB49,LastName50,FirstName50,Mr.,02/04/1985,Address,City50,Region50,SL1 5BG,Italy,035-640230,035-640231
BBB50,LastName51,FirstName51,Mr.,03/04/1985,Address,City51,Region51,WG2 7LT,Belgium,(02) 201 24 67,(02) 201 24 68
BBB51,LastName52,FirstName52,Mr.,04/04/1985,Address,City52,Region52,SW1 8JR,Canada,(514) 555-8054,(514) 555-8055
BBB52,LastName53,FirstName53,Mr.,05/04/1985,Address,City53,Region53,EC2 7JR,Germany,0342-023176,NULL
Ln 1, Col 1
```

Figure A.3: Customers.CSV

A.4 Test Data - Orders Table

Column Header

OrderID,CustomerID,EmployeeID,OrderDate,DispatchDate

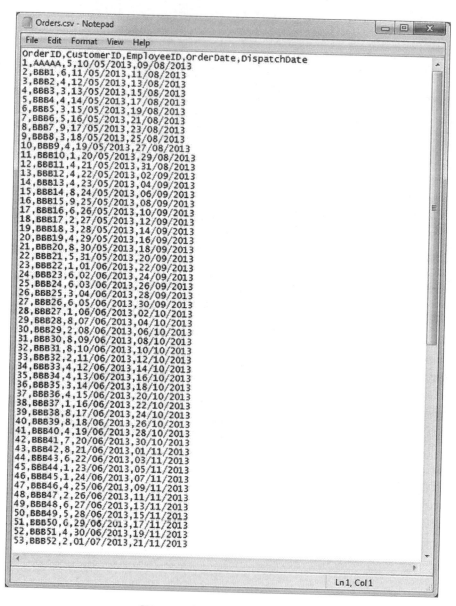

Figure A.4: Orders.CSV

A.5 Test Data - OrderDetails Table

Column Header
OrderID,ProductID,UnitPrice,Quantity,Discount,GiftWrap,PriceMatch

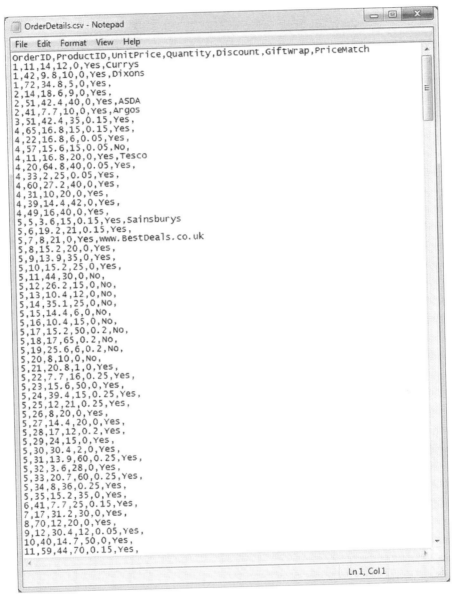

Figure A.5: OrderDetailss.CSV

A.6   Test Data - SalesTransactions.CSV

Column Header

OrderID,CustomerID,ProductID,EmployeeID,OrderDate,DispatchDate,
PriceMatch, UnitPrice,Quantity,Discount,GiftWrap

```
SalesTransactions.csv - Notepad
File  Edit  Format  View  Help
OrderID,CustomerID,ProductID,EmployeeID,OrderDate,DispatchDate,PriceMatch,UnitPrice,Quantity,Discount,Giftwrap
1,AAAAA,11,5,14/05/2013,17/08/2013,Currys,14,12,0,Yes
1,AAAAA,42,5,15/05/2013,19/08/2013,Dixons,9.8,10,0,Yes
1,AAAAA,72,5,16/05/2013,21/08/2013,,34.8,5,0,Yes
2,BBB12,14,6,17/05/2013,23/08/2013,,18.6,9,0,Yes
2,BBB13,41,6,18/05/2013,25/08/2013,Argos,7.7,10,0,Yes
2,BBB14,51,6,19/05/2013,27/08/2013,ASDA,42.4,40,0,Yes
3,BBB14,51,4,20/05/2013,29/08/2013,,42.4,35,0.15,Yes
4,BBB20,11,3,21/05/2013,31/08/2013,Tesco,16.8,20,0,Yes
4,BBB20,20,3,22/05/2013,02/09/2013,,64.8,40,0.05,Yes
4,BBB20,22,3,23/05/2013,04/09/2013,,16.8,6,0.05,Yes
4,BBB20,31,3,24/05/2013,06/09/2013,,10,20,0,Yes
4,BBB20,33,3,25/05/2013,08/09/2013,,2,25,0.05,Yes
4,BBB20,39,3,26/05/2013,10/09/2013,,14.4,42,0,Yes
4,BBB20,49,3,27/05/2013,12/09/2013,,16,40,0,Yes
4,BBB20,57,3,28/05/2013,14/09/2013,,15.6,15,0.05,No
4,BBB20,60,3,29/05/2013,16/09/2013,,27.2,40,0,Yes
4,BBB20,65,3,30/05/2013,18/09/2013,,16.8,15,0.15,Yes
5,BBB25,5,4,31/05/2013,20/09/2013,Sainsburys,3.6,15,0.15,Yes
5,BBB25,6,4,01/06/2013,22/09/2013,,19.2,21,0.15,Yes
5,BBB25,7,4,02/06/2013,24/09/2013,www.BestDeals.co.uk,8,21,0,Yes
5,BBB25,8,4,03/06/2013,26/09/2013,,15.2,20,0,Yes
5,BBB25,9,4,04/06/2013,28/09/2013,,13.9,35,0,Yes
5,BBB25,10,4,05/06/2013,30/09/2013,,15.2,25,0,Yes
5,BBB25,11,4,06/06/2013,02/10/2013,,44,30,0,No
5,BBB25,12,4,07/06/2013,04/10/2013,,26.2,15,0,No
5,BBB25,13,4,08/06/2013,06/10/2013,,10.4,12,0,No
5,BBB25,14,4,09/06/2013,08/10/2013,,35.1,25,0,No
5,BBB25,15,4,10/06/2013,10/10/2013,,14.4,6,0,No
5,BBB25,16,4,11/06/2013,12/10/2013,,10.4,15,0,No
5,BBB25,17,4,12/06/2013,14/10/2013,,15.2,50,0.2,No
5,BBB25,18,4,13/06/2013,16/10/2013,,17,65,0.2,No
5,BBB25,19,4,14/06/2013,18/10/2013,,25.6,6,0.2,No
5,BBB25,20,4,15/06/2013,20/10/2013,,8,10,0,No
5,BBB25,21,4,16/06/2013,22/10/2013,,20.8,1,0,Yes
5,BBB25,22,4,17/06/2013,24/10/2013,,7.7,16,0.25,Yes
5,BBB25,23,4,18/06/2013,26/10/2013,,15.6,50,0,Yes
5,BBB25,24,4,19/06/2013,28/10/2013,,39.4,15,0.25,Yes
5,BBB25,25,4,20/06/2013,30/10/2013,,12,21,0.25,Yes
5,BBB25,26,4,21/06/2013,01/11/2013,,8,20,0,Yes
5,BBB25,27,4,22/06/2013,03/11/2013,,14.4,20,0,Yes
5,BBB25,28,4,23/06/2013,05/11/2013,,17,12,0.2,Yes
5,BBB25,29,4,24/06/2013,07/11/2013,,24,15,0,Yes
5,BBB25,30,4,25/06/2013,09/11/2013,,30.4,2,0,Yes
5,BBB25,31,4,26/06/2013,11/11/2013,,13.9,60,0.25,Yes
5,BBB25,32,4,27/06/2013,13/11/2013,,3.6,28,0,Yes
5,BBB25,33,4,28/06/2013,15/11/2013,,20.7,60,0.25,Yes
5,BBB25,34,4,29/06/2013,17/11/2013,,8,36,0.25,Yes
5,BBB25,35,4,30/06/2013,19/11/2013,,15.2,35,0,Yes
6,BBB30,41,3,01/07/2013,21/11/2013,,7.7,25,0.15,Yes
7,BBB31,17,5,02/07/2013,23/11/2013,,31.2,30,0,Yes
8,BBB32,70,9,03/07/2013,25/11/2013,,12,20,0,Yes
9,BBB33,12,3,04/07/2013,27/11/2013,,30.4,12,0.05,Yes
10,BBB34,40,4,05/07/2013,29/11/2013,,14.7,50,0,Yes
11,BBB35,59,1,06/07/2013,01/12/2013,,44,70,0.15,Yes

                                                                    Ln 1, Col 1
```

Figure A.6: SalesTransactions.CSV

A.7 Test Data - SalesTransactions.XLSX

Column Header

OrderID,CustomerID,ProductID,EmployeeID,OrderDate,DispatchDate,
PriceMatch, UnitPrice,Quantity,Discount,GiftWrap

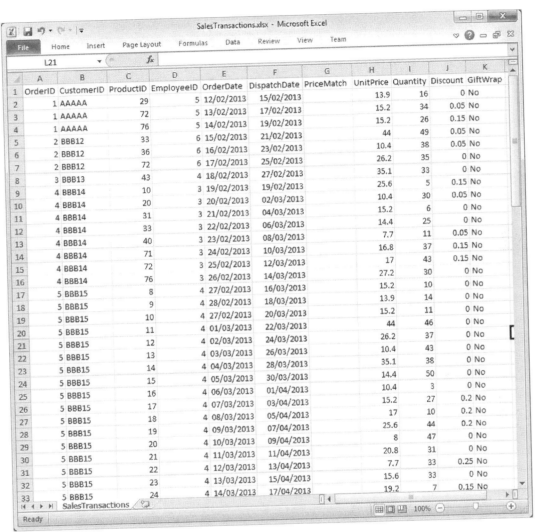

Figure A.7: SalesTransactions.XLSX

A.8   Test Data - SalesTransactions.XLS

Column Header

OrderID,CustomerID,ProductID,EmployeeID,OrderDate,DispatchDate,
PriceMatch, UnitPrice,Quantity,Discount,GiftWrap

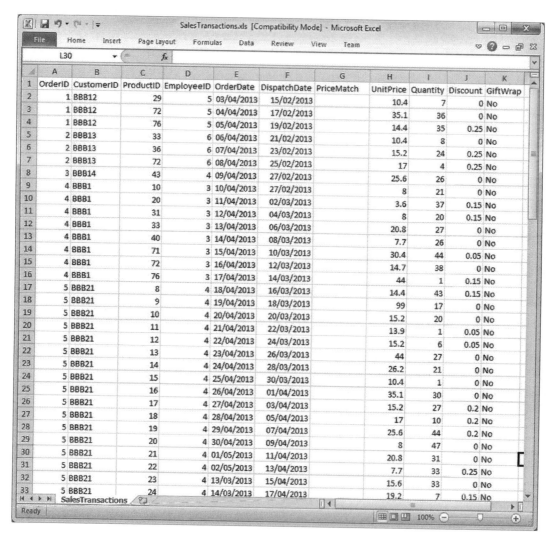

Figure A.8: SalesTransactions.XLS

Index

Made in the USA
Lexington, KY
15 August 2019